JESUS' EMOTIONS IN THE GOSPELS

JESUS' EMOTIONS IN THE GOSPELS

STEPHEN VOORWINDE

t&t clark

Published by T&T Clark International
A Continuum Imprint
The Tower Building, 11 York Road, London SE1 7NX
80 Maiden Lane, Suite 704, New York, NY 10038

www.continuumbooks.com

British Library Cataloguing-in-Publication Data
A catalogue record for this book is available from the British Library

ISBN 13: HB: 978-0-567-62040-8
          PB: 978-0-567-43061-8

Typeset by Pindar NZ, Auckland, New Zealand
Printed and bound in India

Contents

List of Figures and Tables

Foreword

Any book that endeavours to study the life of Jesus as portrayed in the four Gospels is a most worthy undertaking, especially when it addresses a gap in the literature. *Jesus' Emotions in the Gospels* by Stephen Voorwinde is such an undertaking. How do the evangelists portray the emotional life of Jesus? Do the Gospels provide a coherent picture of Jesus' emotions? Are there theological motifs that impart a certain colour to the picture? Does the presentation relate to our understanding of the human and divine natures of Jesus? Are there differences between the Gospels? Furthermore, must Christians experience or imitate the emotions of Jesus – the *imitatio Christi* principle? These questions do not only deal with theological issues, but also with matters of pastoral care and Christian discipleship. The theologian, the pastor, as well as the disciple will discover some solid answers to these questions in *Jesus' Emotions in the Gospels*.

I had the privilege of being one of Stephen's first students when he began teaching at the Reformed Theological College in 1985. As students we experienced the emotions of both joy and trepidation. It was a delight to have had Stephen as one of our first lecturers. Stephen was, as perhaps most young lecturers would be, humble, enthusiastic and very warm towards his first group of students. However, we also experienced much fear. Our minds were often pushed beyond their limits to absorb all the intricacies of New Testament theology and our hands often strained under the attempt to keep up with the speed of delivery.

While our emotions alternated between joy and trepidation, Stephen's alternated between amazement and compassion. Amazement that much of his time over the next four years would be spent on trying to educate a group of four rough simpletons, half of whom struggled to write one coherent sentence in English, for the ministry. When others legitimately frowned and muttered, Stephen exhibited huge amounts of compassion and patience, coaching us through our valleys of ignorance and distress. But what I find even more amazing is that Stephen has maintained the same humility, enthusiasm and warmth he conveyed to us as young students for 25 years. Stephen has pursued his vocation with remarkable zeal and faithfulness.

Stephen is eminently qualified to write about the emotional life of Jesus as portrayed in the Gospels. Erudite scholarship, balanced arguments and considered conclusions have been the hallmarks of his teaching. He has expert knowledge of the Old Testament and the New Testament, is well versed in theology and is up to date with a wide range of research related to the topic. Apart from biblical and theological discussion, there are references to conversations with medical doctors and psychologists. But, what is more, the scholarship stems from a humble and compassionate heart. Stephen is no armchair theologian – his own life has been no stranger to the raft of emotions experienced by Jesus. He has been a pastor to several congregations, scores of students and to his own family. He writes with warm devotion and gentle humanity; it is a subject close to his heart. Indeed, the emotions of Jesus have exercised Stephen's mind for a long time. The questions raised in *Jesus' Emotions in the Gospels* already featured in our encounters over lunch more than 20 years ago. As such, in some ways, the work is Stephen's *magnum opus*; it is the culmination of many years of scholarship, teaching and ministry. The reader will not go away empty.

The book deals with the emotions of Jesus in the four Gospels respectively. As with the emotions of Jesus, there is much more than meets the eye here. The book not only provides an insight into the emotional life of Jesus, but also ample discussion of the theologies of the four Gospels. It is only within the distinctive perspective of the individual evangelists that the emotions of Jesus come into full relief. The conversation is always richly infused with Old Testament spirituality. The emotions of Jesus are small windows through which the observer may perceive larger theological scenes. There are many interesting vistas and surprises. Although readers may not agree with every point of view expressed in *Jesus' Emotions in the Gospels*, they will not be able to brush aside the arguments or be unmoved by the insights. They are substantial, well informed and skilfully argued. Certainly, few will be able to take issue with the main argument of the book. Jesus' emotions can only be rightly understood in light of the cross. The emotions of Jesus point the reader to the significance of Jesus' death on the cross as the God-man who gave his life as for the salvation of the world. The careful reader will not be unaffected by the picture of the Lord that emerges from the pages of the Gospels. Emotions are contagious.

You should read this book. There is a rich smorgasbord of biblical theology. There is a coherent description of the emotional life of Jesus. There is an understanding of Jesus' emotions that is crucial for authentic Christian living and spiritual transformation. But most importantly, you should read this book in order to know the Lord Jesus better – the highest call of both the theologian and the disciple.

Johan Ferreira
Principal
Crossway College

Acknowledgments

Since the publication of *Jesus' Emotions in the Fourth Gospel: Human or Divine?* in 2005, I have frequently been encouraged to write a sequel. Often the encouragement came with the suggestion that the sequel be less technical and more accessible to the thoughtful reader. At times there was the further suggestion that attention be given to the emotions of Jesus in all the Gospels, not just in John. The present work comes in response to such requests.

Although a writer spends many hours in solitude, the final product is never a solitary achievement. I am therefore deeply indebted to those who have enabled me to bring this work to fruition.

My colleagues at the Reformed Theological College deserve my sincere thanks for their unfailing encouragement over many years. They were prepared to take on added responsibilities so as to give me the opportunity to devote myself entirely to the writing of the present manuscript in the second semester of 2009. I am also grateful to the Board of the College for granting me study leave during that period.

My warm gratitude extends to those who gave so generously of their time and expertise through careful proofreading and wise counsel. Family members, friends and colleagues joined forces to check the original manuscript and make helpful comments. My special thanks go to Murray Capill, Allan Harman, Lisa Lowe, Alison McDonald, Alastair McEwen, John Ryall, Anna Thierry-Higgins, Henriet Vanderstocp, Tim Vanderstoep, Christine Verspaandonk and Rebecca Voorwinde. Their areas of speciality ranged from Old Testament, Judaism and English literature to psychology, counselling, pastoral theology, doctoral research and forensic science. Two medical doctors, Barry Edwards and Tim Walker, provided invaluable help at those points where the investigation intersected with their medical interests.

I would like to thank my children and their spouses for their abiding interest and unswerving support for this project over many years. My elderly mother has also assisted me with her keen interest and faithful prayers. A special inspiration for all my work on the emotions of Jesus has come from my wife, Nancy, who has stood by me for almost thirty-seven years. Her chronic struggle with multiple sclerosis for most of her adult life has equipped me for the present study perhaps more than some of the penetrating insights of academic scholarship. Through her suffering she has incarnated the life of Jesus in almost tangible ways. In particular, her strong faith and enduring courage have attuned me to those attributes in the Gospels' portrayals of Jesus.

Above all I thank the God of the Bible for condescending to such an extent as to open himself up to human analysis. Entering into the intimate details of the emotional life of our Lord is to walk on holy ground. One treads carefully and, I hope, accurately. This is the kind of work that is necessarily performed *coram Deo*, in the presence of God. My aim throughout has been to demonstrate to the reader something of the depth and complexity, and yet winsomeness, of the person of Jesus. My prayer is that those readers who begin the book with a mind full of questions will finish it with a heart full of praise.

Stephen Voorwinde
Reformed Theological College
Geelong, Australia
Easter 2010

Abbreviations

AB	Anchor Bible
ABR	*Australian Biblical Review*
ACR	*Australasian Catholic Record*
AJT	*Asia Journal of Theology*
AV	Authorized Version
BAG	Bauer, W., W. F. Arndt and F. W. Gingrich, *Greek-English Lexicon of the New Testament and Other Early Christian Literature* (Chicago: The University of Chicago Press, 1957)
BAGD	Bauer, W., W. F. Arndt, F. W. Gingrich and F. W. Danker, *Greek-English Lexicon of the New Testament and Other Early Christian Literature* (2nd edn; Chicago: The University of Chicago Press, 1979)
BDAG	Bauer, W., F. W. Danker, W. F. Arndt and F. W. Gingrich, *Greek-English Lexicon of the New Testament and Other Early Christian Literature* (3rd edn; Chicago: The University of Chicago Press, 2000)
BDF	Blass, F., A. Debrunner and R. W. Funk, *A Greek Grammar of the New Testament and Other Early Christian Literature* (Chicago, 1961)
BECNT	Baker Exegetical Commentary on the New Testament
BibRev	*Biblical Review*
BST	The Bible Speaks Today
BT	*The Bible Translator*
BTB	*Biblical Theology Bulletin*
BZ	*Biblische Zeitschrift*
CBQ	*Catholic Biblical Quarterly*
CT	*Christianity Today*
CurTM	*Currents in Theology and Mission*
DSS	Dead Sea Scrolls
EDNT	*Exegetical Dictionary of the New Testament* (ed. H. Balz and G. Schneider; ET; 3 vols; Grand Rapids, MI: Eerdmans, 1990–1992)
ESV	English Standard Version
ET	English Translation
EvQ	*Evangelical Quarterly*

ExpTim	*Expository Times*
GNB	Good News Bible
HBT	*Horizons in Biblical Theology*
Holman	Holman Christian Standard Bible
HTR	*Harvard Theological Review*
IBS	*Irish Biblical Studies*
IDS	*In die Skriflig*
Int	*Interpretation*
JB	Jerusalem Bible
JBL	*Journal of Biblical Literature*
JP	*Journal for Preachers*
JSNT	*Journal for the Study of the New Testament*
JSNTSup	Journal for the Study of the New Testament: Supplement Series
JSS	*Journal of Semitic Studies*
JTS	*Journal of Theological Studies*
Kerux	*Kerux: A Journal of Biblical-Theological Preaching*
KJV	King James Version
Knox	The Knox Translation of the Holy Bible
LB	Living Bible
LN	*Greek-English Lexicon of the New Testament: Based on Semantic Domains* (ed. J. P. Louw and E. A. Nida; 2 vols; New York: United Bible Societies, 2nd edn, 1988–89)
LXX	Septuagint
MLB	Modern Language Bible
MM	Moulton, J. H., and G. Milligan. *The Vocabulary of the Greek Testament Illustrated from the Papyri and Other Non-Literary Sources* (London: Hodder and Stoughton, 1930; repr. 1972)
MSJ	*The Master's Seminary Journal*
MT	Masoretic Text
NA	*Novum Testamentum Graece*, Nestle-Aland.
NAB	New American Bible
NASB	New American Standard Bible
NEB	New English Bible
NICNT	New International Commentary on the New Testament
NICOT	New International Commentary on the Old Testament
NIDNTT	*New International Dictionary of New Testament Theology* (ed. C. Brown; 4 vols; Grand Rapids, 1975–1978)
NIV	New International Version
NJB	New Jerusalem Bible
NJKV	New King James Version
NovT	*Novum Testamentum*
NRSV	New Revised Standard Version
NTS	*New Testament Studies*
Phillips	*The New Testament in Modern English*, J. B. Phillips.

PNTC	The Pillar New Testament Commentary
ProEccl	*Pro Ecclesia*
RevExp	*Review and Expositor*
RSV	Revised Standard Version
RTR	*Reformed Theological Review*
RV	Revised Version
TDNT	*Theological Dictionary of the New Testament* (ed. G. Kittel and G. Friedrich; trans. G. W. Bromiley; 9 vols; Grand Rapids, MI: 1964–1976)
TEV	Today's English Version (=Good News Bible)
ThTo	*Theology Today*
TNIV	Today's New International Version
TynBul	*Tyndale Bulletin*
UBS	United Bible Societies
Vid	*Vidyajyoti Journal of Theological Reflection*
Vulg.	Vulgate
WBC	Word Biblical Commentary
WTJ	*Westminster Theological Journal*
WW	*Word and World*
ZNW	*Zeitschrift für die neutestamentliche Wissenschaft und die Kunde der älteren Kirche*

Introduction

In February 1997 *Christianity Today* magazine ran an article with the title 'The Emotions of Jesus and Why We Need to Experience Them.' The article opened on a challenging note:

> The gospel writers paint their portraits of Jesus using a kaleidoscope of brilliant 'emotional' colors. Jesus felt *compassion*; he was *angry, indignant*, and *consumed with zeal*; he was *troubled, greatly distressed, very sorrowful, depressed, deeply moved*, and *grieved*; he *sighed*; he *wept* and *sobbed*; he *groaned*; he was *in agony*; he was *surprised* and *amazed*; he *rejoiced very greatly* and was *full of joy*; he *greatly desired*, and he *loved*.
>
> In our quest to be like Jesus we often overlook his emotions. Jesus reveals what it means to be fully human and made in the image of God. His emotions reflect the image of God without any deficiency or distortion. When we compare our own emotional lives to his, we become aware of our need for a transformation of our emotions so that we can be fully human, as he is.[1]

The article goes on to discuss what has long been a blind spot in Gospel studies and it does so with all the lively vigour and sharp thrust of its opening paragraphs. Fascinating and provocative though the article may be, it raises issues and makes assumptions that need to be carefully addressed. At a most basic level it has to be asked whether the article has correctly identified the emotions of Jesus in the Gospels. Secondly, it assumes that Jesus' emotions are indicators of his full humanity. But is this always the case? Could some of his emotions at least equally indicate his divinity? Finally, on a more experiential level, is it a sign of our Christian maturity or even of our full humanity to reflect the emotions of Jesus as accurately as possible in our own individual lives? Is the extent to which the emotions of Jesus are reflected in a person's life an index to the authenticity of their Christian convictions and experience? For twenty-first century Christians living in a post-modern context these are questions of vital theological and practical importance. Few matters could be weightier than a genuine understanding of the Gospels' presentation of Jesus and the implications that this has for Christian living today.

---

1   G. Walter Hansen, 'The Emotions of Jesus and Why We Need to Experience Them', *CT* 41/2 (1997), p. 43.

1

What gives the present study even greater urgency is the fact that Jesus is seldom thought of in emotional terms. When Christians are asked to list the emotions of Jesus the result often bears only a very imperfect resemblance to his emotions as recorded in the Gospels. Why is this so? Why do those who profess to follow Jesus often have such an imprecise knowledge and understanding of his emotions?

Perhaps one reason is the fact that there are relatively few specific references to Jesus' emotions in the Gospels. There are only sixty such references in all. By far the most are in John, with a total of twenty-eight occurrences. Next is Mark, with sixteen. Matthew has ten, and Luke just six. Compared with the large body of Jesus' teaching, the space devoted to his miracles, the variety of places he visited and the masses of people he encountered, this is a rather small body of data. In some parts of the Gospels references to Jesus' emotions are very sparse indeed.

Apart from the paucity of the data, the emotions of Jesus have seldom been systematically investigated. Perhaps this is the second reason Christians are not as familiar with them as one might expect. Occasionally you might hear a preacher expound a passage which refers to an emotion of Jesus. Rarely, however, will you have the pleasure of hearing a series of sermons that covers a wide range of Jesus' emotions. Some of the most famous hymns in the Christian tradition, such as 'When I Survey the Wondrous Cross', 'Once in Royal David's City' and 'O Sacred Head Now Wounded', briefly touch on some of Jesus' emotions, but they hardly cover the entire spectrum. Although a couple of devotional works with the title *The Emotions of Jesus*[2] have appeared over the past hundred years, there is not a rich tradition of devotional literature on the subject. When it comes to scholarly works the landscape looks bleaker still. What was perhaps the only academic work of note to appear in the twentieth century was the long essay by the Princeton theologian, B. B. Warfield, 'On the Emotional Life of Our Lord', originally published in 1912.[3]

So whether the subject of Jesus' emotions is viewed homiletically, liturgically, devotionally or academically, this is a topic that deserves far more attention than it has received of late. Preachers, song-writers, scholars and writers of devotional books could all do more to address this surprising oversight in Gospel studies. The present work seeks to address this gap. An attempt will be made to give a systematic presentation of all the emotions of Jesus recorded in the four Gospels. The goal of the work is to combine responsible scholarship with richly devotional insights that will inspire preachers and hymn-writers as well as thinking Christians striving to be incarnational in their theology and practice.

For this study to proceed on a sound footing, however, we must first tackle a foundational question: What is an emotion? In the discipline of psychology this remains a vexing problem.[4] In that field, the discussion of emotions has

---

2   Robert Law, *The Emotions of Jesus* (Edinburgh: T. & T. Clark, 1915); Bianca Elliott, *The Emotions of Jesus* (Martinsville, IN: Airleaf, 2006).

3   Benjamin B. Warfield, *The Person and Work of Christ* (Philadelphia: Presbyterian & Reformed, 1950), pp. 93–145.

4   The complexity of the issue currently facing psychologists is well captured by Nico H. Frijda,

covered a broad spectrum of experiences ranging from attitudes, motives and affects to feelings, moods and passions. Needless to say, the issue has sparked intense debate. In the current state of play there are still a number of unresolved questions: How many basic emotions are there? Are emotions universal or are they culturally conditioned? And what is the relationship between emotions, biological reactions and thoughts? In other words, does our emotional experience depend on our perception of a situation (a cognitive approach) or are we predisposed to respond instantaneously to situations without taking the time to evaluate them (a non-cognitive approach)?[5] These are still open questions in the field of psychology.

In spite of these unresolved issues a general definition of emotion is still possible in the context of ongoing discussions: 'Emotion refers to the experience of feelings such as fear, joy, surprise and anger. Like motives, emotions also activate and affect behavior, but it is more difficult to predict the kind of behavior that a particular emotion will prompt.'[6] Even the psychologists who hesitate to define emotions will gladly list examples of emotions. The following recur repeatedly in the literature: joy, fear, anger, grief; disgust, horror, delight; shame, pride, guilt; love, hate, pity, jealousy; wonder, sadness, anxiety, elation, surprise.[7] There is considerable overlap in the lists of examples provided by psychologists. This suggests at least a measure of consensus in their discipline. These areas where they generally seem to agree, together with the examples of emotions that they repeatedly give, provide the broad contours within which emotions can be fruitfully discussed.

When it comes to the emotions of Jesus we will need to restrict the discussion to the Gospel writers' explicit and clear references to his feelings. Otherwise we run the very real risk of reading our own emotions into the text. The discussion will therefore include all those passages where the emotions identified by the psychologists are explicitly mentioned, such as love, joy, anger and sorrow. It will also include actions that clearly signify an underlying emotion, such as weeping and sighing. On the other hand, there are cases where Jesus' words are undoubtedly emotionally charged, but where any attempt to identify the precise emotion involved would be an exercise in speculation. For example, the Greek

'The Psychologists' Point of View', in *Handbook of Emotions*, ed. Michael Lewis, Jeannette M. Haviland-Jones, and Lisa Feldman-Barrett (London: The Guildford Press, 3rd edn, 2008), pp. 68–87.

5 Charles G. Morris and Albert A. Maisto, *Understanding Psychology* (Upper Saddle River, NJ: Prentice Hall, 8th edn, 2008), pp. 294–97.

6 Morris and Maisto, *Psychology*, p. 273.

7 See Rita L. Atkinson, Richard C. Atkinson, and Ernest R. Hilgard, *Introduction to Psychology* (San Diego: Harcourt Brace Jovanovich, 1981), p. 331; David G. Benner (ed.), *Baker Encyclopedia of Psychology* (Grand Rapids, MI: Baker, 1985), 354; Daniel Goleman, *Emotional Intelligence: Why It Can Matter More than IQ* (London: Bloomsbury, 1996), pp. 289–90; David Kretch, Richard S. Crutchfield and Norman Livson, *Elements of Psychology* (New York: Knopf, 2nd edn, 1969), p. 521; Paul D. Meier *et al.*, *Introduction to Psychology and Counseling: Christian Perspectives and Applications* (Grand Rapids, MI: Baker, 1991), pp. 76–77.

particle Ō has an emotive force roughly equivalent to the English interjection 'O.' Jesus uses it to address the Canaanite woman (Matt 15.28), the crowd around the epileptic boy (Matt 17.17; Mark 9.19; Luke 9.41) and the two on the way to Emmaus (Luke 24.25). In spite of its strong emotional overtones it will be left out of consideration. Although this particle 'occurs in contexts suggesting deep emotion on the part of the speaker,'[8] the emotion varies from context to context and is too difficult to define with any degree of accuracy. In the case of the Canaanite woman, for instance, when Jesus says, 'O woman, your faith is great' (NASB), is he expressing admiration or surprise? In the absence of further clues we simply do not know. There are other cases too where his tone of voice would have given away his underlying emotion to his audience. For example, in the case of the seven woes which he pronounces on the scribes and Pharisees (Mt. 23.13-36), Jesus' words were no doubt laced with strong emotion. This would have been perceived immediately by his listeners. In that respect they were in a privileged position. We have only the written text. To try and identify the precise emotion purely on that basis could again prove to be too subjective and risky an undertaking. In a study of this kind some degree of speculation is unavoidable, but every effort should be made to minimize it as much as possible. Unhappily an overly speculative approach may result in a skewed view of Jesus.

The danger of speculation is even more real when it comes to the relationships between the Gospels. Even a casual Bible reader will be aware of the huge over-lap that exists between the Synoptic Gospels (Matthew, Mark and Luke).[9] This has led scholars to seek to determine which Gospel was written first and who borrowed from whom. This is the gist of the so-called 'Synoptic Problem' which has proved to be one of the real cruxes of Gospel studies down the centuries. The traditional solution, originally proposed by Augustine, was that the canonical order was also the chronological order. Matthew was written first. It was then abbreviated by Mark. Later Luke used both Matthew and Mark. This solution became the consensus view and was not seriously challenged until the 1830s.[10] It was then that Markan priority began to gain ascendancy.[11] According to this view Mark was written first. Subsequently both Matthew and Luke borrowed independently from Mark. By the early twentieth century this conclusion was

---

8 Maximilian Zerwick, *Biblical Greek Illustrated by Examples* (Rome: Biblical Institute Press, 1963), p. 36; likewise Daniel B. Wallace, *Greek Grammar beyond the Basics: An Exegetical Syntax of the New Testament* (Grand Rapids, MI: Zondervan, 1996), p. 68.

9 Everett F. Harrison, *Introduction to the New Testament* (Grand Rapids, MI: Eerdmans, 1971), 143, suggests that 93% of Mark, 58% of Matthew and 41% of Luke coincides with the other Gospels, though not 'in exact verbal agreement'.

10 D. A. Carson, and Douglas J. Moo, *An Introduction to the New Testament* (Leicester: Apollos, 2nd edn, 2005), p. 93.

11 The keystone to this development was the observation in 1835 by Karl Lachmann that 'Matthew and Luke never agree in order against Mark, whereas at times Matthew and Mark agree in order against Luke and at times Mark and Luke agree in order against Matthew' (Robert H. Stein, *The Synoptic Problem: An Introduction* [Grand Rapids, MI: Baker, 1987], p. 69).

regarded as one of the assured results of the critical study of the Gospels.[12] Today many scholars still hold to Markan priority but the earlier confidence has been eroded.[13] Alternate theories abound. Not only has Matthaean priority made a comeback, there has also been some support for Lukan priority, or for Matthew and Luke using earlier versions of Mark.[14] It has even been suggested that the Synoptic Gospels were written quite independently of one another and that therefore the Synoptic Problem is merely a figment of scholarly imagination.[15] With scholarly opinion more divided now than it has been for more than a hundred years this is another area where we need to tread carefully.

When it comes to the relationship between the Synoptics and John's Gospel old certainties have also been challenged. The traditional view held that John knew the Synoptics and used them in his own composition.[16] This view can be traced back to the early Fathers and retained its hegemony until the twentieth century when it was challenged by three British scholars, namely Percival Gardiner-Smith, C. H. Dodd and John Robinson. They argued that John was completely independent of the Synoptics. This represented a huge pendulum swing away from the earlier consensus, but later in the twentieth century this new solution was also challenged. The pendulum has come to rest at a midway position. The overlap that exists between John and the Synoptics indicates neither complete dependence nor complete independence, but rather an awareness of the Synoptics. The extent of that awareness, however, still remains an open question.[17]

These developments in recent Gospel scholarship will have implications for the present study. The impact of these developments will be least noticeable in our investigation of Jesus' emotions in John, as the overlap between the emotions of the Synoptic Jesus and those of John's Jesus are almost negligible. Although a couple of verbs are used across the two traditions to indicate emotions of Jesus, they are found in widely differing contexts. Hence John's portrayal of Jesus' emotions may confidently be regarded as unique among the Gospel accounts.

In the relationship between the three Synoptic accounts a more challenging situation presents itself. Although each of these Gospels has a unique contribution

---

12 See Burnett H. Streeter, *The Four Gospels: A Study of Origins* (London: Macmillan, 1956 [first published 1924]), xxix.

13 Cf. Carson and Moo, *Introduction*, p. 103: 'the process through which the gospels came into being was a complex one, so complex that *no* source-critical hypothesis, however detailed, can hope to provide a complete explanation of the situation'.

14 See Robert L. Thomas (ed.), *Three Views on the Origins of the Synoptic Gospels* (Grand Rapids, MI: Kregel, 2002).

15 Thus Eta Linnemann, *Is There a Synoptic Problem? Rethinking the Literary Dependence of the First Three Gospels* (trans. Robert W. Yarbrough; Grand Rapids, MI: Baker, 1992).

16 Stephen Smalley, *John: Evangelist and Interpreter* (Carlisle: Paternoster, rev. edn, 1998), 3.

17 Smalley, *John*, p. 13. For example, John W. Pryor, *John: Evangelist of the Covenant People* (London: Darton, Longman and Todd, 1992), pp. 101–02, argues that 'John knew Mark and/ or Luke (and possibly Matthew), and that while he may not have been heavily dependent on them as a source for his gospel, he may well have occasionally adopted parts of those written traditions.'

to make, these accounts also overlap in significant ways in their presentation of Jesus' emotions. Because of this overlap the Synoptic problem becomes a relevant issue for our investigation. If these Gospels are ostensibly reporting the same incidents in Jesus' life, but in their recording of those incidents they report Jesus' emotions differently, then it is important to know which Gospel has priority and who is borrowing from whom. The problem is that in the current state of Gospel studies these questions cannot be answered definitively.

While it would be appealing to assume Markan priority, as this has been the majority view among scholars for almost two hundred years, this view presents its own difficulties. As we will see, Mark's portrayal of Jesus' emotional life is richer and fuller than the other two. On several occasions he reports Jesus feeling a strong emotion which is either not recorded or is slightly modified in the parallel passages in Matthew and Luke. For example, in Mark 10.14 it says that Jesus was indignant at the disciples for hindering children from coming to him. Although both Mt. 19.13-15 and Lk. 18.15-17 report the same incident they say nothing about Jesus' indignation. Likewise, in the paragraph that immediately follows, we are told that Jesus felt a love for the rich young ruler (Mk 10.21 NASB). Again Matthew and Luke record the same encounter (Mt. 19.16-30; Luke 18.18-30), but make no mention of Jesus' love. Similarly, in the account of Jesus in the Garden of Gethsemane, Mark reports that 'he began to be *deeply distressed* and troubled' (Mk 14.33). Matthew seems to tone down the emotional turmoil somewhat by saying that Jesus 'began to be *sorrowful* and troubled' (Mt. 26.37).[18] These differences can only be observed, not explained. If Markan priority is indeed the correct solution to the Synoptic Problem, what would motivate the other Gospel writers to omit or modify Mark's very clear and interesting references to Jesus' emotions?[19] To look for motivation in cases like this would be another exercise in speculation. The most we can say is *that* the accounts vary, not *why* they vary. For the sake of caution, and because of the current state of flux in Gospel studies, this investigation is not committed to any particular hypothesis with respect to the Synoptic Problem. This is not to deny that the Synoptic Problem exists but simply to say that none of the solutions is secure enough to provide a basis for the present study.

Without a supporting theory of Synoptic origins it is therefore best to consider each Gospel as a literary unit in its own right and to interpret accordingly. Each Gospel account is a literary whole and has its own story to tell. Although we do not know for sure who depended on whom and to what extent, we can compare the various accounts. In the Gospels we have four complementary portraits or four related theological biographies of Jesus. The situation is a little like four paintings of the same scene at different times of the day or in different weather

---

18 Unless otherwise indicated, all Scripture quotations are from the NIV.

19 Hans-Herbert Stoldt, *History and Criticism of the Marcan Hypothesis* (trans. and ed. D. L. Niewyk; Macon, GA: Mercer University Press, 1980), 263, provides an appendix listing 'minor additional details in Mark that extend beyond the text of Matthew and Luke, including passages where either Matthew or Luke is missing.' Among the 180 items listed are some of the Markan references to Jesus' emotions, namely 1.41, 43; 3.5; 6.6; 8.12; 10.21.

conditions. The resulting works of art portray different interplays of light and shade, varying nuances of hue and colour, but they are all recognisably of the same scene. A photographic study of the same human subject in various moods, in different dress and in various life situations could make the point equally well. In this sense the Gospels are like the portraits and photographs of Winston Churchill that can still be seen in Chartwell, his country home from 1922 until his death. The picture of the statesman, the self-portrait, the photograph of the man of war, and a depiction of the artist relaxing by a Swiss lake are all of one and the same man. Yet each tells its own story, evokes its own atmosphere and provokes its own response in the viewer.[20]

Just as it would be inappropriate to superimpose the four images of Churchill on one another, or seek to harmonize them into a single picture, it would be equally inappropriate to do so with the four Gospel portraits of Jesus. The aim of this investigation is not to give the reader a comprehensive personality profile of the earthly Jesus nor even to attempt to demonstrate what made him tick psychologically. The Gospels simply do not give us sufficient data for such an enterprise. Here we will pursue the far more modest and realistic goal of letting each Gospel speak for itself. Like an artist, each Gospel writer handles his subject with unique skill. The resulting portraits of Jesus will be delightfully nuanced and varied. For example, if Matthew is a Jew writing for his fellow-Jews he will no doubt wish to highlight different features of Jesus' person than Luke who is a Gentile writing for another Gentile. But this is not the whole story. Differences between the Gospels will only be partially accounted for by the varying backgrounds of their authors and their original readers. Without compromising historical accuracy each Gospel will also have its own theological concerns and priorities which will colour its presentation of Jesus. It is within this framework that the emotions of Jesus need to be understood. They are no mere literary adornments to make the story more interesting, but are designed to contribute to the overall picture that each Gospel paints of Jesus. This picture in turn is determined by the particular presentation of Jesus that is unique to each Gospel writer. What Alan Culpepper said of John applies equally to the other Gospels as well: 'Every element of the gospel contributes to the production of its meaning'[21] and 'the gospel must be approached as a unity, a literary whole.'[22]

The emotions of Jesus are therefore not depicted in a haphazard or ad hoc manner. They are to be understood within a framework, and this framework is supplied by the complementary theologies of the four Gospels. So rather than devoting a chapter to each emotion of Jesus we are on much surer ground if we devote a chapter to each of the Gospels. Each occurrence of an emotion can then be considered within its own narrative context. Hence its contribution to that Gospel's portrait of Jesus can be carefully assessed. This approach also opens up

---

20 Richard A. Burridge, *Four Gospels, One Jesus? A Symbolic Reading* (Grand Rapids, MI: Eerdmans, 1994), p. 2.

21 R. Alan Culpepper, *Anatomy of the Fourth Gospel: A Study in Literary Design* (Philadelphia: Fortress, 1983), 5.

22 Culpepper, *Anatomy*, 49.

the possibilities of careful exegesis with its potential for fresh insights. It will also enable discerning comparisons to be made between the Gospels both at the level of parallel passages and at that of the overall portraits of Jesus.

An accurate understanding of Jesus' emotions in the Gospels holds the potential for more authentic Christian living. The *imitatio Christi* principle has often been vigorously pursued by those seeking to follow the example of Christ in the realms of morality, life-style and personal relationships. Could it apply equally in the area of emotions? This is a question that can only be answered once the emotions of Jesus in the Gospels have been carefully researched and well understood.

CHAPTER 1

The Compassionate King: Jesus' Emotions in Matthew's Gospel

With his ten references to the emotions of Jesus, Matthew captures a wide range of feelings. Jesus is astonished or amazed (8.10), he sternly warns (9.30), and he has compassion (9.36; 14.14; 15.32; 20.32). In Gethsemane he is sorrowful and troubled (26.37). More than that, he is 'overwhelmed with sorrow to the point of death' (26.38). On the cross, in a climactic expression of emotion, he utters the cry of dereliction (27.46). It is as if Jesus' emotions gain in intensity as the story progresses. A pattern can be discerned. But there is more here than meets the eye. There is a careful symmetry in Matthew's portrayal that operates at a deeper level. To discover this we need to compare Matthew with Mark and Luke.

All three Synoptic Gospels have Jesus' three passion predictions as their centrepiece. In no uncertain terms, and on three separate occasions, he forewarns his disciples that he must go to Jerusalem, be betrayed, suffer at the hands of the religious leaders, be killed and be raised to life on the third day. The first such prediction immediately follows Peter's confession that Jesus is the Christ (Mt. 16.21; Mk 8.31, 32; Lk. 9.22). The second is after the healing of the epileptic boy (Mt. 17.22, 23; Mk 9.31; Lk. 9.44) and the third follows the departure of the rich young ruler (Mt. 20.17-19; Mk 10.32-34; Lk. 18.31-33). These three predictions are pivotal for each of the Synoptic Gospels and mark a turning point in the narrative.

From this evidence we can safely conclude that there is an identifiable 'prediction section' between Peter's confession and the arrival in Jerusalem. Moreover, all these predictions are made on the way from Caesarea Philippi in the north (where Peter made his confession) to Jerusalem in the south (where Jesus will die). Some scholars therefore call this the 'journey' or 'way section',[1] which is flanked

---

1 In this section of Mark the word *hodos* ('way') is found 7x (8.27; 9.33, 34; 10.17, 32, 46, 52). This emphasis is less pronounced in Matthew and Luke, with only two and three occurrences respectively (Mt. 20.17, 30; Lk. 9.57; 10.4; 18.35).

by Jesus' ministry in Galilee on the one side and by his passion in Jerusalem on the other. From this it will be seen that all three Synoptics follow the same basic outline:

Table 1.1 Major Divisions in the Synoptic Gospels

	Galilee	*Journey*	*Jerusalem*
Mark	1.14–8.26	8.27–10.52	11.1–16.8
Matthew	4.12–16.12	16.13–20.34	21.1–28.15
Luke	4.14–9.17	9.18–19.28	19.29–24.53

Each of the Synoptics develops this basic outline in its own way,[2] but these three major sections remain foundational to each. For our purposes it is also important to realize that the emotions of Jesus in the Synoptics fall out along the same lines:

Table 1.2 Jesus' Emotions within the Major Divisions of the Synoptic Gospels

Matthew	*Mark*	*Luke*
	Introduction	
1.1–4.11	**1.1-13**	**1.1–4.13**
–	–	–
	Galilee	
4.12–16.12	**1.14–8.26**	**4.14–9.17**
Amazement (8.10)	Amazement (6.6)	*Amazement* (7.9)
Compassion (9.36;	*Compassion* (1.41; 6.34; 8.2)	*Compassion*
14.14; 15.32)	*A stern warning* (1.43)	(7.13)
A stern warning (9.30)	*Anger* (3.5)	
	Deep distress (3.5)	
	Sighing (7.34)	
	Deep sighing (8.12)	
	Journey	
16.13–20.34	**8.27–10.52**	**9.18–19.28**
Compassion (20.34)	*Compassion* (9.22)	Joy (10.21)
	Indignation (10.14)	Distress (12.50)
	Love (10.21)	

(continued)

2   Matthew, for example, overlays this basic geographical structure by carefully alternating narrative and discourse sections in the main body of his Gospel. Because of his consistent use of opening and closing formulas, five distinct discourses can be recognized: 5.1–7.29; 10.1-42; 13.10-53; 18.1-35; 24.1–25.46. According to Christopher R. Smith, 'Literary Evidences of a Fivefold Structure in the Gospel of Matthew', *NTS* 43 (1997), p. 549, Matthew may be aptly described as the 'gospel of the kingdom' (14.14). These discourses may be said to highlight the kingdom's foundations, mission, mystery, family and destiny respectively.

Matthew	Mark	Luke
	Jerusalem	
21.1–28.20	11.1–16.8	19.29–24.53
Sorrowful and troubled	Deeply distressed and	Weeping (19.41)
(26.37)	troubled (14.33)	[Anguish (22.44)]*
Overwhelmed with	Overwhelmed with sorrow	
sorrow (26.38)	(14.34)	
Cry of dereliction (27.46)	Cry of dereliction (15.34)	

* Square brackets are used here to indicate a textual problem which will be addressed under 3.7 below.

At this point some preliminary observations are in order:

1. No emotions of Jesus are recorded in the introductory sections or in the resurrection accounts. All references are restricted to the main body of each Gospel. They therefore fall between his baptism and temptation on the one hand and his death on the other. Within this framework each Gospel records at least one emotion in each major period of Jesus' ministry.
2. The words in *italics* indicate emotions that accompany the performing of a miracle. Most of these occur in the Galilee section. Matthew and Mark each also record a single occurrence in the journey section.
3. The underlined words indicate emotions that are related to the Passion. In the Jerusalem section the clustering of such emotions is complete.[3] Without exception all Jesus' emotions that are recorded here are associated most intimately with the Passion. An early anticipation of this event is found in Lk. 12.50.
4. The tendency to associate certain emotions with miracles and others with the Passion is most pronounced in Matthew. Without exception, emotions associated with miracles in Matthew are found in the Galilee and journey sections, and those associated with the passion are in the Jerusalem section. Mark and Luke give evidence of the same pattern, but deviate from it somewhat in the first two sections. In the Synoptics there is therefore a high correlation between Jesus' emotions and his miracles and Passion.

From these observations it will be seen that while the words Matthew uses to describe Jesus' emotions overlap completely with the terms found in the other Synoptics, he nevertheless has a unique contribution to make. Only in Matthew are Jesus' emotions aligned perfectly with his miracles in the Galilee and journey sections, and with his Passion in the Jerusalem section. This perfect alignment matches well with his overall presentation of Jesus.

---

3 The relationship of some of Jesus' emotions to his miracles and Passion is not always immediately obvious. For example, his compassion does not appear to be directly related to a miracle in Mt. 9.36, nor his weeping to the Passion in Lk. 19.41. These choices will be defended later in the discussion.

1.1 *Matthew's Presentation of Jesus*

Although the Gospels did not always appear in the order Matthew, Mark, Luke and John (in some early records John followed Matthew), it is perhaps signifi- cant that Matthew has always been placed first. In a way this is as it should be, as Matthew is the logical link between the Old Testament and the New. This becomes apparent as early as the Gospel's opening verse: 'The book of the geneal- ogy of Jesus Christ, the son of David, the son of Abraham' (NASB). This is a far more loaded statement than it might appear at first sight. Each expression is fraught with meaning and forges very strong links with the Old Testament, but especially with the opening and closing passages of the Hebrew Bible. It also sets the tone for all that follows in Matthew's Gospel.[4]

The book of the genealogy is a far more suggestive expression in the original Greek, which reads *biblos geneseōs*. It takes little imagination for the English reader to figure out that this means 'the book of Genesis'. This is precisely what would have come to the mind of the Gospel's first readers who were familiar with the Septuagint (LXX), the Greek translation of the Old Testament made in the second and third centuries BC. This means that both the Old and New Testaments begin with the book of Genesis! In the case of the New Testament it is 'the book of the genesis of Jesus Christ'. The actual expression *biblos geneseōs* is found in the Greek Old Testament on only two occasions – and both in the book of Genesis. In Gen. 2.4 it refers to 'the account of the origin' of the heavens and the earth. Then in Gen. 5.1 these words refer to the list of Adam's descendants. In the LXX, therefore, *biblos geneseōs* refers to both the beginning of creation and the beginning of humanity. Hence, in his very opening words, Matthew is strongly hinting that God is making a new beginning through Jesus Christ.[5]

Jesus Christ should, of course, not be understood in the contemporary sense of a Christian name and a surname. As Matthew will explain in v. 21, the name 'Jesus' means 'Saviour'. It was the Greek name for Joshua in the Old Testament. It was also a name commonly given to Jewish baby boys in the first century. For Matthew, however, the birth of this particular Jesus was anything but ordinary. In both his birth (vv. 18-19) and his naming (vv. 20-21) Matthew sees the fulfil- ment of prophecy (vv. 22-23). This Jesus will also be called 'Immanuel' (v. 23) in fulfilment of Isa. 7.14. The accompanying interpretations of the names *Jesus* and *Immanuel*, namely 'he will save his people from their sins' (v. 21) and 'God with

---

4 Cf. Warren Carter, 'Kernels and Narrative Blocks: The Structure of Matthew's Gospel', *CBQ* 54 (1992), p. 473, 'The genealogy functions . . . as an interpretative framework which places Jesus' story in a particular context to shape the way in which that story is to be understood.'

5 Warren Carter, 'Matthew and the Gentiles: Individual Conversion and/or Systemic Transformation?', *JSNT* 26 (2004), p. 262, develops this point further by arguing that the phrase *biblos geneseōs* 'evokes not just two isolated verses (Gen. 2.4; 5.1), but the larger Genesis accounts of which they are a part, namely the accounts of God's creation of the world and of humans, as well as accounts of resultant human faithlessness, God's judgement and God's willingness to start again. That is, Matthew's opening phrase evokes the story of God's creative and sovereign purposes for the whole world as the initial context for hearing the story of Jesus.'

us' (v. 23), invite the reader to reflect on the nature of his mission.[6] It is precisely those whom he will save from their sins who will also call him 'Immanuel'.[7] While the name *Jesus* is common enough, in this context it has strong overtones of divinity.[8]

Christ, on the other hand, is a title meaning 'Messiah' or 'Anointed One'. In the Old Testament we have a case of a prophet being anointed (1 Kgs 19.16) and some priests were also anointed (Lev. 4.5, 16; 6.22), but most often the anointed one is a king (e.g. 1 Sam. 2.10; Ps. 2.2; 18.50). This was primarily a royal title.[9] So Jesus Christ is a Saviour and a King who has the hallmarks of divinity. He is the Saviour King. Matthew then proceeds to give us his pedigree. He comes from the purest bloodline. He has the perfect ancestry to be the King.[10]

The son of David, the son of Abraham. With the selection of these two ancestors Matthew traces Jesus' genesis all the way back to Genesis. Yet this raises the question as to why Matthew chose these two forefathers out of the genealogy of the more than forty names that immediately follow. We might be inclined to think that these were the most famous of the forefathers and that they are highlighted for this reason. But the answer is probably to be found at a deeper level. Of all the ancestors listed these are the only ones with whom God made a covenant. In the Davidic covenant God promised David both a dynasty and a temple (2 Sam. 7.11-16, cf. 1 Chron. 17.10-14). Because of this covenant David is assured that his throne and kingdom will last forever. About a millennium earlier God has made an equally generous promise to Abraham (Gen. 12.1-3). The essence of the

---

6   Thus Richard T. France, *The Gospel of Matthew*, NICNT (Grand Rapids, MI: Eerdmans, 2007), p. 53; cf. Mark A. Powell, 'The Plot and Subplots of Matthew's Gospel', *NTS* 38 (1992) p. 199, 'The divine plan is introduced in the first part of the narrative. Jesus is presented as the Son of God, the one through whom God is 'with us' (1.23). God is pleased with Jesus (3.17) and, through Jesus, intends to save people from their sin (1.21).'

7   France, *Matthew*, 58, perceptively observes that the words 'they will call' in the quote from Isa. 7.14 agree neither with the Masoretic Hebrew text ('she will call') nor the LXX ('you will call'). In Matthew's account the nearest antecedent to 'they' (v. 23) are the people who will be saved from their sins (v. 21).

8   Cf. Joseph Neuner, 'Immanuel, God with Us', *Vid* 62 (1998) p. 563, 'According to Matthew's Gospel this text [Isa. 7.14] is fulfilled in Mary's child Jesus: He is Immanuel, God with us; he embodies God's saving presence for his people. The content of this title unfolds in Jesus' *earthly life*, in his mission; his *passion and death* reveal its full implications.'

9   In the LXX *Christos* translates the Hebrew *mashiach* ('anointed one') 36*x*. Apart from the sporadic references to priests (3*x*) and prophets (2*x*), the overwhelming majority of references is to a king, such as Saul (11*x*), David (3*x*) or a monarch in the Davidic line (14*x*).

10 Lidija Novakovic, 'Jesus as the Davidic Messiah in Matthew', *HBT* 19 (1997), pp. 152–53, argues: 'Matthew's primary aim in ch. 1 is to establish the royal identity of the newborn child Jesus. This conclusion is supported not only by the fact that he mentions in 1:1 the designation "Son of David" before the designation "Son of Abraham," but also by the fact that the term "Son of David" occurs again in v. 20, but here applied to Joseph. Because the succession of generations in Matthew's genealogy has been broken between Joseph and Jesus (v. 16), the section 1:18-25 has the task to show that this succession has been restored. Applying the title "Son of David" to Joseph in this context suggests that the crucial point of the continuity is the Davidic line. The adoption of Jesus by Joseph made him a legal descendant of David, the king.'

Abrahamic covenant was that through him all peoples on earth would be blessed. An early hint of this is seen in Jesus' genealogy in Mt. 1.3-6, which contains such prominent Gentile names as Tamar and Rahab (both Canaanites), Ruth (a Moabitess) and Uriah (a Hittite).

The last book of the Old Testament in the Hebrew canon of Matthew's day was not Malachi as in our Bibles, but 2 Chronicles (see Mt. 23.35; Lk. 11.51). By the end of 2 Chronicles the temple lies in ruins and the last of the Davidic kings has been deported to Babylon. With this tragic note on which the Hebrew canon closes, both the Davidic and Abrahamic covenants seem to have been decisively annulled. David's dynasty and Solomon's temple have been destroyed, and Abraham's descendants hardly appear to be a source of blessing to the nations. The only ray of hope comes through the proclamation of Cyrus king of Persia indicating that the Jerusalem temple will one day be rebuilt (2 Chron. 36.22-23). At the same time Cyrus reminds his Jewish subjects that God 'has given me all the kingdoms of the earth' (v. 23). This is precisely the point at which Matthew picks up the thread of redemptive history. By the end of this Gospel, in the giving of the Great Commission, the risen Jesus can confidently say, 'All authority in heaven and on earth has been given to me' (28.18). He is the true son of David as confirmed by his genealogy (1.2-17). The Davidic line, which has for so long been in eclipse, is now at last being restored. As the messianic King he does not come to restore the old Davidic kingdom but to transpose it to a higher key and to establish its authority over the nations (Mt. 3.2; 4.17; 28.18-20).

Matthew, therefore, picks up the story of redemptive history from where it left off at the end of the Old Testament as he knew it. Through his Gospel he is seeking to demonstrate that the covenants with David and Abraham, which seemed to have come to nothing by the end of the Old Testament, are now being gloriously fulfilled in Jesus Christ. As 'great David's greater son' he has come to establish an eternal kingdom. As the true son of Abraham it is in him that all the nations will be blessed as the Great Commission is carried out (Mt. 28.18-20). As the Immanuel he is also the new temple. Rather than dwelling in a physical temple (Mt. 21.12-13), God now dwells with his people in him (Mt. 1.23; 28.20).[11] Although on the surface these may appear to be just incidental references, Mt. 1.23 and 28.20 actually encapsulate one of Matthew's major themes. Matthew is a master of the neat literary device known as *inclusio*, a technique whereby a work (or a section of the work) could end on the same note with which it began, and thus signal a major theme in the intervening material. In Matthew the largest *inclusio* is between 'God with us' (1.23) and 'I will be with you' (28.20). These two short statements are like brackets around the whole narrative. Hence this Gospel ends the way it began – on the reassuring note of God's presence. In Jesus God is present with his people.

Matthew's first chapter therefore gives the reader enormous clues when it comes to the identity of Jesus. From the very beginning Matthew makes it clear

---

11   Cf. Carter, 'Matthew and the Gentiles', p. 263: 'Linking Jesus with Abraham from the outset establishes Jesus as an agent of the divine purposes not just to convert individual Gentiles, but to bless all the nations of the world.'

that Jesus' origins are both human and divine. He is simultaneously the son of David, the son of Abraham and the Immanuel who was conceived of the Holy Spirit (v. 20). This dual identity of Jesus provides the matrix out of which Matthew's entire narrative is developed.[12] It is also the key to understanding his emotions.

1.2 *Amazement (8.5-13)*

⁵ When Jesus had entered Capernaum, a centurion came to him, asking for help.

⁶ 'Lord,' he said, 'my servant lies at home paralysed and in terrible suffering.'

⁷ Jesus said to him, 'I will go and heal him.'

⁸ The centurion replied, 'Lord, I do not deserve to have you come under my roof. But just say the word, and my servant will be healed.

⁹ For I myself am a man under authority, with soldiers under me. I tell this one, "Go", and he goes; and that one, "Come", and he comes. I say to my servant, "Do this", and he does it.'

¹⁰ When Jesus heard this, *he was astonished* and said to those following him, 'I tell you the truth, I have not found anyone in Israel with such great faith.

¹¹ I say to you that many will come from the east and the west, and will take their places at the feast with Abraham, Isaac and Jacob in the kingdom of heaven.

¹² But the subjects of the kingdom will be thrown outside, into the darkness, where there will be weeping and gnashing of teeth.'

¹³ Then Jesus said to the centurion, 'Go! It will be done just as you believed it would.' And his servant was healed at that very hour.

The first emotion that Matthew attributes to Jesus should surprise the thoughtful reader. In saying that Jesus 'was astonished' Matthew uses the Greek verb *thaumazō* which can also be translated 'be amazed', 'marvel' or 'wonder'. This is hardly what one would expect from the bearer of the divine name *Immanuel*. As Matthew's story unfolds, the amazement of Jesus recorded here becomes all the more remarkable. The remaining occurrences of this verb always refer to others being amazed at Jesus. The disciples are amazed at the stilling of the storm (8.27) and the withering of the fig tree (21.20). The crowds were amazed when they saw the dumb speaking, the crippled made well, the lame walking and the blind seeing (9.33; 15.31). The Pharisees were astonished at the aptness of his answer (22.22) and Pilate at his silence (27.14). This sole reference to Jesus' amazement is therefore unusual, exceptional and out of the ordinary. What could have motivated this unique expression of emotion? What was it about the centurion that so greatly impressed Jesus? To answer these questions we not only need to

---

12   Cf. Novakovic, 'Davidic Messiah', p. 172.

precisely understand the centurion's response to Jesus in vv. 8-9, but also the wider context in which these words are found.

At the end of ch. 7 Matthew concludes his version of the Sermon on the Mount (Mt. 5–7) by making the observation that Jesus 'taught as one who had authority' (7.29). In Matthew's further references to Jesus' authority, it turns out that this is the authority of the son of David, the son of Abraham, and the Immanuel, who had been so prominently introduced in ch. 1. Matthew emphasizes Jesus' authority to forgive sins and to heal a paralytic (9.6-8). In the next chapter Jesus is able to delegate to his twelve disciples his authority both to exorcize and to heal (10.1). Early in Passion Week he exercises his authority to cleanse the temple as well as to heal the blind and the lame who came to him there (21.12-17, 23-27). After his resurrection, and as the introduction to his Great Commission, he can climactically declare, 'All authority in heaven and on earth has been given to me' (28.18). When the centurion refers to his own authority (8.9), this must be understood within Matthew's development of the theme of Jesus' authority.

This theme commences with Matthew's reference to Jesus' authoritative teaching (7.29). But not only are his words imbued with divine and messianic authority, so are his deeds. Matthew's reference to Jesus' authority, therefore, not only refers back to the Sermon on the Mount but it also points forward to the three groups of miracles that Jesus performs in chs 8–9. His authority is demonstrated in both his words and his works. It drives not only his teaching but also his miracles, not least the three that are recorded immediately after the Sermon has been concluded (8.1-17). In Matthew's account Jesus' authority is the hinge that links his preaching and his miracles.

In the first triplet of miracles three people are healed – a leper (vv. 1-4), the centurion's servant (vv. 5-13) and Peter's mother-in-law (vv. 14-17). Within the context of first century Judaism the beneficiaries of these miracles would all have suffered some degree of disadvantage.[13] The leper would have been disadvantaged because of his disease, the centurion (and presumably also his servant) because of their race, and Peter's mother-in-law because of her gender. To one degree or another each would have been excluded or at least restricted from full participation in the worship of God, particularly at the Jerusalem temple. These three miracles therefore function as an acted parable indicating that in the kingdom that Jesus is establishing all these barriers will be abolished.[14]

Another feature of the context that should not be overlooked is the fact that two of the healings took place in Capernaum. This town was located on the north-west shore of the Sea of Galilee, about four kilometres west of the mouth of the Jordan.[15] This location made it a frontier town falling just within the

---

13 Thus Christoph Burchard, 'Zu Matthäus 8,5-13', *ZNW* 84 (1993), p. 287.

14 France, *Matthew*, p. 321, comments: 'The point is strongly emphasized in Matthew's telling of the story of the centurion, with this elevation of this Gentile's faith above any in Israel and its revolutionary vision of outsiders welcomed to take their place alongside the Jewish patriarchs at the messianic banquet.'

15 Yohanan Aharoni and Michael Avi-Yonah, *The Macmillan Bible Atlas* (New York: Macmillan; rev. edn, 1977), p. 144.

Galilean domains of Herod Antipas, but not far from the territories of Herod Philip to the north and east. Being on the border as well as on a major trade route it naturally had a toll station (Mt. 9.9).[16] To defend the border and to ensure the collection of customs and taxes it also held a military garrison under the control of a non-Jewish centurion.[17] It is unlikely that there was an officer senior to him.[18]

The Jewish historian Josephus writes of Capernaum and its vicinity in glowing and almost idyllic terms. It is a temperate and fertile region where every plant can flourish. Walnuts, palms, figs, olives and grapes all thrive there. Without a hint of exaggeration he praises the area for being 'wonderful in its characteristics and in its beauty' and 'nature's crowning achievement'.[19] Capernaum was also the place where Jesus settled after John had been thrown into prison (Mt. 4.12-13). It could rightly be called 'his own town' (Mt. 9.1) and 'home' (Mk 2.1), and thus became the base for his Galilean ministry. Jesus taught in the local synagogue (Mk 1.21; Jn 6.59), which the centurion had built (Lk. 7.5). Capernaum was also the scene of some rather impressive miracles (Mt. 17.24-27; Mk 1.23-28; 2.1-12; Lk. 4.23, 31-37; Jn 4.43-54), some of which no doubt had preceded the healing of the centurion's servant. By this time it would be fair to conclude that Jesus was a well known public figure in town. Whether he and the centurion knew each other personally before this point must remain an open question, but there can be little doubt that the centurion knew of Jesus' reputation as a preacher and a healer.

In any event, upon returning to Capernaum from the Galilean hill country Jesus is met by the centurion. He comes to him pleading for help (v. 5). His servant is lying at home paralysed and in terrible suffering (v. 6). From the parallel passage in Luke we learn that the young man's situation is indeed desperate. He is sick and about to die (Lk. 7.2). What precise disease it is we do not know. The identity of the sick man has also been debated by scholars. Matthew describes him as a *pais*, an ambiguous term that can mean 'servant', 'slave', 'child' or 'boy'. Those who see a parallel only with Luke 7.3 opt for 'servant' or 'slave', the unambiguous meaning of the Greek word *doulos* which Luke employs. Those, on the other hand, who also see a parallel in Jn 4.43-54 generally opt for 'child' or 'boy', as the recipient of the healing in that instance is the official's son.[20] Recent scholarship of a more radical stripe has thrown a third option into the mix. According to this view the *pais* is the centurion's 'boy love' within a pederastic

---

16 Jericho was in a similar situation in the south of the country (Lk. 19.1-10).
17 *EDNT* 2, p. 280.
18 Thus J. A. G. Haslam, 'The Centurion at Capernaum: Luke 7:1-10', *ExpTim* 96 (1985), p. 109; cf. France, *Matthew*, p. 311.
19 Flavius Josephus, *The Jewish War* (trans. G. A. Williamson; Harmondsworth, Middlesex, UK: Penguin, 1959), p. 221.
20 Ralph P. Martin, 'The Pericope of the Healing of the Centurion's Servant/Son (Matt 8:5-13 par. Luke 7:1-10): Some Exegetical Notes', in Robert A. Guelich, ed., *Unity and Diversity in New Testament Theology: Essays in Honor of George E. Ladd* (Grand Rapids, MI: Eerdmans, 1978), p. 15, sees parallels between the two passages and further argues that 'it is unlikely that a Roman official would show great concern for a subordinate, especially in view of his own confession of possessing authority.'

relationship.[21] The centurion's reluctance to have Jesus come into his house was due to his fear that Jesus might usurp his place in the boy's affections.[22] The argument on which this understanding is based has already been soundly refuted in the scholarly literature.[23] Furthermore, it stretches credulity to the limit to suggest that the centurion, who may have been a God-fearer, would have enjoyed such a good reputation in the Jewish community at Capernaum (Lk. 7.4-5) had he been a known sexual predator. Nothing in the Gospel text suggests that the mortally ill man was his 'boy love'. Moreover, the healing of the official's son in John 4 is hardly a convincing parallel. Hence the traditional view, that the *pais* was the centurion's servant, is most likely correct. He may have been a soldier acting as the centurion's personal aide, but he could also have been a domestic slave.[24]

Another point of interpretation that has divided scholars is whether Jesus' response to the centurion's implied request that he heal his paralysed servant should be construed as a statement or as a question. Did Jesus say, 'I will go and heal him', or did he ask, 'Will I go and heal him?'? The vast majority of English translations favour taking the saying as a statement. The only dissenting voices are the TNIV and the margin of the NEB which reads, 'Am I to come and heal him?' Greek grammar actually allows equally for either possibility, which is probably the reason for the greater division among scholars than among translations.[25] Recently Richard France, in his magisterial commentary on Matthew, has mounted a compelling case for taking Jesus' response as a question.

France begins by observing that the 'I' (Greek *egō*) in the saying is emphatic.[26] This emphasis on the speaker would make the saying rather pompous if it is taken as a statement, as seen for example in the Jerusalem Bible's rendering, 'I will come myself and cure him.' If that is the case, who would Jesus be comparing himself to? The delegated healings of the disciples do not commence before the beginning of ch. 10. If, on the other hand, the emphatic *egō* belongs to a question its place in the sentence is far more obvious. It draws attention to the highly irregular suggestion that as a good Jew Jesus should visit a Gentile home. Perhaps with a note of disbelief, surprise or even indignation in his voice he asks the centurion, 'You want *me* to come and heal him?'[27]

France further argues that a statement implying Jesus' willingness to enter a Gentile home here would conflict with the hard time that Jesus later gives the

---

21   Thus Theodore W. Jennings, Jr., and Tat-Siong Benny Liew, 'Mistaken Identities but Model Faith: Rereading the Centurion, the Chap and the Christ in Matthew 8:5-13', *JBL* 123 (2004), p. 468.

22   Jennings and Liew, 'Mistaken Identities', p. 484.

23   D. B. Saddington, 'The Centurion in Matthew 8:5-13: Consideration of the Proposal of Theodore W. Jennings, Jr., and Tat-Siong Benny Liew', *JBL* 125 (2006), pp. 140–42.

24   Thus France, *Matthew*, p. 312.

25   Robert A. J. Gagnon, 'The Shape of Matthew's Q Text of the Centurion at Capernaum: Did It Mention Delegations?', *NTS* 40 (1994), p. 136, lists an impressive array of scholars on both sides of the issue.

26   France, *Matthew*, p. 313.

27   France, *Matthew*, p. 313.

Canaanite woman who comes to him with a similar request (Mt. 15.21-28).[28] Why would Jesus make things difficult for the woman when earlier in the narrative he had been more than willing to enter the house of a centurion?[29] The very suggestion makes Jesus uncharacteristically inconsistent. As it turns out, his consistency remains unblemished. In Matthew only the healing of the centurion's servant and the woman's daughter are performed from a distance. The only instance of Jesus entering a Gentile building in the Gospels is when he enters Pilate's headquarters in Jerusalem at his trial. By then he clearly had no choice in the matter. Although entering a Gentile household did not contravene the laws of Moses, it would have been seen as a rather defiant breach of a traditional taboo (cf. Acts 10.28-29).[30]

The centurion's reply to Jesus' understandably piqued question, 'You want *me* to come and heal him?' then makes perfect sense: 'Lord, I do not deserve to have you come under my roof. But just say the word and my servant will be healed' (v. 8). France offers a convincing paraphrase of this verse: 'Of course not; I couldn't expect you to come under my roof; all I am asking for is a word of healing, spoken here where you are.'[31] The statement is more than a culturally sensitive remark on the centurion's part. It also expresses more than merely a concern not to render Jesus ceremonially unclean. Twice the centurion addresses Jesus as 'Lord' (vv. 6, 8), which the context shows to be far more than a term of politeness or respect. The centurion feels unworthy in the face of Jesus' authority. It is precisely Jesus' authority that he underscores so brilliantly when he speaks of his own authority in v. 9, 'For I myself am a man *under authority*, with soldiers under me. I tell this one, "Go", and he goes; and that one, "Come", and he comes. I say to my servant, "Do this"' and he does it.' But why does he say that he is 'under authority' when he really wants to say that he has authority?

What the centurion is doing here is drawing an analogy. He is comparing Jesus' authority to his own. This is not totally clear in the NIV translation. It makes no provision for the little Greek word *kai* (meaning 'too' or 'also') at the beginning of the sentence. Literally the centurion is saying, 'For I *too* am a man under authority . . .' What at first sounds rather counter-intuitive now becomes perfectly clear. Being the good military man that he is, he realizes that he has authority only because he is under authority. The same is true of Jesus. The difference is that, while the centurion is under imperial authority, Jesus is under divine authority. As Carson has pointed out, 'Precisely because Jesus was under God's

28 France, *Matthew*, p. 314; cf. Gagnon, 'Shape of Matthew's Q Text', p. 136: 'The decisive consideration is that for Jesus to acquiesce so willingly to the centurion's request renders incomprehensible Matthew's version of the Syrophoenician woman, where Matthew lays great stress on the reluctance of the disciples and Jesus to assist this 'Canaanite' woman (15.23-24; cf. 10:5-6).'

29 Craig S. Keener, *Matthew* (Downers Grove: Inter-Varsity Press, 1997), p. 173, also reads v. 7 as a question and adds: 'Here Jesus erects a barrier the Gentile must surmount, as in 15:24, 26.'

30 See W. F. Albright and C. S. Mann, *Matthew* (AB 26; New York: Doubleday, 1971), p. 93.

31 France, *Matthew*, p. 313. Keener, *Matthew*, p. 173, comments: 'Rather than protesting, the centurion acknowledges his questionable merit before Jesus.'

authority, he was vested with God's authority, so that when Jesus spoke, God spoke. To defy Jesus was to defy God; and Jesus' word must therefore be vested with God's authority that is able to heal sickness . . . [H]is authority was God's authority, and his word was effective because it was God's word.'[32] Just as the centurion is backed by the full authority of the Roman Empire which he represents to his troops, Jesus is backed by the very authority of God.

Coming from a Gentile centurion this is a penetrating insight into the identity of Jesus. His perceptive analogy draws forth Jesus' amazement. Jesus is truly astonished at the man's level of spiritual awareness. With so much emphasis falling on Jesus' divinity in this context, such an expression of genuine surprise introduces a delightfully human touch. So overwhelmed is Jesus by the centurion's insight that he solemnly declares, 'I tell you the truth, I have not found anyone in Israel with such great faith' (v. 10). This is as strong a commendation for the centurion as it is a piercing rebuke to Israel. Time and again in Matthew's Gospel Jesus rebukes the crowds, the disciples and even Peter for having 'little faith' (Mt. 6.30; 8.26; 14.31; 16.8; 17.20). By contrast, the centurion is credited with great faith. What does Jesus find so astonishing and so great about this man's faith?

At a most basic level the centurion believed that all Jesus needed to do to heal his servant was to 'say the word' (v. 8). This is remarkable because up to this point in Matthew Jesus had not healed in this way. The first miracles that are performed merely 'with a word' are the exorcisms recorded in v. 16. The only other healing from a distance that Matthew records is that of the Canaanite woman's daughter. This woman is the only other character in this Gospel who is commended for her great faith (Mt. 15.28), and she too was a Gentile.

Another level at which the centurion lifted the standard of faith to new heights comes with his christological insight. Although we should avoid the temptation of reading a full-blown Christology into his analogy, he has a remarkable understanding of Jesus' identity. Ironically, he has penetrated the mystery of Jesus' person more profoundly by his simple analogy than any Jew had managed to do up to this point. In Jesus he has seen something of the Immanuel.

But the centurion has seen still more. In his own way he has also recognized Jesus as the true son of Abraham. Even though he was a Gentile he did not see himself as being beyond the pale of messianic blessings. Whether he was conscious of it or not, he was making his request of the one in whom all the nations of the earth would be blessed. With the eye of faith he could see that, although he was not an Israelite and had no privileges by virtue of his birth, Jesus could extend his authority to heal his mortally ill servant.

No wonder Jesus is amazed. He is filled with delighted surprise because this centurion believes he can heal with a word, has a remarkable insight into his identity and anticipates the Gentile mission. This outsider has grasped some of the grandeur of Jesus' person as the son of David, the son of Abraham, and the Immanuel. This certainly outstrips any faith that Jesus has seen in Israel up to this

---

32   D. A. Carson, 'Matthew', *The Expositor's Bible Commentary* (Grand Rapids, MI: Zondervan, 1984), vol. 8, pp. 201–202.

point, even among his own disciples. Although this Gentile considered himself unworthy to have Jesus come under his roof, Jesus declares that he is worthy to dine at the messianic banquet with Abraham, Isaac and Jacob (v. 12).

In granting the coveted healing for the centurion's servant Jesus picks up the thread of Gentile inclusion that runs through this Gospel from beginning to end. Jesus' genealogy includes Gentiles (Mt. 1.3-6). The first to pay him their respects as the newborn king of the Jews were Gentiles (Mt. 2.1-12). When he began his public ministry it was in 'Galilee of the Gentiles' (Mt. 4.15). Those whom he commended for their great faith were Gentiles (Mt. 8.10; 15.28). In the Olivet Discourse he predicts that the gospel of the kingdom will be preached to all the nations (24.14). Finally, having returned again to Galilee of the Gentiles, he commands his disciples to 'go and make disciples of all the nations' (Mt. 28.19). The Gentile thread is therefore woven carefully through Matthew's Gospel, but when Jesus initially observes the faith of a Gentile firsthand he is genuinely amazed.

1.3 *A Stern Warning (9.27-31)*

27 As Jesus went on from there, two blind men followed him, calling out, 'Have mercy on us, Son of David!'
28 When he had gone indoors, the blind men came to him, and he asked them, 'Do you believe that I am able to do this?' 'Yes, Lord,' they replied.
29 Then he touched their eyes and said, 'According to your faith will it be done to you';
30 and their sight was restored. *Jesus warned them sternly*, 'See that no-one knows about this.'
31 But they went out and spread the news about him all over that region.

Throughout chs 8 and 9 Jesus continues to demonstrate his authority through his miracles. Following the healing of the centurion's servant, while still in Capernaum, he cures Peter's mother-in-law of a fever, drives out demons and heals the sick. Because of the thronging crowd he leaves Capernaum by boat and heads for the other side of the lake. But by the beginning of ch. 9 he is back. More miracles follow. A paralytic is put back on his feet (9.1-8). A woman who had been subject to bleeding for twelve years touched the edge of Jesus' cloak and was healed (9.20-22). A ruler's daughter is raised from the dead (9.23-25). Capernaum has indeed become the scene of some spectacular miracles (cf. 11.4-6).[33]

Small wonder then that, after Jesus had left the ruler's house, he finds himself being followed by two blind men. They cry out for his assistance. The wording of

---

33 Donald A. Hagner, *Matthew 1-13* (Word Biblical Commentary; Waco: Word, 1993), p. 252, 'By turning from the raising of the dead to the healing of the blind, Matthew continues to document the sovereign power of Jesus in terms of a full range of miracles, corresponding closely to those expected with the coming of the messianic age.'

their plea is significant, 'Have mercy on us, Son of David!' (9.27). These two men may not have sight, but they certainly have insight. The way they understand Jesus is precisely the way Matthew has portrayed him at the beginning of his Gospel. In fact, in this Gospel they are the first ones explicitly to have this understanding. In that sense their understanding of Jesus is even more precise than that of the centurion. In hailing Jesus as the Son of David they will later be joined by the Canaanite woman (15.22), the two blind men at Jericho (20.30-31), the crowds at the triumphal entry (21.9) and the children in the temple (21.15). Ironically, it is the nobodies of Jewish society who recognize the messianic significance of Jesus, while the religious leaders remain blind to his true identity (12.22-24; 22.41-46).

Remarkably then, it is the blind who are the first to see Jesus for who he really is. Not only do they correctly call him 'Son of David', they also plead 'Have mercy on us' and in a moment they will address him as 'Lord' (9.28). The language is actually quite stunning. Similar wording will later be found on the lips of the Canaanite woman (15.22), the father of the epileptic boy (17.15), and the two blind men in Jericho (20.30, 31). In each case the cry is heeded and followed by a miracle. These pleas all include the well known Greek words that have become famous through traditional hymnody, *Kyrie Eleison* ('Lord, have mercy'.) As it turns out, these words occur as a recurring refrain in the LXX version of the Psalms (Pss. 6.2; 9.13; 25.16; 26.11; 27.7; 30.10; 31.9; 41.4, 10; 51.1; 56.1; 86.3, 16; 119.29, 58, 132; 123.3). In the Psalter this refrain is exclusively addressed to Yahweh. These blind men are therefore using the loftiest possible language to address Jesus.

Nevertheless, in spite of their impeccable christological insight, Jesus treats these two blind men a little strangely. At first he keeps them at arm's length. He does not speak to them until they are all indoors or, more literally, 'in the house' (9.28). This could either have been Matthew's house (9.10) or Jesus' own house in Capernaum. He wants privacy perhaps because he can do without unnecessary and potentially harmful publicity. He does not want to be hailed loudly with messianic titles out on the street.[34] He also first enquires as to whether these men have faith (a requirement made only here in Matthew's Gospel),[35] and so he asks, 'Do you believe that I am able to do this?' (9.28). On hearing their affirmative answer he touches their eyes and pronounces them healed. 'According to your faith will it be done for you', he declares (9.29). It was an effective pronouncement, much like Jesus' statement to the centurion at the end of their conversation (8.13). 'It is', says France, 'what the philosophers call a "performative utterance," not stating that something will happen, still less merely wishing it, but making it happen.'[36]

In the case of the centurion this is where the story ended. With the blind men, however, it is at this point that the story takes a surprising twist. Once their sight is restored Jesus warns them sternly by swearing them to secrecy, 'See that no one knows about this' (9.30). Not only is this an unusual request, it is also made in

---

34 Thus Herman N. Ridderbos, *The Bible Student's Commentary – Matthew* (trans. Ray Togtman; Grand Rapids, MI: Zondervan, 1987), p. 190.

35 France, *Matthew*, p. 367.

36 France, *Matthew*, p. 320.

rather harsh terms. The stern warning comes from the Greek verb *embrimaomai*, a rare word that has overtones of anger and indignation.[37] There are only four other occurrences in the New Testament, three of which refer to strong emotional reactions on the part of Jesus himself (Mk 1.43; Jn 11.33, 38). The only other reference is to those at the home of Simon the Leper *scolding* the woman who anointed Jesus for wasting the expensive perfume rather than selling it and giving the money to the poor (Mk 14.5). In this instance anger is explicitly mentioned in the context. In the previous verse we are told that some who were present at the dinner were angry or indignant at what was happening. This anger then spilled over into their speech rebuking the woman. 'They scolded her' (ESV, NRSV). 'They criticized her harshly' (TEV). 'They snarled' (LB). 'They turned upon her with fury' (NEB). 'They were angry with her' (JB). These attempts at translating the same verb in a different context are instructive. Perhaps translators are too diffident to refer an emotion of such obvious sharpness to Jesus.

But why would Jesus speak to these formerly blind men in such strident tones? Why should he address them with overtones of anger and indignation when they had just addressed him with the utmost respect and theological accuracy? They had come in faith and had identified him even more precisely than the centurion who had inspired Jesus with wonder and amazement. So why does he seem to turn on them like this? If we understand Jesus' emotions at a purely human level, his reaction seems quite inappropriate. But he has just been addressed as God is addressed. So we must understand this as a divine reaction. They have just called him the 'Son of David' and they have addressed him as 'Lord'. They have recognized that his authority is both royal and divine, but now they are going to disregard it. They are going to disobey. They had faith, but not obedience. In spite of his insistence that no one should know about it, 'they went and spread the news about him all over that region' (v. 31).

So why is Jesus angry? Why does he speak harshly to these men? Because he knows that they are going to spread the news like wildfire. They are going to make his mission dangerous and his ministry more difficult.[38] This becomes apparent in the next scene (vv. 32-34). When Jesus has exorcized a demon the crowd is impressed, but the Pharisees are critical, 'It is by the prince of demons that he drives out demons' (v. 34). This is the very kind of situation he had wanted to prevent. It is the beginning of a conflict that will escalate into the so-called 'Beelzebub controversy' (12.22-37). As Lidija Novakovic has observed, 'His fame as the Son of David has been publicly spread, which gives rise to the first big conflict with the Jewish leaders.'[39] In sternly warning the two men who have just

---

37 MM, p. 206: 'We can produce no fresh evidence to throw light on the meaning of this difficult verb in the NT, but the LXX usage [Dan. 11.30] . . . is in favour of the meaning "am angry", "express violent displeasure", perhaps with the added idea of "within oneself."' LN 1, p. 295 gives the following entry for this verb: 'to have an intense, strong feeling of concern, often with the implication of indignation – "to feel strongly, to be indignant."'

38 Cf. Carson, 'Matthew', p. 233, re *embrimaomai*: 'This rather violent verb reveals Jesus' intense desire to avoid a falsely based and ill-conceived acclaim that would not only impede but also endanger his true mission.'

39 Novakovic, 'Davidic Messiah', p. 165.

been healed of their blindness, Jesus could foresee the looming storm. It is little wonder then that his words are laced with anger and indignation.

The first two reported expressions of Jesus' emotions in Matthew's Gospel therefore contrast quite sharply. In both cases there is a request for a healing miracle and the supplicants address Jesus respectfully and correctly, but at an emotional level his reactions are very different. The centurion inspires his wonder and amazement. The formerly blind men elicit a stern and angry warning. In the faith of the one Jesus foresees the Gentile mission. In the loose tongues of the others he foresees trouble with the Jewish leadership. As we will see throughout the Gospels, it is often his prescience that gives us the best clue to his true feelings.

1.4 *Compassion*

Compassion is the dominant emotion attributed to Jesus in Matthew's Gospel, accounting for no less than four out of the ten references. It is therefore a strong Matthaean emphasis. Jesus' compassion is directed mainly to crowds. Initially Matthew indicates that Jesus had compassion on the crowds 'because they were harassed and helpless, like sheep without a shepherd' (9.36). Later Jesus has compassion on the five thousand and demonstrates it by healing their sick and feeding the entire multitude (14.13-21). He also has compassion on the four thousand and feeds them (15.29-39). Both feedings take place by the Sea of Galilee. In Matthew's journey section, as Jesus and his disciples are leaving Jericho, he has compassion on two blind beggars and restores their sight (20.34).

Standing behind these four occurrences is the Greek word *splanchnizomai*, a verb which expresses strong emotion. It means 'to have great affection and compassion for someone'.[40] As Robert Roberts further explains, 'Compassion is a form of love, but distinguishable from other forms of love by the terms of its fellowship. Friendship, family affection, love of spouse, and love for fellow believers all differ from compassion in that the terms of this latter fellowship are suffering or deficiency.'[41] The New Testament use of *splanchnizomai* is confined to the Synoptics where it is used exclusively of Jesus and a few parable characters – the master of the unmerciful servant (Mt. 18.27), the Good Samaritan (Lk. 10.33) and the father of the prodigal son (Lk. 15.20). In the parables these are all decidedly Christ-like and God-like figures. None of the twelve occurrences of *splanchnizomai* in the Gospels therefore is ever used of a human emotion pure and simple. This has led Köster to conclude that it 'is always used to describe the attitude of Jesus and it characterises the divine nature of his acts'.[42]

---

40 LN 1, p. 295.

41 Robert C. Roberts, *Spiritual Emotions: A Psychology of Christian Virtues* (Grand Rapids, MI: Eerdmans, 2007), pp. 179–80.

42 *TDNT* 7, p. 553; cf. Walter, *EDNT* 3, p. 265, 'This primitive application of the vb. to Jesus thus allows him – as the 'Son' – to act in the role of God himself as eschatological Savior.'

Is this the case in Matthew's Gospel? In highlighting Jesus' compassion on the crowds, in his feeding the masses and healing the blind, does Matthew again want his readers to see traces of the Immanuel? And when Mark and Luke report on Jesus' compassion will they also be underscoring his divinity? Only a careful look at the evidence will satisfactorily answer these questions.

1.4.1 COMPASSION ON THE CROWDS (9.35-38)

35   Jesus went through all the towns and villages, teaching in their synagogues, preaching the good news of the kingdom and healing every disease and sickness.
36   When he saw the crowds, *he had compassion on them*, because they were harassed and helpless, like sheep without a shepherd.
37   Then he said to his disciples, 'The harvest is plentiful but the workers are few.
38   Ask the Lord of the harvest, therefore, to send out workers into his harvest field.'

Matthew is a master of the *inclusio*. He perfects the technique at several levels. At the macro level, as we have seen, the 'Immanuel' *inclusio*, spanning from 'God with us' (1.23) to 'I will be with you' (28.20), dominates the entire Gospel. With this subtle use of *inclusio* Matthew indicates to his readers that the life and ministry of Jesus has been a powerful demonstration of God's presence with his people.

Matthew also uses *inclusio* as a very effective literary device at the micro level. In Jesus' beatitudes (5.3-10) the first and the last end with the same blessing – 'for theirs is the kingdom of heaven' (5.3, 10). With the kingdom of heaven bracketing the entire series, it becomes clear that the beatitudes are kingdom declarations. The attendant blessings, such as inheriting the earth, being shown mercy and seeing God, are therefore all kingdom blessings.

In the paragraph under consideration Matthew uses the device of *inclusio* at an intermediate level, this time bracketing neither the entire Gospel nor merely a set of pronouncements, but rather a major discourse-narrative section of his work. He introduces the paragraph with a summary statement that is strongly reminiscent of a similar statement several chapters earlier: '*Jesus went* through all the towns and villages, *teaching in their synagogues, preaching the good news of the kingdom and healing every disease and sickness*' (v. 35). The words in italics are a verbatim reproduction of 4.23, where Matthew gives a crisp summary of Jesus' early ministry in Galilee. The strong verbal connection between the two statements suggests that in the intervening chapters Jesus has been engaged in precisely this kind of activity. In this section he has been preaching and teaching, and healing every disease and illness. Put more simply, he has been proclaiming the kingdom in both word (the Sermon on the Mount in chs 5–7) and deed (his miracles in chs 8–9).

Furthermore, the most intimate possible connection exists between the summary statement in v. 35 and what follows in v. 36, 'When he saw the crowds he had compassion on them, because they were harassed and helpless, like sheep without a shepherd.' Here we are given insight into the motivation that drove the activity of the previous chapters. Matthew puts it all down to Jesus' profound sense of compassion. As France explains, 'His response is described by the strongly emotional Greek verb *splanchnizomai*, which speaks of a warm, compassionate response to need. No single English term does justice to it: compassion, pity, sympathy, and fellow feeling all convey part of it, but "his heart went out" perhaps represents more fully the emotional force of the underlying metaphor of a "gut response."'[43]

Jesus' compassion is focused particularly on the crowds. In the preceding narrative these crowds have been playing a prominent though ambivalent role. They enter the narrative in the early phase of Jesus' public ministry and come from all points of the compass (4.25). They seem attracted to Jesus, at least initially, through his healing ministry (4.24). When Jesus is about to preach the Sermon on the Mount he sees the crowds, but it is his disciples who come to him (5.1). By the end of the Sermon, however, Matthew can report that the crowds were impressed with the authoritative nature of Jesus' teaching (7.28-29). Even so, he can still refer to '*their* teachers of the law', hence suggesting their ongoing allegiance to the religious leaders. At the same time their recognition that Jesus' authority is greater also creates distance. The crowds were again present at the healing of the leper (8.1-4) and when the paralytic was healed 'they were filled with awe; and they praised God, who had given such authority to men' (9.8). At the healing of the demon-possessed man who could not talk, they are again amazed (9.33), as they had been with the Sermon on the Mount (7.28). Therefore Jesus' words and works equally amaze them and make them aware of his authority.

Yet not all references to the crowd are positive. There are times when Jesus wants to get away from the crowd (8.18) and before the ruler's daughter is raised from the dead the crowd is put outside (9.25). In terms of their response to Jesus they occupy a position midway between the disciples and the religious leaders. In Matthew's narrative the opposition of the scribes and Pharisees does not begin to surface until ch. 9. At first they keep their thoughts to themselves, inwardly accusing Jesus of blasphemy (9.3). They then approach the disciples questioning Jesus' practice of dining with social outcasts (9.11). Finally, in response to the last miracle recorded in this section, they openly attribute Jesus' exorcism to the devil (9.34). Their opposition to Jesus is beginning to mount. The crowds, however, never echo the criticism of their leaders, but neither do they respond with the faith of the disciples, small though that faith at times may be (8.26). The most that can be said for the crowds is that 'they exhibit awareness that God is doing something special in Jesus'.[44]

It is this mixed reaction to Jesus' ministry up to this point – the growing antagonism of the religious leaders and the ambivalence of the crowds – that

---

43 France, *Matthew*, p. 373; cf. James L. Bailey, 'Church as Embodiment of Jesus' Mission (Matthew 9:36-10:39)', *CurTM* 30 (2003), p. 190, 'The Greek word translated "compassion" implies a visceral response to the plight of others, allowing one to connect with their pain.'
44 Thus Warren Carter, 'The Crowds in Matthew's Gospel', *CBQ* 55 (1993), p. 59.

inspires Jesus' compassion. The spiritual condition of the crowds especially concerns him. 'When he saw the crowds he had compassion on them, because they were harassed and helpless, like sheep without a shepherd' (v. 36). The spiritual need of the crowds is described in graphic terms. They are 'harassed' like a straying flock of sheep left alone and exposed to the dangers of a desolate, inhospitable wilderness. They are also 'helpless', which 'refers to the state to which such sheep are finally reduced; they give up and lie down in exhaustion'.[45] Their situation is desperate and their plight pitiful. The reason for this sad state of affairs is that they are 'like sheep without a shepherd'. This simile is a stinging indictment on the religious leaders whose own spiritual condition is betrayed by their growing hostility to Jesus. Their reaction shows that they have ceased to be shepherds to the sheep. The expression is also fraught with Old Testament associations. This imagery occurs repeatedly, particularly during times of crisis when a leadership vacuum exists among God's people (Num. 27.17; 1 Kgs 22.17; 2 Chron. 18.16; Ezek. 34.5; Zech. 10.2). Significant for our purposes are those who fill the vacuum by taking up the reins of leadership and assuming the role of shepherd. Joshua is appointed to succeed Moses (Num. 27.12-23). Yahweh will tend his flock, the house of Judah (Zech. 10.3). As for the scattered and wandering sheep of Ezekiel's day, Yahweh himself will search for them and look after them (Ezek. 34.11-16) and he will place his servant David as shepherd over them (Ezek. 34.23-24). The way Matthew describes the crowds as 'harassed and helpless, like sheep without a shepherd' sounds very much like the sheep described in Ezek. 34. In a further allusion to this chapter Jesus will soon refer to the crowds as 'the lost sheep of the house of Israel' (10.6 NASB). The least that can be said is that this language is highly evocative and suggestive. Is Matthew hinting that Jesus' compassion is a reflection of Yahweh's? Is this a subtle indication that Jesus is here fulfilling the role of both Yahweh and his servant David? Do these Old Testament echoes again suggest that Jesus' compassion is in character with his introduction as the Son of David and Immanuel in ch. 1?

In the next verse, in a bold switch of metaphor, Jesus declares, 'The harvest is plentiful, but the workers are few' (v. 37). The crowds are not only shepherd-less sheep, but also a harvest to be reaped. In the crowds Jesus sees an opportunity. Bringing in the harvest is bringing in new recruits for the kingdom of God. As the disciples pray to the Lord 'to send out workers into his harvest field' (v. 38), they soon become the answer to their own prayer. In the next chapter Jesus 'gave them authority to drive out evil spirits and to cure every kind of disease and sickness' (10.1). He also commanded them to preach, 'The kingdom of heaven is near' (10.7). The implications are obvious. The authority that Jesus exercised in his preaching and healing in the previous chapters he is now delegating to his disciples. It is another expression of his compassion for the crowds.

The present paragraph is a bridging passage between two major discourse-narrative sections in Matthew's Gospel (i.e. chs 5–9 and 10–12). In its pivotal

45 Ridderbos, *Matthew*, p. 194.

position it is both retrospective and prospective. Central to this paragraph and the motivating factor both for what precedes and follows is Jesus' compassion for the crowds. His heart goes out to them and he is deeply affected by their precarious spiritual condition. It is this compassion that is the driving force behind his preaching and teaching, his healings and his exorcisms. When he commissions his disciples to be workers in the harvest, he is spurred on by the same compassion. It drives the whole missionary enterprise. Jesus' compassion is therefore of a different order to his amazement and his stern warning. Those emotions were directed at individuals; his compassion is for entire multitudes. Those emotions at most might dominate a pericope;[46] his compassion undergirds entire chapters. It is one of the major motivators for Jesus' ministry in Matthew's Gospel.

1.4.2 COMPASSION ON THE FIVE THOUSAND (14.13-21)

13 When Jesus heard what had happened, he withdrew by boat privately to a solitary place. Hearing of this, the crowds followed him on foot from the towns.

14 When Jesus landed and saw a large crowd, *he had compassion on them* and healed their sick.

15 As evening approached, the disciples came to him and said, 'This is a remote place, and it's already getting late. Send the crowds away, so that they can go to the villages and buy themselves some food.'

16 Jesus replied, 'They do not need to go away. You give them something to eat.'

17 'We have here only five loaves of bread and two fish,' they answered.

18 'Bring them here to me,' he said.

19 And he directed the people to sit down on the grass. Taking the five loaves and the two fish and looking up to heaven, he gave thanks and broke the loaves. Then he gave them to the disciples, and the disciples gave them to the people.

20 They all ate and were satisfied, and the disciples picked up twelve basketfuls of broken pieces that were left over.

21 The number of those who ate was about five thousand men, besides women and children.

The hostility to Jesus' ministry that is latent in ch. 9 becomes patent in the chapters that follow. Compared to the numerous miracles recorded in chs 8–9, in the next narrative section (chs 11–12) Jesus' miracles are few and far between. The miracles that are depicted, however, dramatically intensify the conflict between Jesus and the religious leaders. The opposition of the Pharisees that had been merely verbal in ch. 9 now turns deadly. When Jesus healed a man with a shrivelled hand in a synagogue on the Sabbath, Matthew reports that 'the Pharisees

---

46   A pericope is any self-contained unit of Scripture. In the Gospels it is generally made up of a parable, miracle story, teaching section or pronouncement by Jesus.

went out and plotted how they might kill Jesus' (12.14). This forms the backdrop to the Beelzebub controversy (12.22-37). After the healing of a demon-possessed man who was blind and mute (12.22), the Pharisees again attribute the exorcism to the devil (12.24; cf. 9.34), an accusation which Jesus classifies as blasphemy against the Holy Spirit and therefore an unforgivable sin (12.31-32). Nonplussed by Jesus' stinging rebuke, the scribes and Pharisees ask for yet another miracle (12.38). Jesus is not very accommodating to their request and refers them to the rather cryptic and still future sign of Jonah (12.40-41). Matthew 12 is therefore a watershed. The hostility between Jesus and the religious leaders has become intractable. From this point on they will be his most determined and deadly opponents (16.21; 20.18-19; 21.15; 22.15; 26.3-4, 65; 27.41).

Danger also lurks in another quarter. Opposition comes not only from a religious but also from a political direction. Just prior to the feeding of the five thousand Matthew reports the execution of John the Baptist at the hands of Herod Antipas, the tetrarch of Galilee (14.3-12). Not only did Jesus, as a resident of Capernaum, fall under Herod's jurisdiction, the tetrarch also held to the disturbing superstitious belief that Jesus was *Johannes redivivus*, John the Baptist risen from the dead (14.2). This made matters doubly dangerous for Jesus. With his reputation for miracles and his ability to pull a crowd, would he be Herod's next target?

Not wanting to take his chances with such an unpredictable ruler, Jesus considers it judicious to move out of harm's way. So 'he withdrew by boat privately to a solitary place' (14.13). From parallel accounts in the other Gospels we learn that this solitary place was on the other side of the Sea of Galilee.[47] Being in the territory of Herod Philip this was therefore a safe haven beyond Antipas' political reach. Jesus' withdrawal for reasons of his own personal safety is a recurring emphasis unique to Matthew. Earlier he had withdrawn at the news of John's imprisonment (4.12) and again when the Pharisees' hostility became deadly (12.15). It was also a policy that had been adopted by the magi and Joseph at earlier threats from the Herodian dynasty (2.12, 13, 14, 22). Whenever the verb 'withdraw' (*anachōreō* in Greek) relates to Jesus or those involved with him, it therefore means withdrawing from danger or confrontation. It underscores the fact that Jesus had to walk a political tightrope if his ministry was not to be prematurely aborted. While parallel accounts give other reasons for the excursion to the far side of the lake, such as some much needed rest and relaxation (Mk 6.31), in Matthew the political reason is paramount.[48] For the time being at least, Jesus is a political refugee from Galilee. His associations with John the Baptist pose too great a risk at this point in time. Herod has become too much of a menace. Discreet withdrawal is therefore Jesus' best option.

No sooner has Jesus disembarked than he is met by a large crowd. In spite of

---

47 According to Lk. 9.10 Jesus and the apostles withdrew to Bethsaida, while Jn 6.1 reports that 'Jesus crossed to the far shore of the Sea of Galilee.'

48 Cf. Jose B. Fuliga, 'The Man Who Refused to be King', *AJT* 11 (1997), p. 141, 'Knowing his life was in danger, Jesus withdrew from Herod's area of jurisdiction. He had "to escape from the dominion of Herod" [R. V. G. Tasker]. Moreover Jesus needed the solitude for he was bereaved.'

opposition from other quarters he seems to have lost none of his popularity with Galilee's *hoi polloi*. In the face of threats from both the religious and political leadership the masses appear to remain loyal to Jesus. But again the chapters between Mt. 9.35-38 and the present passage are instructive. The crowds remain ambivalent. All is not as it seems.

Crowds are present when Jesus explains the significance of John the Baptist (11.7-19). His explanation ends with a telling comparison of 'this generation' to children sitting in the market places (11.16-19). The point of the parable is that neither Jesus nor John sang or danced to the tune of 'this generation'. John did not dance and Jesus did not mourn. In both cases the people are like surly children sitting along the street complaining. The comparison is Jesus' unflattering diagnosis of the crowds' spiritual condition.

The aptness of Jesus' diagnosis soon becomes clear. In the lead-up to the Beelzebub controversy the crowds side neither with Jesus nor with the Pharisees. In response to the exorcism they are again astonished, but then ask an insightful question, 'Could this be the Son of David?' (12.23). They are entertaining the possibility that Jesus might be the Messiah, couching their question in language that exactly echoes the way Matthew has introduced Jesus in his opening verse (1.1). They come tantalizingly close to recognizing Jesus' true identity. Their question falls in the grammatical category of 'hesitant questions'.[49] Yet the mere suggestion that the crowds should publicly acclaim Jesus as the Messiah is too much for the Pharisees. They repudiate the very thought with their blasphemous assertion that Jesus drives out demons by Beelzebub (12.24). The smouldering wick of the crowd's tentative faith seems to have been quickly snuffed out.

The crowds' failure to affirm Jesus' identity will have implications. In ch. 13 Jesus begins to speak in parables. While the parables are spoken to the crowds (13.2, 34), the explanations of the parables of the Sower (13.18-23) and the Weeds (13.36-43) are given in the hearing of the disciples only. Jesus is therefore making a deliberate distinction between the two groups. The reason for such discrimination is because 'the knowledge of the secrets of the kingdom of heaven' has been given to the disciples, but not to the crowds (13.11).[50] Jesus' parables are therefore intentionally veiled. The responsibility for this change in teaching strategy is placed squarely on the shoulders of the crowds, 'because while seeing they do not see, and while hearing they do not hear, nor do they understand' (13.13 NASB). Like the people of Judah in Isaiah's day, their ears are dull, their eyes dim and their hearts calloused (13.14-15; cf. Isa. 6.10). As was the case in 9.36, their spiritual condition remains precarious. Only now, with their consistent failure to recognize Jesus' true identity, matters are far worse. The fact that they considered John the Baptist to be a prophet (14.5) is hardly a mitigating factor.

---

49   In Greek their question is introduced by *mēti*. Like most English translations, the NIV correctly gives the question a note of uncertainty.

50   Carter, 'Crowds in Matthew's Gospel', p. 62, notes that '[i]n this respect, the crowds are qualitatively different from the disciples . . . Those who understand Jesus gain more instruction (13:36b-43), while Jesus leaves the crowds who do not understand (13:36a).'

Given this background of Jesus' recent dealings with the crowds, his response to them in the present context is quite unexpected. Whatever his desire may have been for privacy (14.13), perhaps also including the need to grieve over John's tragic death (14.3-12), Jesus is nevertheless prepared to shelve his own plans at the sight of the crowd. Rather than seeing the crowd as an intrusion or a nuisance, Luke observes that Jesus actually welcomed them (Lk. 9.11). Matthew takes matters even a step further. Like Mark, he traces Jesus' positive reaction to a deeper level. Jesus is once again motivated by compassion for the crowds (14.14; cf. Mk 6.34). Considering the political danger that he is seeking to avoid, this is impressive. Ridderbos' comments are perceptive: 'He could not escape the people, no matter how dangerous they were to Him. Nevertheless He was ready to give Himself to them at once. In spite of their unspiritual reasons for following Him (cf. 9:36), the Mediator's compassion could not be suppressed.'[51]

Despite the crowds' spiritual obtuseness, their inability to recognize his true identity, and their surly and childish responses to both Jesus and John, Jesus is nevertheless driven by an irrepressible compassion for them. This comes to immediate expression in his healing their sick (14.14). It would appear that Jesus' popular appeal still lay in his ability to heal just as it had done at the beginning of his Galilean ministry (4.23-24). It has already been noted that Matthew's first reference to Jesus' compassion (9.36) is linked to both his 'healing every disease and sickness' (9.35) and his giving his disciples the authority to do the same (10.1, 8). In that sense nothing has changed. The disappointing responses of the crowd notwithstanding, Jesus continues to show them compassion by healing their sick.

As in the earlier example, however, Jesus' healing does not exhaust his compassion. It would therefore be arbitrary to confine Jesus' compassion in this pericope to the verse where the reference to the compassion is found (v. 14). Surely Jesus' compassion also spills over into the feeding miracle that follows. Unlike the disciples, Jesus is unwilling to send the crowds away at the end of the day (v. 15). Jesus' healing activity, combined with his teaching mentioned in the other Synoptics (Mk 6.34; Lk. 9.11), obviously took longer than expected. The disciples therefore remind him of the lateness of the hour. But Jesus insists that the crowd does not need to go away and challenges the disciples to give them something to eat. While Jesus had earlier conferred some of his miraculous powers to the disciples (10.1, 8), *creatio ex nihilo* was certainly not among them! The best they can come up with are just five loaves of bread and two fish (v. 17). Jesus takes this humble fare and performs a spectacular miracle.[52] Although the menu was simple, Matthew notes that there was more than enough food for the huge crowd. The twelve basketfuls of leftovers suggest abundance, a sure sign that the messianic age has dawned (Gen. 49.11-12; Isa. 25.6; Jer. 31.12-14; Amos 9.13-14). Whether or not one gives the feeding associations with the Eucharist,

---

51 Ridderbos, *Matthew*, p. 277.
52 N. S. L. Fryer, 'Matthew 14:14-21. The Feeding of the Five Thousand: A Grammatical-historical Exegesis', *IDS* 84 (1987), p. 37, notes that 'John mentions that the loaves were made of barley flour' and that this bread was food 'of the coarsest and cheapest kind, the food of the working man'.

sees symbolism in the twelve baskets, or draws connections to the manna in the wilderness,[53] the least that can be said is that this is a miracle of messianic proportions, a mighty demonstration of divine compassion.

1.4.3 COMPASSION ON THE FOUR THOUSAND (15.29-39)

[29] Jesus left there and went along the Sea of Galilee. Then he went up on a mountainside and sat down.

[30] Great crowds came to him, bringing the lame, the blind, the crippled, the mute and many others, and laid them at his feet; and he healed them.

[31] The people were amazed when they saw the mute speaking, the crippled made well, the lame walking and the blind seeing. And they praised the God of Israel.

[32] Jesus called his disciples to him and said, '*I have compassion for these people*; they have already been with me three days and have nothing to eat. I do not want to send them away hungry, or they may collapse on the way.'

[33] His disciples answered, 'Where could we get enough bread in this remote place to feed such a crowd?'

[34] 'How many loaves do you have?' Jesus asked. 'Seven,' they replied, 'and a few small fish.'

[35] He told the crowd to sit down on the ground.

[36] Then he took the seven loaves and the fish, and when he had given thanks, he broke them and gave them to the disciples, and they in turn to the people.

[37] They all ate and were satisfied. Afterwards the disciples picked up seven basketfuls of broken pieces that were left over.

[38] The number of those who ate was four thousand, besides women and children.

[39] After Jesus had sent the crowd away, he got into the boat and went to the vicinity of Magadan.

Between the two feeding miracles in Matthew's Gospel the geographical movements of Jesus continue to be propelled by conflict. After dismissing the crowd of five thousand (14.22) Jesus returns to the Galilean side of the lake, arriving at Gennesaret (14.34) which is located southwest of Capernaum about halfway to Magdala. Word of Jesus' arrival soon spreads and again he heals all those who are brought to him (14.35-36). Jesus also attracts the attention of some high ranking scribes and Pharisees (15.1) who, it would appear, have come all the way from Jerusalem specifically to confront him about his disciples' non-observance of the tradition of the elders (15.2). The precise complaint is that 'they don't wash their hands before they eat!' This is more than a matter of hygiene. It was

---

53   See Donald A. Hagner, *Matthew 14–28* (WBC; Dallas: Word, 1995), p. 419.

seen as a breach of acceptable religious practice. Eating with unwashed hands rendered the disciples ceremonially unclean. Jesus makes no attempt to defend his disciples but immediately goes on the offensive. He demonstrates how the tradition of the elders conflicts with the higher authority of Scripture and accuses his opponents of teaching what amounts to no more than 'rules taught by men' (15.9; cf. Isa. 29.13). Although the Pharisees were offended by Jesus' riposte (15.12), he does not hesitate to call them 'blind guides' (15.14). The encounter again serves to illustrate the escalating conflict and deepening rift between Jesus and the religious leaders.

For safety's sake Jesus therefore needs to withdraw (15.21). Once again Matthew uses the now loaded verb *anachōreō*. The confrontation with these 'heavies' from Jerusalem has again placed Jesus and his disciples in a dangerous situation. This time he seeks shelter not on the far side of the lake but in the more distant districts of Tyre and Sidon. Yet even in this thoroughly Gentile area he cannot remain anonymous. He is met by a Canaanite woman. Addressing him as 'Lord, Son of David', she pleads for her desperately demon-possessed daughter (15.22). Her christological understanding is surprising, and so is her great faith (15.28). Nevertheless, it is only very reluctantly that Jesus grants her request, protesting that he was sent 'only to the lost sheep of Israel' (15.24). The point is clear. Jesus has not come here on a mission, but rather to escape the political heat that has been building up in Galilee. Once again he is a temporary refugee from his own homeland. Precisely how long he stayed in the area of Tyre and Sidon is impossible to say.

Although the geographical indicators are vague, Matthew intimates that Jesus returns to more familiar territory. Now he is recognized not just by a solitary needy individual, but by 'great crowds' who bring their lame, blind, crippled and dumb for healing (15.30). The reason for Jesus' magnetic attraction with the crowds remains unaltered. They come for healing and he does not disappoint. How could he? The lame, blind and dumb are the very kind of people who will be healed at the dawning of the messianic age (Isa. 29.18; 35.5-6). True to form, the crowds are amazed (15.31). On earlier occasions when they had been amazed at similar miracles they had praised God (9.8) and exclaimed, 'Nothing like this has ever been seen in Israel' (9.33). On this occasion, Matthew notes, 'they praised the God of Israel' (15.31). Although this is a positive reaction, it does not represent a significant advance on the crowds' earlier exclamations of praise at Jesus' miraculous healings. There is no indication that the secrets of the kingdom have now been revealed to them as they have been to the disciples (13.11). The most that can be said for the crowds is that they still remain sympathetic outsiders when it comes to the kingdom of heaven.

In spite of the ongoing spiritual ambivalence of the crowd Jesus nevertheless declares to his disciples, 'I have compassion for these people' (15.32). His heart now goes out to the four thousand in exactly the same way as it had earlier gone out to the five thousand (14.14). There is, however, a slight change of emphasis. In both contexts healings (14.14; 15.30-31) are followed by a miraculous feeding (14.15-21; 15.32-39). In the case of the five thousand, Jesus' compassion comes to immediate expression in his healing the sick (14.14), while in the case of the four thousand, his compassion is shown specifically in his feeding the hungry (15.32). But while the two accounts are perhaps intended to be complementary in this respect, the compassion of Jesus is not to be understood as restricted to the sick in the first account or to the hungry in the second. Clearly it embraces both groups. In these contexts, Matthew would have his readers see Jesus' compassion extend to all – the sick, the disabled and the hungry. This is no place for artificial boundaries or arbitrary distinctions. With crowds of this size Jesus' compassion is breath-taking in its scope.

Yet with the feeding of the four thousand we are faced with a problem of interpretation that goes back to ancient times and that continues to confound scholars and commentators to the present day. What was the ethnic identity of the crowd? Were they Jews or Gentiles? Is Matthew's account of this miracle almost a carbon copy of the previous one because he intends to demonstrate that Jesus' compassion extends equally to Jews and Gentiles? Could it therefore be said that the feeding of the five thousand was the Jewish feeding, while the feeding of the four thousand was the Gentile feeding? Moreover, was the feeding of the Gentiles anticipated by Jesus' debate with the scribes and Pharisees about the clean and the unclean (15.1-20) and by his subsequent encounter with the Canaanite woman and his granting her request (15.21-28)? Furthermore, does the earlier feeding of the five thousand suggest Jewish priority in the covenant purposes of God?

The way these questions are answered will carry wide implications not only for our present study but also for our overall understanding of Matthew's Gospel and his portrayal of Jesus' ministry. The arguments will therefore need to be carefully considered. The view that the four thousand were a Gentile crowd depends on four main arguments:

The first argument is topographical. When Jesus left the region of Tyre and Sidon, Matthew simply notes that Jesus 'went along the Sea of Galilee' (15.29). But in the parallel passage Mark gives a far more detailed itinerary. 'Jesus left the vicinity of Tyre and went through Sidon, down to the Sea of Galilee and into the region of the Decapolis' (Mk 7.31). Because of the growing pressure on Jesus in Galilee from both the political and the religious establishment, it would be attractive to suggest that he spent a prolonged period in Gentile territory. After healing the Canaanite woman's daughter near Tyre, Jesus headed north to Sidon and from there he presumably cut a broad swathe through Gentile territory to the north and east of Galilee until finally arriving in the part of the Decapolis that skirts the south-eastern quadrant of the Sea of Galilee.[54] Appealing as this solution may be, it depends on two unsubstantiated assumptions that could seriously undermine its credibility. The less significant assumption is that Jesus took a long detour through Gentile territory on his return journey from Tyre and Sidon. Neither Matthew nor Mark demands this. 'The most straightforward route from this district to the shore of the Sea of Galilee is through Galilee.'[55] But neither the longer nor the shorter route can be demonstrated from the available

---

54   Thus Aharoni and Avi-Yonah, *Bible Atlas*, p. 231.
55   J. R. C. Cousland, 'The Feeding of the Four Thousand *Gentiles* in Matthew? Matthew 15:29-39 as a Test Case', *NovT* 41 (1999), p. 10.

evidence. The more crucial assumption is that the Decapolis was considered an exclusively Gentile area. While the population may have been predominantly Gentile in the first century, the district had belonged to the land of the Jews since ancient times. Hence, as Ridderbos has argued, 'Jesus apparently included its inhabitants in the "lost sheep of Israel," among whom He intended to display the powers of the kingdom.'[56] Early in his Gospel Matthew has already indicated that, because of Jesus' reputation as a healer, large crowds from the Decapolis followed him (4.24-25). The later exorcism of two demon-possessed men in the same area (8.28-34; cf. Mk 5.1-20) would have made Jesus even better known in the region. Jesus' present ministry in the Decapolis would therefore hardly represent a new departure as far as Matthew is concerned. This conclusion is only enhanced by the vagueness of Matthew's geographical references.[57] All we know from him is that Jesus was near the Sea of Galilee at the time (15.29). The other geographical information has to be imported from Mark.

The second argument for the view that the four thousand were a Gentile crowd is that 'they praised the God of Israel' (15.31). It is commonly assumed that this 'could be naturally said only by Gentiles'.[58] France further argues, 'This is never said about the Galilean crowds, and the terminology suggests that the crowd are Gentiles, recognizing the special power of the Jewish Messiah.'[59] Of all the arguments for the Gentile identity of the crowd this is probably the strongest. Appeal can even be made to the Old Testament to bolster this view. When the ark of the covenant came into the possession of the Philistines they refer to it several times as 'the ark of the god of Israel' (1 Sam. 5.7, 8, 10, 11; 6.3). Their priests and diviners even suggested that they 'pay honour to Israel's god' (1 Sam. 6.5). This comes very close to Matthew's remark that 'they praised the God of

56 Ridderbos, *Matthew*, p. 290. The territory had at one time been incorporated into the Davidic kingdom (2 Sam. 8.5-15) and was later retaken during the reign of the Hasmonean king Alexander Jannaeus (103–76 BC) who forced its inhabitants to accept the Jewish religion. Although Pompey established Roman authority over the region in 63 BC, the cities of the Decapolis were given municipal autonomy and were attached to the province of Syria. In the first century AD there were significant Jewish communities in these cities, but there is also evidence of strong hostility toward them on the part of their Gentile neighbours. See Craig A. Evans and Stanley E. Porter, *Dictionary of New Testament Background* (Downers Grove: Inter-Varsity Press, 2000), p. 267.

57 The fact that after dismissing the crowd of four thousand Jesus 'got into the boat and went to the vicinity of Magadan' (15.39) does not help much, as 'not only the site, but even the existence of such a place-name is uncertain' (Bruce M. Metzger, *A Textual Commentary on the Greek New Testament* [Stuttgart: Deutsche Bibelgesellschaft, 2nd edn,1994], p. 32). In the parallel passage Mark gives the destination as 'the region of Dalmanutha' (Mk 8.10). Unfortunately this is 'an equally unknown site and name' (Metzger, *Textual Commentary*, p. 33). All that can be said with some degree of confidence is that this must have been Jewish territory. Soon after his arrival Jesus is confronted by Pharisees and Sadducees (16.1; cf. Mk. 8.11).

58 Carson, 'Matthew', p. 357.

59 France, *Matthew*, p. 597.

Israel'. Could Matthew have seen the Philistine episode as a prototype of the crowd's response?[60]

This suggestion would have some merit if the expression 'the God of Israel' was used only by Gentiles in the Old Testament. This is far from being the case. It is often found on the lips of pious Israelites in contexts of praise (e.g. 1 Kgs 1.48; Pss. 41.13; 72.18; 106.48; Isa. 29.23). In fact, in its various forms this appellation is found some two hundred and four times in the Hebrew Bible, and only eleven times in the mouth of a non-Jew. When almost 95% of the occurrences are not attributed to Gentiles, it does become rather problematic to suggest that the expression 'could be naturally said only by Gentiles'.[61] The problem only intensifies when evidence more contemporary to Matthew is taken into account. From his research J. R. C. Cousland has concluded that '"Israel" figures extremely rarely in Greek and Roman authors; perhaps only twice in the period before the end of the first century AD. In both these instances Israel refers to the patriarch and not to the people.'[62] In the first century the Gentiles referred to the people of Israel simply as 'the Jews'. It was only the Jews who thought of themselves as the people of Israel. This distinction is carefully reflected in the Gospels, including Matthew. When Jesus is called 'king of the Jews' the expression is always used by Gentiles (Mt. 2.2; 27.11, 29, 37). On the other hand, when he is referred to as 'the king of Israel' it is always by other Jews (Mt. 27.42; cf. Mk 15.32; Jn 1.49; 12.13). It would therefore be very unlikely that Matthew would say of a crowd of Gentiles that 'they praised the God of Israel' (15.31).

A third argument, often used in conjunction with the first two, trades on the numerical symbolism associated with the two feedings. Thus the twelve baskets of fragments left by the five thousand would, by virtue of the twelve tribes and the twelve patriarchs, be associated with Israel. The seven baskets, on the other hand, point to fullness and perfection and therefore 'may well symbolize the meeting of the needs of the Gentiles, that is, the fullness of messianic provision for the entire world'.[63] One could push matters further and suggest that the five loaves that fed the five thousand represent the books of the law, while the seven loaves used to feed the four thousand represent the worldwide mission. The process breaks down, however, when it comes to the fish. In the first miracle two fish were used (14.17-19), while in the second their number is not specified (15.34-35). The fact that it is pointless to compare the numbers of fish casts serious doubt on any endeavour to compare the numbers of baskets and loaves. The whole interpretive enterprise runs the very real risk of allegorization, of seeking deeper meanings where none were intended. When it comes to numerical symbolism in cases like this, Richard France has sounded a salutary note of caution: 'Such suggestions are as hard to refute as they are to prove, but I see little in the way Matthew tells the story to encourage such speculation.'[64]

---

60   Cf. Cousland, 'Feeding of the Four Thousand', p. 8.
61   Cousland, 'Feeding of the Four Thousand', p. 18.
62   Cousland, 'Feeding the Four Thousand', p. 15.
63   Hagner, *Matthew 14-28*, p. 452.
64   France, *Matthew*, p. 600.

The final argument for the Gentile identity of the four thousand is flimsier still. Masked by most English translations is the distinction between the two kinds of baskets used to collect the leftovers. The basket used in the first instance was the *kophinos* (14.20; 16.9; Mk 6.43; 8.19; Lk. 9.17; Jn 6.13), while in the second it was the *spuris* (15.37; 16.10; Mk 8.8, 20). The distinction between the two kinds of basket is maintained consistently across all the Gospel accounts. The question is whether the distinction is at all significant and whether it helps identify the Jewish nature of the first crowd and the Gentile nature of the second. Some scholars suggest that *kophinos* was the more specifically Jewish word for basket and that it was used to carry kosher food. The more general term *spuris* may therefore be a pointer to a non-Jewish cultural setting.[65] Comments of this kind are often dependent on Bauer's lexicon of the Greek New Testament. This lexicon is to New Testament Greek what the Oxford Dictionary is to contemporary English. If you really want to know the meaning of a Greek word this will generally be regarded as the lexicon of choice. Yet even here there are pitfalls for the unwary. Entries into this lexicon do not always remain constant from one edition to the next. Thus while the earlier editions say that the *kophinos* was 'considered typical of the Jews',[66] this comment is omitted from the third edition.[67] The most that can be said is that the *spuris* was probably the more flexible and larger of the two. The apostle Paul was lowered through an opening in the wall of Damascus in a *spuris* (Acts 9.25). This is the only place in the New Testament where either word is used apart from the feeding miracles. To my knowledge no interpreter has yet suggested that Paul was lowered in a *spuris* because he had just recently embraced the Gentile mission. The baskets available to collect the leftovers after the miraculous feedings were therefore culturally irrelevant.

None of the arguments used to demonstrate that the four thousand were a Gentile crowd is convincing – either individually or cumulatively. There is nothing in Matthew's report to suggest that they were anything other than a predominantly Jewish multitude. If the Canaanite woman could barely manage to scrape some crumbs from the messianic table, would Jesus now suddenly be feeding thousands of loaves to a Gentile crowd? Until now he has confined his own mission (15.24) and that of his disciples (10.6) to the people of Israel. Although his encounter with the woman resulted in a warm commendation of her faith (15.28), it meant neither a change of heart nor a change of policy as far as the focus of his mission was concerned. We must not interpret the feeding of the four thousand and the healing miracles that preceded it in such a way that the narrative of the Canaanite woman becomes absurd. Had Matthew intended Gentiles, he would have made that clear.[68] There is indeed a Gentile thread that runs through this Gospel, but this is not a point where it surfaces. In this regard Cousland's conclusion is worth quoting in some detail:

---

65 Thus Carson, 'Matthew', p. 359; France, *Matthew*, p. 603.
66 BAG, p. 448; BAGD, p. 447.
67 BDAG, p. 563.
68 Thus Hagner, *Matthew 14-28*, p. 446.

Matthew takes what Jesus says very seriously. Thus when he has Jesus say he was 'sent only to the lost sheep of the house of Israel' (15:24), he has Jesus act in a manner that accords with Jesus' utterance. The Evangelist is certainly aware of the coming mission to the Gentiles, but Jesus does what he says he will do. Thus, Jesus engages in a particularist mission to the Jewish people, and his disciples do the same. The feeding and healing of the four thousand, therefore, are designed to reflect the covenantal relationship between Yahweh and his people, with Jesus figuring as its culmination. It is only after his death and resurrection that he will enjoin the universal mission on the disciples, so that all nations may join in the praise of the God of Israel as well.[69]

So when Jesus says, 'I have compassion for these people' (15.32), he says it of what must have been mainly a Jewish crowd. His focus has not now suddenly shifted to the Gentiles. Their time has not yet come. Strictly speaking, this is still the era of the old covenant and it is to God's old covenant people that his heart goes out.[70] It is these crowds that he himself has called 'sheep without a shepherd' (9.36) and 'the lost sheep of Israel' (10.6; 15.24). To find these sheep and show them compassion he is prepared to traverse the length and breadth of Israel.

Even so, his ministry is about to reach a major turning point. Returning by boat from the feeding of the four thousand, Jesus again finds himself hounded by his religious opponents (16.1-4; cf. Mk 8.11-13). For the first time these opponents include Sadducees as well as Pharisees. This is an ominous development. With the temple as their power base and their headquarters in Jerusalem these Sadducees seem to have gone out of their way to confront Jesus. This is the only place in the New Testament where they are found outside Judea. Counting the high priest and the chief priests among their number, this is the group that will be ultimately responsible for Jesus' death (16.21; 20.18; 21.15; 26.1–27.56). Their collusion with the Pharisees on this occasion is also highly unusual. The two parties were often at loggerheads (Acts 23.1-10). So they must have seen Jesus as a serious threat. Their encounter with him is undoubtedly hostile. They test him by demanding a spectacular sign (16.1). In his rebuff Jesus refers to them as a 'wicked and adulterous generation' (16.4). Jesus' relations with the religious establishment are not improving. Rather they are rapidly deteriorating and Jesus' personal safety again becomes an issue. Once more he seeks asylum by crossing the lake (16.4-5). From there he goes deep into Gentile territory

---

69   Cousland, 'Feeding of the Four Thousand', p. 23.

70   This point has been further developed by Allan M. Harman, 'Missions in the Thought of Jesus', *EvQ* 41 (1969), p. 138, 'Because Jesus was the last messenger of the old covenant it is not surprising in the least that He should have directed His ministry almost exclusively to Israel since the Old Testament period has not yet run its course. The historical Israel was still in existence. The thought of the old covenant giving way to the new covenant brings us to the significance of the death of Jesus for the universal mission. Through the suffering and death of the Messiah salvation was to be opened "for many," Isaiah had foretold (Isa. 53.11-12; cf. also Jesus' own words, Mk. 10.45). Until that messianic death had taken place the guests could not be invited. To use the language of one of Jesus' own parables, all was not yet ready, the table had not been set.'

until he reaches the region of Caesarea Philippi (16.13), a town safely within the domain of Herod Philip who had a reputation for being the most moderate of the Herods. It is there that Jesus begins to predict his suffering and death at the hands of the elders, scribes and chief priests (16.21; cf. 17.22-23; 20.17-19). Matthew's Galilee section has drawn to a close. The fateful journey to Jerusalem is about to begin.

With this shift of focus much will change in Jesus' ministry. His compassion, however, remains a constant. It is his only emotion to be recorded in Matthew's journey section.

1.4.4 COMPASSION ON TWO BLIND MEN (20.29-34)

> [29] As Jesus and his disciples were leaving Jericho, a large crowd followed him.
> [30] Two blind men were sitting by the roadside, and when they heard that Jesus was going by, they shouted, 'Lord, Son of David, have mercy on us!'
> [31] The crowd rebuked them and told them to be quiet, but they shouted all the louder, 'Lord, Son of David, have mercy on us!'
> [32] Jesus stopped and called them. 'What do you want me to do for you?' he asked.
> [33] 'Lord', they answered, 'we want our sight.'
> [34] *Jesus had compassion on them* and touched their eyes. Immediately they received their sight and followed him.

Jericho is Jesus' last stop before he arrives in Jerusalem (21.1-11). With the healing of the two blind men the journey section (16.13–20.34) therefore draws to a close. This part of Matthew's Gospel is of quite a different character to the Galilee section that preceded it. Much attention is devoted to the more private times that Jesus has with his disciples, as he instructs them and prepares them for what lies ahead. The crowds which thronged him for most of his Galilean ministry have not entirely disappeared, but they are far less prominent.[71] The miracles have begun to recede as well.[72] Strikingly, but not unexpectedly, the presence of crowds correlates perfectly with the only recorded miracles – the exorcism of the epileptic boy (17.14-21), the healings in Perea (19.1-2) and the restoring of sight to the blind men in Jericho (20.29-34). Even the confrontations with opponents have diminished. The only flashpoint on the journey occurs in Jesus' single encounter with the Pharisees. As he travels through the Transjordan area of Perea, which fell within the jurisdiction of Herod Antipas, they approach him with the question, 'Is it lawful for a man to divorce his wife for any and every reason?' (19.3). They are hardly seeking his pastoral advice. Matthew says they came to test him, no doubt hoping to impale him on the horns of a

---

71 The word *ochlos*, the only word Matthew uses to refer to the crowds, occurs 34x in chs 4–15, but only 4x in chs 16–20.

72 In the Galilee section there are twenty-three references to miracles, while in the journey section this number is reduced to three (17.14-21; 19.1-2; 20.29-34).

double dilemma. Not only was divorce a hot topic in religious circles, so that any answer was bound to give offence in some quarter, the Pharisees' question was also politically loaded. It was, after all, John the Baptist's pronouncement on Herod Antipas' divorce and subsequent remarriage that had landed John in prison in the first place (14.3-5). Were the Pharisees hoping Jesus would suffer a similar fate? Whatever the precise motives behind their question, Jesus carefully avoids their trap. Moreover, their hostility no longer determines his movements. His itinerary is now driven by another agenda. He is on the way to the cross (16.21; 17.22-23; 20.17-19, 22, 28).

As Jesus is leaving Jericho, it is not surprising that a large crowd follows him (20.29). Jericho was only a day's journey from Jerusalem. It was therefore a logical stopping point on the way to the Passover for Galilean pilgrims who wanted to avoid the shorter but more hazardous route through Samaria (cf. Lk. 9.51-53). As Jesus would have been known to many from Galilee, it is understandable that they would attach themselves to him as they all journeyed to the same destination. On their arrival in Jerusalem some of their provincial pride comes through in the way they identify their hero. 'This is Jesus, the prophet from Nazareth in Galilee' (21.11).

For all their adulation, however, the spiritual condition of the crowd is still not what it ought to be. When the blind men cried out to Jesus, 'Lord, Son of David, have mercy on us!' the crowd rebuked them and told them to be quiet (20.30-31). Perhaps they did not want a figure of Jesus' calibre to be interrupted by a couple of beggars. They probably wanted him to get on with the business of setting up the kingdom they hoped he would establish (21.9).[73] At the very least they wanted to see and hear Jesus and not be disturbed by these men shouting out for pity.[74] But whatever their reason for seeking to hush the two blind men, the crowd was acting in character. They once again 'exhibit some perception that God is at work in a special way in Jesus, yet they lack both the faith and understanding manifested by the disciples and the hostility displayed by the Jewish leaders'.[75]

In their lack of compassion the crowds also act as a foil to the welcoming attitude of Jesus. The crowd's initially hostile reaction throws the attention and compassion of Jesus into sharper relief.[76] While they had been ready to silence the blind men and keep them out of the way, Jesus was too compassionate for such harsh treatment of people in need. For a moment he ignores the crowd of people thronging around him and pays attention to these two insignificant beggars.[77] Sympathetic to their plight he asks, 'What do you want me to do for you?' (20.32). Although their need for sight was obvious, Jesus gave them the

---

73   Thus Keener, *Matthew*, p. 311.
74   Thus Leon Morris, *The Gospel According to Matthew* (Grand Rapids, MI: Eerdmans, 1992), p. 515.
75   Carter, 'The Crowds in Matthew's Gospel', p. 64.
76   Thus France, *Matthew*, p. 764.
77   See Morris, *Matthew*, p. 515.

opportunity to voice their need[78] as well as express their faith through their request (20.33).[79] Then Jesus acted in compassion (20.34).

This expression of compassion is unique in Matthew. On earlier occasions Jesus had been moved with compassion only for the crowds. Now it is these two unfortunates who are the very particular and personal focus of his compassion. This brief episode provides a remarkable insight into his priorities and values. His compassion for these two marginalized individuals triumphs over the expectations of the crowd. At a time when his mind might be expected to be on his imminent arrival in Jerusalem and the fate which awaited him there, Jesus still has time to notice and respond to the needy.[80] More than that, his compassion comes to tangible expression as he touches their eyes (20.34). This is not the first time that Jesus has healed by touch. He had done the same for a leper (8.3), Peter's mother-in-law (8.15) and the two blind men he had healed earlier (9.29). But only here is his touch seen as a direct expression of his compassion. These two blind beggars at Jericho are therefore uniquely blessed. Their healing is instantaneous. So is their decision to follow Jesus, presumably not only as fellow pilgrims but also as faithful disciples.

Moving as this scene may be, the episode raises a curious problem. Matthew has already recounted the healing of two blind men in an earlier passage (9.27-31). So great are the similarities between the two accounts that scholars are sometimes inclined to see the two passages as 'doublets', namely, two versions of the same story. The common elements between the two pericopes are particularly striking: (1) both concern two blind men (9.27; 20.30), who (2) cry out with nearly the same cry, 'Lord [not in 9.27], Son of David, have mercy on us' (9.27; 20.30, 31),[81] (3) to Jesus as he passes by (9.27; 20.30), and (4) whom Jesus heals by touching their eyes (9.29; 20.34).[82] Jesus also asks the blind men fairly similar questions – 'Do you believe I am able to do this?' (9.28) and 'What do you want me to do for you?' (20.32). These striking similarities are, however, more than counterbalanced by the obvious differences. The first miracle took place in Capernaum, the second in Jericho. The first was performed indoors (9.28), the second outdoors and before a large crowd (20.29-31). The response of the blind men is also significantly different in each case. Upon receiving their sight the second pair simply followed Jesus (20.34), while the first pair 'went out and spread the news about him all over that region' (9.31). For our purposes the most important difference lies in the sharply contrasting emotional reactions of Jesus to the two men. He scolds the one pair and has compassion on the other. Why the difference?

---

78 Keener, *Matthew*, p. 311.
79 Hagner, *Matthew 14-28*, p. 587.
80 France, *Mattthew*, p. 766.
81 Although 'Lord' is not found in 9.27, it does appear in 9.28. In some ancient manuscripts it is also missing from 20.30, 31, so that the blind men would have addressed Jesus in identical terms in both passages. However, 'it is more likely that copyists, influenced by Matthew's earlier account of the healing of the blind men, produced by assimilation an exact parallel to 9.27' (Metzger, *Textual Commentary*, p. 43).
82 Hagner, *Matthew 14-28*, pp. 585–86.

The plight of both sets of men was equally great. The way they addressed Jesus was equally reverential and theologically accurate. Presumably their faith was equally genuine. So why is there such a great discrepancy between Jesus' emotions on the two occasions? Why a mix of anger and indignation on the one hand and a touching display of compassion on the other? How can two similar situations evoke such contradictory emotions? The answer to these questions must lie in the respective contexts of both accounts. A key factor is the opposition from the religious authorities that has been a consistent feature for much of Matthew's narrative. In ch. 9 the conflict is just beginning to simmer. Jesus needs to take precautions to prevent it from boiling over prematurely. Hence his harsh words to the blind men at Capernaum. By the time Jesus reaches Jericho, however, the ultimate showdown is inevitable. In the journey section he has already predicted it three times. So when the blind men loudly yell out, 'Lord, Son of David, have mercy on us!' the crowd rebukes them but not Jesus (20.31). Such public acclamation now poses no danger. Earlier in ch. 20 Jesus had taken the twelve disciples aside for the third time to tell them that they would go up to Jerusalem where he would suffer, die and rise (20.17-19). Nothing can deflect him from his course. In such a setting compassion is completely in place. It is Jesus' response to pleas for mercy. What he is about to do in Jerusalem is the greatest demonstration of mercy imaginable. Jesus' compassion for these blind men is therefore the gospel in microcosm.

Our discussion of the last four passages has shown that compassion is the major emotion attributed to Jesus in Matthew's Gospel. He has compassion on the harassed and helpless crowds that are like sheep without a shepherd (9.36). He has compassion on the five thousand and heals their sick (14.14) as well as on the four thousand whose hunger he satisfies (15.32). Finally, in his last miracle before entering Jerusalem, he has compassion on two blind men outside Jericho (20.34). The objects of Jesus' compassion form a noteworthy combination. In showing compassion as he does, Jesus is doing the works of God and ushering in the messianic age. The divine nature of his activities is epitomized in Ps. 146 where God 'gives food to the hungry' (v. 7; cf. Exod. 16) and 'the LORD gives sight to the blind' (v. 8; cf. Isa. 42.6). The restoration of sight is also one of the gifts of the messianic age (Isa. 29.18; 35.5; 42.7). In the Old Testament healing is also regarded as an exclusively divine prerogative. The Hebrew verb for 'heal' (*rapha*) occurs 67*x*, but whether this word is used literally or metaphorically, it is only God who heals successfully (e.g. Exod. 15.26; 2 Kgs 20.5; Pss. 103.3; 147.3). When it comes to tending sheep without a shepherd, the Old Testament foresees a future messianic age where this task will be a joint venture carried out by Yahweh and his servant David (Ezek. 34). Hence the way Matthew selects and portrays Jesus' acts of compassion is not random or sporadic but has deep taproots in the Old Testament.

The Greek verb *splanchnizomai* ('show/have compassion'), which the Synoptics use exclusively of Jesus and a few parable characters, is also one of the

New Testament counterparts to the *racham* word group in the Old Testament.[83] This group is made up of words commonly translated 'compassion', 'compassionate' and 'have compassion'. It is attested precisely 100x in the Hebrew Old Testament, and is used with reference to God no less than 85x. It would therefore appear that God has something of a monopoly on compassion in the Old Testament. In the Gospels the same is true of Jesus. Furthermore, this compassion comes to supreme expression in a covenant context. It is out of love that God enters into the covenant (Deut. 7.6-13; Jer. 31.1-3; Hos. 11.1-4). His jealousy or zeal arises from the intensity and exclusiveness of the covenant bond (Exod. 20.4-6; 34.12-16; Num. 25.11-13; Deut. 4.23, 24). When his partner breaks the covenant he reacts with anger/wrath (Exod. 32.10-13; Lev. 26.14-33; Num. 25.1-5; Deut. 31.16, 17; Josh. 7.1-26; Judg. 2.20; 1 Kgs 11.9-11; 2 Kgs 17.7-18; Ezek. 16.8-63; Hos. 8.1, 5). Subsequently it is in compassion that he restores the covenant relationship (Exod. 33.19; 34.6; Deut. 4.29-31; 30.3; Neh. 9.5-38; Hos. 2.14-23; Zech. 10.6). The theme of restoration is particularly prominent in Isaiah and Jeremiah, and it is precisely within this context that there is also a strong emphasis on divine compassion (Isa. 49.8-13; 54.7-10; 60.10; Jer. 12.14, 15; 30.18; 31.15-20; 33.23-26; 42.12). Upon restoration God again rejoices and delights in his covenant partner (Deut. 30.9, 10; Isa. 42.1-6; Jer. 32.40, 41).

In his various expressions of compassion Jesus therefore lives up to what is said of him in Matthew 1. He is the son of David in whom the messianic age has dawned. He is also the Immanuel who does the kinds of miraculous deeds previously ascribed only to Yahweh, the covenant God of Israel.[84] Whenever Matthew specifically mentions Jesus' compassion, the recipients are therefore always Jews, the old covenant people of God. The question now needs to be asked whether Jesus also resembles the God of the Old Testament in that he does his deeds of compassion in a context of covenant renewal and restoration.

1.5 *Overwhelming Grief*

As has been observed throughout this chapter, all the emotions of Jesus in the Galilee and journey sections are connected with miracles. He is amazed at a

---

83 *TDNT* 7, p. 552.
84 Although the compassion of Jesus so closely resembles God's compassion in the Old Testament, the two cannot simply be equated. Care must be taken not to regard Jesus' compassion as a 'divine' emotion that is to be solely attributed to his divine nature. Paul Helm, 'B. B. Warfield on Divine Passion', *WTJ* 69 (2007), p. 104, in his discussion of Jesus' anger, provides a helpful analogy: 'Jesus' anger occurred at particular times – the death of Lazarus, the cleansing of the Temple; it had a beginning and an end. No doubt the welling up of such anger made Jesus' heart race. It is human anger in sinless expression. Is God's anger like that? It would be rash to conclude that it is.' God is expressing his impassioned emotions in the person of his Son in his assumed human nature. It would therefore be more accurate to say that in showing compassion Jesus is fulfilling his role as Immanuel in Matthew's Gospel, rather than claiming that his compassion is a divine emotion as such.

centurion who has the faith that his servant can be healed at a distance by a mere word. He fiercely rebukes two men whose sight he has just restored. He has compassion on two hungry crowds and two blind beggars. Even the harassed and helpless to whom his heart goes out are those who witness his miracles. There is therefore a perfect correlation between Jesus' emotions and miracles. In the Galilee and journey sections this is always the pattern.

In the Jerusalem section this pattern changes dramatically. There is only one overriding emotion expressed by Jesus and that is overwhelming grief. Here the miracles are few and far between and no connections are made with Jesus' emotions.[85] The grief of Jesus really comes in waves, in two devastating tsunami waves of sorrow. The first is Gethsemane and the second is Calvary.

Before we look at Gethsemane and Calvary, however, we need to backtrack a little so that we can get some perspective on Jesus' overwhelming grief. In the journey section, as we have seen, Jesus predicts his suffering, death and resurrection three times (16.21; 17.22-23; 20.17-19). He seems to make this prediction very matter-of-factly. There is not a trace of emotion, not the slightest disturbance of mind. The only ones who seem to get emotional are the disciples. At the first prediction Peter begins to rebuke him (16.22) and with the second prediction all the disciples are deeply grieved (17.23). But with Jesus there doesn't seem to be even a ripple of feeling. He sets his sights on Jerusalem. He doesn't waver. He perseveres with his journey until he reaches his destination. He knows what's coming and he seems to steel himself for what lies ahead.

But Jesus not only knows *that* he is going to die, he also knows *why* he is going to die. Soon after the last passion prediction, while they are still on the journey, he declares to his disciples: 'The Son of Man did not come to be served, but to serve, and to give his life as a ransom for many' (20.28). He then spells this out even more clearly at his Last Supper with them in the upper room (26.26-29):

26 While they were eating, Jesus took bread, gave thanks and broke it, and gave it to his disciples, saying, 'Take and eat; this is my body.'

27 Then he took the cup, gave thanks and offered it to them, saying, 'Drink from it, all of you.

28 This is my blood of the covenant, which is poured out for many for the forgiveness of sins.

29 I tell you, I will not drink of this fruit of the vine from now on until that day when I drink it anew with you in my Father's kingdom.'

Particularly significant are the words of v. 28 with its reference to the 'blood of the covenant'.[86] Coupled with Jesus' prediction that he would give his life as a

---

85 Apart from the resurrection of Jesus the only miracles recorded in the Jerusalem section are the healing of the blind and lame in the temple (21.14) and the cursing of the fig tree (21.18-22).

86 In some ancient manuscripts this is the 'blood of the *new* covenant', a reading that has also been adopted by some English translations and paraphrases (e.g. KJV, LB, Phillips), but the word 'new' seems to be a later scribal insertion from Lk. 22.20.

ransom for many (20.28) this pronouncement indicates that Jesus knew precisely what he was doing when he died. This was not the death of a masochist, nor was it the death of a victim. For the sake of his disciples he gives the meaning of his death ahead of time. He will give his life as a ransom for many, for whom he will pour out his blood for the forgiveness of sins, and the blood that he pours out is the blood of the covenant. All of this language is highly allusive, picking up several important Old Testament themes. The blood of the covenant recalls the blood that was shed to inaugurate God's original covenant with Israel at Sinai (Exod. 24.8). Jesus' blood will be shed for the forgiveness of sins, the chief blessing associated with the new covenant as foretold by Jeremiah (Jer. 31.31-34). The many for whom this blood will be poured out as a ransom can be identified as the many whom the Servant of the Lord will justify as he bears their sins and iniquities (Isa. 53.11-12). From these strong allusions to the Old Testament it is clear that Jesus has come to renew the covenant and to restore God's relationship with his people. Because of the covenant in his blood they will be ransomed and their sins will be forgiven. In him God is once again showing compassion to his people.

If Jesus is indeed consciously alluding to Isaiah's fourth Servant Song (Isa. 52.13–53.12), he would also have recalled that the suffering Servant would be stricken and smitten by God (Isa. 53.4). Not only would he be 'despised and rejected by men' (Isa. 53.3), it was also 'the LORD's will to crush him and cause him to suffer' (Isa. 53.10). At its deepest level this suffering involved a seismic shift in his relationship with God. The Son whom God loves and with whom he is well pleased (3.17; 17.5) is precisely the one whom God is about to strike, smite and crush. It is this divine dimension to his suffering that seems to have affected Jesus most deeply.

What is latent in the apparent allusion to Isaiah becomes more transparent in the next paragraph, where Jesus predicts the disciples' desertion (26.31-35). Jesus' prediction is based on an Old Testament prophecy, 'I will strike the shepherd, and the sheep of the flock will be scattered' (Zech. 13.7). The way Jesus quotes the prophecy strongly emphasizes the fact that the striking of the shepherd is an act of God. The form of the quotation does not agree with its Hebrew source which begins with an imperative, 'Strike the shepherd'. The difference between source and quotation is not as substantial as it may appear, however, since in the original context 'the imperative is addressed by God to his sword, so that in effect it is God who is striking'.[87] The way Jesus quotes the verse makes the divine initiative unmistakable. He knows he is about to be struck by God and this forms an important prelude to his overwhelming grief.

Inseparably bound to this aspect of his grief is Jesus' deep disappointment in his disciples. As the sheep of the flock they will be scattered, and this will involve desertion (26.56), denial (26.69-75) and betrayal (26.47-50). His acute awareness of the ways the disciples were about to fail him must also have contributed to Jesus' overwhelming grief in the garden. At the same time the striking

---

87 France, *Matthew*, p. 998.

of the shepherd and the scattering of the sheep form the lynch pin to a significant theme that Matthew has been developing. Soon after Jesus' birth Matthew
draws attention to the prophecy of Micah that he 'will be the shepherd of my
people Israel' (2.6; Mic. 5.2). The realization of this expectation will unfold
gradually over the course of the narrative. Jesus' initial compassion is aroused
by the crowds who were 'like sheep without a shepherd' (9.36). Although this is
an indictment of the people's religious leaders, there is as yet no indication that
Jesus will step in to be their shepherd. But soon there are hints. Jesus' disciples
are to go to 'the lost sheep of Israel' (10.6), to whom (in a dramatic shift of
imagery) he sends them 'as sheep among wolves' (10.16). So the disciples are
also compared to sheep, as are the man with the shrivelled hand (12.9-12) and
the little children (18.10-14). Although he 'was sent only to the lost sheep of
Israel' (15.24), Jesus is never compared to a shepherd until the final judgement
when 'he will separate the people from one another as a shepherd separates the
sheep from the goats' (25.32). The only time in this Gospel that Jesus is specifically called a shepherd is in the very verse that we are currently considering
(26.31). Paradoxically, it is only when God strikes the shepherd and when the
flock of disciples is scattered like the harassed and helpless crowds, that Jesus
is constituted the true shepherd of the flock.[88] It is when God strikes him, when
the blood of the covenant flows, that the covenant is renewed. But the prospect
deeply distresses Jesus. Was there no other way? That is his anguished question
in Gethsemane.

1.5.1 GETHSEMANE (26.36-46)

[36] Then Jesus went with his disciples to a place called Gethsemane, and he
said to them, 'Sit here while I go over there and pray.'

[37] He took Peter and the two sons of Zebedee along with him, and *he began
to be sorrowful and troubled.*

[38] Then he said to them, '*My soul is overwhelmed with sorrow to the point
of death.* Stay here and keep watch with me.'

[39] Going a little farther, he fell with his face to the ground and prayed, 'My
Father, if it is possible, may this cup be taken from me. Yet not as I will,
but as you will.'

[40] Then he returned to his disciples and found them sleeping. 'Could you men
not keep watch with me for one hour?' he asked Peter.

[41] 'Watch and pray so that you will not fall into temptation. The spirit is
willing, but the body is weak.'

---

88 Cf. David R. Bauer, 'The Major Characters of Matthew's Story: Their Function and
Significance', *Int* 46 (1992), p. 358, 'Jesus is the Davidic ruler who governs by "shepherding"
the people of God. The broader context of the Gospel indicates just what this shepherding
involves: Jesus rules as one who dies on behalf of his people in order to bring salvation to
them (1.21; 20.28; 26.27-28).'

42 He went away a second time and prayed, 'My Father, if it is not possible for this cup to be taken away unless I drink it, may your will be done.'

43 When he came back, he again found them sleeping, because their eyes were heavy.

44 So he left them and went away once more and prayed the third time, saying the same thing.

45 Then he returned to the disciples and said to them, 'Are you still sleeping and resting? Look, the hour is near, and the Son of Man is betrayed into the hands of sinners.

46 Rise, let us go! Here comes my betrayer!'

Nowhere else in Matthew's Gospel are Jesus' emotions as intense as in the Garden of Gethsemane. It is precisely this feature that makes the narrative so attractive to the modern reader. As Kevin Madigan explains:

> To many modern readers, there is hardly a more moving spectacle in the New Testament than Jesus collapsing in the garden and praying to his father in fear and trembling . . . Almost nowhere else in the gospels does Jesus appear so impressively human. Nowhere does he seem more nakedly vulnerable to human vicissitude. His lonely nocturnal vigil in Gethsemane appears to be marked neither by sovereign control of his destiny nor by serene assurance of divine oversight, but by helplessness and loss of control. Here, Jesus appears to distinguish himself not by some divinely given immunity to the passions but by the cruel intensity with which he experiences them. His prayer is striking because of his vehement resistance to the divine will rather than quiet surrender to it.[89]

Elsewhere Madigan probably overstates his case when he describes Jesus in Gethsemane as 'powerless, ignorant, and recalcitrant',[90] but Matthew's portrayal of Jesus in the Garden is so arresting partly because there is so little in the preceding narrative that has prepared us for it. Up to this point Matthew's Jesus has always seemed so self-controlled, in charge of every situation. But now for the first time he seems to 'lose it' as his emotions unravel completely. While the modern reader may find this scene appealing, the thoughtful reader will also find it disturbing and even shocking. This is not the Jesus he thought he had come to know from reading Matthew's Gospel. In the overall narrative Gethsemane gives a twist that is totally unexpected.

The account starts on an ironic note. En route to the Garden, Jesus has predicted that all his disciples will fall away (26.31), but it is now these very disciples on whom he leans for support. This is a particularly strong motif in Matthew who 'strikingly emphasizes Jesus' longing for community with the

---

89 Kevin Madigan, 'Ancient and High-Medieval Interpretations of Jesus in Gethsemane: Some Reflections on Tradition and Continuity in Christian Thought', *HTR* 88 (1995), p. 160.

90 Madigan, 'Jesus in Gethsemane', p. 157.

disciples' (vv. 36, 37, 40).[91] Perhaps even more telling is the singling out of Peter, James and John once again to be his closest companions (26.37). This privileged little trio had earlier been the only disciples to witness the splendour of Jesus' Transfiguration (17.1-8). Now in stark contrast they are called upon to be the closest witnesses of his emotional distress. Between these two events it is also these disciples who, more than the others, had pledged Jesus their unwavering support – even to the extent of being prepared to drink his cup (20.22) and to stand true even if all others fall (26.33). These three stalwarts, whose failure he has just predicted, now become Jesus' confidants in Gethsemane. They see him in his deepest distress and it is to them that he discloses the true state of his soul.

In the presence of his three closest but over-confident friends Jesus 'began to be *sorrowful* and *troubled*' (26.37).[92] These two highly descriptive words 'together depict a state of extreme agitation'.[93] Taken individually, the two Greek verbs that Matthew uses are even more illuminating of Jesus' emotional condition. The first (*lupeisthai*) is commonly used to express human sorrow. This is the word that was used to express the disciples' grief at Jesus' second passion prediction (17.23) and at the prospect that one of them would betray him (26.22). There is therefore a sense in which Jesus has now become just like his disciples as he faces a fearful future. The least that can be said is that his grief is very human. Matthew also attributes the same emotion to Herod Antipas (14.9) and the rich young ruler (19.22). Jesus is therefore giving expression to a common human emotion. The second Greek verb (*adēmonein*) is far less common. It is not attested in the LXX. In the New Testament it is found only in the Markan parallel (Mk 14.33) and in Phil. 2.26 where it refers to the distress of Epaphroditus. Bauer's lexicon lists its range of meanings as *be in anxiety, be distressed, troubled*. These two Greek verbs therefore form a very powerful combination. This has led to some enlightening English translations and paraphrases: 'Grief and anguish came over him' (TEV); '(He) began to be in terrible pain and agony of mind' (Phillips); 'Sadness came over him, and great distress' (JB); '(He) began to be grieved and agitated' (NRSV); 'Anguish and dismay came over him' (NEB). It would not be too much to say that Gethsemane was a terrifying experience for Jesus.

Matthew's description is corroborated by Jesus' own confession, one of those

---

91   Rudolf Schnackenburg, *The Gospel of Matthew* (trans. Robert R. Barr; Grand Rapids, MI: Eerdmans, 2002), p. 271.

92   Madigan, 'Jesus in Gethsemane', p. 165, notes that Jerome, the fourth century Church Father, made much of the fact that Jesus '*began* to be sorrowful and troubled', claiming that 'it is one thing to be saddened, another *to begin* to be saddened.' This distinction, found in Jerome's *Commentary on Matthew*, arose out of his view that as finite and sinful human beings we suffer passions which 'dominate the soul', while Christ experienced only 'half-passions' (*propassiones*) which did not overcome his human soul. The distinction is arbitrary and the resulting interpretation is best regarded as a historical curiosity. A more natural interpretation of the expression is that Jesus now entered a state of extreme distress that was very intense but of relatively short duration (cf. his question to Peter in v. 40, 'Could you not keep watch with me for *one hour*?') and that was resolved through prayer. By the end of this scene Jesus is ready to face his betrayer (vv. 45-46).

93   France, *Matthew*, p. 1000.

few occasions when Jesus reveals his true feelings,[94] 'My soul is overwhelmed with sorrow to the point of death' (26.38). If anything, this is an even more poignant description of his inward state. The expression 'overwhelmed with sorrow' translates the Greek adjective *perilupos*, which is rarely found in the Greek Bible. The only others who are described this way in Scripture are Cain (Gen. 4.6), the Psalmist (Pss. 42.5, 11; 43.5), Herod Antipas (Mk 6.26) and the rich young ruler (Lk. 18.25). Needless to say, Jesus' greatest affinity is with the Psalmist whose words he echoes in his grief. His confession is drawn from the threefold refrain that punctuates Psalms 42–43, 'Why are you downcast, O my soul? Why so disturbed within me?' These are emotions with which Jesus can now readily identify. Like the Psalmist he is about to be taunted and oppressed by the enemy (Pss. 42.3, 9, 10; 43.2). But he can also identify with the Psalmist at a deeper level. Behind the machinations of men the Psalmist detects the heavy hand of God. He therefore laments that 'all your waves and breakers have swept over me' (Ps. 42.7). Both the Psalmist and Jesus are downcast and overwhelmed with sorrow not only because of human opposition but because of a difficult providence.

Of course Jesus does more than repeat a refrain from the Psalms. He is 'overwhelmed with sorrow *to the point of death*'. Yet even here he does not seem to outstrip the experience of the Psalmist who claims, 'My bones suffer mortal agony' (Ps. 42.10). Even so, what does the expression mean? Is Jesus so sorrowful that he could die of sorrow? Or is he saying that he would rather die in Gethsemane than at Calvary? Or does he mean that his sorrow will last until he dies? It is probably best to understand the expression as an indication of the intensity of his sorrow.[95] Perhaps the expression is somewhat akin to such colloquial expressions as 'scared to death' or 'worried to death'.[96] A rough paraphrase of Jesus' words would then be, 'I am so overwhelmed with sorrow that it's killing me.' Such was his humanity. His heart is about to break with grief. At this point Jesus' feelings are very low and he is deeply disturbed. For moral and spiritual support he asks his three friends, 'Stay here and keep watch with me.'

But why have Jesus' feelings reached such a dangerously low ebb? Could it be because he foresaw his disciples falling away and scattered after his arrest and death? Or could it be the prospect of his own death that so deeply depresses him? Or is he again thinking of himself as the shepherd whom God will strike?

The answer to these questions lies in Jesus' prayer in the next verse, 'Going a little farther, he fell with his face to the ground and prayed, "My Father, if it is possible, may this cup be taken from me. Yet not as I will, but as you will"'

---

94 This is probably the clearest case of Jesus' emotional self-disclosure in the Gospels. Apart from the parallel in Mk 14.34 other instances can be found in Mt. 27.46 (cf. Mk 15.34); Luke 12.50; Jn 11.15; 12.27; 13.34; 15.9-13.

95 These various possibilities are well laid out by Raymond E. Brown, *The Death of the Messiah: From Gethsemane to the Grave* (2 vols; New York: Doubleday, 1994), 1, p. 155. Brown also understands the expression as an indication of intensity and finds Old Testament precedent to back his claim. Delilah nagged Samson so much that 'he was tired to death' (Judg. 16.16)!

96 Thus France, *Matthew*, p. 1004.

(26.39). In his extremity Jesus naturally resorts to prayer. His posture reflects his attitude. Like Abraham he falls facedown before God (Gen. 17.3, 17) indicating his humble submission.[97] His posture also matches his petition. He asks that the cup be taken away, but is prepared to submit to the Father's will. His own will is quite evidently that the cup be removed, and he prays that this may be the Father's will as well. But if not, there will be no clash of wills. He is prepared to do the Father's will, a commitment that he makes three times (vv. 39, 42, 44). As he prayed for more than an hour (v. 40), there was obviously more to his prayer than this single petition, but this was the heart of it. The essence of his prayer was for the removal of the cup. But precisely what did this cup entail? From what ordeal is Jesus so earnestly pleading to be spared?

The cup is not a new concept for Matthew. It was introduced in the journey section when James and John make the rash claim that they can drink the cup Jesus is going to drink (20.22). At this point Jesus makes no attempt to explain the metaphor. The first hint of this comes at the Last Supper. All the disciples present are offered the cup (26.27). Jesus then declares, 'This is my blood of the covenant, which is poured out for many for the forgiveness of sins.' For the disciples this is a cup of blessing, as they are reckoned among the many whose sins are forgiven. For Jesus at this point the cup is anything but a cup of blessing. In Gethsemane he grapples with the awful realization of what the cup means for him. To put it graphically, he now looks into the cup and sees with burning clarity that its contents are none other than his own blood. The cup contains his blood of the covenant. As he peers into the cup he shrinks from it in horror and revulsion. Understandably, he pleads with the Father whether there might not be some other way. In the infinite realm of divine possibility is there no other way in which the sins of the many can be forgiven? The silence of Gethsemane is his answer and after praying three times he bows to the Father's will. The die has been cast. The matter is resolved. Until then his turmoil continues.

Again the Old Testament provides a deeper perspective on Jesus' emotions at this point. There the cup is a common metaphor that can be understood either positively or negatively. Positively it stands for blessing and salvation (Pss. 16.5; 23.5; 116.13) and it is in this sense that the disciples are to drink the wine at the Supper (26.27). But for Jesus the cup has a very different meaning. He will experience the dark side of the metaphor. In the Old Testament the cup represents more than a tragic fate or an unwelcome destiny. It often stands for the wrath and judgement of God (Pss. 11.6; 75.8; Isa. 51.17, 22; Jer. 25.15-17; 49.12; Lam. 4.21; Ezek. 23.31-34; Hab. 2.16). The cup of the Lord is his terrifying judgement of the wicked and the nations. The prime Old Testament example is the Babylonian invasion and captivity. This is the cup of God's wrath that Jerusalem has 'drained to its dregs, the goblet that makes men stagger' (Isa. 51.17). When the nations drink this cup 'they will stagger and go mad because of the sword I will send among them' (Jer. 25.16). To drink the cup is to undergo the judgement and suffer the wrath of God. This is also what drinking the cup would mean

---

97   Thus Craig A. Smith, 'A Comparative Study of the Prayer of Gethsemane', *IBS* 22 (2000), p. 107.

for Jesus. His passion would involve more than humiliation and pain. Jesus was about to be subjected to divine judgement of the most excruciating and terrifying kind.[98]

This Old Testament background therefore gives us remarkable insight into Jesus' unspeakable sorrow and anguish (26.37-38). Behind these emotions lies not the fear of a dark fate or a cringing before physical suffering and death, but horror at the prospect of a judgement which will deliver Jesus up to the wrath of God. His approaching passion is not fate but judgement.[99] His is 'the horror of the Holy One at coming under God's judgment on human sin'.[100] In the present context Jesus' heart-rending emotions are bracketed by two metaphors for divine judgement. The first is the striking of the shepherd (26.31) and the second is the drinking of the cup (26.39, 42). This is why 'he began to be sorrowful and troubled' (26.37) and confessed to his inner circle of disciples, 'My soul is overwhelmed with sorrow to the point of death' (26.38). While his sorrow may have been compounded by the knowledge of his friends' desertion and by the prospect of an agonising physical death, these factors do little to account for the uncharacteristic intensity of Jesus' grief in Gethsemane. His loss of composure would then compare unfavourably with the earlier courage of the Maccabaean martyrs[101] and with the later unflinching determination of some of his own followers in the face of certain death.[102] His death was of a different order to theirs. Only of *his* shed blood could it be said that it was the 'blood of the covenant, which is poured out for many for the forgiveness of sins' (26.28). Gethsemane was the crushing realization of that reality.

Portraying Jesus' emotions in the Garden as he does, Matthew presents his readers with a paradox. Jesus' sorrow and anguish are all too human, distressingly human. We see him as we have never seen him before, as weak, vulnerable and emotionally out of control. He is overcome by powerful passions. To some he might even seem to cut a pathetic figure. But there is more here than meets the eye. These overwhelming emotions are ultimately driven not so much by human

---

98   Cf. James L. Mays, '"Now I Know": An Exposition of Genesis 22:1-19 and Matthew 26:36-46', *ThTo* 58 (2002), pp. 522–23: 'the metaphor of drinking the cup as the key to the meaning of the will of God reveals that Jesus knew that his human judgment was the form and instrument of the wrath of God. We are to read about this human miscarriage of justice as the paradoxical enactment of a cosmic, transcendent purpose.'

99   Thus *TDNT* 6, p. 153.

100 *TDNT* (abridged), p. 844.

101 See especially the book of 4 Maccabees which commemorates the martyrdom of Eleazar and of a mother with her seven sons who all faced horrendous tortures with great equanimity (cf. 2 Macc. 6.12–7.42) and thus demonstrated that 'devout reason is sovereign over the emotions' (4 Macc. 1.1; 13.1).

102 A notable example is Polycarp, the bishop of Smyrna, who was martyred in the mid-second century. When the proconsul threatened to have him burnt, Polycarp replied, 'You threaten the fire that burns for an hour, and after a little while is quenched; for you are ignorant of the fire of the judgement to come, and of everlasting punishment reserved for the ungodly. But why delay? Do what you wish' (*The Martyrdom of Polycarp* 11:2. See J. Stevenson, ed., *A New Eusebius: Documents Illustrative of the History of the Church to A. D. 337* [London: SPCK, 1968], p. 21).

frailty as by divine foreknowledge. Jesus would not have experienced such intensity of emotion had it not been for his prescience of what lay immediately before him.[103] Not only does he possess a detailed and incisive knowledge of prophetic Scripture, he can also predict the future with an uncanny accuracy. Hence his emotions do not arise out of some dark foreboding of what lies ahead. They arise from a foresight and understanding that are uniquely his as the Immanuel. He is 'God with us'. But will God always be with him?

1.5.2 THE CROSS (27.45-56)

⁴⁵ From the sixth hour until the ninth hour darkness came over all the land.

⁴⁶ About the ninth hour Jesus cried out in a loud voice, '*Eli, Eli, lama sabachthani?*'[104] – which means, '*My God, my God, why have you forsaken me?*'

⁴⁷ When some of those standing there heard this, they said, 'He's calling Elijah.'

⁴⁸ Immediately one of them ran and got a sponge. He filled it with wine vinegar, put it on a stick, and offered it to Jesus to drink.

⁴⁹ The rest said, 'Now leave him alone. Let's see if Elijah comes to save him.'

⁵⁰ And when Jesus had cried out again in a loud voice, he gave up his spirit.

⁵¹ At that moment the curtain of the temple was torn in two from top to bottom. The earth shook and the rocks split.

⁵² The tombs broke open and the bodies of many holy people who had died were raised to life.

⁵³ They came out of the tombs, and after Jesus' resurrection they went into the holy city and appeared to many people.

⁵⁴ When the centurion and those with him who were guarding Jesus saw the earthquake and all that had happened, they were terrified, and exclaimed, 'Surely he was the Son of God!'

⁵⁵ Many women were there, watching from a distance. They had followed Jesus from Galilee to care for his needs.

⁵⁶ Among them were Mary Magdalene, Mary the mother of James and Joses, and the mother of Zebedee's sons.

This scene is one of high drama. After three torturous hours on the cross Jesus' suffering becomes even more unbearable. At midday the sky mysteriously turns pitch-black and darkness covers the land. Some three hours later Jesus screeches

---

103 Cf. Matthew Elliott, *Faithful Feelings: Emotion in the New Testament* (Leicester: Inter-Varsity Press, 2005), p. 205: 'Jesus' full understanding of the suffering before him was the reason for the overwhelming nature of this sorrow.'

104 This is the reading of the NIV footnote. The main text reads, '*Eloi, Eloi, lama sabachthani.*' In this respect the NIV is unusual among English translations, most of which have '*Eli, Eli*' here, and '*Eloi, Eloi*' in Mk 14.34. These differences between the two versions of Jesus' cry will be considered in the discussion of the Markan parallel.

into the blackness, 'My God, my God, why have you forsaken me?' But why is this the setting for Jesus' anguished cry? Why does night come at high noon? What caused the darkness and what does it mean?

If the darkness is understood as a purely natural phenomenon, it becomes difficult to explain. A solar eclipse might readily suggest itself as the cause, but with Passover being observed at full moon this would be an astronomical impossibility. Another suggestion would be that the sun was obscured by the sirocco, a hot, dust-laden desert wind that can blow so hard that the sun becomes invisible.[105] There is, however, no indication of this in any of the Gospel accounts. Other possibilities that have been suggested are sunspots, solar storms, a thunderstorm or the aftermath of a volcanic eruption in Arabia or Syria.[106] But once again there is nothing in the Gospel text to support such suggestions.

The darkness is therefore best understood as a direct act of God. The clearest Old Testament precedent for such an event is the plague of darkness that befell the land of Egypt just prior to the exodus. This was a darkness that could be felt (Exod. 10.21). It was a total darkness that covered all Egypt for *three* days (Exod. 10.22). As the ninth plague it also immediately preceded *the death of the firstborn* (Exod. 11–12). These parallels with the crucifixion are hardly incidental. There are strong connections between the darkness in Egypt and the darkness that now envelops Jerusalem and its environs. The judgement of God has descended on the land.

There are further Old Testament examples where darkness is a sign of judgement. Especially telling are the words of Amos 8.9-10 which belong to a divine judgement oracle against Israel, 'I will make the sun go down at noon and darken the earth in broad daylight . . . I will make that time like mourning for an only son and the end of it like a bitter day.' The prophet Zephaniah likewise speaks of the great day of the Lord as 'a day of darkness and gloom, a day of clouds and blackness' (Zeph. 1.15). This is precisely also the language of Joel as he predicts a plague of locusts that will devour the land (Joel 2.2). In all these cases darkness is associated with divine judgement.[107] The darkness that came over Egypt and that was predicted by the prophets has now come over the land.[108] It has also come over Jesus. He is suffering God's judgement. He is drinking the cup.[109]

---

105 Ridderbos, *Matthew*, p. 531, notes that this phenomenon was observed by visitors in Palestine around the Passover of 1913.

106 Brown, *Death of the Messiah* 2, p. 1040.

107 This connection is commonly made by commentators, e.g. Carson, 'Matthew', p. 578; Hagner, *Matthew 14-28*, p. 844; Morris, *Matthew*, p. 720; Ridderbos, *Matthew*, p. 531.

108 The events recorded in v. 51 – the tearing of the temple curtain, the earth shaking and the rocks splitting – should also be seen as acts of divine judgement. In the Greek text all the verbs in this verse are in the passive voice and can be legitimately regarded as 'divine' or 'theological' passives, which means that God is the unexpressed agent behind the action of all three verbs. Like the darkness that covered the land these are therefore all acts of God.

109 The darkness may hold more secrets still. Greg Forbes, 'Darkness over All the Land: Theological Imagery in the Crucifixion Scene', *RTR* 66 (2007), pp. 83–96, also sees the ratification ceremony of God's covenant with Abraham in Genesis 15 as significant background to the darkness at the crucifixion. He draws attention to the darkness that came over

It is into this deep darkness of divine judgement that Jesus screams, 'My God, my God, why have you forsaken me?' It hardly needs to be said that this is a deeply emotional cry. But Matthew wants to leave his readers in no doubt. The verb translated 'cried out' (*anaboaō*) is found only here in the New Testament, although in some ancient manuscripts it is also used of the crowd clamouring for Barabbas (Mk 15.8) and of the father of the epileptic boy desperately pleading with Jesus for his only son (Lk. 9.38). It would therefore seem to carry some emotional overtones. Added to this is the fact that Jesus cried out 'in a loud voice'. He does so again in v. 50, just before he gives up his spirit. This latter cry is left unidentified, but the effect of these two loud cries is impressive. In Matthew no one else cries out or shouts in a loud voice. In the other Synoptics such loud cries describe the screeches of the demon-possessed (Mk 1.26; 5.7; Lk. 4.33; 8.28), the praises of those who have experienced and witnessed Jesus' miracles (Lk. 17.15; 19.37), the screams of those clamouring for his crucifixion (Lk. 23.23), as well as to Jesus' own shouts from the cross (Mk 15.34, 37; Lk. 23.46). It is noteworthy that Matthew restricts such loud cries to the crucified Jesus, the one of whom he had said that 'no one will hear his voice in the streets' (12.19; cf. Isa. 42.2). Only in his direst extremity does he raise his voice.

The emotional intensity is heightened by the contents of his cry, particularly his use of the double vocative, 'My God, my God'. This puts Jesus' words in the same category as some of the best known emotive utterances in Scripture, such as David's anguished cry, 'O my son Absalom! O Absalom, my son, my son!' (2 Sam. 19.4); God's urgent summons, 'Abraham! Abraham!' (Gen. 22.11), 'Jacob! Jacob!' (Gen. 46.2), 'Moses! Moses!' (Exod. 3.4) and 'Samuel! Samuel!' (1 Sam. 3.10); and Jesus' own pleas, 'Martha, Martha' (Lk. 10.41), 'O Jerusalem, Jerusalem' (Lk. 13.34), 'Simon, Simon' (Lk. 22.31), and 'Saul, Saul' (Acts 9.4; 22.7; 26.14).[110] In some of these examples it is difficult to identify the precise emotion involved. Suffice it to say that in times of high emotion speakers tend to repeat words or phrases. Repetition is natural in emotion.[111]

Given the emotionally charged nature of Jesus' words, the question still needs to be asked as to precisely what emotion is involved. Traditionally theologians have spoken of 'the cry of dereliction'. This terminology can be traced all the way back to the Latin of Jerome's Vulgate translation of the fourth century, which reads, 'Deus meus, Deus meus, ut quid *dereliquisti* me?' Jerome consistently uses the verb 'dereliquisti' in Mt. 27.46, Mk 15.34 and Ps. 22.1. It is the perfect

---

Abraham (v. 12) and to the fact that the covenant was ratified only when the sun had set and darkness had fallen (v. 17). If this insight is correct, it further highlights the covenant context in which Jesus' death occurs (cf. Mt. 26.28).

110 Further examples of the double vocative are dotted throughout Scripture (2 Sam. 18.33; 2 Kgs 2.12; 13.14; Mt. 7.21; 23.37; 25.11; Lk. 6.46; 8.24; cf. Est. 13.9 LXX; Dan. 14.37 LXX; 3 Macc. 2.2). Particularly powerful is Jeremiah's triple vocative, 'O land, land, land, hear the word of the LORD' (Jer. 22.29).

111 A. T. Robertson and W. Hersey Davis, *A New Short Grammar of the Greek Testament* (New York: Harper, 10th edn, 1933), p. 400, refer such repetition to the figure of speech known as 'climax', giving Lk. 8.24, Jn 19.6 and Acts 19.34 as examples.

tense of *derelinquo*, which means 'to forsake wholly', 'abandon', 'desert'.[112] It is therefore an appropriate translation of the underlying Greek word which carries the same range of meaning. While nowadays 'dereliction' can still mean 'the condition of being forsaken or abandoned', this meaning has become rare.[113] A more common meaning is 'neglect' in the sense of failure to carry out one's obligations. This can make the traditional terminology slightly misleading. In his cry from the cross Jesus is not implying that God is guilty of dereliction of duty! But he is asking why God has forsaken, abandoned, and deserted him.

After about six hours of excruciating pain on the cross, almost three of them in utter darkness, Jesus understandably has the feeling of being abandoned and deserted by God. He experiences a sense of total desolation. But can this emotion be identified still more closely? The fact that Jesus is quoting Ps. 22.1 may give a clue. This Psalm was traditionally ascribed to David. So it would seem appropriate that, as the Son of David, Jesus should now quote the words his forefather uttered in his deepest distress. Before Jesus quotes the Psalm, Matthew has carefully interwoven allusions to Psalm 22 into his crucifixion narrative, thereby demonstrating the many similarities between the sufferings of David and those of Jesus. Even in his deepest sufferings Jesus remains the true antitype of David. This is seen in several ways. When he was crucified, 'they divided up his clothes by casting lots' (27.35), a humiliation also suffered by David (Ps. 22.18). As Jesus hung on the cross the passers-by 'hurled insults at him, shaking their heads' (27.39). Those who mocked David did the same (Ps. 22.7). The religious leaders also mocked Jesus in words echoing those used against David, 'He trusts in God. Let God rescue him now if he wants him' (27.43; cf. Ps. 22.8).

Matthew has therefore carefully set the stage for Jesus' cry of abandonment. Jesus is not quoting Psalm 22 out of context! He can relate all too painfully to the experiences of David. Yet to how much of the Psalm does Jesus relate? How much of its context should be used to interpret Jesus' cry? The Psalm naturally falls into two parts. The first part (vv. 1-21) consists of an individual lament where David pours out his heart to God. His laments, however, alternate with strong pleas and affirmations of faith which become ever more personal and contemporary (vv. 3-5, 9-11, 19-21). In the second part of the Psalm (vv. 22-31) the genre shifts from a lament to a vow of praise that moves out in ever widening circles until it reaches the ends of the earth. The Psalm ends on a very triumphant note. Since Matthew is at pains to have his readers understand that Jesus is quoting v. 1 in context, just how much of this context should be read back into the quote? Is it a lament, an expression of faith or a shout of triumph?

If the darkness and the cup both symbolize the judgement of God, then it follows that Gethsemane and the cry of dereliction interpret one another.[114] What Jesus dreads most at Gethsemane is the prospect of being forsaken by God. On

---

112   Charlton T. Lewis and Charles Short, *A Latin Dictionary* (Oxford: Clarendon, 1962), p. 553.
113   William Little, H. W. Fowler and J. Coulson, *The Shorter Oxford English Dictionary* (Oxford: Clarendon, 3rd edn, 1956), p. 487.
114   On both occasions Jesus alludes to or quotes a Psalm of lament (26.38 = Pss. 42.5, 11 and 43.5; 27.46 = Ps. 22.1).

the cross he cries out in anguish because he is now drinking to the dregs the cup of God's judgement and wrath. It is therefore a cry of utter abandonment and desolation. No interpretation of these words should be allowed to minimize their bitter anguish. Although Psalm 22 ends on a note of triumphant vindication, the wider context should not annul what the text so evidently affirms.[115] What can and must be said, however, is that although not a cry of triumph this is nevertheless a cry of faith. Jesus echoes the faith of the Psalmist by calling out '*my* God, *my* God'. In this darkest of darkest hours the communion between the Father and the Son that had been unbroken for all eternity is now mysteriously broken. In the agony of 'God-forsakenness' Jesus howls out into the darkness. But in the midst of it all he still strikes a note of trust. Just as in the Garden he had said '*my* Father', so now he cries '*my* God, *my* God'. His terrible shout does not express a loss of faith, but rather a temporary loss of contact.[116] At this point in history something happened that had never occurred in all eternity. The fellowship between the Father and the Son was broken. For what must have seemed an eternity to Jesus there was an inseparable barrier between him and the Father. That barrier was the sins of the people whom he had come to save (1.21), the sins of the many who would be forgiven and for whom his blood of the covenant would be shed (26.28). This separation between the Father and the Son is one of the most impenetrable mysteries of the entire Gospel narrative.[117] Because of this unfathomable mystery Matthew's narrative is riddled with paradoxes at this point.

In the cry of abandonment this Gospel finds both its zenith and its nadir. Here the story peaks and troughs at the same time. In the previous chapter Jesus' disciples have betrayed (26.48-50), deserted (26.56) and denied him (26.69-75). The crowds that had been so ambivalent earlier in the Gospel have decisively turned against him (26.47, 55; 27.15, 20-24). The religious leaders have condemned him (26.66; 27.1) and mocked him (27.41-43). Now even God himself seems to concur with this unanimous human verdict by forsaking Jesus (27.46). Mystery of mysteries, the Immanuel, 'God-with-us', is abandoned by God. It would seem that all is lost. Yet it is precisely here that Matthew's story reaches its culmination. As Kingsbury explains:

> Ironically, however, what the religious authorities do not perceive is that God and Jesus, too, will the death of Jesus. Jesus wills his own death because he is the perfectly obedient Son of God. God wills Jesus' death because, through it, he will renew his covenant and proffer all humans everywhere the forgiveness of sins and salvation (1:23; 20:28; 26:28). To demonstrate that Jesus' death is in line with his saving purposes, God raises Jesus from the dead on

---

115 Carson, 'Matthew', p. 579; cf. William J. Kenneally, "Eli, Eli, Lamma Sabachthani?' (Mt. 27.46)', *CBQ* 8 (1946), p. 132, who rightly contends that the cry can only 'insinuate complete victory' if it is assumed that Jesus recited all of Psalm 22 from the cross, but there is no evidence whatsoever that this was the case.

116 France, *Matthew*, p. 1077.

117 Hagner, *Matthew 14-28*, p. 845.

the third day (28:5-6). In raising Jesus, God both vindicates him and exalts him . . . From the standpoint of the religious authorities, the cross attests to Jesus' destruction and their victory. From the standpoint of Matthew and the reader, however, the cross stands as a sign of the victory that Jesus has won. By the twist of irony, the cross attests, not to the destruction of Jesus, but to the salvation that God henceforth proffers through Jesus to all humankind.[118]

This universal salvation is foreshadowed by the reaction of the pagan centurion and his men. Standing at the foot of the cross, they witnessed the earthquake and no doubt also the splitting of the rocks and the darkness. They would also have heard Jesus' loud cries. With all these momentous events surrounding his death they reacted in sheer terror and exclaimed, 'Surely he was the Son of God' (27.54). Although their level of understanding can be debated, it is remarkable that these raw Gentiles identify Jesus in the way God had introduced him at the outset of his ministry (3.17; cf. 17.5). The disciples are the only other humans to have identified Jesus in this way (14.33; 16.16). Like the other centurion we met earlier in this Gospel, this centurion and his soldiers have also displayed a faith beyond 'anyone in Israel' (8.10). They, too, represent the many who will come from east and west to join the Jewish patriarchs in the kingdom of heaven (8.11-12).[119] It is a tragic irony that while the Jewish leaders mock Jesus for being the Son of God (27.41-43), these pagans acknowledge him as such. It is a sign of things to come.

In a final twist of irony, the authority which the religious leaders had challenged so strenuously (21.23-27) is now affirmed by the risen Jesus to encompass both heaven and earth (28.18). On this basis the disciples are to go and make disciples of all nations (28.19). Because of his death and resurrection the Son of David is establishing an eternal kingdom by which all the nations will be blessed.

Conclusion

Matthew is the most Jewish of the four Gospels. It is steeped in the language of the Old Testament. Its author has a keen eye for the fulfilment of Old Testament prophecies, types and symbols in the life and ministry of Jesus. Underpinning this theme of fulfilment Matthew is adamant to demonstrate that in the coming of Jesus God has proved himself faithful to all the covenants he made with Israel and its leaders. The Gentile thread that runs throughout the Gospel, culminating in the Great Commission (28.18-20), shows that the covenant with Abraham is beginning to be fulfilled. The eternal kingdom Jesus has come to establish fulfils God's covenant promises to David. Jesus sheds the blood of the covenant, the antitype of the blood that sealed the covenant with Moses (Exod. 24.8). Finally, Jesus' blood is poured out for the forgiveness of sins, the greatest blessing of

---

118   Jack D. Kingsbury, 'The Plot of Matthew's Story', *Int* 46 (1992), p. 355.
119   France, *Matthew*, p. 1085.

the new covenant (Jer. 31.34). Because of his shed blood the new covenant is established to replace the Mosaic. As a result, the fulfilment of the covenants with Abraham and David can become a reality. As the inaugurator of the new covenant through his blood Jesus becomes the king of the nations and his throne is eternal.

It is within this covenant framework that Jesus' emotions in Matthew make most sense. He is amazed when a Gentile is the first to recognize his true authority as the Son of David, and he reacts with anger when he knows that this same authority is about to be snubbed. His God-like compassion for the covenant people through his miracles of healing the sick, feeding the hungry and restoring sight to the blind suggests that the covenant is about to be renewed. This renewal of the covenant comes at great cost to himself, the cost of his own blood. The contemplation of this at Gethsemane and the experience of it at Calvary overwhelm him with grief.

CHAPTER 2

The 'Man of Sorrows':
Jesus' Emotions in Mark's Gospel

No Gospel writer allows us to gaze more deeply into Jesus' soul than Mark. If a psychological analysis of Jesus' personality were possible, this would be the place to begin. Mark captures a wider range of Jesus' emotions than any other Gospel. To describe the variety of Jesus' emotional reactions he uses fourteen different expressions, compared with seven in Matthew and five in Luke. Mark's variety is even greater than John's. Although there are twenty-eight references to Jesus' emotions in John (compared with sixteen in Mark), only nine different words are used. This is because some of the Fourth Gospel's favourite emotions (such as love and joy) are attributed to Jesus again and again. The reason for this delightful diversity in Mark's portrait of Jesus is the stuff of speculation. Perhaps something is to be said for Peter's involvement in the production of Mark's Gospel, which can be traced back to a very ancient tradition.[1] Whatever the case, Mark was privy to the inside story of Jesus and has given us unique insights into his person.

Mark has all the emotions of Jesus found in Matthew, but sometimes with slightly different turns and nuances. Thus Jesus is again amazed, but this time not at the faith of a centurion but at the unbelief of his own townsfolk in Nazareth (6.6). Again he issues a stern warning, not now to two blind men but to a leper he has healed (1.43). As in Matthew he shows compassion to crowds (6.34; 8.2), but also to needy individuals such as a leper (1.41) and an epileptic boy and his

---

1 Papias, who was the bishop of Hierapolis in Asia Minor in the second century, is quoted in this regard by Eusebius, the fourth-century church historian: 'Mark, having become Peter's interpreter, wrote down accurately everything he remembered, though not in order, of the things either said or done by Christ. For he neither heard the Lord nor followed him, but afterwards, as I said, followed Peter.' See Michael W. Holmes (ed.), *The Apostolic Fathers: Greek Texts and English Translations of Their Writings* (trans. and ed. J. B. Lightfoot and J. R. Harmer; Grand Rapids, MI: Baker, 2nd edn, 1992), p. 569.

59

desperate father (9.22). In Gethsemane and at Calvary, Mark also pictures Jesus overwhelmed by grief, but at times his wording is subtly different from Matthew's (14.33; 15.34; cf. Mt. 26.37; 27.46).

There are also instances where Mark goes beyond Matthew. At times he highlights emotions of Jesus which, for his own reasons, Matthew has chosen to leave to one side. In most cases these are found in passages that have a Matthaean parallel. Thus, as he is about to heal the man with the shrivelled hand, he looks at his opponents 'in anger, deeply distressed at their stubborn hearts' (3.5). When the Pharisees test him, wanting a sign from heaven, Jesus sighs deeply (8.12). When the disciples try to stop little children from coming to Jesus he is indignant (10.14) and when he looked at the rich young ruler he loved him (10.21). He also sighs at the healing of a deaf-mute (7.34), a miracle for which Matthew seems to have no exact parallel.

From these preliminary observations it would appear that Mark gives his readers a more emotionally detailed picture of Jesus than Matthew. At the same time the neat pattern, whereby Matthew links Jesus' emotions to miracles in the Galilee and journey sections, can be detected in Mark only in part. While in both Gospels the Jerusalem section is dominated by overwhelming grief, Mark does not connect all of Jesus' emotions to miracles in the Galilee and journey sections. Although in most cases there is such a connection, there are also some notable exceptions to the pattern. Jesus' amazement in Nazareth (6.6), his deep sighing in response to the Pharisees (8.12), his indignation with his disciples (10.14) and his love for the rich young ruler (10.21) are all quite independent of a miracle.

Again like Matthew, references to Jesus' emotions in Mark are distributed across the major sections of his Gospel, although in slightly different proportions. Mark has nine references in Galilee, three on the journey and four in Jerusalem, compared to Matthew's five, one and four respectively. These subtle differences between the two accounts produce the colour, perspective and depth unique to each of their portraits of Jesus. Mark's portrait is more complex and nuanced than Matthew's, not only because of the greater number of references and the wider variety of terms employed, but also because he sometimes presents Jesus as having mixed emotions. Thus Jesus has compassion on a leper but also sends him away with a stern warning (1.41-43), while his reaction to his opponents is a combination of anger and deep distress (3.5). Mark has succeeded in producing a very detailed and fascinating picture of Jesus.

2.1 *Mark's Presentation of Jesus*

A Gospel writer's first comments about Jesus provide an early clue to his overall presentation. Such opening remarks are like an artist's rough sketch that will be filled out by the more detailed and intricate portrait of the subject. This rough sketch will not only lay down some of the subject's major features, it also prepares the canvas for the work of art that is based upon it. In Mark's case this preliminary sketch of Jesus is drawn in the introduction to his Gospel (1.1-13).

As the main subject of Mark's masterpiece Jesus is sketched in increasing detail at three points in this opening section: (a) in the title to the work (v. 1), (b) in the Old Testament quote that expands on this title (vv. 2-3), and (c) in the declaration from heaven at Jesus' baptism (v. 11).

Mark comes closer to having a title for his work than any other Gospel writer. His opening verse, 'The beginning of the gospel about Jesus Christ, the Son of God,'[2] is not a grammatical sentence complete with subject and predicate. It therefore reads more like a title to the work that follows. The 'beginning' to which Mark refers is best understood as the opening section of his Gospel which includes the ministry of John the Baptist and the baptism and temptation of Jesus (1.4-13). This forms the introduction to 'the gospel about Jesus Christ, the Son of God.' Alone among the Gospel writers Mark specifically states that he is setting out to write a Gospel. The grand subject of this Gospel is 'Jesus Christ, the Son of God'. This is the key to Mark's understanding of Jesus. More than anything, he intends to portray Jesus as the Christ (or Messiah) and the Son of God. This double designation of Jesus is supported by an Old Testament quote (1.2-3) and confirmed by the declaration at the baptism of Jesus (1.10-11). It also provides a rough outline for the Gospel as a whole. As William Lane explains:

> The initial verse of the Gospel dictates the structure of the account which follows. Mark's witness in the first half of the document reaches a point of climax with the confession of Peter at Caesarea Philippi that Jesus is the Messiah (Ch. 8:29). All that has preceded has prepared for this moment of recognition. All that follows, as Jesus directs his way to Jerusalem and the Passion, clarifies what messiahship entails. The climax to the second half of the Gospel is provided in the confession of the centurion in charge of the crucifixion that Jesus is the Son of God (Ch. 15:39). Through the vehicle of these two confessions, one uttered by a representative of Israel and the other by a spokesman for the Gentile world, Mark bears witness to the faith that undergirds his document.[3]

Lane has come up with a simple and convincing outline of this Gospel. The contents of the Gospel fit his twofold structure particularly well. Peter's confession comes at a significant turning point in the whole account. Geographically, Caesarea Philippi represents the most northerly point in the narrative and from here the journey heads south towards Jerusalem. The Passion predictions also begin here. Before this there was little hint that Jesus would turn out to be a suffering Messiah. In fact quite the opposite. Up until this point the ministry of Jesus

---

2 The NIV footnote alerts the reader to a textual problem in this verse, 'Some manuscripts do not have *the Son of God*.' The omission has some early and important manuscripts in its favour, but the general manuscript evidence weighs heavily against it. The NIV, which here represents the English translation tradition as a whole, has therefore correctly retained the title.

3 William L. Lane, *The Gospel according to Mark* (NICNT; Grand Rapids, MI: Eerdmans, 1974), pp. 1–2.

has been defined mainly in terms of exorcisms, healings, miracles and other acts of power. In fact, of the twenty-three references to Jesus' miraculous activity in this Gospel, no fewer than nineteen occur before Peter's confession. In the first eight chapters of Mark Jesus cuts a triumphant and compelling figure. There is little to prepare the disciples (or the reader) for what lies ahead.

Although Lane's simple outline has an obvious appeal to a tidy mind, it could use further refinement. This is suggested by the next two verses. Immediately following the superscription to Mark's Gospel (1.1) a strong link is forged with the Old Testament (1.2, 3): 'It is written in Isaiah the prophet: "I will send my messenger ahead of you, who will prepare your way" – "a voice of one calling in the desert, 'Prepare the way for the Lord, make straight paths for him.'"'

By quoting Isa. 40.3 in v. 3, Mark wants his readers to be thinking of Isaiah's New Exodus section (Isa. 40–66) at the very outset of his Gospel. Both verses stand as introductory landmarks to all that follows. This provides the reader with an overall perspective on Mark's Gospel. Mark is implicitly inviting us to read his Gospel in the light of Isaiah's New Exodus. (There is more here as well since v. 2 is not a quote from Isaiah at all but from Malachi. We will return to this difficulty in a moment. For now it is important to see the connections between Mark and Isaiah.)

In each case a threefold structure can be detected:[4]

First, the Isaianic New Exodus develops three major themes:

(a) Yahweh as Warrior and Healer delivers his people from bondage among the nations, especially from Babylon and her idol gods (40.10ff.; 51.9ff.; 52.10-12).
(b) He leads the 'blind' along a New Exodus way (40.3-5; 41.17-20; 43.19, 20).
(c) The destination is Jerusalem (40.9ff.; 54.11ff.).

These divisions are not clear-cut, but rather are intertwined throughout this prophetic material. In Mark the divisions stand out far more clearly:

(a) Jesus' powerful ministry in Galilee and beyond with its strong emphasis on healing and exorcisms (1.16ff.). The casting out of the demons closely parallels the overthrow of Babylon's idol gods. Jesus is now the Yahweh–Warrior figure (1.16–8.26).
(b) His journey along the way (8.27–10.52). The failure of the disciples to understand the nature of his messiahship shows that they are still spiritually blind. Unlike the journey in Matthew, Mark's journey section is bracketed by accounts of blind men being healed (i.e. 8.22-26; 10.46-52). These blind men are indicative of the spiritual condition of the disciples. Not surprisingly, the word *hodos* ('way') occurs frequently in this section (8.27; 9.33, 34; 10.17, 32, 46, 52) – a total of seven times.

---

4 A detailed argument for the connections between Isaiah 40–66 and Mark's Gospel can be found in Rikki E. Watts, *Isaiah's New Exodus and Mark* (Tübingen: Mohr Siebeck, 1997), pp. 53–368.

(c) His arrival in Jerusalem (11.1ff.). While for Isaiah the goal of the New Exodus is the enthronement of Yahweh in a restored Jerusalem, Mark has a tragic twist at this point. Jesus does not come to restore Jerusalem but to pronounce judgement. His first acts upon arrival are ominous – the cleansing of the temple and the cursing of the fig-tree (11.11-21). Even in Jesus' ministry the Isaianic New Exodus is still only partially fulfilled. While the quote from Isa. 40.3 heralds a time of promise and fulfilment, the quote from Mal. 3.1 in 1.2 strikes a note of warning. Both strands will be worked out as this Gospel unfolds. Still the question remains as to why Mark seems to attribute a verse from Malachi to Isaiah.

There are two explanations. First, it was common practice to attribute a combined quotation from two prophets to the greater of those prophets, e.g. Mt. 27.9-10 contains allusions to Zech. 11.12, 13 and to Jer. 18.2; 19.2, 11; 32.6-9, but is introduced by the words, 'Then what was spoken by Jeremiah the prophet was fulfilled . . .'

Secondly, Mark loves his 'sandwiches'. For example, the episode of the cursing of the fig tree in 11.12-14, 20-21 is interrupted by the cleansing of the temple in 11.15-18 (cf. Mt. 21.12-21). The implication is that it too is cursed and barren. Likewise the woman's loving response in anointing Jesus is contrasted with the plotting taking place around it (14.1-11). As Richard Burridge explains, 'In each case, the story on the inside illuminates the surrounding narrative, by way of commentary, comparison, or contrast.'[5] This is certainly the case in Mk 1.2, 3. The quote from Mal. 3.1 in v. 2b is the 'filling in the sandwich' between the introductory formula to the quote in v. 2a and the citation of Isa. 40.3 in v. 3. The warning of judgement in 1.2b stands as an ominous counterpoise to Isaiah's promise of fulfilment in 1.3. Yes, Jesus does travel the New Exodus way and he will be enthroned in Jerusalem – but on a cross! In Mark's Gospel Jesus is hailed as 'King of the Jews (Israel)' no less than six times, but all of these occurrences are in ch. 15 (vv. 2, 9, 12, 18, 26, 32) and only in connection with his crucifixion. In fact, these are the only references to Jesus as King in this entire Gospel. He comes to inaugurate his kingdom, but his throne is a cross. As Paul Barnett points out:

> The dominant theme running through this chapter [15] is 'the king of the Jews' . . . But, ironically, it is in his crucifixion on a trumped-up charge of high treason that Jesus ultimately reveals himself to be 'the king of the Jews.' Although Jesus has announced that the *kingdom* of God is 'near' (1.14, 15), Mark does not say directly that it has arrived. The repetition of the similar sounding word *king* in this chapter, however, is Mark's way of saying, 'The kingdom of God has now come, in – of all things – the death of the king.'[6]

---

5 Richard A. Burridge, *Four Gospels, One Jesus? A Symbolic Reading* (Grand Rapids, MI: Eerdmans, 1994)., p. 39. Other 'sandwiches' can be found in 3.20-35; 5.21-43; 6.6-30; 14.54-72.

6 Paul Barnett, *The Servant King: Reading Mark Today* (Sydney: Anglican Information Office, 1991), p. 284.

The strength of the view that links the outline of Mark to Isaiah 40–66 lies in the fact that it anchors the idea of a suffering Messiah at deeper level. The very concept with which Peter and the other disciples had so much trouble is at the heart of Isaiah's New Exodus, that is, the suffering Servant of Isaiah 53. This is echoed in Jesus' climactic statement in 10.45, towards the end of the journey section. He was going to Jerusalem 'to give his life a ransom for many'.[7] He was indeed the 'man of sorrows' (Isa. 53.3).

What has been said editorially by Mark in 1.1-3 is confirmed by the announcements attending Jesus' baptism. John the Baptist, who is both Malachi's messenger and Isaiah's 'voice' (1.2-3), declares that Jesus is more powerful than he (1.7). He will demonstrate his power not by baptizing people with water as John did, but by baptizing them with the Holy Spirit (1.8). What John may not have realized was that in order to baptize with the Holy Spirit Jesus first needed himself to be baptized with the Holy Spirit. It was this baptism by the Holy Spirit that would confirm Jesus' messianic identity. Only when he is thus anointed by the Holy Spirit does Jesus become the Anointed One, the Messiah, the Christ. It is this divine anointing that occurs in v. 10: 'As Jesus was coming up out of the water, he saw *heaven being torn open* and the Spirit descending on him like a dove. Mark's language is unusual. In Matthew and Luke it simply says that 'heaven was opened'. Only Mark says that Jesus saw 'heaven being *torn* open'. Why does he put it that way? Again he seems to be echoing the language of Isaiah's New Exodus. Now at last the prayer of Isaiah the prophet is being answered: 'Oh, that you would *rend* the heavens and come down!' (Isa. 64.1). Now the heavens have been torn open and the Holy Spirit has come down. The descent of the Spirit on Jesus in v. 10 constitutes him as the Christ.

In the next verse he is declared to be the Son of God: 'And a voice came from heaven: "You are my Son, whom I love; with you I am well pleased."' This is an extremely loaded statement and programmatic for Jesus' entire ministry. It sets the stage for everything that follows. Very emphatically the heavenly voice declares: 'You are my Son.' Again we need to read this statement in the light of the Old Testament where we find there is more than one candidate for the title. In Exod. 4.22-23 God says to Pharaoh: 'Israel is my firstborn son, and I told you, "Let my son go, so he may worship me."' So Israel is the son of God. This is confirmed in Hos. 11.1 where God recalls at a much later date: 'Out of Egypt have I called my son.'[8] But Israel is not the only son of God in the Old Testament. As the representative and as the embodiment of the nation, the king of Israel is also the son of God. This is what God said about King David in Psalm 89: 'I will also appoint him my firstborn, the most exalted of the kings of the earth' (v. 27). This is again reflected in the promise that God made to David about Solomon, 'I will be his father, and he will be my son' (2 Sam. 7.14). The Old Testament comes closest to the words at Jesus' baptism in Psalm 2, which is an enthronement Psalm for a Davidic king. It is when that king is enthroned that God decrees:

---

7 Cf. Isa. 53.11, 'by his knowledge my righteous servant will justify *many*, and he will bear their iniquities'.

8 Cf. Isa. 63.16; Jer. 31.20.

'You are my Son; today I have become your Father' (v. 7). This declaration is fulfilled directly in Jesus. He is great David's greater Son. He is the king of Israel par excellence. Anointed with the Holy Spirit he is now the ideal king of Israel. All the earlier kings of Israel find their fulfilment in him.

Not only is Jesus God's Son in some royal, official sense. The declaration continues, 'You are my Son, whom I love; with you I am well pleased.' In Psalm 2 the wording had been rather different: 'You are my Son; today I have become your Father.' So the heavenly voice is not quoting the Psalm exactly. So where does the rest of the declaration come from? At the beginning of Isaiah 42 we have the first Servant Song, and there the Servant of the Lord is introduced with these words: 'Here is my servant, whom I uphold, my chosen one *in whom I delight*; I will put my Spirit on him and he will bring justice to the nations.' There are some pertinent parallels between this pronouncement and the declaration at Jesus' baptism. God delights in his Servant; God is well pleased with his Son. God puts his Spirit on his Servant; the Holy Spirit descends on his Son. God has chosen his Servant and he loves his Son. It all sounds very similar. The Son and the Servant are the same person. In Isaiah the Servant of the Lord becomes the suffering Servant of ch. 53. Mark will devote more of his Gospel to the Passion of Christ than any other. The beloved Son and the Servant of the Lord turn out to be one and the same.

The statement from heaven almost buckles under the weight of meaning that every part carries: 'You are my Son, whom I love, with you I am well pleased.' It is a heavily loaded statement.[9] Jesus is the King of Israel, but he is also the Servant of the Lord. Yes, he is a king, but he is a special kind of king. He is the Servant-King. As such, he 'did not come to be served, but to serve and to give his life a ransom for many' (Mk 10.45). As the King of Psalm 2 he will rule the nations with a rod of iron (vv. 7-8). As Isaiah's Servant, the central figure of the New Exodus, the Lord will lay on him the iniquity of us all (53.6).

Mark's introduction (1.1-13) is therefore a tightly constructed unit. He introduces Jesus as the Christ and the Son of God (1.1), an identity that is substantiated by Scripture (1.2-3), by John the Baptist (1.7-8) and by God himself (1.10-11). Further confirmation is found in Jesus' encounter with the devil in the desert (1.12-13). Unlike the other Synoptics, Mark says nothing about the outcome. The remainder of his first chapter, however, leaves the reader in no doubt. The Yahweh–Warrior figure has come to do battle with his foes and to establish his kingdom.

---

9 The declaration could also be a veiled allusion to Gen. 22.2 where God commands Abraham, 'Take your son, your only son Isaac, *whom you love*, and go to the region of Moriah.' If this allusion is intentional, it is an early pointer to the crucifixion.

2.2 *Mixed Emotions*

Early in his Gospel, Mark presents us with some puzzling combinations. Jesus is filled with compassion for a leper (1.41), but then immediately after his cleansing sends him away with a strong warning (1.43). Overtones of anger are not far from the surface. Compassion laced with anger is an unusual mix to say the least and has caused commentators considerable consternation. The next set of mixed emotions also proves intriguing. Anger and deep distress come together as Jesus looks around at his opponents before healing the man with the shrivelled hand (3.5). But how well does anger combine with either compassion or deep distress? Is it psychologically plausible? Is Mark presenting a credible portrait of Jesus?

To answer these questions we need to appreciate the context in which Jesus experiences these mixed emotions. In both cases there is a healing. A leper is cleansed and a shrivelled hand is restored. These miracles also stand at the climax of the sections in which they are found. The healing of the leper comes at the end of the beginning of Jesus' ministry in Galilee (1.14-45). The man with the shrivelled hand is healed at the conclusion of Mark's first controversy section (2.1–3.6; cf. 3.20-30; 7.1-21; 12.1-40). Events escalate in the lead up to both miracles and they are performed in an emotionally charged atmosphere.

Jesus' ministry in Galilee commences with an emphatic declaration. 'The time is fulfilled and the kingdom of God is at hand' (1.15 NASB). These are the first words of Jesus to be quoted by Mark. What precisely does Jesus mean by 'the time is fulfilled'? A paraphrase of his words may suffice: 'The great prophetic future predicted in the Old Testament is now here. What the prophets prophesied has now arrived. What the seers dreamed of has become reality. What the patriarchs longed for – it's now happening before your eyes. The great hope of Israel has finally come.'

Why can Jesus say this? What does he base it on? How can he make such a grand and lofty claim? Again Mark's introduction has made this abundantly clear. There are three key events that form the background to Jesus' statement – the ministry of John the Baptist, the baptism of Jesus, and the temptation of Jesus. So is it any wonder that he can say, 'The time is fulfilled'? John the Baptist has done his work. Jesus has been baptized and withstood the temptations of Satan. So now at last a new age has dawned. Finally God's Old Testament promises are being fulfilled.

His next statement is therefore a little unexpected, 'The kingdom of God is near.' After the fulfilments Mark has just recorded, that is not what we would expect. We would have anticipated a simple equation: the King is here and the kingdom is here. Jesus' two opening statements are not exactly synonymous. 'The time is fulfilled' and 'the kingdom is near' are not one and the same. Some scholars have tried to argue that they are.[10] But Jesus doesn't say that the kingdom has arrived. He says that the kingdom has approached. He doesn't say that

---

10   See, for example, C. H. Dodd, *The Parables of the Kingdom* (London: James Nisbet, 1935).

the kingdom is here, but that the kingdom is near. Its nearness is evidenced by the events that immediately follow.

As the messianic King and Yahweh–Warrior figure Jesus is on the warpath. He is out to establish his kingdom. There are enemies to be overcome. In some of his early triumphs he defeats the dreaded duo of demons and disease, thereby displaying his messianic authority (1.22, 27). Because he is the Christ whom the Spirit has empowered for ministry he has the authority to cast out an evil spirit in the synagogue at Capernaum (1.23-27). That same day after the synagogue service he heals Peter's mother-in-law of a fever (1.31). That evening he heals many and drives out many demons (1.34). Later as he travels throughout Galilee he drives out more demons (1.39). All this is clear evidence that the showdown with Satan in the wilderness went Jesus' way. Under his messianic authority the kingdom of God is advancing in spectacular fashion. But of the healings and exorcisms recorded in ch. 1 no miracle was more spectacular than the healing of the man with leprosy (1.40-45). Healing leprosy was regarded by the rabbis as equivalent to raising the dead.[11] Only God could heal leprosy.[12] This is was the epitome of Jesus' miracles in ch. 1.

Because of these miracles Jesus became an instant celebrity not only in Capernaum (1.33) but throughout Galilee (1.28, 45). Even without the glare of the media, celebrity status in the first century had its downsides. There was the obvious lack of privacy (1.35-37, 45), but the more troublesome companion was controversy. Then, as now, celebrity and controversy were constant companions. This aspect dominates ch. 2. In reporting on Jesus' teaching in the Capernaum synagogue Mark had dropped in the aside that Jesus taught as one having authority and not as the scribes (1.22). It is an early indication of things to come. It was not long before the scribes saw Jesus as a threat. By the beginning of ch. 2 they are watching his every move. When he forgives the sins of the paralytic, they think, 'Why does this fellow talk like that? He's blaspheming! Who can forgive sins but God alone?' (2.7). On this occasion they were prepared to keep their thoughts to themselves. The next encounter occurs at Levi's place. This time the Pharisaic scribes are not as reticent, but they still do not approach Jesus directly. Instead they confront his disciples, 'Why does he eat with tax collectors and "sinners"?' (2.16). Out in the grain fields on the Sabbath the Pharisees are more forthright and tackle Jesus directly over the behaviour of his disciples, 'Look, why are they doing what is unlawful on the Sabbath?' (2.24). In the next confrontation with the religious authorities it is Jesus who goes on the offensive, 'Which is lawful on the Sabbath: to do good or to do evil, to save life or to kill?' (3.4). His challenge is met with a stony silence. It is what lay behind this silence that so angered and distressed Jesus (3.5). After he had healed the man with the shrivelled hand, the Pharisees begin to plot with the Herodians how they might kill him (3.6). Already

---

11 Lane, *Mark*, p. 89.
12 In the Old Testament the cleansing of leprosy was regarded as a sign of God's presence (Exod. 4.1-7; Num. 12.10-15; 2 Kgs 5.8, 15), and in Mt. 11.5 and Lk. 7.22 it is cited as evidence that Jesus is the Coming One.

at this early stage the conflict turns deadly.[13] Jesus knows it, and his emotions are deeply stirred.

The healing of the leper and of the man with the withered hand both have parallel accounts in Matthew and Luke (Mt. 8.1-4; Lk. 5.12-16 and Mt. 12.9-14; Lk. 6.6-11 respectively). For reasons best known to themselves these Evangelists record no emotional reaction on Jesus' part. This is where Mark makes a unique contribution. Where the others report no emotion he has two. Within the flow of his narrative the appearance of these two pairs of emotions is highly appropriate. In the lead up to each the emotional temperature has been steadily rising. The heat is on Jesus. Celebrity causes it in the first instance and controversy in the second. The fact that Jesus becomes emotional is therefore very understandable, but the precise mix of emotions remains somewhat baffling.

2.1.1 COMPASSION WITH A STERN WARNING (1.40-45)

40 A man with leprosy came to him and begged him on his knees, 'If you are willing, you can make me clean.'
41 *Filled with compassion*, Jesus reached out his hand and touched the man. 'I am willing,' he said. 'Be clean!'
42 Immediately the leprosy left him and he was cured.
43 Jesus sent him away at once with a *strong warning*:
44 'See that you don't tell this to anyone. But go, show yourself to the priest and offer the sacrifices that Moses commanded for your cleansing, as a testimony to them.'
45 Instead he went out and began to talk freely, spreading the news. As a result, Jesus could no longer enter a town openly but stayed outside in lonely places. Yet the people still came to him from everywhere.

The leper who approached Jesus for cleansing was in a desperate situation.[14] Although the NIV footnote correctly points out that the Greek word for 'leprosy' could indicate 'various diseases affecting the skin – not necessarily leprosy',[15] this should not be understood as minimising the man's plight. He seems to have been afflicted with a particularly severe form of the disease. In the parallel account Luke, with a fine eye for medical detail, observes that the man 'was covered with leprosy' (Lk. 5.12). His skin condition may therefore have affected him from head

---

13   Mark's narrative reaches this point at a remarkably early stage (cf. Mt. 12.14; Lk. 19.47; Jn 5.18).

14   For the medical comments in this section I am grateful for the advice of Dr Timothy D. Walker MBBS (Hons), MPHTM, FRACP and of Dr Barry N. Edwards MBBS, Dip Obs, RCOG, OAM, member of the National Council and Victorian Advisory Council of the Leprosy Mission Australia.

15   Under the entry *lepra* ('leprosy') BDAG cautiously comments that the word 'in LXX and NT may at times refer to what is generally termed leprosy, but probability extends to such skin diseases as psoriasis, lupus, ringworm, and favus, and in the absence of more precise data it is best to use the more general term *serious skin disease* Mt. 8.3; Mk 1.42; Lk. 5.12f.' (592).

to toe and made him an ugly sight. Because of the disease his life was reduced to a pitiful existence. In biblical times leprosy was a skin disease that was difficult to diagnose and heal.[16] The Law of Moses, mainly in Leviticus 13–14, had prescribed in great detail how such diseases were to be treated.[17] It provided for their diagnosis, the separation of the sufferer and the law of his cleansing, all of which were the responsibility of the priest.[18] What these regulations could not provide was a cure. Healings were extremely rare. Moses' sister Miriam and Naaman the Syrian were the only victims of the disease whom the Old Testament records as having been healed. From Jesus' instructions to the healed leper to go and show himself to the priest and offer the sacrifices that Moses commanded (1.44) it would also appear that the Levitical regulations were still in force. In that case the leper would be obliged to wear torn clothes, let his hair go unkempt, cover the lower part of his face and cry out 'Unclean! Unclean!' (Lev. 13.45). He was also to live alone 'outside the camp' (Lev. 13.46). The social ostracism suffered by the leper was acute. Leprosy was therefore far more than a medical condition. As James Edwards further explains:

> This is not simply the description of an illness. It is a *sentence*, the purpose of which was to protect the health of the community from a dreaded contagion . . . Lepers were victims of far more than the disease itself. The disease robbed them of their health, and the sentence imposed on them as a consequence robbed them of their name, occupation, habits, family and fellowship, and worshiping community. To ensure against contact with society, lepers were required to make their appearance as repugnant as possible. Josephus speaks of the banishment of lepers as those 'in no way differing from a corpse'

16 This is no longer the case with modern leprosy. In private correspondence with the author on 14 October 2009 Dr Barry Edwards defined leprosy as 'a mildly infectious disease of the nerves and skin.' He also commented that it is not really difficult to diagnose and is treatable. 'Since 1984 multi-drug therapy arrived which renders the patient non-infectious after 48 hours and cured of the bacterial infection in 6 to 18 months. Surgery for deformity and vocational training, social and moral healing, and rehabilitation back to their usual abode will complete the treatment.'

17 Philip Eichman, 'The History, Biology & Medical Aspects of Leprosy', *The American Biology Teacher* 61 (1999), pp. 490–95, has argued that the signs and symptoms described in Leviticus 13–14 do not appear to be consistent with leprosy as it is defined today. Modern leprosy, which since the late nineteenth century has been known as 'Hansen's disease', should probably be distinguished from biblical leprosy. The earliest written records describing true leprosy are from India dating back to around 600 BC, and it was there that the disease may have originated. It may then have been spread to the Mediterranean world by the soldiers of Alexander the Great returning from their Indian campaign (ca. 327–326 BC), although this cannot be proved. In any event, leprosy as it is known today was definitely described by the Greek physicians and it appears to have become a fairly common disease by Greek and Roman times. Thus the leper encountered by Jesus could have been suffering from leprosy as it is known today. On the other hand he could have been afflicted by one of the serious skin diseases described in Leviticus 13–14. Since after his cleansing Jesus instructs him to follow the Mosaic regulations, the latter alternative still remains a distinct possibility.

18 See C. H. Cave, 'The Leper: Mark 1.40-45', *NTS* 25 (1979), p. 247.

(*Ant.* 3.264). The reference to Miriam's leprosy in Num 12:12 prompted various rabbis to speak of lepers as 'the living dead', whose cure was as difficult as raising the dead. The diagnosis of leprosy thus encompassed both medical and social dimensions.[19]

The leper who approached Jesus therefore lived in a constant state of physical and mental anguish. The way he approaches Jesus reflects his desperate plight. He comes to Jesus literally '*begging* him and *falling* on his knees'. In the Greek these two participles add a double pathos that prepares for Jesus' compassion.[20] In approaching Jesus in this way the man is breaking through social barriers and religious taboos, including the restrictions laid down by Moses. He defies the social ban that kept him in places away from the towns. In his desperation the leper has only one thing on his mind, 'If you are willing, you can make me clean' (1.40). The request is precisely put. He asks not for healing but for cleansing. Other diseases might be healed; leprosy had to be cleansed (cf. Mt. 11.5).[21] In making this request the leper is not only showing great faith, he is also running a great risk. By crashing through the barriers he has shown aggressive disrespect for the Law.[22] It is an act of reckless faith. Will Jesus also be prepared to cross the boundaries or will he recoil in horror at the thought and refuse the man's request? What will have the priority – religious ritual or human need?[23]

No doubt to the man's great relief Jesus feels compassion and responds accordingly.[24] He shows it by reaching out his hand and touching him – an unthinkable act.[25] As he was not troubled by the threat of the disease or by the

19   James R. Edwards, *The Gospel according to Mark*, PNTC (Grand Rapids, MI: Eerdmans, 2002), pp. 68–69 (italics his).

20   Thus Robert H. Gundry, *Mark: A Commentary on His Apology for the Cross* (Grand Rapids, MI: Eerdmans, 1993), p. 95.

21   Thus Edwards, *Mark*, p. 69.

22   Cf. William Loader, 'Challenged at the Boundaries: A Conservative Jesus in Mark's Tradition', *JSNT* 63 (1996), p. 56.

23   George B. Telford, Jr., 'Mark 1:40-45', *Int* 36 (1982), p. 56, has shown just how much is at stake for Jesus: 'if he accepts the challenge and is drawn into this farthest outpost of the profane, if he touches this untouchable, then he will, at least for a while, be disqualified for preaching in those towns where it is known what he has done. And perhaps not just for a while, for more is at stake here than becoming ceremonially unclean. For Jesus is touching and healing a sinner, breaking a major taboo.'

24   In a small minority of manuscripts the verb *splanchnizomai* ('have/show compassion') is replaced by *orgizomai* ('be angry'), a reading reflected in the NEB, 'In warm indignation Jesus stretched out his hand.' Robert H. Stein, *Mark* (BECNT; Grand Rapids, MI: Baker, 2008), p. 106, has some sympathy for this reading, but finally concludes that it yields an intolerable sense: 'I must admit that if "being angry" is the correct reading, we simply do not possess a clear understanding of why Jesus was angry or how Mark understood it. On the other hand, "moved with compassion" has far better textual support and describes Jesus in 6:34 and 8:2 (cf. also 9:22).'

25   Michal Wojciechowski, 'The Touching of the Leper (Mark 1, 40-45) as a Historical and Symbolic Act of Jesus', *BZ* 33 (1989), p. 118, elaborates, 'A voluntary touching of a leper is absolutely shocking and difficult to compare with anything. Jesus acted in a great passion which certainly inspired this extraordinary gesture.'

possibility of contracting ceremonial uncleanness, Jesus is probably the first 'clean' human being to have touched this social outcast in some time. Jesus' words also reinforce his compassion. His verbal response perfectly echoes the man's request. 'I am willing,' he says. 'Be clean!' (1.41). Jesus therefore shows his compassion in both word and deed. By reflecting the man's words back to him he indicates how sympathetic he is to his request; and his touch turns out to be the healing touch whereby the request is granted.[26] In compassion Jesus touches the untouchable and cures the incurable. Jesus' compassionate response is as scandalous as the leper's audacity. Rather than turning from the leper he turns to him. 'Unlike an ordinary rabbi,' says Edwards, 'Jesus is not polluted by the leper's disease; rather the leper is cleansed and healed by Jesus' contagious holiness.'[27]

Jesus' compassion comes to its finest expression, of course, not so much in his touch or in his words, but in the healing itself. The way Mark describes it, this is a stupendous miracle. 'Immediately the leprosy left him and he was cured' (1.42). Although Mark uses the word 'immediately' rather profusely, the temporal dimension here should be given its full weight. Like most of Jesus' other miraculous healings this healing from leprosy was instantaneous and complete. The leprosy simply went away and the man was cured. The change that came over him was visible and dramatic. Although we cannot know the extent of the leper's disfigurement, he was transformed before the very eyes of any onlookers who may have been present. In a moment of time his skin was restored to a healthy condition. Perhaps like Naaman's, his 'flesh was restored and became clean like that of a young boy' (2 Kgs 5.14). But while Naaman had to dip into the Jordan seven times, this man's flesh was cleansed in a flash. It was a mighty miracle.

Although the cleansing of the leper was an outstanding miracle, its significance should also be sought at a deeper level. The rare occurrences where the disease was cured in the Old Testament were commonly understood as direct acts of God. Jesus has therefore performed a divine act in much the same way as the restoration of sight to the blind and feeding the hungry were seen as divine acts (see ch. 1.4 above). Just as those miracles were associated with Jesus' compassion in Matthew's Gospel, it is important to note that here too Jesus' compassion comes to expression in a miracle that had hitherto been attributed only to God. As the healing of leprosy is God-like, so too is the emotion of compassion. Hence both the miracle and the accompanying emotion carry overtones of the divine. In both respects Jesus is true to his role as the divine Warrior–Healer figure of Isaiah's New Exodus. In the restoration passages of Isaiah 40–66 there is a strong emphasis on divine compassion (Isa. 49.10, 12, 15; 54.7, 8, 10; 60.10).

---

26 Pieter J. Lalleman, 'Healing by Mere Touch as a Christian Concept', *TynBul* 48 (1997), p. 361, has argued that 'it appears that the miracles of healing by a mere touch of his hand ascribed to Jesus are unique'. There are no pre-Christian parallels in Greek and Hellenistic literature and only rarely are precursors for this practice found in the Old Testament (only in 2 Kings) and the Dead Sea Scrolls (the *Genesis Apocryphon*). Following Jesus, however, it became a Christian practice among the apostles and in the early church. In this way Jesus 'broke the barriers of uncleanness reaching out to the sick and allowing them to touch him'.

27 Edwards, *Mark*, p. 70.

Throughout the Galilee section in Mark Jesus therefore resembles the Yahweh of the New Exodus. He casts out demons, heals diseases and shows compassion.

Up to this point in the story Jesus has been acting in character, but then quite suddenly the account seems to strike a discordant note. Unexpectedly and without warning his emotions appear to turn ugly as compassion gives way to anger. 'Jesus sent him away at once with a strong warning' (1.43). In Greek the language sounds quite harsh. The verb 'sent away' is the same word that is commonly used elsewhere for the casting out of demons. Although the verb may be used in a weakened sense here, Jesus is hardly treating the man gently. He sends him packing.[28] This is further emphasized by the 'strong warning' that accompanies the man's expulsion. This is another occurrence of the rare word *embrimaomai*, the same word used of Jesus' stern warning to two blind men he had just healed (Mt. 9.30). The situations are very similar. Two blind men have had their sight restored and a leper has been cleansed. As soon as they are healed he dismisses them with a warning. 'See that no one knows about this,' he tells the formerly blind men (Mt. 9.30). 'See that you don't tell this to anyone,' he says to the cleansed leper (Mk 1.44). Understandably and yet culpably both parties ignore Jesus' clear request. The once blind men 'went out and spread the news about him all over that region' (Mt. 9.31), while the man cured of leprosy 'went out, and began to talk freely, spreading the news' (Mk 1.45). Apart from the conditions that were cured the parallels are quite astounding.

Because of these great similarities the two passages must be allowed to interpret one another. Jesus is angry with the healed leper for exactly the same reason that he is angry with the two men who once were blind. He has not now suddenly, but belatedly, become angry because the leper had overstepped the mark, broken a taboo and caused him ritual defilement. He is not angry about anything that the leper *has done*. It is what the man *will do* that so angers him. Like the previously blind men he will snub Jesus' authority and defy his clear command. That is why Jesus turns on him in sudden anger. He is exasperated because he foresees the man's disobedience.[29] Again the force of the verb *embrimaomai* must not be played down as is so often the case in English translations. Even the TEV's 'Jesus spoke harshly with him' is too domesticated. Perhaps it would be no exaggeration to say that Jesus roared at the man, as the verb was used in Classical Greek to denote 'scarce-controlled animal fury'.[30] Although not without some exaggeration, Cave's imaginative comments admirably capture the tense atmosphere: 'As he charged the leper . . . he stumbled over the words, the loud and harsh tone of his voice indicating his agitation.'[31] George Telford continues in a similar vein: 'What is described here are the inarticulate sounds which escape from persons who are physically overcome by a great wave of emotion. Jesus apparently

---

28   Thus Edwards, *Mark*, p. 70.
29   Thus Lane, *Mark*, p. 87.
30   Richard T. France, *The Gospel of Mark: A Commentary on the Greek Text* (Grand Rapids, MI: Eerdmans, 2002), p. 118, quoting Campbell Bonner, 'Traces of Thaumaturgic Technique in the Miracles', *HTR* 20 (1927), p. 174.
31   Cave, 'The Leper', p. 247.

experienced this very human anger and emotion, as he experienced much else human.'[32] Quite simply, the man's prompt disobedience infuriates Jesus.

In this emotionally charged reaction we again catch a glimpse of the complexity of Jesus' person. While the verb used here to describe Jesus' intense feeling as he dismisses the cleansed leper is used elsewhere by Mark to describe an all too human reaction (14.5), and earlier literature had even used the word to describe the sounds of animals,[33] the driving force behind Jesus' emotion is divine fore-knowledge.[34] Had it not been for his prescience of what the healed leper was about to do, his angry outburst would have been quite out of place. His emotions are not always driven by ordinary human motivations.

Further insight into Jesus' angry response can be gained from an examination of the rationale behind Jesus' request of the cleansed leper. It is important to realize that the request consists of three parts: (a) 'See that you don't tell this to anyone,' (b) 'Go, show yourself to the priest,' and (c) 'Offer the sacrifices that Moses offered for your cleansing, as a testimony to them' (1.44). In a sense these are three distinct commands, but they are also phrased in such a way as to be intimately related and dependent on one another. Rather than publicising the miracle the man is to promptly go and show himself to the priest (in obedience to the Mosaic regulations prescribed in Leviticus 13) and to offer the sacrifices that Moses commanded (as prescribed in Leviticus 14). The man would probably have been able to present himself to a priest residing locally in Galilee. The offering of the prescribed sacrifices was another story and would have necessitated a trip to the Jerusalem temple. Jesus was therefore asking the man to undergo a long and involved process that would take time and effort on his part, as the only legitimate way for him to be rehabilitated into Jewish society was by following the prescribed ritual. It would seem that the man took the easy way out by ignoring all three of Jesus' related requests.

Mark specifically points out that when it came to Jesus' first command, namely to keep the miracle quiet and not tell anyone, the man did the exact opposite. 'He went out and began to talk freely, spreading the news' (1.45). There is no way of putting a positive spin on what the man did.[35] He is acting in defiant disobedience of Jesus' clear instructions, and Mark makes no attempt to whitewash his defiance. Rather he states that the man's rash behaviour had major implications for Jesus' early ministry in Galilee. 'As a result, Jesus could no longer enter a town openly but stayed outside in lonely places. Yet the people still came to him from everywhere.' Ironically, in retreating to 'lonely places', Jesus

---

32 Telford, 'Mark 1:40-45', p. 54.

33 Max Zerwick and Mary Grosvenor, *A Grammatical Analysis of the Greek New Testament* (Rome: Biblical Institute Press, 1981), p. 104, claim that the verb was properly used for the snorting of horses. In a transferred sense it could also apply to 'persons snorting with inward rage or indignation.'

34 Cf. France, *Mark*, p. 119, 'it is possible that it [the verb] reflects Jesus' knowledge of and displeasure at the still future response.'

35 *Contra* Robert H. Stein, *Mark* (BECNT; Grand Rapids, MI: Baker, 2008), p. 108, 'The preaching and spreading of the word by the leper emulate the actions of Jesus in 1:14, 38, 39. As a result his similar action should not be considered as negative.'

has now traded places with the leper. This is not intended to be a positive assessment of the situation. Because of the suffocating presence of the crowds Jesus' early Galilean ministry has ground to an untimely halt. In a dynamic and at times anachronistic explanation of the situation Garland has observed that, whenever someone breaks Jesus' command to keep the news of his miracles quiet, 'the next scene begins by mentioning the crush of the crowds. The hubbub restricts Jesus' free movement as he is harried by the increasing numbers of supplicants and autograph hounds (3:9). He is no longer able to enter a town openly, and people from miles around seek him out (1:45). The leper's disobedience forces Jesus to avoid the cities and to retreat to deserted places, but even they are no longer deserted. Throngs who come from all over mob him (see also 6:32-33; 7:24).'[36] A few days later Jesus seems to have no choice but to go back home to Capernaum, but even there the crowd is hanging from the rafters (2.1-4). The healed leper's disobedience has profoundly disrupted Jesus' ministry.

But the repercussions of the man's disregard for Jesus' clearly stated wishes do not stop there. Although Mark does not tell us in so many words, it seems likely that the man also failed to carry out the Mosaic requirements to show himself to the priest and offer sacrifices. This would set the stage for the controversy section that immediately follows in 2.1–3.6. The man's failure to observe the levitical regulations would appear to attract the unwelcome attention of the religious authorities for the first time. By the very next scene (2.6) they begin to watch Jesus' every move and become his most determined, and eventually deadly, opponents. No doubt unwittingly the healed leper has prepared the way for the escalating controversy that is about to unfold. When Jesus gave him his marching orders he could foresee his disobedience and its consequences. The very thought made him understandably irate.

2.2.2 ANGER AND DEEP DISTRESS (2.23–3.6)

23 One Sabbath Jesus was going through the cornfields, and as his disciples walked along, they began to pick some ears of corn.

24 The Pharisees said to him, 'Look, why are they doing what is unlawful on the Sabbath?'

25 He answered, 'Have you never read what David did when he and his companions were hungry and in need?

26 In the days of Abiathar the high priest, he entered the house of God and ate the consecrated bread, which is lawful only for priests to eat. And he also gave some to his companions.'

27 Then he said to them, 'The Sabbath was made for man, not man for the Sabbath.

28 So the Son of Man is Lord even of the Sabbath.'

---

36 David E. Garland, *Mark: The NIV Application Commentary* (Grand Rapids, MI: Zondervan, 1996), p. 77.

¹ Another time he went into the synagogue, and a man with a shrivelled hand was there.

² Some of them were looking for a reason to accuse Jesus, so they watched him closely to see if he would heal him on the Sabbath.

³ Jesus said to the man with the shrivelled hand, 'Stand up in front of everyone.'

⁴ Then Jesus asked them, 'Which is lawful on the Sabbath: to do good or to do evil, to save life or to kill?' But they remained silent.

⁵ He looked round at them in *anger* and, *deeply distressed* at their stubborn hearts, said to the man, 'Stretch out your hand.' He stretched it out, and his hand was completely restored.

⁶ Then the Pharisees went out and began to plot with the Herodians how they might kill Jesus.

The episode of the man with the withered hand brings Mark's first controversy section (2.1–3.6) to a head. At the beginning of ch. 2 Jesus has had to return to Capernaum because of the oppressive crowds, and it would appear that Capernaum is the scene for all the controversies in this section. All the locations – Jesus' home (2.1), the lakeside (2.13), Levi's house (2.15), the cornfields (2.23) and the lake (3.7) – suit Capernaum and its vicinity extremely well. The synagogue in which the showdown between Jesus and the Pharisees occurs is therefore most likely the one at Capernaum. On a previous Sabbath it was the congregation at Capernaum that had been amazed at his authoritative teaching and witnessed a dramatic exorcism (1.21-28). It was also in their town that many – including Peter's mother-in-law – had been healed of various diseases and where Jesus had driven out many demons (1.29-34). This was also where the paralytic had had his sins forgiven and his health restored (2.1-12). But more sinister developments were also beginning to unfold.

Jesus' spectacular successes in ch. 1 – his magnetic attraction of disciples and crowds, his healings and exorcisms – are contrasted with the groundswell of opposition that begins to mount steadily in ch. 2. Among the religious leadership he is gaining a reputation as a blasphemer (2.7), a fraternizer with sinners (2.13-17), an apostate from religious custom (2.18) and a Sabbath breaker (2.24).[37] By the end of the chapter the Sabbath issue becomes the sharpest point of contention and it spills over into the synagogue scene at the beginning of ch. 3. The stakes are high. In the cornfields the Pharisees have warned Jesus about his disciples' laxity when it comes to Sabbath observance, a neglect for which they hold him responsible (2.24). He defends their behaviour by citing David as an Old Testament precedent (2.25-26), but he is not content to leave matters at that. A higher principle is involved and Jesus states it quite emphatically, 'The Sabbath was made for man, not man for the Sabbath. So the Son of Man is Lord even of the Sabbath' (2.27-28). It is a climactic announcement with huge implications. Garland's comments are apposite:

---

37 Thus Edwards, *Mark*, pp. 98, 101.

This segment begins with the statement, 'The Pharisees said . . .' (2:24). In the conclusion it is clear that it makes no difference what they say. The narrative to this point has demonstrated that the authority of Jesus far outstrips that of the teachers of the law. This statement boldly affirms that as Lord the Son of Man is the one who decrees what is lawful and unlawful, permissible and impermissible, and any customs ordained by the Pharisees or their traditions are thereby rendered null and void. It is Jesus who makes plain the humanitarian purpose of the Sabbath, and his word is final. The Pharisees with their rules and regulations, quibbles and fusses, misrepresent the will of God.[38]

Clearly the Pharisees will have none of this. The chapter division notwithstanding, it is reasonable to assume that the Pharisees who accost Jesus in the cornfields (2.23-28) are the same Pharisees who now join him for worship in the Capernaum synagogue (3.1-6) – presumably on the same Sabbath (cf. Mt. 12.9).[39] If so, the situation in the synagogue is very tense indeed. The Pharisees' motives for attending the service are highly suspect. They 'were looking for a reason to accuse Jesus' (3.2). Their intentions are obviously hostile. Treacherously they watch his every move. They want to see if he will heal on the Sabbath in violation of their interpretation of the Law. Such a violation, like blasphemy, could incur the death penalty. Their purpose is to bring legal charges against him. But Jesus seizes the initiative.

In a command that is as provocative as it is authoritative, Jesus addresses the man with the shrivelled hand, 'Stand up in front of everyone' (3.3). For him to make the first move like this is quite exceptional. With the other healings so far recorded by Mark Jesus has always been requested to heal the sick person or the sick have been brought to him (1.30, 32, 40; 2.3). Only here in the Synoptics does Jesus heal a man without having been asked to do so. The man's condition is not life threatening, but he is suffering from a serious handicap. Again with the careful historian's attention to detail Luke points out that it is the man's *right* hand that is withered (Lk. 6.6). The chances are that he would therefore have found it difficult to make a living. But even so, it is important to realize that he does not approach Jesus for healing. The way Mark tells the story, the healing is almost incidental. Throughout the whole episode the man says nothing and is never further identified. Perhaps to the man's embarrassment Jesus suddenly makes him the centre of attention. He had come to synagogue to worship, not to be healed. Similarly Jesus is not so much out to heal as to make a point. Just as the healing of the paralytic had demonstrated that he had authority to forgive sins (2.5-12), so this healing will prove that he is Lord of the Sabbath (2.28). Although the handicapped man no doubt welcomes the healing and is happy to comply with Jesus' requests to stand up in front of everyone (3.3) and stretch

---

38 Garland, *Mark*, p. 107.
39 France, *Mark*, p. 148. The opening words of ch. 3, which the NIV renders, 'Another time he went into the synagogue', are more literally translated, 'And he went into the synagogue again', and therefore probably cast a backward glance to Jesus' earlier attendance at the Capernaum synagogue in 1.21-28.

out his hand (3.5), he plays no more than a supportive role in the story. There is a sense in which he is a pawn in a struggle larger than his own. In the best sense of the term Jesus is prepared to make a public spectacle of this man for the purpose of silencing his enemies. It is Jesus' authority that is the bone of contention. Throughout Mark's narrative the degree of authority claimed either for Jesus or by him has been steadily rising. During his first visit to the synagogue the congregation recognized that, unlike their scribes, he taught with authority (1.22). During the same service Jesus had the opportunity to demonstrate that authority by exorcising a demon (1.23-27). In the next chapter he claims to have the authority to forgive sins (2.10) and most recently that he is the Lord of the Sabbath (2.28). As his claims to authority intensify, so does the antagonism of his opponents.

It is therefore with all the authority of the Christ and the Son of God, and in his capacity as the Warrior–Healer figure, that Jesus issues his curt commands to the hapless invalid in the synagogue. He is determined to heal him, but as the Warrior he is also doing battle with his opponents. He is out to prove that he is Lord of the Sabbath, the authoritative figure whom Mark introduced to his readers at the beginning (1.1-13). He is the compassionate Healer on the warpath. The question which Jesus directed to the Pharisees is therefore a weapon of war wielded with grace, 'Which is lawful on the Sabbath: to do good or to do evil, to save life or to kill?' (3.4).

Simple though the question is, it is worded with the utmost skill. In the tradition of Hebrew poetry Jesus uses the device of synonymous parallelism, an artful way of saying the same thing twice. Hence to save life is to do good, and to kill is to do evil. The equation is simple and the question straightforward. Why then should it stump Jesus' opponents so completely? The answer lies in the dynamics of the story. The context allows further equations to be made. By healing the man with the shrivelled hand Jesus is saving life and doing good (3.5). By hindering his healing ministry and plotting how they might kill Jesus the Pharisees are doing evil (3.6). By his question Jesus shows that he has read the Pharisees' minds, as he had earlier read the minds of the scribes (2.8). He is fully aware of what they are thinking (cf. Lk. 6.8). With divine insight he is able to reduce his opponents to silence with a question easy enough for a Sunday School child to answer. It allows only for an affirmative answer. Who would dare say publicly that it is lawful to do evil or to kill on the Sabbath or on any day? Yet that is precisely what the Pharisees were plotting to do. On the other hand, had they answered in the affirmative it would undermine their whole approach to the Sabbath and the basis of their objections to Jesus.[40] So either way they are caught. Jesus' clever question has left them no escape. He has demonstrated that their understanding of the Law is completely untenable. He has also subjected them to a public humiliation for which they will never forgive him.

The Pharisees' silence is therefore not only a stony but also a guilty one. Jesus has exposed their motives and their true intentions. According to Robert Gundry,

---

40 Thus France, *Mark*, p. 150.

'Jesus doubtless knows that a violation of the Pharisees' earlier warning is liable to prompt capital proceedings against him . . . The Pharisees will try to take this illegal alternative as a result of Jesus' taking the legal alternative of saving life.'[41] The outcome is filled with irony. The same Pharisees who earlier that day had accused Jesus' disciples of doing what is unlawful on the Sabbath (2.24) are now plotting to kill, the very epitome of doing evil on the Sabbath (3.6).

The irony is not lost on Jesus. This is what gives rise to his mixed emotions. Their guilty silence prompts his anger, their stubborn hearts his deep distress (3.5). Little reflection is needed to realize that this is no ordinary human reaction. In normal circumstances a speaker or debater who silences his opponents is not angry or distressed. A measure of self-satisfaction or even gleeful pride would be the order of the day. But this is not a normal situation, nor is Jesus your average debater. His divine insight leads him in quite a different direction.

Jesus' initial reaction is one of anger. He is angry as he surveys the synagogue scene, especially his silent opponents. On several occasions Mark has Jesus looking around before saying or doing something dramatic (3.34; 5.32; 10.23; 11.11). It is a tense moment as he directs his angry gaze at the silenced opposition. 'Not one of those sullen countenances escaped the search-light of that gaze, and it was a gaze of indignant wrath.'[42] But what is it about their silence that angers him? They are silent because they are unwilling to allow Jesus to do good and to save life, while at the same time they themselves are prepared to do evil by plotting to kill him. By not allowing Jesus to do good for a man for whom the Sabbath was made (2.27), they have overlooked the mercy and grace of God in favour of their own legalistic requirements. Their indifference to divine grace and human needs angers Jesus, as does his awareness of their murderous design.

But not only is he angry at their silence, he is also 'deeply distressed at their stubborn hearts'. Here Mark is probing the state of Jesus' soul at a deeper level. Behind his angry mien lies a deep distress, just as behind the Pharisees' silence are 'their stubborn hearts' (or, more accurately, 'their hardness of heart'). To be hard-hearted is not the same as being cold-hearted. It is rather the conscious refusal to believe in Jesus. In it lies the ultimate cause of the Pharisees' hostility. Elsewhere in the New Testament such hardening is attributed to ignorance and unbelief (Rom. 11.25; Eph. 4.18). In the Old Testament the archetype of the hard-hearted was Pharaoh who persisted in his unbelief in the face of irrefutable evidence. Now the Pharisees are doing the same. It is a spiritual condition from which not even the disciples are immune when they relapse into old ways of thought and fail to understand the significance of Jesus' miracles (6.52; 8.17). But why does the Pharisees' hardness of heart cause Jesus such deep distress when no such emotion is expressed when later the disciples clearly manifest the same condition?

The answer must lie in the Pharisees' reaction which Mark reports in v. 6. Rather than responding in faith and wonder to Jesus' dramatic miracle, 'the Pharisees went out and began to plot with the Herodians how they might kill

41   Gundry, *Mark*, p. 151.
42   Law, *Emotions of Jesus*, p. 97.

Jesus.' Their hardness of heart is more than the disciples' later spiritual obtuseness. The plot they are hatching with the Herodians is completely unwarranted. Healing by speaking was no breach of the Sabbath.[43] Theologically they have no case against Jesus. So they strike a deal with the politically minded supporters of Herod.[44] In desperation they enter into an uneasy and unholy alliance against a common threat. In Jerusalem the Pharisees and Herodians will team up again to ask Jesus a trick question about the legality of paying taxes to Caesar (12.13-17; cf. Mt. 22.15-22). They will try to set a deadly trap which Jesus deftly avoids. But already in the aftermath of the synagogue healing their conflict with Jesus has become deadly. The Pharisees' spiritual stubbornness expressed itself first in silence and then in their malicious plot to do away with Jesus altogether. He is deeply grieved at such callousness. To underscore the intensity of Jesus' grief Mark uses the rare compound verb *sullupeomai*, which is found only here in the New Testament and can mean either 'be deeply grieved' or 'feel sorry for'.[45] But Jesus is not grieved *for* the Pharisees but *at* them. The hardness of their hearts, which lies behind their conniving and scheming, affects him deeply. Not insignificantly, Mark draws attention to Jesus' distress in connection with the first direct mention of his death. Not only is he the Lord of the Sabbath, he is also the 'man of sorrows'.

In this episode Mark therefore gives his readers a penetrating insight into Jesus' psyche. Rather than being incompatible, his anger and distress actually complement one another. But precisely how do they complement one another? Commentators will sometimes claim that Jesus' anger is tempered by his grief.[46] But this is not entirely correct. It would be more accurate to say that anger is the outward emotion and distress the inward. His anger could be felt by all who sat under his wrathful gaze during that tense and hushed moment in the synagogue. His distress lay deeper, however, in the inner recesses of his soul. With perceptive insight into human nature Benjamin Warfield has observed that 'the fundamental psychology of anger is curiously illustrated by this account; for anger always has pain as its root, and is a reaction of the soul against what gives it discomfort.'[47] The hardness of the Pharisees' hearts hurt Jesus and his anger rose in response to the cause of his pain. 'There are thus two movements of feeling brought before us

---

43 Thus Garland, *Mark*, p. 109.

44 According to Craig A. Evans and Stanley E. Porter, *Dictionary of New Testament Background* (Downers Grove: Inter-Varsity Press, 2000), p. 493, the Herodians 'in the Gospel narratives are not portrayed as either domestic servants or officers of Herod but as influential people whose outlook was friendly to the Herodian rule and consequently to the Roman rule upon which it rested.'

45 In the two occurrences of this verb in the LXX (Ps. 69.20; Isa. 51.19) the latter meaning is more suitable. The TEV also wants to import this sense into Mk 3.5: 'Jesus was angry as he looked round at them, but at the same time *he felt sorry for them* . . .' Not only is this rendering unusual among English translations, it also links anger and sympathy – a more difficult combination than anger and grief.

46 For example, Lane, *Mark*, p. 124.

47 Benjamin B. Warfield, *The Person and Work of Christ* (Philadelphia: Presbyterian & Reformed, 1950), p. 108.

here,' Warfield continues. 'There is the pain which the gross manifestation of the hardness of heart of the Jews inflicted on Jesus. And there is the strong reaction of indignation which sprang out of this pain.'[48] The angry glance was fleeting, and the emotion it expressed was undoubtedly short-lived (cf. Eph. 4.26). Not so Jesus' deep-seated grief. It will surface again and again throughout this Gospel until it finally breaks Jesus' heart in Gethsemane and at Calvary.

2.3 Amazement (6.1-6a)

1 Jesus left there and went to his home town, accompanied by his disciples.
2 When the Sabbath came, he began to teach in the synagogue, and many who heard him were amazed. 'Where did this man get these things?' they asked. 'What's this wisdom that has been given him, that he even does miracles?[49]
3 Isn't this the carpenter? Isn't this Mary's son and the brother of James, Joseph, Judas and Simon? Aren't his sisters here with us?' And they took offence at him.
4 Jesus said to them, 'Only in his home town, among his relatives and in his own house is a prophet without honour.'
5 He could not do any miracles there, except lay his hands on a few sick people and heal them.
6 And *he was amazed* at their lack of faith.

In Mark 5 Jesus has performed some of his most remarkable miracles. He has cast out a legion of demons (5.1-20). He has healed a woman who had been subject to bleeding for twelve years (5.25-43). Then, to cap this magnificent chapter, Jairus' daughter is raised back to life (5.40-43). The last two of these miracles have also been attended by commendable faith (5.34, 36). This backdrop forms a stunning contrast to the current passage where few miracles are performed because of the people's lack of faith (6.5-6a). The difference is quite dramatic. The successful, all-conquering Jesus who has shown himself as master over demons, disease and death seems to be defeated by the unbelief that he strikes in – of all places – his old hometown. His miraculous activity is curbed. The great Warrior–Healer appears to have almost been stopped in his tracks. In closing this segment Mark describes a very human Jesus who 'was amazed at their lack of faith' (6.6a).

But why is Jesus so surprised at their lack of faith? There are other occasions in the Gospels where Jesus encounters unbelief. The father of the epileptic boy

---

48 Warfield, *Person and Work of Christ*, p. 108.
49 The NIV (together with the NAB, RSV and NRSV) has an exclamation mark here rather than a question mark. As the earliest surviving Greek manuscripts have no punctuation, this is a legitimate editorial decision. But the fact that this sentence is preceded by a question and followed by further questions makes it unlikely that an exclamation is intended (Stein, *Mark*, p. 281).

admits to his unbelief (Mk 9.24) and Jesus rebukes the crowd of onlookers for being an 'unbelieving generation' (Mt. 17.17; Mk 9.19; Lk. 9.41). When Jesus' brothers challenge him to attend the Feast of Tabernacles, the comment is made that 'even his own brothers did not believe in him' (Jn 7.5). But on neither of these occasions does Jesus respond in amazement. So what makes this passage different? Why is this the only time in the Gospels that Jesus is surprised by unbelief?

If psychiatrists are correct when they say that emotions are contagious, then maybe there is a clue in the amazement of the many who heard Jesus teach in the Nazareth synagogue (6.2). Early in this pericope the Nazarenes are amazed at Jesus, but at the end he is amazed at them. Is there a connection? Admittedly two different Greek words are used, but they are synonymous enough for the NIV to correctly translate both as 'be amazed'.[50] In other contexts the kind of amazement shown by the synagogue audience is seen by Mark to be positive. On four occasions it describes a reaction to Jesus' teaching (1.22; 6.2; 10.26; 11.18) and once to a miracle (7.37). On two of these occasions Jesus is teaching in a synagogue – first in Capernaum (1.22) and then here in Nazareth (6.2). There is every reason to believe that in both synagogues the initial responses to Jesus' teaching were equally positive. People were genuinely impressed and sincerely amazed. In Nazareth, however, this initially positive response seems to have been short-lived. By the end of the very next verse Mark states that 'they took offence at him' (6.3). The swift transition from amazement to offence is unusual and can no doubt be attributed to the fickleness of the crowd. But the sudden switch is not inexplicable. The key lies in the five intervening questions (6.2b-3) expressing the people's astonishment that soon mutates into offence.

Where did this man get these things? This initial question is not disparaging and should not be understood as expressing contempt for Jesus. As a general question it simply introduces the second which is decidedly positive.

What's this wisdom that has been given him, that he even does miracles? The congregation's response to Jesus' 'wisdom', a word occurring only here in Mark, arises logically from their having heard him teach.[51] But this is more than simply a positive response to a sermon. The passive participle 'given' is a divine passive. They recognize that Jesus' wisdom as displayed in his teaching was given by God. Their question could therefore correctly be paraphrased, 'What is this wisdom that God has given to him?'[52] It is on a par with the earlier question asked by the congregants at Capernaum, 'What is this? A new teaching – and with authority!' (1.27). If we allow these two reactions to Jesus' synagogue teaching to shed light on each other, the people at Nazareth are at least raising the possibility that Jesus' message was 'a wisdom pronouncement, which as a gift of God

---

50 Mark uses *ekplēssō* for the people and *thaumazō* for Jesus. The difference between these two verbs is no greater than between 'astonish' and 'amaze' in English. Margie Doty, '"Amazed" in Mark', *Notes on Translation* 4 (1990), p. 57, at the end of her study of the eight different words for amazement used by Mark concludes: 'There is a great deal of overlap among their semantic components.'

51 Thus Robert A. Guelich, *Mark 1-8:26* (WBC; Dallas: Word, 1989), p. 309.

52 Stein, *Mark*, p. 281.

is an authoritative form of address, and therefore powerfully contrasts with all human talents (v. 3).'[53] They were also impressed with his 'miracles', the same word that will be used in v. 5 of the few healings that Jesus performed in their town. Perhaps these had already happened and were sufficient to amaze them.[54] On the other hand, Jesus' reputation may have gone before him with reports of his earlier miracles already having reached Nazareth. Either way the people were amazed. They are astonished by his God-given wisdom and impressive miracles. But the tide is about to turn.

Their next question is not quite as positive. *Isn't this the carpenter?* It is not that they are looking down on him for being a labourer. As Jews they did not share the general Graeco-Roman outlook that took a dim view of manual work. The question is not derogatory. The point is that they are beginning to take offence, and the offence lies not so much in the carpenter's lowly status as in his familiarity. Such a tradesman is a reassuring symbol of normality, not the kind of person from whom you would expect wisdom and miracles.[55] They took offence not because he was beneath them, but because he was just like them. They were offended not so much by his lowliness as by his ordinariness.

His ordinariness would also seem to be the point of their fourth question. *Isn't this Mary's son and the brother of James, Joses, Judas and Simon?* Again this question is not intended to be pejorative. Nor should the reference to Jesus as 'Mary's son' be understood as an insult. There is no hint here of illegitimacy or anything unsavoury. The most that can be read into the identification is that Joseph has by now probably died and Mary is the only parent still living in the village. The naming of Jesus' four brothers would also suggest no more than that they were well known figures around town. They were an ordinary family with whom everyone was familiar.

Their final question, about the unnamed sisters, makes the same point. *Aren't his sisters here with us?* They too are just ordinary folk about town with whom everyone is well acquainted.

The last three questions that the villagers raise about Jesus' occupation and family background imply that Jesus is just another one of the village children who has grown up and returned for a visit.[56] He is 'a local son, a common, ordinary man with a trade and family known to all'.[57] In spite of his wise words and miraculous deeds they knew who he *really* was – just one of them.

Their conclusion may sound innocent enough, but it has serious implications. While the questions in v. 2 voice the people's astonishment, the questions about Jesus' occupation and family in v. 3 indicate that 'they took offense at him.' If we transliterate, rather than translate, the underlying Greek verb, the comment

---

53   Erich Grässer, 'Jesus in Nazareth (Mark VI. 1-6a): Notes on the Redaction and Theology of St Mark', *NTS* 16 (1969), p. 14.

54   Thus Gundry, *Mark*, p. 291. He bases this interpretation on the fact that these miracles were literally 'done through *his hands*' (v. 2) and that Jesus placed '*his hands*' on a few sick people' (v. 5).

55   Thus France, *Mark*, p. 243.

56   Edwards, *Mark*, p. 175.

57   Guelich, *Mark 1-8:26*, p. 310.

would read that 'they were *scandalized* at him.' Throughout the New Testament this is a very loaded term that sometimes carries the sense of being shocked and angered.[58] Although it might be tempting to see the villagers' mood change from amazement to shock and anger, that does not seem to be the meaning here. To be scandalized by Jesus can also mean to be repelled by him and thus refuse to believe in him (cf. Mt. 11.6; 13.57).[59] So what Mark is saying is that the villagers stumbled over Jesus' ordinariness and so did not come to faith.[60] It is therefore not so much an emotional response as a faith response that is in view. As Gustav Stählin explains: 'This cannot simply mean that they took offence at the irreconcilable contradiction between His origin and His work, which also carried with it an unmistakable claim. It means rather that on this account they refused to believe in Him.'[61] While in v. 2 the Nazarenes are open to the possibility that God may be at work in Jesus, they have dismissed that possibility by the end of v. 3. Jesus' background is far too humble and prosaic for that. Even they seem convinced that nothing this good can come from Nazareth (cf. Jn 1.46).[62]

The offence that the townspeople took at Jesus was therefore tantamount to unbelief. Their initial amazement soon evaporated when they considered his familiar origins and was quickly replaced by a settled cynicism and suspicion. It is the sudden transformation of their astonishment into hardened unbelief that amazed Jesus. He was not surprised at their unbelief pure and simple. On other occasions unbelief as such never amazed him. What caught him by surprise in Nazareth was the rapidity at which the change from astonishment to unbelief took place. Hence his disbelief at their unbelief.

Their unbelief was to have immediate repercussions, both for Jesus and for themselves. Because of their lack of faith Jesus did not receive the honour that was his due. As a result the old proverb that 'a prophet is without honour only in his hometown' (cf. Mt. 13.57; Lk. 4.24; 13.33; Jn 4.44) again proved to be remarkably apt.[63] But because of their unbelief the townspeople lost out as well. In Nazareth Jesus' miraculous activity was severely curtailed. The few healings

---

58 BDAG, p. 926 (entry 2)

59 BDAG, p. 926 (entry 1b).

60 *EDNT* 3, p. 248.

61 *TDNT* 7, p. 350.

62 Garland, *Mark*, p. 233. In Jesus' day Nazareth was an obscure village. It is never mentioned in the Old Testament, Josephus, the Mishnah or the Talmud. Apart from the thirty or so occurrences of 'Nazareth' and 'Nazarene' in the Gospels and Acts, the first recorded mention of Nazareth is by Julius Africanus some two centuries after Jesus' birth. According to Edwards, *Mark*, p. 169, Nazareth was 'an obscure hamlet of earthen dwellings chopped into sixty acres of rocky hillside, with a total population of five hundred – at the most.' Jesus' background was inauspicious and inconspicuous in the extreme, a fact which the Nazarenes themselves knew only too well.

63 According to Edwards, *Mark*, p. 174, different versions of the saying were 'not uncommon in antiquity, including both Jewish and Greco-Roman contexts'. A later example comes from the *Gospel of Thomas* 31, 'No prophet is acceptable in his village, no physician heals those who know him.'

that he did perform would seem to indicate that there were at least some exceptions to the pervasive lack of faith.

All in all, Jesus' visit to Nazareth makes for a sad story. He had not anticipated the people's disappointing reaction. Although he could quote a well known proverb to describe what happened, this did not necessarily make the situation any more acceptable. When he responds in amazement at their unbelief it is therefore a poignantly human emotion that comes to the fore.[64] As Robert Guelich explains:

> Faced with the general rejection of himself and his ministry by those who knew him so well, Jesus' amazement expresses his humanness, the very issue that had blinded those who knew him best! His puzzlement reflects personal and compassionate pain. Their lack of faith meant not only their personal rejection of him (6:2b-3) but precluded his offering to them what God was doing through him (6:5a).[65]

The rejection at Nazareth is a sign of things to come. It is another reminder that for Mark, Jesus is not only the triumphant Warrior–Healer but also the suffering Servant and 'man of sorrows.' Even in Galilee there are early indications of the gathering storm (3.1-6, 20-35; 6.1-29; 7.1-13). What made this so personally painful for Jesus was the fact that the opposition and rejection came not only from the religious leaders but also from his own townspeople and even his own family (3.20-21; 6.4). His surprise would therefore seem to be tinged with sorrow at the unbelief of those who, humanly speaking, should have been his nearest and dearest (cf. 3.31-35). In Matthew and Luke, Jesus is pleasantly surprised by the faith of a centurion who was a foreigner and a Gentile. Here he is unpleasantly surprised by the unbelief of those who should have known him best.

2.4 *Compassion*

For Mark, as for Matthew, compassion is an important emotion. Each of these Gospels mentions Jesus' compassion four times. Two of the four instances overlap. Both Evangelists refer to it in connection with the feeding of the four thousand (Mt. 15.29-39; Mk 8.1-10) and the five thousand (Mt. 14.14-21; Mk 6.30-44). In Mark we have already witnessed Jesus' compassion for a leper (1.40-45) and will see it again at the healing of the epileptic boy (9.14-32). In Matthew, Jesus also shows compassion for two blind men (Mt. 20.29-34). The pattern that was discovered in Matthew therefore repeats itself in Mark, namely that the compassion of Jesus is invariably related to miracles.

There is further similarity in the kinds of miracles that give expression to

---

64 The verb *thaumazō* that is used here is found elsewhere in Mark exclusively to indicate the amazement of others at Jesus (5.20; 6.51; 12.17; 15.5, 44).

65 Guelich, *Mark 1-8:26*, p. 312.

Jesus' compassion. In both Gospels large crowds are fed and those suffering from chronic conditions are healed, whether from leprosy, epilepsy or blindness. In these feeding and healing miracles Jesus does what in the Old Testament only God could do. This emphasis is present equally in both Gospels. But the similarities do not end there.

Of the four references to Jesus' compassion three are found in the Galilee section and one in the journey section. Perhaps the main difference between the two is that Jesus' compassion comes to expression near the beginning of Mark's journey section and at the end of Matthew's. The epileptic boy is healed soon after the Transfiguration (Mk 9.14-32), whereas the two blind men have their sight restored outside Jericho (Mt. 20.29-34). In portraying Jesus' compassion these Gospels are therefore remarkably similar, although by no means identical.

2.4.1 COMPASSION ON THE FIVE THOUSAND (6.30-44)

30 The apostles gathered round Jesus and reported to him all they had done and taught.

31 Then, because so many people were coming and going that they did not even have a chance to eat, he said to them, 'Come with me by yourselves to a quiet place and get some rest.'

32 So they went away by themselves in a boat to a solitary place.

33 But many who saw them leaving recognized them and ran on foot from all the towns and got there ahead of them.

34 When Jesus landed and saw a large crowd, *he had compassion on them*, because they were like sheep without a shepherd. So he began teaching them many things.

35 By this time it was late in the day, so his disciples came to him. 'This is a remote place,' they said, 'and it's already very late'.

36 'Send the people away so that they can go to the surrounding countryside and villages and buy themselves something to eat.'

37 But he answered, 'You give them something to eat.' They said to him, 'That would take eight months of a man's wages! Are we to go and spend that much on bread and give it to them to eat?'

38 'How many loaves do you have?' he asked. 'Go and see.' When they found out, they said, 'Five – and two fish.'

39 Then Jesus directed them to have all the people sit down in groups on the green grass.

40 So they sat down in groups of hundreds and fifties.

41 Taking the five loaves and the two fish and looking up to heaven, he gave thanks and broke the loaves. Then he gave them to his disciples to set before the people. He also divided the two fish among them all.

42 They all ate and were satisfied,

43 and the disciples picked up twelve basketfuls of broken pieces of bread and fish.

44 The number of the men who had eaten was five thousand.

Jesus' disappointing reception in Nazareth did nothing to damage his popularity in other parts of Galilee. His personal magnetism continues unabated. So much is this the case that even his disciples attract a popular following. He confers his authority on them by giving them power over evil spirits and sending them on a mission. This mission of the Twelve (6.7-13) seems to have been a singular success. Mark can report that the disciples drove out *many* demons and healed *many* sick people (6.13).

What follows makes it clear that we have another example of a Markan 'sandwich'.[66] Mark again picks up the story of the disciples' mission when they report back to Jesus (6.30), which he uses as a lead-in to his account of the feeding of the five thousand (6.31-44). Sandwiched between the mission of the Twelve and the miraculous feeding is the execution of John the Baptist (6.14-29). As the story on the inside of the sandwich, this grisly tale illuminates the surrounding narrative by way of commentary, comparison and contrast.[67] By way of commentary the death of John the Baptist is a strong reminder that Jesus' popularity is politically dangerous and that he runs the very real risk of suffering the same fate as John. The lavish birthday party thrown by Herod Antipas for Galilee's upper crust is compared unfavourably to the simple fare by which Jesus feeds the multitude. The greatest contrast, however, lies in the end result in each case – the gruesome death of 'a righteous and holy man' (6.20, 27) and a large crowd eating and being satisfied, with food enough to spare (6.42-44).[68]

Such is the setting for the next demonstration of Jesus' compassion. The ministry of the disciples is having the same effect as the earlier ministry of Jesus. The crowds are milling around them so constantly that they don't even have time to eat (6.31; cf. 3.20). So Jesus makes the welcome suggestion that they get some much needed rest and relaxation, 'Come with me by yourselves to a quiet place and get some rest' (6.31). So Jesus and the disciples sail away by boat to a solitary place (6.32), but even these best laid plans are easily thwarted. Outsmarted by an eager crowd that was fleet of foot, Jesus and the disciples soon realize that their destination has become anything but 'a solitary place'. But rather than letting his heart sink at the sight of the crowd, Jesus' heart goes out to them in compassion. His compassion 'takes precedence over his concern for his disciples or for himself. Bone-tired or not, "he began to teach them many things".'[69]

Mark does not leave his readers guessing what the reason for Jesus' compassion might be. What motivated Jesus was the fact that the large crowd 'were like sheep without a shepherd' (6.34). This is precisely the same simile that Matthew had used to explain the driving force behind Jesus' compassion on the crowds (Mt. 9.36). Again a Gospel writer is employing the Old Testament imagery that describes a leadership vacuum among God's people. The first to use the expression was Moses, who prayed for a successor 'so the Lord's people will

---

66   See footnote 5 above.
67   Burridge, *Four Gospels*, p. 39.
68   Cf. Edwards, *Mark*, pp. 189–90: 'Jesus' compassion on the multitudes and the manner in which he satisfies their needs are a dramatic contrast to Herod's self-serving and deadly party.'
69   Lamar Williamson Jr., 'An Exposition of Mark 6:30-44', *Int* 30 (1976), p. 170.

not be like sheep without a shepherd' (Num. 27.17). This could be a convincing antecedent to the present passage which has a number of allusions back to the time of Moses. The 'solitary place' to which Jesus takes his disciples is literally a 'desert' place, a designation it is given three times (6.31, 32, 35). Mark obviously wants to give this feature some emphasis. It is there that Jesus feeds the five thousand, a miracle reminiscent of the manna in the wilderness (Exod. 16). Also, in a detail unique to Mark, under Jesus' direction the people 'sat down in groups of hundreds and fifties' (6.39-40). This arrangement recalls the order of the Mosaic camp in the wilderness (Exod. 18.21). Mark angles the story in such a way that exodus motifs stand out.

Although it would be an attractive possibility to see Jesus as a new Moses,[70] this would not exhaust the Old Testament imagery that lies behind the account. In other instances of a leadership vacuum it is Yahweh himself, or his servant David, who assumes the role of the shepherd of his people (Ezek. 34.11-24; Zech. 10.3). In Ezekiel 34 the shepherd image is again associated with the wilderness. As there is no shepherd for the sheep, Yahweh promises a faithful shepherd, 'my servant David' (Ezek. 34.23), who will tend his sheep so that they will live in the desert in safety (Ezek. 34.25).[71] So Jesus is not only the successor to Moses. By this miracle he also demonstrates that he is the new David, the promised shepherd of God's people. In this role he contrasts sharply with Herod Antipas whose decadent feast and murderous activity Mark has just described in some detail. As Lane observes: 'In spite of the tetrarch's pretensions to royalty, the people are as leaderless as sheep who have no shepherd. In contrast to the drunken debauchery of the Herodian feast, Mark exhibits the glory of God unveiled through the abundant provision of bread in the wilderness where Jesus is Israel's faithful shepherd.'[72]

But even the Mosaic and Davidic imagery does not do full justice to the Old Testament background that lies behind this passage. The great Shepherd of Israel is of course Yahweh himself. On significant occasions he has stepped in when the people had no shepherd (Ezek. 34.11-16; Zech. 10.3). Therefore when Jesus has compassion on the crowd he does it also in this capacity. The miracle that he performs was analogous to the manna, a miracle performed not by Moses but by God (cf. Jn 6.32). Even Jesus' direction to have the people recline in groups on the green grass (6.39) could be an allusion to the great Shepherd Psalm, where Yahweh 'makes me lie down in green pastures' (Ps. 23.2). In this passage Jesus is the Yahweh–Warrior figure showing his gentler side. He is also the Good Shepherd of his people, a theme by no means foreign to Isaiah's New Exodus. One of this section's earliest descriptions of God is that 'he tends his flock like a shepherd' (Isa. 40.11).

This is precisely what Jesus is doing when he shows God-like compassion to the crowd. As their shepherd he does so in two ways. He meets their spiritual

---

70 Cf. Alan Richardson, 'The Feeding of the Five Thousand (Mark 6:34-44)', *Int* 9 (1955), p. 145, 'St. Mark implies that the disciples should have understood that Jesus was the new Moses whom it was believed God would raise up in the last days.'

71 Lane, *Mark*, p. 226.

72 Lane, *Mark*, p. 227.

needs by teaching them many things (6.34) and he satisfies their physical needs by feeding them with bread and fish (6.39-44).[73] Both his teaching and feeding are expressions of his compassion. By feeding the hungry he is again doing what ultimately God alone can do (Pss. 145.15-16; 146.7).

2.4.2 COMPASSION ON THE FOUR THOUSAND (8.1-10)

1. During those days another large crowd gathered. Since they had nothing to eat, Jesus called his disciples to him and said,
2. '*I have compassion for these people*; they have already been with me three days and have nothing to eat.
3. If I send them home hungry, they will collapse on the way, because some of them have come a long distance.'
4. His disciples answered, 'But where in this remote place can anyone get enough bread to feed them?'
5. 'How many loaves do you have?' Jesus asked. 'Seven,' they replied.
6. He told the crowd to sit down on the ground. When he had taken the seven loaves and given thanks, he broke them and gave them to his disciples to set before the people, and they did so.
7. They had a few small fish as well; he gave thanks for them also and told the disciples to distribute them.
8. The people ate and were satisfied. Afterwards the disciples picked up seven basketfuls of broken pieces that were left over.
9. About four thousand men were present. And having sent them away,
10. he got into the boat with his disciples and went to the region of Dalmanutha.

Between the two feeding miracles Jesus travels considerable distances. Although Mark mentions specific place names – Gennesaret (6.53), Tyre (7.24), Sidon, the Sea of Galilee and the Decapolis (7.31) – it is impossible to plot an exact itinerary. As was the case in Matthew, Jesus' movements seem to be dictated by conflict with opponents. Mark has another major controversy section in 7.1-23, where he records a confronting encounter between Jesus and the Pharisees who have come to him with some scribes from Jerusalem. Jesus' sharp and incisive retort to their challenge makes it judicious for him and the disciples to withdraw to safer territory. Initially, during Jesus' sojourn in the vicinity of Tyre (7.24-31), this is indisputably Gentile territory. He would then seem to remain in Gentile lands until he reaches the region of Dalmanutha (8.10). Although its exact location is unknown, this area must have been on the Jewish (western) side of the Sea of Galilee as Jesus is immediately accosted again by the Pharisees (8.11-12). On this basis it can be argued that the feeding of the four thousand, which happened just before the arrival in Damanutha, took place in Gentile territory, presumably in the Decapolis where a deaf-mute had been miraculously healed (7.31-37). From

---

73   According to Stein, *Mark*, p. 313, the two activities are closely related: 'In Jewish literature the "feeding" of Israel is often associated with their being taught the Torah (2 Bar. 77.13-15).'

this it is concluded that the four thousand who were fed were Gentiles, while the five thousand who had been fed earlier were Jews.[74]

The Gentile identification of the four thousand is very difficult to maintain in Matthew's parallel account, as has been argued in some detail in the previous chapter. Those arguments do not need to be repeated here. Since Mark makes no reference to Jesus being 'sent only to the lost sheep of the house of Israel' (Mt. 15.24), it may seem more plausible to suggest that he has a Gentile multitude in mind. But to argue from his rather general geographical references is precarious at best. Even if Mark is intending to locate the feeding of the four thousand in the Decapolis, as it is the last mentioned place name (7.31), the Gentile nature of the crowd is not necessarily a foregone conclusion. In the first century of our era there were still significant Jewish communities in the region.[75] After considering both sides of the argument Lane draws a moderate conclusion: 'In view of the mixed population of the area . . . it is probable that both Jews and Gentiles sat down together in meal fellowship on this occasion, and this prefigured Jesus' intention for the Church. This seems to be a more realistic approach to the historical situation than the desire to find an exclusively Gentile audience in Ch. 8:1-9.'[76]

Whatever the precise make-up of the crowd, they are a testimony to Jesus' personal magnetism. If the gathering is in the Decapolis the assembly of a large crowd around Jesus is not surprising. He has had plenty of publicity there, most recently because of the healing of the deaf-mute (7.36-37) and earlier through the man who had been exorcized of a legion of demons (5.20). What is surprising is that they have been with him for three days and have stayed on even when their provisions have run out. They are clearly an eager and enthusiastic crowd. What transpired during their three days with Jesus we are not told. Either he held them spellbound through his teaching or amazed them with his miracles. Perhaps it was a combination of both. Whatever the attraction, they are in a remote place and some have come long distances. This situation concerns Jesus. He doesn't want to send them home hungry or they might collapse on the way. So he tells his disciples, 'I have compassion for these people.' Only here and in Matthew's parallel (Mt. 15.32) does Jesus speak of his compassion. In most other instances the Gospel writers identify Jesus' compassion by way of an editorial comment. Here Jesus gives voice to his own compassion. His first person dialogue is very effective. He has a very direct and lively concern for the hungry crowd. Edwards'

---

74 See Eric K. Wefald, 'The Separate Gentile Mission in Mark: A Narrative Explanation of Markan Geography, the Two Feeding Accounts and Exorcisms', *JSNT* 60 (1995), pp. 14, 20. Wefald develops an elaborate theory claiming that Jesus made four journeys to 'the other side', i.e. the Gentile side of the Sea of Galilee. The feeding of the four thousand takes place on the third such journey (7.24–8.10). What this theory overlooks is the fact that these journeys were not always missions but efforts to find temporary asylum from the mounting conflicts and controversies in Galilee. Moreover, the argument depends on a precision of geographical detail that is simply not present in the text. In the case of the feeding of the four thousand the argument also places far too much weight on numerical symbolism (21–25).

75 See above, ch. 1, footnote 56.

76 Lane, *Mark*, p. 275.

suggestion that Jesus expresses 'gut-wrenching emotion on behalf of the crowd'[77] is perhaps a trifle overdrawn, based as it is on the etymology of the verb *splanchnizomai* rather than on the dictionary definition of the word. Nevertheless, Jesus' feelings for these people are obviously very strong.

What prompts his compassion is the sight of a crowd with almost no food. It is their physical need that stirs him. This reaction is complementary to his reaction to the five thousand. Then it was primarily the crowd's spiritual need that had aroused his compassion. 'They were like sheep without a shepherd' (6.34). His compassion is first expressed in his teaching them many things and only later in satisfying their hunger. Although the two are complementary and cannot be separated, the main focus is on meeting the crowd's spiritual need through his teaching. In the case of the four thousand they have already been with him for three days, a time that presumably included teaching. So it would be safe to assume that their spiritual needs have already been addressed. Now it is time for their physical needs to be met. In both cases Jesus meets the needs of the whole person. In the first the focus is on the crowd's spiritual needs, while in the second the emphasis falls on the physical, but in neither case is it the one without the other. Jesus exercises a compassionate and holistic ministry. Both miracles, moreover, 'indicate that Jesus Christ, the Son of God, can do what God does! He is able to do what no other person, only God alone, can do (2.7; 3.27; 5.3; 9.22-23, 28-29).'[78] The same point will be made in the next example.

2.4.3 COMPASSION ON THE EPILEPTIC BOY (9.14-29)[79]

14   When they came to the other disciples, they saw a large crowd around them and the teachers of the law arguing with them.

15   As soon as all the people saw Jesus, they were overwhelmed with wonder and ran to greet him.

16   'What are you arguing with them about?' he asked.

17   A man in the crowd answered, 'Teacher, I brought you my son, who is possessed by a spirit that has robbed him of speech.

18   Whenever it seizes him, it throws him to the ground. He foams at the mouth, gnashes his teeth and becomes rigid. I asked your disciples to drive out the spirit, but they could not.'

19   'O unbelieving generation,' Jesus replied, 'how long shall I stay with you? How long shall I put up with you? Bring the boy to me.'

20   So they brought him. When the spirit saw Jesus, it immediately threw the boy into a convulsion. He fell to the ground and rolled around, foaming at the mouth.

---

77   Edwards, *Mark*, p. 230.
78   Stein, *Mark*, p. 369.
79   Dr Tim Walker kindly read the first draft of this section and I am again indebted to his advice and professional insights.

21 Jesus asked the boy's father, 'How long has he been like this?' 'From child-
    hood,' he answered.
22 'It has often thrown him into fire or water to kill him. But if you can do
    anything, *have compassion on us*[80] and help us.'
23 'If you can?' said Jesus. 'Everything is possible for him who believes.'
24 Immediately the boy's father exclaimed, 'I do believe; help me overcome
    my unbelief!'
25 When Jesus saw that a crowd was running to the scene, he rebuked the
    evil spirit. 'You deaf and mute spirit,' he said, 'I command you, come out
    of him and never enter him again.'
26 The spirit shrieked, convulsed him violently and came out. The boy looked
    so much like a corpse that many said, 'He's dead.'
27 But Jesus took him by the hand and lifted him to his feet, and he stood up.
28 After Jesus had gone indoors, his disciples asked him privately, 'Why
    couldn't we drive it out?'
29 He replied, 'This kind can come out only by prayer.'

Of all the references to Jesus' compassion in the Gospels this is the only occasion
it is referred to by way of a request. After witnessing a violent epileptic attack
(9.20) Jesus empathetically asks the victim's desperate father, 'How long has he
been like this?' (9.21). The boy has been possessed by an evil spirit since childhood, the man answers, and with almost fatal results. 'It has often thrown him
into fire or water to kill him.' Then comes the father's anguished plea: 'But if
you can do anything, have compassion on us and help us' (9.22). Significantly,
the man not only asks that Jesus show compassion to his son but to himself as
well. The father and the son are in this together. Recovery for the boy would also
bring great relief to the father. Such would seem to be the reasoning behind his
impassioned petition. But that is not exactly the way things turn out. Jesus will
show compassion to the father before showing compassion to the son. The father
will experience Jesus' compassion in a way he had never expected.

The father's heart-rending request is riddled with doubt, a point that Jesus
picks up immediately. Unlike the leper in ch. 1, this man does not preface his
request with 'if you are willing', but with 'if you can do anything'. He does not
question Jesus' willingness but his ability. In view of the disciples' earlier failure to cast out the evil spirit (9.18) the man's hesitation is understandable, but
Jesus does not take it kindly. He fires back, '"If you can"?' Whatever the precise
emotion lying behind the sharp retort (is it anger, exasperation or frustration?),[81]

---

80 For the sake of consistency the translation 'have compassion on us' (ESV, Holman, KJV,
    NKJV) is adopted here to translate *splanchnizomai*, although the NIV's 'take pity on us' is
    also a perfectly adequate rendering.
81 According to Bart D. Ehrman, 'Did Jesus Get Angry or Agonize? A Text Critic Pursues the
    Original Jesus Story', *BibRev* 5 (2005), p. 22, in Mark 'Jesus' anger erupts when someone
    doubts his willingness, ability or divine authority to heal.' Ehrman therefore interprets Jesus'
    reply as 'an angry response.' On the other hand Craig A. Evans, *Mark 8:27-16:20* (WBC
    34B; Nashville: Thomas Nelson, 2001), p. 52, comments, 'Jesus' exasperated response . . .
    repeats the father's words and stems from his frustration with his generation's lack of faith.'

Jesus is clearly unimpressed with the man's doubting his ability. When he had first brought his son's plight and the disciples' failure to Jesus' attention (9.17-18), it drew a stinging rebuke from Jesus. 'O unbelieving generation,' he exclaimed, 'how long shall I stay with you? How long shall I put up with you?' (9.19). Again the precise emotion behind Jesus' exclamation is hard to pinpoint. It seems to have overtones of exasperation.[82] By phrasing his request the way he does, the father betrays his lack of faith and thus identifies himself with the 'unbelieving generation' that has just been so roundly rebuked by Jesus. Jesus therefore pulls him up short.

Jesus' sharp '"If you can"?' is, however, not intended to rob the man of hope. For he immediately continues, 'Everything is possible for him who believes.' This is a terse and cryptic sentence made all the more difficult because in Greek it is verbless. Some commentators argue that this is a reference to Jesus who, in the midst of an unbelieving generation, is the only one still to have faith.[83] In the context this is a possible interpretation, but it makes more sense to see it as a challenge to the doubting man. Perhaps it is therefore wisest to follow Stein who supplies the verb that is to be understood here and offers the following cautious paraphrase: 'All things [are] able [to be done] *for* the one who believes.'[84]

This is certainly how the father takes Jesus' remark. Feeling justly rebuked for his unbelief and at the same time challenged to greater faith, he now cries out to Jesus even more desperately, 'I do believe; help me overcome my unbelief!' (9.24). His is a classic case of doubt. Torn between faith and unbelief, he has reached a point of spiritual crisis. With a foot in each camp he believes and disbelieves at the same time. He is in a precarious spiritual condition. Momentarily his thoughts are no longer on his epileptic son. Now he does not cry 'help us' but 'help me'. The focus of his request has changed dramatically. Foremost in his mind at this particular point in time is not his son's horrific epilepsy, but his own lack of faith. He needs Jesus' help not only for his son's epilepsy but also for his own unbelief. He needs Jesus' compassion in ways that he had initially never imagined, and the beauty of the story is that Jesus grants the man more than he ever thought he needed. In compassion Jesus will not only heal the boy's epilepsy, he will also help the father overcome his unbelief. But before the man's unbelief is overcome, the little faith that he has will be tested in the strongest possible way.

Mark never calls the boy an epileptic, but there can be little doubt that this would be a correct diagnosis. Matthew says as much in the way he reports the father's plea: 'Lord, have mercy on my son. He is an epileptic[85] and is suffer-

---

82 Daniel B. Wallace, in *Greek Grammar beyond the Basics: An Exegetical Syntax of the New Testament* (Grand Rapids, MI: Zondervan, 1996, p. 68) claims that exclamations introduced by O (as here) indicate 'deep emotion', which in this case Zerwick identifies as 'grief at the people's lack of faith' (Maximilian Zerwick, *Biblical Greek Illustrated by Examples* [English edn, adapted from the 4th Latin edn by Joseph Smith S. J.; Rome: Biblical Institute Press, 1963, p. 12]). Zerwick could be correct but ultimately it remains a subjective judgment.

83 See France, *Mark*, pp. 367–68.

84 Stein, *Mark*, p. 434 (emphasis his).

85 This statement translates the Greek verb *selēniazomai*, which BDAG renders 'to experience epileptic seizures, *be an epileptic*' (919). The KJV's unfortunate 'lunatic' was replaced by

ing greatly' (Mt. 17.15). The boy seems to have an extremely severe case of the disease, so much so that each of the Synoptic Gospels puts it down to demonic causes. Even so, the boy's symptoms, which are described in greatest detail by Mark, are very similar to what is known as epilepsy today. John Wilkinson, a medical doctor with a theological degree, offers this insight:

> The evangelists do not give us an exact medical description of the convulsions such as we might find in a modern text-book of neurology, and we have no right to expect this from them. Even so, the detail given and the words used give us a very vivid picture of the seizures, and leave us in no doubt that this boy suffered from the major form of epilepsy or *le grand mal* of the French neurologists.[86]

Wilkinson continues by identifying the usual five stages of a grand mal seizure in the details provided by the three Gospel accounts.[87] For the medical layperson his article makes for comprehensible and even fascinating reading, but the simple identification of the boy's condition as epilepsy is not without its problems. Although the similarities between the two are quite astounding, it should not be forgotten that all three Gospel accounts portray Jesus' activity not primarily as a healing but as an exorcism. Wilkinson is therefore also careful to point out that in this instance demon possession and epilepsy are not necessarily mutually exclusive. 'Epilepsy', he says, 'is due to a sudden disturbance of nerve endings and may have many causes . . . Therefore to arrive at a diagnosis of epilepsy does not automatically exclude demon possession as the cause of his disease.'[88] Hence this boy has symptoms characteristic of grand mal epilepsy which we are told are the result of demon possession. The medical diagnosis and the underlying spiritual cause would seem to be complementary pieces of information, not contradictory ones. Such an explanation allows for a true regard for the miracle. In discerning and treating the underlying cause Jesus provides a cure that is both spiritual and medical.

Jesus' response to the father's importunate plea to take pity on him and his son and show them compassion therefore comes in two stages which will culminate at the same point. He first addresses the father's unbelief and only then does he deal with the boy's condition. As a demonstration of Jesus' compassion it is

---

'epileptic' in the Revised Version of 1881. This has been the choice of most English translations ever since (including the NKJV), although 'lunatic' still persists in some quarters (e.g. JB, Phillips). The LB paraphrase, 'he is mentally deranged', misses the point entirely. The only other occurrence of *selēniazomai* in the New Testament is in Mt. 4.24 where epileptics are brought to Jesus for healing along with paralytics, the demon-possessed and those suffering severe pain.

86 John Wilkinson, 'The Case of the Epileptic Boy', *ExpTim* 79 (1967), pp. 40–41. A more detailed medical explanation of the boy's condition by the same author can be found in *The Bible and Healing: A Medical and Theological Commentary* (Grand Rapids, MI: Eerdmans, 1998), pp. 121–30.

87 Wilkinson, 'Epileptic Boy', pp. 41–42.

88 Wilkinson, 'Epileptic Boy', p. 42.

unique. Never again in the Gospels does Jesus' compassion come to expression through an exorcism. In the verses that follow the father's final plea (9.25-27) this is clearly what is taking place.

The exorcism is hastened when Jesus sees a crowd running to the scene. At times seeking privacy for his miracles (cf. 5.37, 40; 7.33-36; 8.23), Jesus does not want this difficult exorcism to become a public spectacle. He begins by rebuking the demon, 'You deaf and dumb spirit.' This need not imply that the demon itself was deaf and dumb. Otherwise how could it hear Jesus' rebuke! What it probably means is that during seizures the evil spirit would afflict the boy with deafness and dumbness.[89] Jesus then commands the spirit to come out of the boy and never enter him again. It was precisely at this point that the disciples' earlier attempt had been such a dismal failure (9.18). Although Jesus had given them the authority to cast out demons when he first appointed them to be apostles (3.14-15) and later reaffirmed that authority (6.7) so that they exercised it successfully (6.13), on this occasion their efforts had resulted only in public embarrassment (9.14-16) – a situation that the scribes seemed only too eager to exploit (9.14). Stung by their failure, they later ask Jesus privately why they had not been able to cast out the demon. They are met with a terse reply, 'This kind can come out only by prayer' (9.29). Jesus' answer is puzzling. Was this a particularly difficult case of demon possession? Or was it simply that the disciples had forgotten the basic requirement of prayer? Whatever the precise answer to these questions, the situation drips with irony. Neither Mark nor the other Gospels give any indication that Jesus had prayed before the exorcism. The salient point is that he doesn't need to. The disciples have to pray. All Jesus has to do is to command the demon to leave the boy and never come back.

The evil spirit reacts in typically demonic fashion. Like the demon in the synagogue at Capernaum (1.26) he lets out a shriek and violently shakes his victim by convulsing him one last time (9.26). Then he comes out of him. But, like an epileptic in a postictal state (the altered state of consciousness experienced after a seizure), the boy is left limp and seemingly lifeless.[90] A casual spectator might be excused for thinking that the sufferer has died. That was certainly the thought that was going through the minds of many in the crowd. 'The boy looked so much like a corpse that many said, "He's dead"' (9.26). Like the father who was rebuked for his lack of faith, they give evidence for the accuracy of Jesus' diagnosis of their spiritual condition when he referred to them as an 'unbelieving generation' (9.19). In their own way they were saying that the operation was a success (the demon had gone) but the patient had died (the boy looked like a corpse).[91]

---

89   In private correspondence with the author dated 16 October 2009 Dr Tim Walker commented, 'Interestingly some forms of epilepsy (e.g. absence seizures, complex partial seizures) can cause both episodes of muteness (and altered consciousness such that the boy could not "hear" others) and be associated with generalized seizures like those described in the account. The two sets of symptoms are quite consistent.'

90   Thus Wilkinson, 'Epileptic Boy', p. 42.

91   Cf. Garland, *Mark*, p. 356.

But at the very point when all seems lost Jesus steps in once again. He took the boy 'by the hand and lifted him to his feet, and he stood up' (9.27). Although concealed in English translation, Mark describes the miracle in resurrection language. The expression 'lifted him to his feet' is more literally rendered 'raised him' (NASB). It translates the verb *egeirō* which Mark not only uses in healing contexts (1.31; 2.9-12; 3.3; 10.49) but also with respect to raising the dead (5.41; 6.14, 16; 12.26; 14.28; 16.6). Likewise, 'he stood up' could equally well be translated 'he arose' (KJV). The Greek verb here is *anistēmi*, which Mark also uses in resurrection contexts (5.42; 9.9-10; 12.23, 25), and particularly to refer to Jesus' resurrection in his three passion predictions (8.31; 9.31; 10.34). These two verbs also come together in the raising of Jairus' daughter (5.41-42). To bring out the resurrection connections a little tautology might be quite in order, 'he raised him up and he arose'. So Mark would have his readers see this miracle not only as an exorcism but as a direct pointer to the resurrection of Jesus. Lane's comments are therefore apt:

> the accumulation of the vocabulary of death and resurrection in verses 26-27, and the parallelism with the narrative of the raising of Jairus' daughter, suggest that Mark wished to allude to a death and resurrection. The dethroning of Satan is always a reversal of death and an affirmation of life. There is a nuance in this instance, however, which must be appreciated. There appears to be a definite heightening of demonic resistance to Jesus which can be traced in the sequence Ch. 1:23-27 – Ch. 5:1-20 – Ch. 9:14-29. In this instance the disciples are powerless before the demon's tenacious grip upon the child and Jesus is successful only by the costly means of death and resuscitation. The healing of the possessed boy thus points beyond itself to the necessity of Jesus' own death and resurrection before Satan's power can be definitively broken.[92]

If by 'the costly means of death and resuscitation' Lane means to imply that the boy actually died, he is outstripping the evidence supplied by the text. It says that he looked '*like* a corpse', not that he actually died.[93] One can only wonder whether the father was among the many who exclaimed, 'He's dead.' At the very least his hesitant faith – like his son's tortured body – must have been violently shaken. Jesus' raising up the boy would have had the double effect of restoring both the man's faith and the boy's health. The compassion for which the father asked therefore exceeded his greatest expectations. Thus far in Mark's Gospel it is the greatest demonstration of Jesus' compassion – exceeding even the healing of the leper and the feeding of the crowds. But more is yet to come. What happened to the boy foreshadows the greater things that will happen to Jesus. The boy seemed to be dead; Jesus will be killed. The boy was raised to his feet; Jesus will be raised from the dead. The death and resurrection of Jesus are foretold not

---

92 Lane, *Mark*, pp. 334–35.
93 'A postictal state can look mortal to an untrained observer, but the boy would be medically expected to gradually awake from it. The healing is from the recurrent seizure disorder caused by the evil spirit, not from the self-limited postictal state' (Dr Tim Walker, 16 October 2009).

only by the surrounding passion predictions, which form the heart of this section of Mark, but are also adumbrated by what happened to this lad. The greatest expression of Jesus' compassion still lies ahead.

Jesus' spectacular success in exorcising a very tenacious demon is set against the backdrop of the disciples' failure. In Mark's journey section the disciples constantly act as a foil to Jesus. In the journey from Caesarea Philippi to Jerusalem he heads for his destination as the Yahweh–Warrior figure who leads his blind people along a New Exodus way. As we have seen, this entire section (8.27–10.52) is bracketed by the healing of blind men – the man at Bethsaida (8.22-26) and Bartimaeus outside Jericho (10.46-52). These two blind men are symbolic of the spiritual state of the disciples who, in spite of Peter's ringing confession of Jesus as the Christ (8.29), remain strangely blind to the true nature of his messiahship. This section of Mark teems with examples of their blunders, spiritual immaturity, plain stupidity and lack of understanding (8.33; 9.5-6, 10, 17-18, 28-29, 32, 33-37, 38-41; 10.13-16, 32, 35-40, 41). The present miracle is a case in point. The disciples fail because of their prayerlessness, while Jesus the Warrior achieves perhaps his greatest victory to date.

When read against the background of Isaiah's New Exodus, Mark's choice of specific examples of Jesus' compassion is remarkably apt. Rich in references to divine compassion (Isa. 49.8-13; 54.7-10; 60.10) these chapters in Isaiah portray God acting mightily on behalf of his people. The same is true of the Markan Jesus. By healing leprosy, teaching those who are 'like sheep without a shepherd', feeding the hungry and successfully performing a very difficult exorcism, he is doing the works of God. All of these actions accord with the way he was introduced at the beginning. He is the Christ and the Son of God (1.1). He is more powerful than John the Baptist (1.7). Supremely endowed with the Holy Spirit (1.10) he is the beloved Son with whom God is well pleased (1.11). His acts of compassion give substance to all these affirmations.

2.5 Sighing

On two occasions in the Gospels Jesus sighs. Both are recorded only by Mark and in close proximity to one another. But Jesus' sighing is in response to very different situations. First he lets out a sigh in the process of healing a deaf-mute (7.34). Next he sighs deeply in response to the Pharisees' request for a sign from heaven (8.12). The situations that evoke Jesus' sighs are so different that it is tempting to ask whether he is giving vent to the same emotion in each case. Everything in the two contexts seems so different – the people, the request they make, Jesus' response to their request, and the surroundings in which these events take place.

In the first instance Jesus appears to be in the Decapolis, on the predominantly Gentile side of the Sea of Galilee (7.31). From there he sails to the unknown location of Dalmanutha (8.10), which was presumably on the Jewish side of the lake as he is immediately confronted by the Pharisees (8.11). Both incidents therefore bring us back to Mark's Galilee section (1.14–8.26), although only the latter episode would appear to have taken place in Galilee itself. The healing of the deaf-mute most convincingly belongs to Jesus' long detour through mainly Gentile lands (7.24–8.10) away from the pressure of Herod Antipas and the religious leaders.[94] Could these different locations – the more relaxed Gentile environment in the Decapolis and the more hostile setting in Galilee – perhaps suggest that the emotions conveyed by Jesus' sighing are not the same?

The underlying vocabulary in the two passages also differs. Although some English translations (including the NIV) give the same translation on both occasions, the Greek actually uses two different words. It first uses the simple verb *stenazō* (7.34) and then the compound *anastenazō* (8.12). Strictly speaking, Jesus only sighs over the deaf-mute, but sighs deeply at the Pharisees. Is this just a matter of emphasis or is Mark suggesting a different underlying emotion in each case? This is a difficult question well worth exploring.

2.5.1 SIGHING AT THE PLIGHT OF A DEAF-MUTE (7.31-37)

31 Then Jesus left the vicinity of Tyre and went through Sidon, down to the Sea of Galilee and into the region of the Decapolis.

32 There some people brought to him a man who was deaf and could hardly talk, and they begged him to place his hand on the man.

33 After he took him aside, away from the crowd, Jesus put his fingers into the man's ears. Then he spat and touched the man's tongue.

34 He looked up to heaven and *with a deep sigh* said to him, 'Ephphatha!' (which means, 'Be opened!').

35 At this, the man's ears were opened, his tongue was loosened and he began to speak plainly.

36 Jesus commanded them not to tell anyone. But the more he did so, the more they kept talking about it.

37 People were overwhelmed with amazement. 'He has done everything well,' they said. 'He even makes the deaf hear and the mute speak.'

Jesus' travels again bring him to the Decapolis where earlier in his ministry he had delivered a man from a legion of demons (5.1-20). Quite deliberately Jesus had denied the man's request to go with him. Instead he was to tell his people how much the Lord had done for him (5.19), a command that the man seems to have carried out with enthusiasm. He began to tell in the Decapolis how much Jesus had done for him so that all the people were amazed (5.20). The man's proclamation may well have set the stage for the present miracle. Jesus now has a reputation in the region as a healer so that when he returns to the area some people begged him to heal a man with a serious physical disability. To modern ears what follows sounds like one of the strangest and most bizarre miracles

94 *Contra* Stein, *Mark*, pp. 357–59. He argues that Jesus' itinerary (7.31) took him *through* the Decapolis and back to the western side of the lake, but this is not the most natural reading of the text.

ever performed by Jesus. Everything about it seems dramatic and unusual. Jesus sighing and spitting, and putting his fingers into the man's ears – it all sounds so foreign to us and so unlike Jesus. Why did he go to such extraordinary lengths to heal this man?

Part of the answer may lie in the nature of the disability. The man is significantly challenged in two related areas, but apparently not to the same extent. He 'was deaf and could hardly talk' (7.32). He was completely deaf and as a result it seems that his speech was badly impaired. His speech impediment is indicated by the rare Greek word *mogilalos*, which in the entire Bible is found only here and in Isa. 35.6 (LXX). This term might suggest that he was completely mute because of his deafness, but it more probably indicates that he spoke only with great difficulty.[95] The latter is the more likely possibility in view of the outcome of the miracle – 'he began to speak *plainly*' (7.35). He may therefore have been a stammerer and unable to articulate himself properly. Whatever the precise nature of his speech difficulty, the fact that he was also deaf makes his healing a remarkable fulfilment of the messianic prophecy in Isaiah 35:

> Then the eyes of the blind shall be opened,
> and *the ears of the deaf shall hear*;
> then the lame shall leap like a deer,
> and *the tongue of stammerers shall be clear* (vv. 5-6a LXX).[96]

These are the kinds of miracles that will take place when God comes to save his people (Isa. 35.4). This prophecy is echoed by those who later hear of the healing of the deaf-mute. Overwhelmed with amazement at Jesus they declare, 'He has done everything well. He even makes the deaf hear and the dumb speak' (7.37). Their praise is lavish and abundant. Whether consciously or unwittingly they liken the works of Jesus to the activity of God at creation, who 'saw all that he had made, and it was very good' (Gen. 1.31). In this miracle Mark wants us to see the dawning of the messianic age and a hint of the new creation.

The healing of this man should therefore be seen against the broad canvas of God's eschatological purpose and the coming of the new creation. This broad perspective also helps to explain the actions and emotions of Jesus. His actions surrounding the miracle will not seem as strange when it is appreciated that he is showing empathy to the disabled man and seeking to enter his world. Jesus is not imitating pagan magical incantations, as some have assumed. Rather, he is using a kind of sign language in a effort to communicate with the man. He puts his fingers in the man's ears. Then he spits and places the saliva on the man's tongue. Perhaps these are gestures indicating what Jesus is about to do. He is about to open the man's ears and loosen his tongue. Whatever this sign language

---

95 See BDAG, p. 656, which allows for both possibilities.
96 Unless otherwise indicated, LXX quotations are from Albert Pietersma and Benjamin G. Wright (eds), *A New English Translation of the Septuagint and the Other Greek Translations Traditionally Included under That Title* (Oxford: Oxford University Press, 2007). The italics are the author's.

means exactly, Jesus then looks up to heaven, possibly indicating prayer. Then he sighs and says, '*Ephphatha*!' (meaning 'Be opened!').[97] As a result the man is instantly healed.

But why does Jesus sigh? In the literature various trends can be detected in the answers to this question. Some interpreters emphasize Jesus' deep emotional involvement with the man and take his sighing as a sign of sympathy and compassion. Others understand it as a gesture of prayer (cf. Exod. 2.24; 6.5; Judg. 2.18) seeking God's power for healing and maybe also drawing attention to the extreme difficulty of the case. Still others, who link the healing to pagan magic, describe the sighing as a standard healing technique, perhaps indicating an expression of power.[98] These lines of interpretation are rather different, and difficult to reconcile. They also underscore the complexity of the question before us. A fresh look at the biblical evidence is therefore in order.

In the canonical LXX, with which Mark was no doubt familiar, the verb *stenazō* is associated with weeping (Job 30.25), mourning (Job 31.38; Isa. 19.8; 24.7), lament (Nah. 3.7), affliction (Lam. 1.8, 21), and the prospect of bitter grief (Ezek. 21.6, 7) and disaster (Ezek. 26.15). Sighing in the LXX therefore 'expresses deep distress of spirit'[99] and is an 'expression for human lament and powerless suffering in situations that people cannot change on their own.'[100]

In the New Testament *stenazō*, usually translated 'sigh' or 'groan', is sometimes still associated with grief (Heb. 13.17). Most of its six occurrences, however, open up a completely new dimension. This is particularly evident in the Pauline references. Paul describes the eschatological groaning of those who eagerly await the redemption of their bodies (Rom. 8.23), which he also describes more picturesquely as 'being clothed with our heavenly dwelling' (2 Cor. 5.2, 4).

---

97 Scholars have debated whether '*Ephphatha*' is Aramaic or Hebrew. Strong arguments have been mounted on both sides, but if France is correct 'the issue is apparently not capable of definitive resolution' (*Mark*, p. 304). The scholarly stalemate had earlier been aptly described by S. Morag, '*Ephphatha* (Mark VII. 34): Certainly Hebrew, Not Aramaic?', *JSS* 17 (1972), p. 202, 'when its grammatical interpretation is examined in the light of the phonology of the Western Aramaic dialects, one must reach the conclusion that the possibility of regarding the word as Aramaic is as valid as that of considering it to be Hebrew'. The most that can be said is that Jesus was using a Semitic language, which could possibly be an argument for the disabled man being a Jew. This does not necessarily place the miracle in Galilee, however. In Jesus' day Aramaic was still widely spoken throughout the Middle East. So the term proves nothing as to the ethnicity of the man nor of those who brought him to Jesus. The location of the miracle in the Decapolis is equally non-determinative 'since there were sizeable colonies of Jews in nearly all the cities' (Lane, *Mark*, p. 266). While in the preceding narrative the ethnicity of the Syro-Phoenician woman is clearly pointed out, there are no such markers in the present pericope. This consideration leads to Gundry's cautious comment: 'Mark does not identify anyone in this narrative as Gentile. The same observation will hold for the feeding of the four thousand (8:1-9). Mark never identifies regions as Jewish or Gentile and hardly expects his audience to do so' (*Mark*, p. 382). Hence neither 'Decapolis' nor '*Ephphatha*' decisively determines the question of ethnicity.

98 See Stein, *Mark*, p. 360 for a helpful summary of the various views.

99 *TDNT* 7, p. 600.

100 *EDNT* 3, p. 272.

The sighing still has the element of grief and distress (as in the LXX) but this is radically tempered by the hope of the resurrection body. Although their distress is still painfully real, the sighing of believers 'expresses their eager expectation and longing . . . for the final fulfilment of the promised salvation already given to them in faith'.[101] In their groaning believers are not alone but are joined by the whole creation (Rom. 8.22) and even by the Holy Spirit (Rom. 8.26). In this symphony of sighs Paul expresses most poignantly the eschatological tension between the 'already' and the 'not yet'. Encrypted within the sighing are both the painful distress of the old order and the sure hope of the world to come. Caught in the tension between their present distress and their future hope, the believers' most appropriate response is to sigh. In sympathy the Holy Spirit sighs with them and helps them in their weakness.

Jesus' sighing at the healing of the deaf-mute is a precursor of the later work of the Holy Spirit. It expresses Jesus' empathy for the man's plight as he enters into his distress. To that extent Jesus is the man of sorrows who 'took up our infirmities and carried our diseases' (Isa. 53.4; Mt. 8.17). But at the same time Jesus' sigh expresses his hope for the new age that is still to come and that is foreshadowed so clearly by the miracle he is about to perform. He too longs for the ultimate fulfilment of the messianic prophecy in Isaiah 35. On that great eschatological Day not only will the deaf hear and the dumb shout for joy (Isa. 35.5-6), but all the redeemed of the Lord 'will enter Zion with singing; everlasting joy will crown their heads. Gladness and joy will overtake them, and sorrow and sighing will flee away' (Isa. 35.10; 51.11). Jesus therefore sighs for the Day when sighing will be no more. He longs for the New Jerusalem, the destination to which he will lead his people along a New Exodus way.

2.5.2 SIGHING AT THE TESTING OF THE PHARISEES (8.11-13)

11 The Pharisees came and began to question Jesus. To test him, they asked him for a sign from heaven.
12 *He sighed deeply* and said, Why does this generation ask for a miraculous sign? I tell you the truth, no sign will be given to it.'
13 Then he left them, got back into the boat and crossed to the other side.

No sooner has Jesus set foot again in Galilee than he is confronted by the very people he had been trying so hard to avoid – the Pharisees. It was his last encounter with the Pharisees and some Jerusalem scribes (7.1-13) that had prompted his sojourn in the regions of Tyre and Sidon (7.24-31) and his long detour through the Decapolis (7.31–8.10). But in his absence his adversaries had not forgotten about him. In earlier confrontations with Jesus the Pharisees had shown themselves to be strict sabbatarians in the most legalistic sense (2.23–3.6) as well as sticklers for ceremonial purity (2.16; 7.1-5). They had taken issue with Jesus

---

101 *EDNT* 3, p. 273.

on both counts and Mark has already alerted his readers to the fact that the Pharisees' antagonism towards Jesus was deadly (3.6). Up to this point they have therefore been cast consistently in an adversarial role. True to form they now come to Jesus asking for a sign from heaven.

On the surface their request would seem legitimate enough. As guardians of a sacred tradition they would appear to have every right to test Jesus' orthodoxy. Earlier they have noticed him fraternizing with undesirable characters, taking a lax view of the Sabbath and allowing his disciples to eat with unwashed hands, thus defying the tradition of the elders. Hence it would seem to be their duty to question his non-conformist ways and if necessary protect the wider public from his dubious influence. But Mark soon sweeps away any aura of respectability that the Pharisees might have in the way they approach Jesus. He unmasks their motives by revealing that they asked him for a sign 'to test him' (8.11). The Greek verb for 'test' is *peirazō*, which can just as well be translated 'tempt' (as in the KJV). In Mark this verb always has strongly negative connotations. It is first used of Satan tempting Jesus in the wilderness (1.13). On the three other occasions it is used of the Pharisees trying to test or trap Jesus. In Perea they set a trap with their question about divorce (10.2). In Jerusalem they again act in collusion with the Herodians with their testing question about paying taxes to Caesar (12.15). Their test questions therefore link the Pharisees with some unsavoury characters. Not only are they in collusion with the Herodians, they are also in league with the devil. In Mark the temptations initiated by Satan are continued by the Pharisees. These connections cast the Pharisees and their request in a very negative light. Their request for a sign presents Jesus with an alluring temptation.

On the face of it their demand seems ironical and almost nonsensical. By this stage in Jesus' ministry Mark has no less than eighteen references to his miracles, some of which were witnessed by the scribes and Pharisees themselves (2.1-12; 3.1-6). So the request for yet another miracle would seem rather pointless. The fact is, however, that the Pharisees are not asking for a miracle but for a sign. The difference is significant. While Jesus' miracles are regularly referred to as 'signs' in John's Gospel, this is not the case in the Synoptics. As A. M. Hunter explains, 'whereas for St John "sign" is mostly a favourable term for miracle, in the synoptic tradition it is definitely a "bad" word. There it means some thaumaturgical *tour de force* – a visible manifestation of overmastering power which, so to speak, would write the truth of Jesus' claims plain against the sky.'[102] So the Pharisees are not just asking Jesus for another 'garden-variety' miracle, but for a spectacular sign that will settle his claims once and for all. But what would this kind of sign look like?

It should be noted that the Pharisees are asking Jesus for 'a sign *from heaven*'. This is more than a circumlocution for 'a sign from God', since it was commonly supposed that all genuine miracles had their source in God. So this should help further define what the Pharisees had in mind. They are demanding something truly extraordinary. But beyond that do they leave the matter open? After a

---

102 A. M. Hunter, *According to John* (London: SCM, 1972), p. 67.

careful study of the word 'sign' in Scripture (and with a special focus on Mk 8.11-12; 13.22) Jeffrey Gibson concludes that 'it is clear that according to Mark the "sign" is a phenomenon whose content is apocalyptic in tone, triumphalistic in character, and the embodiment of one of the "mighty deeds of deliverance" that God had worked on Israel's behalf in rescuing it from slavery.'[103] In other words the Pharisees are asking Jesus to recapitulate one of the mighty signs that God performed on Israel's behalf at the time of the exodus.[104] For Jesus this would have been a very powerful and seductive temptation. One of Jesus' greatest temptations – one that began in the wilderness and continued even as he hung on the cross – was to be the political Messiah of contemporary Jewish expectations.[105] The Pharisees' request is just another guise for this recurring temptation.

The request for a sign is therefore anathema to Jesus and he repudiates it vigorously. This is the force of his reaction in v. 12. 'He sighed deeply and said, "Why does this generation ask for a miraculous sign? I tell you the truth, no sign will be given to it."' Given the strength and subtlety of the temptation he is facing, Jesus' response is understandably charged with emotion. But once again the precise emotion is difficult to pinpoint accurately. It is unlikely that the deep sighing this time is synonymous with the sigh that he let out at the healing of the deaf-mute. There is little suggestion that this is a fine blend of distress, empathy and hope! Jesus sighs again but the underlying emotion that inspires it seems to be quite different. In their attempts to identify the emotion commentators offer conflicting solutions. Lane calls it 'an expression of indignation' and 'a note of exasperation'.[106] Guelich puts it down to the 'spiritual excitement' experienced by a prophet who is 'moved deeply in his person prior to an utterance or an action'.[107] For Richard France the sighing suggests 'an internal emotional upheaval' indicating Jesus' distress over the unresponsiveness of the Pharisees.[108] This diversity of opinion again highlights the complexity of the issue at hand.

What makes matters so difficult is the rarity of the verb *anastenazō*. It occurs

---

103   Jeffrey Gibson, 'Jesus' Refusal to Produce a "Sign" (Mk 8.11-13)', *JSNT* 38 (1990), p. 53.

104   In the Old Testament the Hebrew word for 'sign' is *oth*. Whenever it designates miraculous, redemptive signs *oth* refers almost exclusively to the exodus, especially the ten plagues (e.g. Exod. 7.3; 8.23; 10.1-2; Deut. 34.10-11; Neh. 9.10; Pss. 78.43; 105.27; Jer. 32.20-22).

105   Oscar Cullmann, *The Christology of the New Testament* (trans. Shirley C. Guthrie and Charles A. M. Hall; Philadelphia: Westminster, rev. edn, 1963), p. 122, sees another version of this same temptation in Peter's rebuke of Jesus following the first passion prediction (Mk 8.32): 'The same Satan who met Jesus openly in the wilderness after his baptism and tried to impose on him the role of a political Messiah – that Satan now uses the disciple Peter to prevent him from fulfilling his real task and again to persuade him to play the role of a Jewish political Messiah. The extraordinary vehemence with which Jesus rejects this demand in Caesarea Philippi indicates how deeply the temptation of Peter affects him. He does not want to be the king of Israel in this way . . . he must fulfil his task in suffering and dying, not in establishing a political kingdom.'

106   Lane, *Mark*, p. 277.

107   Guelich, *Mark 1-8:26*, p. 414.

108   France, *Mark*, p. 312.

only once in the New Testament, once in the canonical LXX,[109] three times in the Apocrypha,[110] and fewer than thirty times in the entire body of ancient Greek literature.[111] A thorough investigation of the data was made by Gibson on two separate occasions. His initial research led him to the conclusion that, where '*anastenazō* is used with a verb of speaking, it is consistently employed to express neither exasperation nor indignation, but dismay, particularly dismay over the realization that one has been forced into a set of circumstances where one's commitment to a given divine decree may be found wanting or foolish.'[112] Several years later Gibson examined further data that had become available. This only confirmed his earlier conclusions. 'In every one of the additional instances, what is conveyed by the verb is always a sense of *dismay*, and never a sense of resentment or acrimony, vexation or ire.'[113] In both investigations Gibson therefore reaches exactly the same conclusion with respect to Mk 8.12 – Jesus sighed deeply because 'he experienced something which tried not his patience but his faithfulness'.[114]

On this interpretation Jesus' deep sigh is a natural response to a particularly powerful temptation. He is being tempted to forego the way of suffering in favour of the more attractive road of a political messiahship that would fulfil the earthly dreams of his compatriots.[115] It is a temptation that he repudiates vehemently. 'I tell you the truth,' he says, 'no sign will be given to this generation.' The first statement is an 'amen' saying that Jesus uses to lend added weight and authority to what he is saying (cf. 3.28).[116] The second statement could be more accurately translated 'If a sign will be given to this generation . . .' The sentence is incomplete and the grammar unusual. Scholars agree that it is a self-imprecatory oath.[117] The

---

109   In Lam. 1.4 the priests of Zion *groan* because of her destruction.
110   The husband of the wicked woman 'involuntarily *groaned* bitter things' (Sir. 25.18). Faced by a moral dilemma Susanna *groaned* (Sus. 22) while Eleazar *groaned aloud* before his martyrdom (2 Macc. 6.30).
111   Edwards, *Mark*, p. 236.
112   Jeffrey B. Gibson, 'Mark 8.12a: Why Does Jesus "Sigh Deeply"?', *BT* 38 (1987), p. 123.
113   Jeffrey B. Gibson, 'Another Look at Why Jesus "Sighs Deeply" in Mark 8:12a', *JTS* 47 (1996), p. 138 (italics his).
114   Gibson, 'Why Does Jesus "Sigh Deeply"?', p. 125; 'Another Look', p. 140.
115   Typical of the nationalistic, messianic hopes of the first century are the pseudepigraphical *Psalms of Solomon*: 'And he shall have the peoples of the nations to be subject to him under his yoke and he shall glorify the Lord in the mark (perhaps 'sight') of the earth, and he shall purify Jerusalem in holiness as it was at the beginning so that all nations may come from the end of the earth to see his glory' (17.30-31a). See Pietersma and Wright, *Septuagint*, p. 775.
116   Literally translated 'Amen I say to you', this introductory formula is very common in the Synoptics, while in John it is modified to the double 'amen.' The formula is found only on the lips of Jesus and was never used by the apostles. As the unique bearer of divine truth he speaks with unparalleled authority. It is his way of underlining or italicising what immediately follows.
117   According to BDF, p. 189, 'if' in oaths is a strong Hebraism meaning 'certainly not.' C. F. D. Moule, *An Idiom Book of New Testament Greek* (Cambridge: Cambridge University Press, 2nd edn, 1959), p. 179, further explains that the verb following the 'if' expresses vigorous denial. Other examples of this uniquely Hebrew construction are found in Gen. 14.23; Num.

ellipsis needs to be filled in with an expression such as 'may God's judgment fall upon me', 'may God strike me down' or 'may I be accursed of God'.[118] In using this grammatical construction Jesus is repudiating the Pharisees' request in the strongest possible way. Rather than yield to their temptation he would sooner be cursed by God. In the event that is of course exactly what happened. Whatever it takes, he must fulfil his calling as the man of sorrows.

To underline his intentions Jesus abruptly left the Pharisees, 'got back into the boat and crossed to the other side' (v. 13). He set sail for Bethsaida (8.22), a lakeside village across the Jordan inflow from Galilee. From there he will head almost due north to the Gentile district of Caesarea Philippi (8.27). He has decisively parted ways with the Pharisees. His public ministry in Galilee is over. The journey to Jerusalem with its predictions of the Passion will soon begin.

If read superficially Mark's two references to Jesus' deep sighing (7.34; 8.12) could be taken as expressions of a single underlying emotion. A little probing, however, quickly shows that this is not really the case. The sighing that accompanies the healing of the deaf-mute indicates Jesus' empathy for the man's suffering by sharing in his distress, but the prospect of the healing that is about to occur adds the dimension of longing for a better Day when all such afflictions will be a thing of the past. Jesus' sigh on this occasion gives voice to a complex web of emotions. On the other hand, when Jesus sighs deeply at the Pharisees' request for a sign it is simply an expression of dismay, without any admixture of anger or exasperation. He is dismayed by their stubborn unbelief and the brazenness of their seductive temptation.

2.6 Indignation (10.13-16)

13 People were bringing little children to Jesus to have him touch them, but the disciples rebuked them.

14 When Jesus saw this, *he was indignant*. He said to them, 'Let the little children come to me, and do not hinder them, for the kingdom of God belongs to such as these.'

15 I tell you the truth, anyone who will not receive the kingdom of God like a little child will never enter it.'

16 And he took the children in his arms, put his hands on them and blessed them.

Jesus rebuking the disciples and blessing the children falls within the journey section (8.27-10.52). Here he leads his blind followers along a New Exodus way. Of all the incidents recorded as they travelled from Caesarea Philippi to Jerusalem this must have been the disciples' most myopic moment. Blinded by

　　　32.11; Deut. 1.35; 1 Sam. 3.17; 1 Kgs 3.14; 2 Kgs 6.31; Ps. 95.11; Heb. 3.11; 4.3, 5 (Stein, *Mark*, p. 377).

118 See Garland, *Mark*, p. 308; Stein, *Mark*, p. 374.

the general disregard of children and the low esteem in which they were held in contemporary culture, the disciples have not yet been enlightened by the actions and teaching of Jesus. Not only had the beneficiaries of some of Jesus' most spectacular miracles been children – namely Jairus' daughter (5.39-41) and the epileptic boy (9.24) – Jesus had just recently given the disciples specific instruction as to how children ought to be received. On their latest visit to Capernaum Jesus had given his disciples a most valuable object lesson. Ironically, immediately after their failure to drive the evil spirit out of the epileptic boy (9.14-29), the disciples had been arguing along the way about which of them was the greatest (9.33-34). In response to their quibbling Jesus stood a child among them, embraced the child and said, 'Whoever welcomes one of these little children in my name welcomes me; and whoever welcomes me does not welcome me but the one who sent me' (9.37).

Sadly, Jesus' salutary lesson was soon lost on his status-seeking disciples. Their journey had taken them from Capernaum (9.33) across the Jordan (10.1) and would eventually bring them to Jericho (10.46). So the present encounter seems to have taken place in Perea, the territory of Herod Antipas that lay across the Jordan and south of the Decapolis. It would appear then that somewhere between Capernaum and Perea Jesus' lesson about children had simply been forgotten. So when people tried to bring little children to Jesus for the simple reason that he might touch them, the disciples rebuked them (10.13). This must be seen for the negative and hostile reaction that it is. The disciples were being more than an obstruction or a hindrance. Their rebuke is a reminder of the other rebukes in Mark, which have to do with exorcisms (1.25; 3.12; 9.25), opponents of God's will (4.39; 8.30-33) and outright censure (10.48).[119] The disciples' rebuke (whether of the children or of those who brought them is not clear) is therefore the polar opposite to Jesus' clear instruction back in Capernaum about the way children ought to be received. Garland has imaginatively reconstructed the situation:

> The disciples act like truculent bouncers. They rebuke these parents and try to block their children's access to Jesus. Again, they want to throw their weight around and exercise control by keeping at bay others who come from outside their circle. These aspiring leaders want to be gatekeepers, who determine not only who can use Jesus' name (9:38), but also who can have admission to his presence.[120]

In response Jesus is indignant[121] with his disciples. They have stoked his ire and he has lost his cool. Although Jesus has been angry before – with the healed leper who was about to defy his orders (1.43) and with the Pharisees for their stony

---

119 Thus Edwards, *Mark*, p. 306.
120 Garland, *Mark*, p. 381.
121 This translates the Greek verb *aganakteō*, which occurs seven times in the New Testament, and only in the Synoptic Gospels. The cognate noun *aganaktēsis* is found only in 2 Cor. 7.11 and Est. 8.13.

silence (3.5) – this is the only time in all the Gospels that Jesus gets angry with his disciples. Although Matthew and Luke have their own versions of this episode (Mt. 19.13-15; Lk. 18.15-17), neither mentions Jesus' indignation. If we assume that they made use of Mark in their own accounts, the omission could become an interesting point of speculation. Was Mark too radical for them at this point? Could a reference to Jesus' indignation impugn his sinlessness? We have no way of knowing the answer, nor can we know for sure whether these questions are legitimate in the first place. Even so, it would appear that Mark is attributing a rather unpleasant emotion to Jesus. The other contexts in which he mentions indignation are never positive. The ten other disciples are indignant with James and John for asking Jesus for special places of honour in his coming kingdom (10.41; Mt. 20.24). Later, at the home of Simon the Leper, the disciples were wrongly indignant at the woman who anointed Jesus because it was such a waste of money (14.4; Mt. 26.8). By attributing indignation to Jesus Mark seems to link him to his disciples at times when they were clearly not at their best.

Outside of Mark references to indignation are rare, but such as there are suggest just how bold he has been in attributing this emotion to Jesus. Matthew notes the indignation of the scribes and Pharisees when the children in the temple were shouting, 'Hosanna to the Son of David' (Mt. 21.15). The sole occurrence in Luke concerns the synagogue ruler who was indignant because Jesus had healed a crippled woman on the Sabbath (Lk. 13.14). In these Gospel references it is only the opponents of Jesus who seem to get indignant!

The canonical LXX has no references to indignation (indicated by *aganakteō*, the verb used for Jesus' indignation in Mk 10.14), but there are four occurrences in the Apocrypha. In their suffering the Egyptians are *incensed* at their gods (Wis. 12.27).[122] When the Babylonians heard that Bel and the dragon had been destroyed they were very *indignant* at their king and conspired against him (Bel 28). The divine justice *was angered* by the conspiracies of Jason (4 Macc. 4.21). The word can also be used metaphorically of the *raging* of the sea (Wis. 5.22). These four references indicate the breadth and flexibility of the word, but the common denominator is always the force and vehemence of the emotion.

So why was Jesus indignant, vexed, angry or perhaps even enraged at this disciples? There can be no denying that a powerful emotion was involved, but why did Jesus react so vehemently? A partial answer must lie in the fact that the disciples had so dismally failed to put his earlier teaching (9.37) into practice. But a further answer can also be found in the words that follow his expression of indignation: 'Let the little children come to me, and do not hinder them, for the kingdom of God belongs to such as these. I tell you the truth, anyone who will not receive the kingdom of God like a little child will never enter it' (10.14-15). From the next verse it is obvious that Jesus' irritation with the disciples' self-importance quickly subsided, giving way to an outpouring of warm affection for the children.

---

122 The words in italics in this paragraph are the renderings of *aganakteō* in the NRSV translation of the Apocrypha. The apocryphal writings cited are generally dated in the first and second centuries BC.

The disciples had hindered from coming to Jesus the very kind of people to whom the kingdom of God belongs. But what is it about children that makes them such suitable candidates for the kingdom? In answer to this question a veritable host of childlike characteristics have been suggested. They include such qualities as the receptivity of children, their utter dependence, childlike faith, their simplicity and the fact that a child knows he is helpless and small, without claim or merit.[123] The variety of answers given to the question accentuates the danger of imposing our views of the nature of children onto this statement of Jesus. The text actually says nothing of the qualities of these children, either objective or subjective, which adults are to emulate. But perhaps that is the point. In context these children are contrasted with the rich man who thought he could merit the kingdom (10.17-31). To his ideas of earning his way, Jesus says 'no', but to these children who bring nothing he says 'yes.' The children, and not the rich man, are models for kingdom entry. Jesus' point is that entry into the kingdom is by grace, and by grace alone. What is required is an attitude that accepts the kingdom as a gift and realizes that one can in fact do nothing to deserve it.

What really incenses Jesus is not only that the disciples have such a tenuous understanding of God's grace but that they also manage to stand in its way. By aggressively hindering the children's access to Jesus they are also obstructing God's grace. As a result they earn Jesus' ire. It cannot have been a pleasant experience for the disciples to be on the receiving end of his indignation, but an important lesson needed to be learned. The lesson is not that the disciples learn 'to be in solidarity with the most vulnerable'.[124] However valuable a lesson that might be in other contexts, it is not Jesus' main point here. Here the focus remains on God's grace – how to receive it and not to stand in its way. The account closes with an acted parable of God's grace, an illustration of what Jesus has just been teaching about children and their place in the kingdom. As he did with the individual child at Capernaum (9.36), he took these children in his arms (10.16). He had been asked to touch them, but he does more. He 'put his hands on them and blessed them' (10.16). His actions are a public display of the grace of which he has just spoken. Within the brief compass of this account one cannot help but notice the contrast between Jesus' tenderness towards these children and his indignation with his disciples. The contrast may not have been lost on the disciples either. Perhaps this time they would learn a lesson they would never forget.

123 See Larry L. Eubanks, 'Mark 10:13-16', *RevExp* 91 (1994), p. 401. Eubanks' own solution lies in translating the phrase '*like* a little child' by '*when* a little child.' Hence only those who receive the kingdom in their childhood will enter it. While this translation is possible grammatically, there are more realistic ways of understanding Jesus' words.

124 Thus James L. Bailey, 'Experiencing the Kingdom as a Little Child: A Rereading of Mark 10:13-16', *WW* 15 (1995), p. 66.

2.7 *Love (10.17-22)*

17 As Jesus started on his way, a man ran up to him and fell on his knees before him. 'Good teacher,' he asked, 'what must I do to inherit eternal life?'
18 'Why do you call me good?' Jesus answered. 'No-one is good – except God alone.'
19 You know the commandments: 'Do not murder, do not commit adultery, do not steal, do not give false testimony, do not defraud, honour your father and mother.'
20 'Teacher,' he declared, 'all these I have kept since I was a boy.'
21 *Jesus looked at him and loved him.* 'One thing you lack,' he said. 'Go, sell everything you have and give to the poor, and you will have treasure in heaven. Then come, follow me.'
22 At this the man's face fell. He went away sad, because he had great wealth.

The juxtaposition of this paragraph to the preceding is remarkable. Some of the contrasts could hardly be greater. Little children who have done nothing to deserve it receive the kingdom of God, while a man who has kept the commandments since he was a boy fails to inherit eternal life. Yet Mark says of this man what is said of nobody else in the Synoptics, namely that Jesus loved him (10.21). On the other hand, the previous paragraph records the only instance of Jesus' indignation with the disciples. These contrasts have a mystifying effect. Jesus is indignant with his own disciples who have left all to follow him (10.28), but he loves a man who will reject the invitation to follow because he is unprepared to make the necessary sacrifices (10.21-22). In his emotional responses Jesus sometimes comes across as such a mysteriously puzzling figure. How can this particular puzzle be resolved?

We can appreciate Jesus' indignation with the disciples because they so blatantly get in the way of God's grace. But why did this anonymous figure deserve the only specific mention of Jesus' love in the Synoptics? While Matthew describes him as a young man (Mt. 19.20, 22) and Luke refers to him as a ruler (Lk. 18.18), Mark maintains the man's anonymity throughout the account. Only at the end of the story does he declare his hand by saying that he had great wealth (10.22). So why is this otherwise unknown rich man the only (and very unlikely) recipient of Jesus' love in the Synoptic tradition? In John this is a privilege enjoyed by a number of people – all of them followers of Jesus. In Mark it is pointedly a non-follower who so remarkably receives the love of Jesus.[125] But why should this be so?

The man's initial approach to Jesus has all the hallmarks of eagerness and sincerity. He runs up to Jesus and falls on his knees before him (10.17). He is respectful, deferential and earnest – and his question is a weighty one: 'Good teacher, what must I do to inherit eternal life?'

In comparison Jesus' reply comes across as quite brusque. 'Why do you call

---

125 In their parallel accounts (Mt. 19.16-22; Lk. 18.18-23) Matthew and Luke say nothing of Jesus' love for the rich young ruler.

me good?' he asks. 'No one is good – except God alone' (10.18). This unexpected reproof for the man's use of an unusual title of respect recalls the scribes' earlier question, 'Who can forgive sins but God alone?' (2.7). Yes, who indeed! Mark often uses questions as subtle pointers to Jesus' divinity (cf. 4.41) and this may be another example. But that is scarcely the main point here. So Jesus returns to the man's question. In answer to what he must *do* to inherit eternal life, Jesus recites the commandments in the so-called 'second table' of the Decalogue, but he replaces 'do not covet' by 'do not defraud' (10.19). There is some plausibility to the suggestion that Jesus makes this adaptation for the sake of the rich man, who was more likely to defraud others than covet their wealth.[126]

Relieved that his hunch about his good prospects for the age to come has been confirmed by a religious specialist, the man declares, 'Teacher, all these things I have kept since I was a boy' (10.20). There is no need to doubt the sincerity of this announcement nor should we assume that 'the man was hypocritical in bringing his report card to Jesus.'[127] The man was sincerely convinced of the genuineness of his own Torah-observance. He was a good man after all and a good teacher has just assured him it was so. He could hardly have been expecting what Jesus is about to say next!

But before Jesus speaks Mark wants his readers to understand what lay behind Jesus' challenge to the young man. 'Jesus looked at him and loved him' (10.21). This was more than a fleeting glance. The Greek word (*emblepō*) suggests that he looked intently.[128] Jesus took a good hard look at the man. He studied him, and as he did so he was moved with affection for him. There was something about the young man that was deeply appealing to Jesus. His answer had not been hypocritical or arrogant. 'Given Jesus' affection for the man,' writes Edwards, 'it seems more reasonable to assume that his ready presentation of his goodness was childlike, unreflective perhaps, but not arrogant . . . There must have been something rare and admirable in the man, for of no one else in the Gospel does Mark say that Jesus "loved him."'[129] Perhaps no more is indicated here than the warmth of natural human affection. Gundry, taking his cue from Jesus just having embraced the children, suggests that it meant 'Jesus' putting his arm around the man, patting him, or doing some other such thing in physical demonstration that he "loved" him.'[130] Craig Evans is also open to the idea that 'Jesus actually hugged him or took him by the shoulders as a sign of affection.'[131] There is no hint of physical contact in the text, however, and these scholars may be reading their own cultural practices back into the situation. The least that can be said is that the man passed Jesus' careful scrutiny, and that Jesus is duly impressed.[132] Jesus has found no traces of hypocrisy or insincerity. Nor does he

---

126 Edwards, *Mark*, pp. 310–11.
127 Edwards, *Mark*, p. 311.
128 Thus BDAG, p. 321.
129 Edwards, *Mark*, pp. 311–12.
130 Gundry, *Mark*, p. 554.
131 Evans, *Mark 8:26-16:20*, p. 98.
132 France, *Mark*, p. 403.

scoff at the man's spiritual naïvety for claiming that he has kept all the commandments. He takes the man's statement at face value and believes what he says. But
this is also a case of tough love.

Because he loves this young man Jesus is not afraid to challenge him. The
words of v. 21 are not meant to put him off, but they do lay bare the true state
of his soul: 'One thing you still lack. Go, sell everything you have and give to
the poor, and you will have treasure in heaven. Then come, follow me.' In these
simple words Jesus puts his finger on the man's deepest spiritual problem. In
citing the commandments in v. 19 Jesus had carefully confined his examples to
the 'second table' of the Law. Nothing had been said about the man's devotion to
God. The 'one thing' the man lacked was not that he had failed to liquidate his
assets and distribute them to the poor. His problem was far more fundamental
than that. In his heart of hearts he had allowed his wealth to come between him
and God. He was more devoted to his wealth than he was to God and had therefore made an idol of his possessions. So while he might claim to have kept many
of the other commandments, he had failed to keep the first: 'You shall have no
other gods before me' (Exod. 20.3). By selling everything he had and giving it to
the poor and then following Jesus, he would demonstrate beyond the shadow of
a doubt that he was obeying the commandments that he knew so well. Stripped
of all his possessions he would also become like one of those little children to
whom the kingdom of heaven belongs (10.14).

Given the man's dangerous spiritual condition, the most loving response to his
naïve complacency is to shake it to the core – which is precisely what Jesus does.
In the event it rattles the man completely. Faced with the stark choice between
'treasure in heaven' (10.21) and his own 'great wealth' (10.22), he opts for the
latter. But the decision he made gave him no joy. His face clouded over, etched
with disappointment and sorrow.[133] He left the interview with Jesus a sad man.

Jesus' contrasting emotions in these passages – his indignation at his disciples
and his love for the rich young ruler – only make sense in the context of his overall kingdom message (10.14-15), which is a message of grace. He is indignant
with his disciples because they get in the way of God's grace. He loves the young
man and is prepared to shake his life to its very foundations so that he will throw
himself upon God's grace. These two emotions are therefore not contradictory
but profoundly complementary. His passion to see the grace of God in human
lives drives both his indignation and his love.

2.8 Overwhelming Grief

Mark's record of Jesus' emotions overlaps almost completely with Matthew's in
the Jerusalem section (11.1–16.8). Their references to his emotions in Gethsemane
and on the cross are nearly identical. Both describe Jesus as being 'troubled' in

---

133 See Lane, *Mark*, p. 368.

Gethsemane. To this Matthew adds that he was 'sorrowful' (Mt. 26.37), while Mark says at this point that he was 'deeply distressed' (14.33). Jesus' self-disclosure to Peter, James and John, 'My soul is overwhelmed with sorrow to the point of death' (14.34), agrees word for word with Mt. 26.38. On the cross the cry of dereliction and its translation into Greek (15.34) differ slightly from Mt. 27.46, although both record the cry in Aramaic. In both Gospels Jesus' Passion forms the climax to the narrative, and it is here that we see his emotions in their greatest intensity.

Because of the significant overlap between Matthew and Mark in their depictions of Jesus in Gethsemane and on the cross, the reader is referred to ch. 1.5 for a more detailed discussion of Jesus' emotions at these climactic moments. In the remainder of this chapter the focus will be on the slight variations in detail between Mark and Matthew's portrayals of some of Jesus' most harrowing emotions.

2.8.1 GETHSEMANE (14.32-42)

32 They went to a place called Gethsemane, and Jesus said to his disciples, 'Sit here while I pray.'

33 He took Peter, James and John along with him, and *he began to be deeply distressed and troubled.*

34 '*My soul is overwhelmed with sorrow to the point of death*,' he said to them. 'Stay here and keep watch.'

35 Going a little farther, he fell to the ground and prayed that if possible the hour might pass from him.

36 'Abba, Father,' he said, 'everything is possible for you. Take this cup from me. Yet not what I will, but what you will.'

37 Then he returned to his disciples and found them sleeping. 'Simon,' he said to Peter, 'are you asleep? Could you not keep watch for one hour?

38 Watch and pray so that you will not fall into temptation. The spirit is willing, but the body is weak.'

39 Once more he went away and prayed the same thing.

40 When he came back, he again found them sleeping, because their eyes were heavy. They did not know what to say to him.

41 Returning the third time, he said to them, 'Are you still sleeping and resting? Enough! The hour has come. Look, the Son of Man is betrayed into the hands of sinners.

42 Rise! Let us go! Here comes my betrayer!'

Mark's version of the events in Gethsemane is remarkably similar to Matthew's. Even the surrounding context is the same. Prior to his agony in the Garden Jesus institutes the Lord's Supper as a covenant ceremony, declaring as the wine is drunk, 'This is my blood of the covenant, which is poured out for many' (14.24). He also cites the prophecy, 'I will strike the shepherd, and the sheep will be scattered' (14.27; Zech. 13.7), and predicts that Peter will disown him three times

(14.30). Again, as in Matthew, Jesus' prayers in Gethsemane are immediately followed by his arrest (14.43-52).

Not only is the context virtually identical in each case, so is the account itself. Variations between the two versions are strictly minor. In recording Jesus' prayer Mark adds a characteristically Aramaic touch by noting that Jesus addresses his Father as 'Abba' (14.36). 'The two sons of Zebedee' (Mt. 26.37) are identified as 'James and John' (14.33). Peter is singled out for special castigation, 'Simon, are you asleep?' (14.37), and when Jesus returns to the slumbering trio for the third time Mark candidly adds that 'they did not know what to say to him' (14.40). Perhaps the most significant variation from Matthew is Mark's addition to Jesus' prayer 'that if possible the hour might pass from him' (14.35). Thus to the metaphor of the cup Mark adds that of the hour. It is the hour that commences with Jesus' betrayal (14.41; Mt. 26.45). Luke's description is more graphic. At his arrest Jesus tells his opponents, 'This is your hour – when darkness reigns' (Lk. 22.53). It was from this hour of darkness, as well as from the cup of God's wrath and judgement, that the Markan Jesus prayed to be spared.

Within this context of general concord between Matthew and Mark, Jesus' emotions are typical of the vast overlap and minor differences that characterize the two accounts. The only difference is that whereas Matthew notes that Jesus 'began to be *sorrowful* and troubled' (Mt. 26.37), Mark increases the volume as it were by observing that 'he began to be *deeply distressed* and troubled' (14.33). Mark definitely uses the stronger expression of the two. The Greek verb which the NIV translates 'to be deeply distressed' is *ekthambeomai*. It is found four times in Mark and nowhere else in canonical biblical literature.[134] But even within Mark it allows for a range of meanings. When the people saw Jesus after he had come down from the Mount of Transfiguration, 'they *were overwhelmed with wonder* and ran to greet him' (9.15). On Easter morning when Mary Magdalene, Mary the mother of James, and Salome entered Jesus' tomb, 'they saw a young man dressed in a white robe sitting on the right side, and *they were alarmed*' (16.5). The young man tries to reassure them. '*Don't be alarmed*,' he says. 'You are looking for Jesus the Nazarene, who was crucified. He has risen!' (16.6). But even this most joyful news does little to reassure them. They flee from the tomb trembling, bewildered and afraid (16.8).

With such a variety of meanings spread over just a few examples it is not easy to pinpoint the exact sense in which *ekthambeomai* is used in Gethsemane. What precisely was Jesus feeling soon after he had entered the Garden? In an effort to do justice to all four examples of the verb in Mark, Bauer's dictionary defines its meaning as 'to be moved to a relatively intense emotional state because of someth[ing] causing great surprise or perplexity'.[135] In Mark this 'relatively intense emotional state' comes to expression in the crowd's excitement (9.15), Jesus' distress (14.33) and the women's alarm (16.5-6). In Gethsemane Jesus more closely resembles the alarmed women than the excited crowd. He too is

---

134   It is used once in the Apocrypha (Sir. 30.9), in the active voice, of spoiled children who 'shock' (NEB) or 'terrorize' (NRSV). All the occurrences in Mark are in the passive voice.

135   BDAG, p. 303.

overwhelmed and perplexed, bewildered and afraid. France explains that in Mark *ekthambeomai* is 'a particularly strong term for people's surprise or shock on seeing something remarkable and unexpected . . . the verb contains an element of fear. Jesus' "shock" here, however, is not caused by an event already witnessed, but by the prospect of what is to follow.'[136] So once again we have an instance where Jesus' emotion is driven by his foreknowledge of what lies ahead. But in anticipation of the dreaded cup and dark hour that lie before him, perhaps 'shock' is too tame a word to express Jesus' overpowering emotion. Perhaps it would be truer to say that 'Jesus is in the grip of a shuddering horror as he faces the dreadful prospect before him.'[137]

The reason for Jesus' horror in Gethsemane is well captured by Lane's comments:

> The dreadful sorrow and anxiety, then, out of which the prayer for the passing of the cup springs, is not an expression of fear before a dark destiny, nor a shrinking from the prospect of physical suffering and death. It is rather the horror of the one who lives wholly for the Father at the prospect of the alienation from God which is entailed in the judgment upon sin which Jesus assumes. The horror thus anticipates the cry of dereliction in Ch. 15:34. Jesus came to be with the Father for an interlude before his betrayal, but found hell rather than heaven opened before him, and he staggered.[138]

If anything, Mark's depiction of Jesus in Gethsemane is even more poignant than Matthew's. He is let down not only by his inner circle of friends, but especially by Simon Peter, the one who had declared his messiahship (8.29) and had vowed to stay loyal (14.29). He prays not only for the cup to be taken away, but also for the hour to pass him by. Foreseeing what lies before him, Jesus begins not so much to be 'sorrowful' as 'deeply distressed'. This deep distress is a shuddering horror at what is about to transpire. In Mark the cross casts a deep and black shadow over Gethsemane.

---

136 France, *Mark*, p. 582.

137 Garland, *Mark*, p. 539.

138 Lane, *Mark*, p. 516; cf. the similar explanation by Klaas Schilder, *The Schilder Trilogy: Christ in His Suffering* (trans. Henry Zylstra; Grand Rapids, MI: Baker, 1979), p. 296: 'Christ's *task* differs from that of any other human being. His task is to suffer the *penalty* sin has deserved. Hence it is part of His calling to quail in anguish before our God . . . *One would need to have been in hell for some time* in order to understand what it is that is tearing Jesus apart in the garden' (italics his). Lane and Schilder have both seen more than Karen E. Smith, 'Mark 14:32-42', *RevExp* 88 (1991), p. 435, whose explanation of Jesus' prayer for the removal of the cup is insightful, but does not go far enough: '. . . this prayer was not grounded in fear of death, but perhaps the crushing sorrow of Jesus was over the loss of relationship. Perhaps the worst part of the cup of suffering was that he faced isolation, aloneness, and forsakenness.' What this explanation fails to account for is the reason for this loss of relationship.

2.8.2 THE CROSS (15.33-41)

33   At the sixth hour darkness came over the whole land until the ninth hour.
34   And at the ninth hour Jesus cried out in a loud voice, '*Eloi, Eloi, lama sabachthani?*' – which means, '*My God, my God, why have you forsaken me?*'
35   When some of those standing near heard this, they said, 'Listen, he's calling Elijah.'
36   One man ran, filled a sponge with wine vinegar, put it on a stick, and offered it to Jesus to drink.' Now leave him alone. Let's see if Elijah comes to take him down,' he said.
37   With a loud cry, Jesus breathed his last.
38   The curtain of the temple was torn in two from top to bottom.
39   And when the centurion, who stood there in front of Jesus, heard his cry and saw how he died, he said, 'Surely this man was the Son of God!'
40   Some women were watching from a distance. Among them were Mary Magdalene, Mary the mother of James the younger and of Joses, and Salome.
41   In Galilee these women had followed him and cared for his needs. Many other women who had come up with him to Jerusalem were also there.

Like Matthew, Mark has carefully prepared the ground for Jesus' cry of dereliction by permeating his crucifixion account with allusions to Psalm 22. When they had crucified him, the soldiers divided up Jesus' clothes and 'cast lots to see what each would get' (15.24), a humiliation also suffered by his forefather David (Ps. 22.18). Like the Psalmist Jesus is also mocked and insulted by the passers-by who shake their heads at him (15.29; Ps. 22.7). So when he utters his ghastly cry, 'My God, my God, why have you forsaken me?' the reader familiar with the Psalter will appreciate the appropriateness of these anguished words.

Mark's account of the death of Jesus resembles Matthew's in all the important details except that there is no reference to the earth being shaken, the rocks being split, the tombs being broken open and many dead saints being raised to life (Mt. 27.51-53). These acts of God are all unique to Matthew, and Mark is prepared to leave them to one side. Mark does, however, record other acts of God which are sufficient to provide a dramatic context for the death of Jesus. The cry of dereliction is uttered at the end of the three hours of darkness that God had brought upon the land (15.33) and prior to the temple curtain being torn in two from top to bottom (15.38). The setting is therefore one of divine judgement. All these major features are shared by these two Evangelists. The differences lie in the details.

The most intriguing and difficult difference in detail between Matthew and Mark lies in the original wording of Jesus' cry of dereliction. After six hours on the cross – three of them in pitch blackness – did Jesus cry '*Eli, Eli*, lama sabachthani?' or '*Eloi, Eloi*, lama sabachthani?'? Although the manuscript tradition is confusing, it would seem that Matthew originally wrote '*Eli, Eli*' and Mark '*Eloi*,

Eloi.'[139] Although some English translations (such as the NIV) try to harmonize the two versions, most are prepared to live with the discrepancy.[140] From this it could be concluded that while in Mark the entire saying represents an Aramaic original, the Matthaean parallel is partly Hebrew ('Eli, Eli') and partly Aramaic ('lama sabachtani').[141] In many ways this is an attractive solution as bilinguals will often switch languages when they are under emotional stress.[142] However, by the time of Jesus 'Eli' ('my God') may have been adopted into Aramaic as a Hebrew loan-word, in much the same way that we use 'Yahweh' in English today. In fact the Aramaic Targum of the Psalms uses 'Eli' in its exposition of Psalm 22.1.[143] Therefore a strong case can probably be made that both Matthew and Mark intended to reproduce Jesus' saying in Aramaic which was Jesus' mother tongue as well as the language he used to expound Scripture.[144]

If both Matthew and Mark intended to reproduce Jesus' question in Aramaic, this still leaves the nagging question as to why they seem to have reproduced Jesus' words differently. Why does Matthew have 'Eli, Eli' and Mark 'Eloi, Eloi'? Is the discrepancy simply best left for what it is or is some kind of resolution possible? There are two plausible ways of approaching the problem, which need not necessarily be mutually exclusive.

First, it needs to be remembered that Jesus is crying out in extreme agony. It is noteworthy that even after six excruciating hours of pain and torment on the cross Jesus succeeds in raising a loud cry both here and just before he breathes his last (v. 37). Nevertheless it should not be imagined that, just because his cry is loud, his words will be enunciated distinctly. In these circumstances his language

---

139   Metzger, *Textual Commentary*, p. 58, 100. 'Eli, Eli' conforms to the Hebrew text of Ps. 22.1, while 'Eloi, Eloi' appears to be the rendering of an Aramaic original in Greek script.

140   Thus ESV, GNB, Holman, JB, KJV, Knox, NASB, NJB, NKJV, NRSV, RSV, RV. The major Dutch and French translations as well as the Latin Vulgate and Zwingli's German translation also leave the passages unharmonized. Some translations harmonize in the direction of 'Eli, Eli' (e.g. LB, MLB, NEB), while the NIV seems to be alone in harmonizing in the direction of 'Eloi, Eloi.' Luther's German translation reads 'Eli, Eli, lama asabthani?' in both cases, thereby harmonizing both Matthew and Mark with the Hebrew of Ps. 22.2.

141   Metzger, *Textual Commentary*, p. 100.

142   François Grosjean, *Life with Two Languages* (Cambridge, Mass.: Harvard University Press, 1982), p. 275: 'Bilinguals also report switching from one language to the other when they are very tired, angry, or excited. They may revert to their mother tongue or to whatever language they usually express their emotions in. Stress may also cause more interference, problems in finding the appropriate words, and unintentional switching.'

143   See *Biblia Rabbinica: A Reprint of the 1525 Venice Edition Edited by Jacob Ben Hayim Ibn Adoniya* (Jerusalem: Makor, 1972), p. 20. Given that very little is known of the textual history of the targum to the Psalms, it would be rash to conclude that the reading in this edition is the same as that familiar to Jesus and his hearers. Nevertheless, it would probably be fair to say that the Aramaic of the time would have been influenced by Hebrew especially where biblical portions are concerned.

144   France, *Mark*, p. 652. According to John McRay, *Archaeology and the New Testament* (Grand Rapids, MI: Baker, 1991), p. 375, the discovery that some Aramaic texts used the word *El* for God 'means that the words . . . which Jesus spoke on the cross (Matt. 27:46), were not part Hebrew and part Aramaic, but all Aramaic.'

is going to be laboured and anguished rather than clear as a bell. One bystander might hear 'Eli, Eli' and another 'Eloi, Eloi'. That there was some misunderstanding is evidenced by the fact that some of the bystanders immediately respond by saying, 'He's calling Elijah' (15.35; Mt. 27.47). As it is safe to assume that this comment came from Aramaic speaking Jews rather than from the Roman soldiers, then even those who understood Jesus' native language could not make out precisely what he was saying. The slight linguistic discrepancy between Matthew and Mark does therefore not detract from but rather adds to the authenticity of their accounts. They give every indication of being based on ear-witness reports.

Secondly, both Matthew and Mark are attempting to transliterate an Aramaic saying into Greek script.[145] This was never going to be easy as the Greek script is unable to render the exact Aramaic pronunciation. Moreover, Greek is not very consistent in rendering Aramaic/Hebrew letters.[146] The original Aramaic must have sounded very much like: 'Elahi, Elahi, lema šavaqtani?' The attentive reader will realize that, because of the limitations of the Greek script, 'Eli' and 'Eloi' are both equally imperfect attempts to render the Aramaic original. As anyone familiar with languages using different scripts will appreciate, transliteration has never been an exact science but a literary art fraught with inconsistencies. Neither Matthew nor Mark is therefore misquoting Jesus. Both are attempting to use the Greek script for a purpose for which it was never intended – to capture some of the last words of a dying man whose native language was Aramaic.

In Mark's Gospel the cry of dereliction is Jesus' only recorded utterance from the cross. In the trial scenes Mark has been equally sparse in recording the words of Jesus. Before the Sanhedrin the only question Jesus answers is that of the high priest, 'Are you the Christ, the Son of the Blessed One?' (14.61). He also answers just one question before Pilate, 'Are you the King of the Jews?' (15.2). Both questions have to do with his identity. The first question he answers with ringing affirmation in words that resonate with overtones of divinity – the emphatic 'I am' (14.62; cf. Exod. 3.14). His answer to Pilate is far more oblique and sounds almost coy, 'So you say' (15.2 TEV). It is as though Jesus is saying, 'Yes, I am the King of the Jews, but not in the way you think.'

Through the high priest's and Pilate's questions Mark is bringing the reader back to the issue of Jesus' identity, the note on which his Gospel began. There Jesus was identified as the Christ and the Son of God with whom God is well pleased (1.1, 11). But with the authorities' questions regarding Jesus' identity Mark is also looking forward. He wants his readers to see the closest possible link between Jesus' three sole utterances before the Sanhedrin, before Pilate and from the cross. There is a strong connection between his affirmations of his identity as the Christ, the Son of God and the King on the one hand and his

---

145 For the contents of this paragraph I am indebted to personal correspondence received on 2 October 1995 from Dr Pieter van Huyssteen, formerly of the Classics and Ancient History department at the University of Auckland, and currently serving as an ordained minister of the Reformed Churches of New Zealand.

146 As an example of such inconsistency van Huyssteen gives the letter *qof* which the Greek transliterates as a *kappa* in 'Corban' (Mk 7.11) and as a *chi* in 'sabachthani' (Mk 15.34).

cry of dereliction on the other. It is precisely on the cross that he reveals his true identity. He is both the suffering Messiah and the Servant-King. Very fittingly therefore in the moment of his direst extremity he is quoting the words of a king (Ps. 22.1). In the truest sense it is on the cross that Jesus reveals himself to be the very one that Mark (1.1), John the Baptist (1.7-8) and even God himself (1.11) have declared him to be.

Validation for Jesus' claims comes from a most unexpected quarter. It is when the centurion saw how Jesus died that he makes his memorable confession, 'Surely this man was the Son of God' (15.39). It is at this point in Mark's narrative that his story reaches its climax. When this gruff, hardened Roman centurion recognizes Jesus' true identity the narrative reaches its resolution. This Gentile is the first human being to see Jesus as God sees him – as the Son of God (1.11; 9.7). 'That a Roman, for whom crucifixion was an unmentionable obscenity, declares a crucified Jew to be the Son of God is astonishing. Romans only applied that title to the Roman emperor, who was associated with power and triumph. But this soldier applies the title to Jesus – a poor, humiliated, crucified man.'[147] This represents an astounding reversal in values. The centurion sees what the disciples have not yet seen. He also asserts the claim that the Sanhedrin had so abjectly repudiated, the claim that Jesus is God's Son. Therefore 'the centurion's acclamation becomes a vindication of Jesus' claim'.[148] The story has reached both its greatest climax and deepest paradox. The one forsaken by God was the very Son of God.

Conclusion

All of Mark's major themes converge and culminate at the cross. There the suffering Servant suffers the most and the 'man of sorrows' is subjected to sorrow upon sorrow. But in Mark's scheme of things it is also on the cross that the King is enthroned and that his kingdom comes. It is also there that the divine Warrior achieves his greatest victory.

Mark's presentation of Jesus' emotions also coheres most convincingly in the light of the cross. It is on the cross and during its immediate prelude in Gethsemane that Jesus experiences his most intense emotions (14.33-34; 15.34). It is then that he conforms most closely to the 'man of sorrows' who was 'familiar with suffering' (Isa. 53.3). But in Mark his sorrows are not confined to the Passion. The conflict with his opponents that finds its resolution only in his death becomes mortal as early as 3.6. The hardness of heart that lies behind the Pharisees' plot deeply distresses Jesus (3.5). Their later request for a sign fills him with dismay (8.12). Even in his own hometown there are early indications of his ultimate rejection, a reaction at which Jesus is genuinely amazed (6.6). His

---

147 Barnett, *The Servant King*, p. 298.
148 Jack D. Kingsbury, *Conflict in Mark: Jesus, Authorities, Disciples* (Minneapolis: Fortress, 1989), p. 54.

sigh as he heals the deaf-mute (7.34) can best be understood as an expression of sorrowing but hopeful sympathy for the man's plight. Emotionally this sigh is not far removed from the compassion that he shows for the needy (1.41; 6.34; 8.2; 9.22). In these acts of compassion, however, we no longer see so much the man of sorrows as the God of Isaiah's New Exodus who has come to restore his people. At the same time there are also traces of the Yahweh–Warrior figure who gets angry with the defiant (1.43) and stubborn (3.5), and becomes indignant with his own disciples (10.14). But even this Warrior has a gentler side, reaching out in tough love to an earnest seeker for eternal life (10.21).

Mark's configuration of Jesus' emotions is decidedly complex, but then so is his overall presentation of Jesus. The messianic role of the Davidic King from the Psalms is overlaid with features of Isaiah's suffering Servant who in turn is the Yahweh–Warrior figure. These intertwining roles are all played out in Jesus' emotions. The result is a finely nuanced and carefully sketched portrait of Jesus. It is the most emotionally detailed picture of Jesus to be found anywhere in Scripture.

CHAPTER 3

The Sympathetic Son:
Jesus' Emotions in Luke's Gospel

Although Luke is the longest Gospel,[1] it has the fewest references to Jesus' emotions. This is somewhat surprising because Luke mentions the emotions of others more often than each of the other Gospels.[2] It is not that Luke has no interest in emotions; he simply records fewer emotions of Jesus. The reason for this is not easy to ascertain, but it could be a consequence of the way he writes history (1.1-4). By his own admission Luke was not an eyewitness but 'carefully investigated everything' (1.3), drawing on both oral and written sources (1.1-2). Perhaps there is more distance between Luke and the events he records than is the case in the other traditions, although one would have expected that distance to apply equally to the emotions of others as to those of Jesus. Whatever the reason for his reserve on this score, Luke has nevertheless left us with a valuable legacy of insights into Jesus' emotions.

As was the case with Matthew and Mark, Luke refers to the emotions of Jesus across all the major sections of his Gospel. In the Galilee section (4.14–9.17) Jesus is amazed at the centurion in Capernaum (7.9) and his heart goes out in compassion to the widow of Nain (7.13). On the journey (9.18–19.27) he displays two sharply contrasting emotions. He is full of joy on the return of the seventy-two from their mission (10.21), but is distressed at the prospect of his own suffering and death, the baptism he is to undergo (12.50). In the Jerusalem section (19.28–24.53) the only certain reference to an emotion of Jesus is at the beginning. As he approached the city he wept over it (19.41). The other emotion

---

1 In the Greek text, according to the Gramcord program, Luke has 19,496 words, Matthew 18,363, John 15,675, and Mark 11,313. (The Gramcord Grammatical Concordance System is based on the 26th edition of the Nestle-Aland *Novum Testamentum Graece* [Stuttgart: Deutsche Bibelgesellschaft, 1979]).

2 Luke has eighty-six such references, John seventy-seven, Mark fifty-one, and Matthew forty-seven.

that Luke records in Jerusalem is Jesus' anguish in Gethsemane (22.44), but the reference is found in verses that are textually doubtful.[3] This problem will need to be carefully considered. Did Luke actually portray Jesus in anguish or is this a later scribal addition to the text?

Luke's selection of emotions that he attributes to Jesus may be small, but it is both varied and largely unique to his Gospel. Only Jesus' amazement at the centurion is recorded elsewhere (Mt. 8.10). For its small size the wide range of the emotions Luke has selected is impressive. Amazement, compassion, joy, distress and weeping (and possibly anguish as well) capture both the highs and lows of Jesus' emotions. There is a kaleidoscope of emotional colour that reaches from the very bright to the very dark. As the sympathetic Son, Luke's Jesus feels intensely. The mountains are high and the valleys are deep.

3.1 *Luke's Presentation of Jesus*

A Gospel's initial observations about Jesus sketch the outline for the portrait that the Evangelist is about to draw. In the case of Matthew and Mark these were editorial comments made in their opening verses. For Matthew it is crucial that the reader understands Jesus to be the son of David and the son of Abraham, and that he therefore came specifically to fulfill the Abrahamic and Davidic covenants. At the very outset Mark informs his readers that Jesus is the Christ and the Son of God. In the course of his narrative Mark fills both these titles with distinctive meanings, especially through the climactic confessions of Peter and the centurion (Mk 8.29; 15.39). Hence Luke's first comments about Jesus can also be expected to be foundational for his Gospel, although in his case the scenery is somewhat different. His initial comments will prove determinative not only for his Gospel, the first volume of his two-volume work, but also for his second volume, the book of Acts. Another difference is that Luke keeps his readers waiting for almost half a chapter before he says anything about Jesus. Even then the opening words about Jesus are not by way of editorial comment but come from the mouth of the angel Gabriel. He seeks to calm a fearful and greatly troubled Mary with a joyful but solemn announcement (1.30-35):

> 30 'Do not be afraid, Mary, you have found favour with God.
> 31 You will be with child and give birth to a son, and you are to give him the name Jesus.
> 32 He will be great and will be called the Son of the Most High. The Lord God will give him the throne of his father David,
> 33 and he will reign over the house of Jacob for ever; his kingdom will never end.'
> 34 'How will this be,' Mary asked the angel, 'since I am a virgin?'

---

3   In a footnote the NIV cautions: 'Some early manuscripts do not have verses 43 and 44.'

³⁵ The angel answered, 'The Holy Spirit will come upon you, and the power of the Most High will overshadow you. So the holy one to be born will be called the Son of God.'

This angelic annunciation has much to say about the person and status of Jesus. Three features stand out.

The very first comments about Jesus in Luke are Gabriel's words to Mary in v. 31, 'You will be with child and give birth to a son, and you are to give him the name Jesus.' The point to note here is that Jesus is Mary's son. His true humanity is clearly implied by this statement. He is given an ordinary first-century Jewish name. Unlike Matthew, Luke does not dwell on the etymology of the name (cf. Mt. 1.21). Yet Luke cannot have been unaware of the popular etymological understanding of the name 'Jesus' as meaning 'Saviour'. Luke has more references to 'Saviour' and 'salvation' than the other Gospels combined (1.47, 69, 71, 77; 2.11, 30; 3.6; 19.9) and he maintains this theme throughout Acts (4.12; 5.31; 7.25; 13.23, 26, 47; 16.17; 27.34; 28.28). While the meaning of the name is not immediately spelled out, its significance is developed over the course of the entire work.

The second point the angel makes is that Jesus will not only be the son of Mary but also 'the Son of the Most High' (v. 32) and 'the Son of God' (v. 35). This will happen, says Gabriel to Mary, when 'the Holy Spirit will come upon you, and the power of the Most High will overshadow you' (v. 35). The angel speaks with an air of reverent reserve, but the implication is clear. The Holy Spirit will enable Mary to become pregnant even though she is a virgin. Thus in a very real sense Jesus is both the son of Mary and the Son of God.[4] The angel's declaration proclaims not only his humanity but also his divinity. The opening sentence of the angel's answer to Mary in v. 35 is held together by synonymous parallelism. 'The Holy Spirit will come upon you' is synonymous with 'the power of the Most High will overshadow you.' Later a cloud will overshadow those present at the Transfiguration (9.7) and the Holy Spirit will come upon the apostles at Pentecost (Acts 1.8). The imagery indicates both the protection and presence of God (cf. Exod. 40.34-35; Pss. 91.4; 140.7).[5] It is by virtue of the Holy Spirit's coming upon and overshadowing Mary that the holy child to be born to her 'will be called the Son of God' (v. 35b).

Thirdly, Gabriel not only identifies Jesus as the son of Mary and the Son of God, he is also the son of David. 'The Lord God will give him the throne of his father David, and he will reign over the house of Jacob forever; and his kingdom will never end' (vv. 32b-33).[6] This statement obviously draws its inspiration from

---

4   Cf. I. Howard Marshall, *Commentary on Luke: A Commentary on the Greek Text* (NIGTC; Exeter: Paternoster, 1978), p. 68: 'there is reason to suppose that more than a merely adoptive relationship is being set forth. The mention of divine sonship *before* Davidic messiahship suggests that the latter is grounded in the former and should be interpreted in terms of it.'

5   See Darrell L. Bock, *Luke* (BECNT; Grand Rapids, MI: Baker, 1994), p. 122.

6   Bock, *Luke*, p. 115 comments: 'Luke will make much of Davidic descent in this section. The house of David is mentioned in 1:69, the city of David and his house in 2:11. Luke's genealogy

the terms of the Davidic covenant. God had promised not only to establish the kingdom of David's offspring, but also to 'establish the throne of his kingdom forever' (2 Sam. 7.12-13). God's covenant with David meant that he would be blessed with an everlasting succession, an ongoing dynasty and an eternal throne. 'Your house and your kingdom will endure forever before me; your throne will be established forever' (2 Sam. 7.16). The wording of the Davidic covenant in 1 Chronicles takes matters a step further. Whereas in 2 Samuel, David is promised a succession of kings, in 1 Chronicles the emphasis falls not so much on a succession as on one particular successor: 'I will set him over my house and my kingdom forever; his throne will be established forever' (1 Chron. 17.14). As 1 Chronicles is post-exilic, Solomon is long dead. Now the focus falls on a future king.

By the time 1 Chronicles was written this individual focus had already been articulated by Isaiah. He foresaw the reign of a future Davidic king who had both the titles and the attributes of deity: 'For to us a child is born, to us a son is given, and the government will be on his shoulders. And he will be called Wonderful Counsellor, Mighty God, Everlasting Father, Prince of Peace. Of the increase of his government and of peace there will be *no end*. He will reign on *David's throne* and over *his kingdom*, establishing it and upholding it with justice and righteousness from that time on and *forever*' (Isa. 9.6-7 [author's italics]). In the same vein Gabriel speaks of Jesus being given David's throne (1.32), reigning forever and having a kingdom that will never end (1.33).[7] Isaiah further describes the coming Davidic king as the Branch from the stump of Jesse upon whom 'the Spirit of the Lord will rest' (Isa. 11.1-2). Again there would seem to be echoes of this prophecy in the angel's answer to Mary (1.35). The promised Davidic king will be endowed with the Spirit from his mother's womb (cf. 1.15).

Jesus' Davidic origins remain a dominant feature throughout Luke and Acts. He was born in the town of David (2.11). He is hailed as the son of David (18.38-39). He silences his religious opponents with a little theological brain-teaser about David's son also being David's Lord (20.41-44). The Davidic theme continues almost as strongly in Acts. In their first recorded sermons Peter and Paul both quote Psalms of David (Acts 2.25, 29, 34; 13.35-36). They cite David to show that through his resurrection and ascension Jesus is the eternal Davidic king. Through the apostolic proclamation of Jesus' resurrection beginning from Jerusalem (24.46-47) his kingdom expands not only throughout Judea and Samaria, but eventually reaches the ends of the earth (Acts 1.8). This is how 'David's fallen tent' is rebuilt (Acts 15.16) and how God takes 'from the Gentiles a people for himself' (Acts 15.14). The restored Davidic kingdom has Jews, Samaritans and Gentiles as its subjects.

So in Luke and Acts Jesus is the divine Son and the Davidic king, and he fulfils

---

goes through David in 3:31. Jesus' regal Davidic connection is the basic Christological starting point for Luke's presentation of the person of Jesus.'

7 Cf. Joseph A. Fitzmyer, *The Gospel According to Luke: Introduction, Translation and Notes* (AB 28; New York: Doubleday, 1981), p. 348: 'Possibly Luke alludes here to Isa. 9:6 (LXX) or to Dan 7:14, where promise of an everlasting kingdom is made. The endless character of this kingship is thus one of the qualities of the messianic kingdom.'

both roles by being the Saviour – the Saviour of Jews, Samaritans and Gentiles. Matthew ends on a mountain in Galilee with Jesus giving the Great Commission. At the close of Matthew's Gospel Jesus the son of David stands poised to take over the world. Luke–Acts records some of his early conquests. The story ends with the gospel in Rome, the heart of the empire. In both Matthew and Luke Jesus is portrayed as the Davidic king. A major difference is that in Luke–Acts his kingdom is further advanced than in Matthew. In Matthew the King's order has been given. In Acts the order is being carried out and vast territories have already been won. His royal triumph has begun.

3.2 *Amazement (7.1-10)*

1 When Jesus had finished saying all this in the hearing of the people, he entered Capernaum.
2 There a centurion's servant, whom his master valued highly, was sick and about to die.
3 The centurion heard of Jesus and sent some elders of the Jews to him, asking him to come and heal his servant.
4 When they came to Jesus, they pleaded earnestly with him, 'This man deserves to have you do this,
5 because he loves our nation and has built our synagogue.'
6 So Jesus went with them. He was not far from the house when the centurion sent friends to say to him: 'Lord, don't trouble yourself, for I do not deserve to have you come under my roof.
7 That is why I did not even consider myself worthy to come to you. But say the word, and my servant will be healed.
8 For I myself am a man under authority, with soldiers under me. I tell this one, 'Go', and he goes; and that one, 'Come', and he comes. I say to my servant, 'Do this', and he does it.'
9 When Jesus heard this, *he was amazed* at him, and turning to the crowd following him, he said, 'I tell you, I have not found such great faith even in Israel.'
10 Then the men who had been sent returned to the house and found the servant well.

It is again noteworthy that, as was the case with Matthew, the first recorded emotion of Jesus in Luke's Gospel is amazement. Matthew is the Jewish Gospel and Luke the Gentile Gospel, and yet in spite of their differences both record surprise as the first emotion of Jesus. At the outset both Gospels have introduced him in the loftiest terms. For Matthew he is Immanuel and Luke calls him 'the Son of the Most High', but neither Gospel writer has the slightest hesitation to attribute to him the very human emotion of amazement. Throughout Luke this very human reaction is recorded no less than a dozen times, sometimes in response to the words and works of Jesus (4.22; 8.25; 9.43; 11.14, 38; 20.26; 24.12, 41), at other times in response to divinely inspired messages (2.18, 33), and at still other times for more mundane reasons (1.21, 63). Jesus' sense of amazement, wonder and surprise at the centurion's faith is therefore a delightful reminder that for all the divinity that has been ascribed to him Jesus is still the son of Mary, a human being who can be genuinely surprised.

For Matthew and Luke that surprise is expressed for the very same reason. This centurion, of all people, would appear to be the first to recognize Jesus' authority for what it is. He has profound insight into the identity of Jesus. What the angel Gabriel had said to Mary at the beginning about the greatness of Jesus is now recognized by the centurion. He may not have appreciated all that was implied in Jesus' divinity and messiahship, nor did he address him as 'son of David', but he recognized that Jesus had authority from God. He also knew that Jesus could heal his servant even from a distance.

So Matthew and Luke record the same emotion in the same context and for the same reason, but Luke gives more details, so that Jesus' surprise becomes all the more remarkable. Matthew has portrayed the centurion simply as a Gentile, as a raw recruit so to speak. He comes up to Jesus with his request, shows how modest he is and then compares his authority to that of Jesus. Matthew gives the impression that the centurion approached Jesus himself and that he spoke to him directly, but Luke fills out the story in several ways.[8]

First of all, Luke reminds us that the centurion sent some elders of the Jews to Jesus asking him to come and heal his servant. They are even prepared to put in a good word for him: 'This man deserves to have you do this, because he loves our nation and has built our synagogue' (7. 4-5). So this centurion is no raw recruit who has just been plucked from the darkness of paganism. He has

---

8   The differences between the two accounts have given rise to considerable scholarly debate. Robert A. J. Gagnon, 'Luke's Motives for Redaction in the Account of the Double Delegation in Luke 7:1-10', *NovT* 36 (1994), pp. 122–45, has argued that the double delegation of elders and friends who came to Jesus on the centurion's behalf was not part of a common source on which both Gospel accounts may have been dependent. Rather they were a Lukan embellishment added to address issues facing Luke's Christian community. This approach plays fast and loose with historical facts, depriving Luke's account of its credibility. On the other side of the debate stands the attempt at harmonization by Jack R. Shaffer, 'A Harmonization of Matt 8:5-13 and Luke 7:1-10', *MSJ* 17 (2006), pp. 35–50. Shaffer combines the two accounts in such a way that the Lukan delegations approach Jesus first. Then as Jesus nears his house the centurion experiences a change of heart, goes to Jesus and voices his request as per Matthew's account. The difficulty with this solution is that the wording of the centurion's request is virtually identical in both accounts (Mt. 8.8-9; Lk. 7.6-8). This necessitates an artificial reconstruction of the situation. Shaffer suggests that the centurion's friends learned his request off by heart and that later the centurion repeated the same request to Jesus. This is possible, but hardly plausible. Perhaps the answer lies somewhere between these two extremes. Matthew may simply have been using the common convention of having someone speak for himself even when he is using an intermediary. See D. A. Carson, 'Matthew', *The Expositor's Bible Commentary* (Grand Rapids, MI: Zondervan, 1984), p. 200; Craig Blomberg, *The Historical Reliability of the Gospels* (Downers Grove: Inter-Varsity Press, 1987), p. 134.

some redeeming features, none of which are mentioned by Matthew. He loves the Jewish people and has even built them a synagogue.

When Jesus is not far from the house, the centurion sends another delegation. This time he sends his friends to tell Jesus that he doesn't have to come under his roof. All he has to do is say the word and the servant will be healed. Then they tell Jesus what the centurion has asked them to say, comparing his authority to that of Jesus. When Jesus heard this, he was amazed at a centurion whom he had not even met, because he had not found such great faith, even in Israel. All of this makes Jesus' surprise in Luke even more remarkable than in Matthew. Even though Jesus had been told that this man loved the Jewish people and that he had built the local synagogue, he was still surprised. In Matthew Jesus' surprise is understandable. Of course he would not expect a Gentile centurion to comprehend anything of his messianic authority. Faith at any level would have been extraordinary. From Luke we learn that this man is not just any Gentile, nor is he just any centurion. He loves the Jewish people, built the local synagogue and has Jewish friends.

So why is Jesus still surprised? In spite of some of the spiritual advantages that he enjoys, the centurion's insight is exceptional. He seems to know more than he ought. Aware that Jesus has been commissioned by God, he recognizes Jesus' status. Just as he has been commissioned by the Roman military, Jesus has been commissioned by God. While from the scribes and Pharisees Jesus has been getting only questions and criticism (5.21; 6.2), in this foreigner he detects genuine faith and real spiritual insight. At this he is surprised. With a tone of amazement Jesus therefore declares: 'I tell you, I have not found such great faith, even in Israel' (7.9). It is the only statement that Jesus makes in Luke's version of the healing of the centurion's servant. Jesus credits the centurion with great faith. It is a sign of things to come. Later in Luke and Acts there will be more centurions and more Gentiles who will have this same kind of faith. Even at this early stage the Davidic kingdom as restored by Jesus is beginning to make inroads into the Gentile world, a development at which he is truly amazed.

3.3 *Compassion* (7.11-17)

11   Soon afterwards, Jesus went to a town called Nain, and his disciples and a large crowd went along with him.
12   As he approached the town gate, a dead person was being carried out – the only son of his mother, and she was a widow. And a large crowd from the town was with her.
13   When the Lord saw her, *he had compassion on her*[9] and he said, 'Don't cry.'

---

9   The NIV reads 'his heart went out to her.' For the sake of consistency the above translation of the verb *splanchnizomai* has been adopted (as in AV, RSV etc.; cf. Mk 9.22).

[14] Then he went up and touched the coffin, and those carrying it stood still. He said, 'Young man, I say to you, get up!'

[15] The dead man sat up and began to talk, and Jesus gave him back to his mother.

[16] They were all filled with awe and praised God. 'A great prophet has appeared among us,' they said. 'God has come to help his people.'

[17] This news about Jesus spread throughout Judea and the surrounding country.

After Jesus had healed the centurion's servant in the lakeside town of Capernaum, he made his way back into the hill country of Galilee. Some twenty-five miles from Capernaum he arrived in Nain, 'a mere village five miles southeast of Nazareth; situated on a hilly slope it had a gate and wall'.[10] As he approached the town gate with a huge entourage in tow Jesus was greeted by a sad and pathetic sight. The corpse of a dead man who was still quite young was being carried out of town. He was his mother's only son and she was a widow. It was a poignant situation as the woman was now all alone in the world. Nowadays a woman in her situation would probably be consigned to a life of loneliness, but in the first century her situation would have been much worse. Without a male protector and provider she must have been in difficulties. As Luke Johnson explains, 'Luke does not state the obvious consequence of a widow's losing an only son, which is that she would have no economic support.'[11] With few openings for a woman to earn a living, she would have been reduced to a life of poverty.

This widow must have had the sympathy of her townspeople. A large crowd was with her. 'The attendance of a crowd at a funeral is in keeping with Jewish custom, since it ranked as a work of love . . . Mourning was all the greater for an only child.'[12] As this whole procession is going out of the town, Jesus and his disciples with a large crowd following them was about to go in. At that moment of meeting just outside the gate of the village of Nain, with two crowds about to converge, Jesus saw this poor widow and sensed her plight. His heart went out to her and he was filled with compassion. It was the turning point of the story.[13] With deep sympathy for her grief he said to her: 'Don't cry!' From that moment the widow's life would never be the same again. Not only will Jesus restore her son to her, this miracle should also be seen as effecting the restoration of this woman within her community.[14] It should be noted that neither she nor any of the

---

10   Yohanan Aharoni and Michael Avi-Yonah, *The Macmillan Bible Atlas* (New York: Macmillan, rev. edn, 1977), p. 145.

11   Luke T. Johnson, *The Gospel of Luke* (Sacra Pagina; Collegeville, MN: The Liturgical Press, 1991), p. 118.

12   Marshall, *Luke*, p. 285.

13   Jesus' compassion comes at the point in the story where death and sorrow begin to be turned into life and joy. A similar feature can be observed in the parables of the Good Samaritan and the Prodigal Son. The compassion of the Samaritan (10.33) and that of the father (15.20) are central to each parable and mark the turning point in each case. Luke therefore handles his three occurrences of *splanchnizomai* with a sense of artistic consistency.

14   Thus Joel B. Green, *The Gospel of Luke* (NICNT; Grand Rapids, MI: Eerdmans, 1997), p. 290.

other mourners asked Jesus to do anything. There is no mention of any request or even of anyone's faith. The initiative belongs entirely to Jesus. His compassion is the sole driving force behind the miracle.[15] Before he performed the miracle, and in order to bring the funeral procession to a halt, Jesus touched the bier on which the young man's body lay wrapped in a shroud. This meant contracting ritual defilement, but – as in the case where he touched the leper (Mk 1.41) – human need again took precedence over ceremonial requirements.

Then Jesus addresses the corpse: 'Young man, I say to you, get up!' (7.14). The dead man sat up, began to talk and Jesus gave him back to his mother. It was a miracle driven by divine compassion. For the first time in his narrative Luke refers to Jesus as 'the Lord' (v. 13).[16] By raising a dead man Jesus does what only God can do. In the Old Testament there were also two only sons who had been raised from the dead. Elijah had raised the son of the widow of Zarephath (1 Kgs 17.17-24)[17] and Elisha had raised the Shunamite woman's son (2 Kgs 4.32-37),[18] but with a crucial difference. They had prayed fervently to God for the resuscitation of these boys. All Jesus had to do was say the word. He is therefore more than a prophet, since as the Son of the Most High he simply gives the order and the dead man obeys.

This story is unique to Luke and it is only here that compassion is attributed to Jesus in this Gospel. In this instance Jesus' compassion drives an even greater miracle than the miracles motivated by compassion in Matthew and Mark. The awe-struck crowd that witnessed the miracle seems to catch on when they say, 'God has come to help his people' (7.16; cf. 1.68). But the first part of their confession is inadequate, 'A great prophet has appeared among us.'[19] Jesus is more than a prophet. He is in a different league from Elijah and Elisha. They had raised the dead as well, but they had to pray to God, while all he had to do was say the word. They were prophets of God; he was the Son of God. God had indeed visited his people. No wonder the news about Jesus spread throughout

---

15 See Leon Morris, *The Gospel According to St. Luke: An Introduction and Commentary* (London: Inter-Varsity Press, 1974), p. 140.

16 Marshall, *Luke*, p. 285, 'The use of the term reflects the designation of Jesus in the early church as the one exalted by God to be the Lord (Acts 2:36; Rom. 1:4; Phil. 2:11), and indicates that already during his earthly ministry Jesus was exercising the functions of the Lord.' See also 7.19; 10.1, 39, 41; 11.39; 12.42; 13.15; 17.5, 6; 18.6; 19.8; 22.61; 24.34.

17 Thomas L. Brodie, 'Towards Unravelling Luke's Use of the Old Testament: Luke 7.11-17 as an *Imitatio* of 1 Kings 17:17-24', *NTS* 32 (1986), pp. 249–59, sees some major parallels between the two accounts: (a) the meeting with a widow at the town gate, (b) the death of the widow's only son, (c) the resuscitation of the son, (d) the expression 'he gave him to his mother', and (e) the acclamation of the miracle worker as a great prophet or true man of God.

18 See Craig A. Evans, 'Luke's Use of the Elijah/Elisha Narratives and the Ethic of Election', *JBL* 106 (1987), p. 79. Evans discusses Elijah/Elisha themes that surface particularly in 4.25-27, 7.11-17; 9.52-55, 61-62.

19 Cullmann, *Christology*, p. 30, offers a balanced assessment, 'Jesus is simply placed in the prophetic category, a category in which also others belonged. Still, a miracle like the one reported in this passage does show that the Spirit of God is now at work again in an especially powerful way, just as he was earlier at work in the prophets.'

Judea (the land of the Jews) and the surrounding country (probably indicating neighbouring Gentile lands). It was another hint of things to come, when Jesus' own resurrection would be proclaimed in Jerusalem, Judea, Samaria and to the ends of the earth (Acts 1.8).

3.4 *Joy (10.17-24)*

17 The seventy-two returned with joy and said, 'Lord, even the demons submit to us in your name.'
18 He replied, 'I saw Satan fall like lightning from heaven.
19 I have given you authority to trample on snakes and scorpions and to over-come all the power of the enemy; nothing will harm you.
20 However, do not rejoice that the spirits submit to you, but rejoice that your names are written in heaven.'
21 At that time Jesus, *full of joy* through the Holy Spirit, said, 'I praise you, Father, Lord of heaven and earth, because you have hidden these things from the wise and learned, and revealed them to little children. Yes, Father, for this was your good pleasure.
22 'All things have been committed to me by my Father. No-one knows who the Son is except the Father, and no-one knows who the Father is except the Son and those to whom the Son chooses to reveal him.'
23 Then he turned to his disciples and said privately, 'Blessed are the eyes that see what you see.
24 For I tell you that many prophets and kings wanted to see what you see but did not see it, and to hear what you hear but did not hear it.'

This is an absolutely delightful passage. Nowhere else do the Gospels portray Jesus as joyful as he is here. He is beaming and radiant, and bursting with joy. The context makes this rare expression of exuberance all the more remarkable. Luke's journey section (9.18–19.27) has already begun. The journey proper has been anticipated by two passion predictions. Following Peter's confession (9.20) Jesus spells out his coming suffering in telling detail (9.22) and later he reminds his disciples that 'the Son of Man is going to be betrayed into the hands of men' (9.44). Then, by way of an editorial comment, Luke adds that Jesus 'set his face' to go to Jerusalem (9.51 NRSV), 'a phrase which indicates firm resolve to do something unpleasant.'[20] Jesus is therefore fully cognizant of the fact that he is journeying towards his Passion. He knows that at his destination suffering, rejection, betrayal and death await him. Yet despite this grim prospect there is at least one occasion where Jesus can be described as 'full of joy' (10.21). But why should this be the case? Why does the sunshine of joy break through the dark clouds at this particular point?

---

20 I. Howard Marshall, *Luke: Historian and Theologian* (Downers Grove, IL: InterVarsity Press, 3rd edn, 1988), p. 150.

The word used to describe Jesus' fullness of joy is the rare verb *agalliaō*, which is found only in biblical and ecclesiastical Greek.[21] It means 'to be exceedingly joyful, *exult, be glad, overjoyed*'.[22] It is a 'joy which encompasses the whole person and radiates from the person.[23] As William Morrice explains, 'In the New Testament, as in the Septuagint, the Greek verb *agallian* and its cognate [related] noun signify joy of a religious kind. It is a joy that praises God on account of his mighty acts . . .'[24] Others who experienced this quality of joy were Mary (Lk. 1.47), Abraham (Jn 8.56), new believers (Acts 16.34), believers under persecution (1 Pet. 1.6, 8; 4.13), and the chorus of the redeemed (Rev. 19.7). What makes Jesus' expression of this kind of joy distinctive is that it is 'through the Holy Spirit'.[25] This means that Jesus' joy on this occasion cannot be understood without reference to his relationship with the Holy Spirit. In Luke this relationship is particularly well developed.

The implication of Gabriel's opening remarks about Jesus is that he will be conceived by the Holy Spirit (1.35). At Jesus' baptism the Holy Spirit descends on him (3.22) and John the Baptist declares that Jesus will baptize with the Holy Spirit (3.16). After his baptism Jesus is described as 'full of the Holy Spirit' (4.1) and it is the Spirit who leads him into the desert to be tempted by the devil (4.1-2). Having successfully weathered the storm of Satanic temptations, 'Jesus returned to Galilee in the power of the Spirit' (4.14). In Galilee his first port of call is his old hometown of Nazareth. In the local synagogue during a regular Sabbath service he declares his messianic manifesto. As the newly anointed Messiah he has a well defined agenda foretold by Isaiah that depends on the Spirit for its implementation: 'The Spirit of the Lord is on me, because he has anointed me to preach good news to the poor. He has sent me to proclaim freedom for the prisoners and recovery of sight to the blind, to release the oppressed, to proclaim the year of the Lord's favour' (4.18-19).

This statement occupies a pivotal position in Luke's narrative. Jesus was conceived by the Spirit, baptized with the Spirit and filled with the Spirit so that he might carry out this programme of preaching, proclamation, restoration and release. In the remainder of Luke this messianic agenda is accomplished by Jesus. In Acts the day of Pentecost parallels the baptism of Jesus in Luke. As the

---

21 There are ten other occurrences in the New Testament (Mt. 5.12; Lk. 1.47; Jn 5.35; 8.56; Acts 2.26; 16.34; 1 Pet. 1.6, 8; 4.13; Rev. 19.7).

22 BDAG, p. 4.

23 *EDNT* 1, p. 8.

24 William G. Morrice, *'Joy' in the New Testament* (Exeter: Paternoster, 1984), p. 21.

25 Literally the Greek reads '[in] the Holy Spirit.' The precise import of this phrase using [*en* with] the dative case is difficult to determine. According to Marshall, *Luke*, p. 433, 'The force is that Jesus is filled with joy and the Spirit before an inspired saying.' Bock, *Luke*, p. 1009, claims that 'Jesus' rejoicing is described as Spirit directed, thus underscoring its solemnity'. But perhaps in this case the simplest answer may well be the best. 'The one who causes the joy is given in the dat.' (BDAG, p. 4); cf. 1 Pet. 1.8. The Spirit therefore 'plays a role in producing the rejoicing . . . Through the Spirit, Jesus sees clearly how God's purposes are being worked out in Jesus' own ministry and all that extends that ministry': (John Nolland, *Luke* (WBC, vol. 35; Dallas: Word, 1989–93), p. 571).

Holy Spirit came upon Jesus at his baptism, so the Holy Spirit comes upon the apostles at Pentecost. Therefore the outworking of the Nazareth manifesto commences with the ministry of Jesus and is continued by the Spirit-filled church. What is so significant about the mission of the seventy-two in Lk. 10.1-24 is that it anticipates the mission of the church in Acts. Up to this point in Luke the messianic mission as stated in the synagogue at Nazareth has been carried out almost exclusively by Jesus himself. The mission of the twelve disciples to drive out demons, preach the kingdom and heal the sick (9.1-9) had been the only exception up to this point.

Now that messianic ministry had been expanded with the sending out of seventy-two fresh recruits. Going to every town and place where Jesus was about to go, they too healed the sick, proclaimed the kingdom and cast out demons (10.1, 9, 17-20). After their short-term mission, unable to contain their excitement, they report back to Jesus with joy, 'Lord, even the demons submit to us in your name' (10.17). Jesus agrees, but reminds them of an even greater reason for joy, 'Rejoice that your names are written in heaven' (10.20). They are running the very real danger of rejoicing too much in lesser joys. These disciples were rejoicing in their first successes against the powers of darkness, but Jesus needs to remind them that there were greater reasons for joy than exorcisms. They must not be intoxicated with their first flush of success. In the midst of their excitement he teaches them an important lesson. They need to keep their spiritual priorities straight. Greater than the joy of their recent kingdom victories must be the joy of their salvation.

So this passage is brimming with joy. It begins with the seventy-two who are bursting with excitement on returning from what was probably their first mission trip. Their joy must have been similar to that of church youth groups today returning from their first stint of mission work whether at home or abroad. They cannot stop speaking about their experiences. They cannot help themselves. Their emotions are contagious and soon an entire congregation may be caught up in the excitement. Is this the kind of joy that Jesus is experiencing? Is he simply sharing his disciples' excitement? Is he happy because they are happy? Although this is part of the picture, it would be an oversimplified explanation of Jesus' emotional state. Much more is involved.

First, Jesus' joy is far more intense and exuberant than that of his followers. They return 'with joy' (10.17) and 'rejoice' (10.20), but Jesus can be described as 'full of joy' (10.21). While Jesus and the seventy-two share the common denominator of joy, his joy is of a different class. Their joy is indicated by more common Greek words, the noun *chara* ('the experience of gladness') and the verb *chairō* ('to be in a state of happiness and well-being').[26] Both these words fall short of the sense of religious exuberance that Jesus is experiencing at this point. His disciples are happy, Jesus is thrilled. They are glad, he is overjoyed. They are excited, he is exuberant. He is a man on a mission, and now he is beginning to see that mission fulfilled. A task that is close to his heart is being carried out. Others have

---

26   See BDAG, pp. 1077, 1074 respectively.

caught his vision and are beginning to run with it. The mere thought of it gives him a deep sense of satisfaction.

Secondly, his joy in the Holy Spirit comes not just from the sense of a mission being accomplished. He had told his disciples to rejoice because their names were written in heaven. Then he goes on to reveal the reason for his own deepest joy: 'I praise you, Father, Lord of heaven and earth, because you have hidden these things from the wise and learned, and revealed them to little children. Yes, Father, for this was your good pleasure. All things have been committed to me by my Father. No one knows who the Son is except the Father, and no one knows who the Father is except the Son and those to whom the Son chooses to reveal him' (10.21-22).

So why is Jesus so rapturously delighted? Why this unparalleled joy at this point in time? Yes, it was because the mission of the seventy-two was so successful. The gospel had been received by the ordinary townspeople, by the men, women and children of the villages of Galilee. They were the 'little children' to whom the Father had revealed these things. Since they were the ones who received God's revelation rather than 'the wise and learned', they provide another example of Luke's pattern of reversal (1.51-53; 2.31; 6.20-26). Jesus rejoices in the topsy-turvy way God works. More than that, however, Jesus also had his counterpart to the disciples' joy that their names were inscribed in heaven. He rejoiced in the wonderfully intimate relationship that he had with the Father. In the space of just two verses (vv. 21-22) Jesus refers to God as 'Father' no fewer than five times and to himself as 'the Son' three times. The titles 'the Son of the Most High' (1.32) and 'the Son of God' (1.35), with which Gabriel introduced Jesus even before his conception, have now come to their own. Nowhere else in Luke's Gospel is the Father–Son relationship as developed as it is here.[27] In these verses 'we reach a christological peak in the Gospel of Luke'.[28] The focus is on the intimacy and the reciprocity of their relationship. There are depths to that relationship that no human being will ever fathom. There are dimensions to Jesus' person that we will never comprehend, no matter how thoroughly we examine the emotions of Jesus in the Gospels. Jesus has an exclusive and intimate relationship with the Father, and when he reflects on it he is full of joy in the Holy Spirit. It gives us a penetrating insight into the workings of the Trinity. Jesus rejoices in the Holy Spirit because he has such an intimate relationship with the Father. Here Luke offers a Trinitarian perspective comparable to that surrounding Jesus' conception and his baptism (1.35; 3.22).

Jesus' joy on this occasion can therefore be profitably explored at several levels. It is a deeply exuberant joy that springs from several sources. At its most basic level it shares in the gladness and excitement of the seventy-two at the success of their mission. There is a sense in which the happiness of these first-time missionaries rubs off on Jesus. But Jesus' joy far surpasses theirs. As Morrice

---

27 Cf. Morris, *Luke*, p. 186, 'Jesus calls Himself *the Son* in the Synoptic Gospels only here (together with the Matthaean parallel) and in Mark 13:32, though the expression is common in John.'

28 Green, *Luke*, p. 421.

explains, 'The reason for Christ's exultation of spirit was quite different from the motive behind the joy of the returned missionaries. It was not the success of the mission as such that moved him to exult. Rather it was the additional evidence provided of the method of revelation chosen by God that thrilled his heart.'[29] This remarkable outburst of joy 'was due to the fact that God had revealed divine mysteries to ordinary, common people. God had not reserved the revelation of his fatherhood for the educated religious intelligentsia.'[30] This explanation of Jesus' joy is sound as far as it goes, but it does not go nearly far enough. It takes in Jesus' prayer of praise in v. 21, but not his further declaration in v. 22. There he exults in his unique and exclusive relationship with the Father: 'No one knows who the Son is except the Father, and no one knows who the Father is except the Son.' Just as the disciples' highest joy is that their names are written in heaven (10.20), the pinnacle of Jesus' joy is his intimate relationship with the Father. For him this joy is the source of every other. This is divine joy at its most sublime.

Jesus' exultant joy in Lk. 10.21 is therefore the joy of the Messiah, the one supremely anointed by the Holy Spirit. But it is also the joy of the Son of the Most High, the one who has a unique relationship to the Father. These two, however, need not be contrasted nor even juxtaposed, as they are in fact one and the same. At his baptism Jesus was confirmed in his messianic identity by the Holy Spirit. He was also declared by the voice from heaven to be the beloved Son in whom the Father was well pleased. Jesus now reciprocates that good pleasure of the Father by being 'full of joy in the Holy Spirit'.

3.5 Distress (12.49-53)

49 'I have come to bring fire on the earth, and how I wish it were already kindled!

50 But I have a baptism to undergo, and *how distressed I am* until it is completed!

51 Do you think I came to bring peace on earth? No, I tell you, but division.

52 From now on there will be five in one family divided against each other, three against two and two against three.

53 They will be divided, father against son and son against father, mother against daughter and daughter against mother, mother-in-law against daughter-in-law and daughter-in-law against mother-in-law.'

There could hardly be a starker contrast than that between the two emotions that Luke attributes to Jesus in his journey section. From the heights of exultant joy Jesus seems to descend into the depths of great distress. On the surface of it this looks like a mood swing of gigantic proportions. The distress into which Jesus appears to have sunk therefore needs careful investigation. Even some

29 Morrice, 'Joy', p. 87.
30 Morrice, 'Joy', pp. 21–22.

preliminary research will soon reveal that not all translations, commentaries and lexicons are agreed that 'distress' is the best way to describe what Jesus is experiencing at this point. The reason behind this diversity of opinion is the bewildering array of meanings of the verb *sunechō*, which Luke uses here. This word is found a dozen times in the New Testament, seven of them in the passive voice (as here). The wide range of meanings within even these seven occurrences immediately highlights the problems confronting the translator. The passive voice of *sunechō* is used of the sick who are *afflicted* with an illness (Mt. 4.24; Lk. 4.38; Acts 28.8), the Gerasenes who were *gripped* with fear (Lk. 8.37), and of Paul either *devoting* himself to the word (Acts 18.5) or being *torn* (NIV) or *hard pressed* (NASB) between departing to be with Christ and remaining in the body (Phil. 1.23). Although the last example is most akin to the experience of Jesus, there is nothing that even comes close to the baptism that he has to undergo. So while these examples do much to emphasize the difficulty of the problem, they do little to solve it.

The complexity of the issue accounts for the variety among the English translations. While a number clearly favour distress as the emotion being felt by Jesus (ESV, JB, NASB, NIV, NKJV, TEV), others describe him as 'pent up' (LB), 'strained' (Phillips), 'constrained' (RSV) and 'straitened' (KJV). Still others offer further possibilities, 'What constraint/stress I am under' (NEB/NRSV) and 'How it consumes me' (Holman). Some of the commentators come up with even more suggestions. Fitzmyer, for example, suggests that, like Paul, Jesus is 'hard pressed',[31] while John Nolland challenges the general consensus by arguing that the language here is quite unemotional. Jesus is simply indicating that he is pre-occupied, a preoccupation that 'is reflected in 9:51 and the passion predictions'.[32]

The dictionaries also appreciate the complexity of the problem. According to Helmut Köster, Lk. 12.50 'causes the greatest difficulties in interpretation'.[33] The passive use of *sunechō* 'in a transferred sense with no indication of cause would be quite unique and very hard to explain'.[34] Having said that, Köster is still prepared to take issue with the customary translation, 'how troubled/pressed I am'. As an alternative he suggests the strong but unemotional declaration, 'How I am totally governed by this.'[35] Bauer, on the other hand, is quite content to offer a translation with clear emotional overtones, 'how great is my distress' or 'what vexation I must endure'.[36] Although it cannot be denied that on the journey to Jerusalem Jesus is preoccupied with his coming ordeal and even governed by it, by virtue of this very fact it is difficult to divest his statement of emotional content. It is precisely because he is so preoccupied and governed by what is about to transpire that he is distressed. While it might be argued that the passive of

---

31 Fitzmyer, *Luke*, p. 993.
32 Nolland, *Luke*, p. 709. The present context lies between the second and third passion predictions (9.44; 18.31-33).
33 *TDNT* 7, p. 884.
34 *TDNT* 7, p. 884.
35 *TDNT* 7, p. 884.
36 BDAG, p. 971.

sunechō is never used in an emotional sense, this argument overlooks a small but very significant body of evidence from the LXX. On three occasions *sunechō* in the passive voice describes the feelings of Job in his distress. He is '*gripped by fear*' (Job 3.24) and '*tormented* by the bitterness of my soul' (10.1). Most congenial for our purposes is the one occasion where Job gives no indication of the cause of his distress, whether it be fear or bitterness, 'I speak, though I am in anguish; I will open up the bitterness of my soul, though *I am in dire straits*' (7.11). Speaking in the synonymous parallelism of Hebrew poetry Job is equating his dire straits with his anguish. The LXX therefore has an unequivocal example of the passive of *sunechō* 'with no indication of cause' (*contra* Köster), which is also undeniably linked to an emotion. The traditional ascription of an emotion to Jesus in Lk. 12.50 is not without parallel in the LXX.

From the above discussion it would therefore be fair to conclude that the NIV translation 'how distressed I am' can be justified, albeit from a very small body of evidence. The emotional overtones of the expression cannot be eliminated. At the same time the context would also suggest that this is distress of a particular kind. Those who have argued that Jesus is preoccupied with his coming fate should not go unheard. It cannot be denied that on his journey to Jerusalem Jesus is governed by what lies before him. A. Kretzer is therefore correct in concluding that Lk. 12.50 brings to expression both Jesus' 'radical commitment to his calling . . . and his human distress and anxiety at the fate awaiting him'.[37]

Having established that Jesus is in fact experiencing the emotion of distress here, we still need to ask why he is distressed. What is the driving force behind it? What fuels this unique emotion? Although the above discussion has given a preliminary answer to these questions, a more definitive and detailed answer is difficult because of the enigmatic nature of the saying by which Jesus' distress is conveyed: 'I have come to bring fire on the earth, and how I wish it were already kindled! But I have a baptism to undergo, and how distressed I am until it is completed!' (12.49-50). The two statements that Jesus makes are undoubtedly parallel, but the question is whether this is an example of synonymous parallelism or of antithetical parallelism. In other words, is the fire that Jesus has come to cast on the earth the same as the baptism which he will undergo? Likewise, should the distress he feels be identified with his desire to have the fire already kindled? Or, on the other hand, are the fire and the baptism to be understood as being distinct or perhaps even contrasted? The same question should also be asked of Jesus' wish and his distress. Should they be seen in conjunction or in contrast to one another?

Much hinges on the way Luke uses the symbolism of fire in his Gospel and Acts. In the preaching of John the Baptist there is a close association between fire and judgement. Each tree that does not produce good fruit 'will be cut down and thrown into the *fire*' (3.9). Similarly, he predicts that the Christ 'will burn up the chaff with unquenchable *fire* (3.17). It is within this context of judgement that John introduces the Messiah as the one who 'will baptize you with the Holy

---

37   EDNT 3, p. 306.

Spirit and *fire*' (3.16). In John's preaching this would appear to be a prophecy of messianic judgement. The association of fire with judgement is not isolated to John's preaching, however, but is a recurrent theme in Luke and Acts (see also 9.54; 17.29; Acts 2.19). Thus it would appear that when Jesus says that he has come to bring fire on the earth (12.49), he is affirming what John the Baptist had said about him earlier. He has come to execute messianic judgement. But this raises the question as to when such a judgement takes place. Will it occur during Jesus' earthly ministry or at some later date?

Assuming that the parallelism between vv. 49 and 50 is synonymous, Leon Morris argues that the fire of judgement will be kindled at the cross:

> Jesus is saying that God's plan for men is salvation that involves judgment. But it is a judgment that the Messiah will bear for others, not one He will inflict on others. It is not an attractive prospect, but Jesus longs for it to come, for only so can the saving work be accomplished . . . The shadow of the cross hung over Him. He knew it was inevitable: it was the very purpose for His coming. But though he accepted its inevitability nothing could make it attractive.[38]

It is more probable, however, that the saying in its context should be understood with reference to the eschatological judgment. The preceding parables on the theme of watchfulness (12.35-48) certainly have an eschatological focus, which would provide a suitable setting for a symbolical reference to the final judgment in v. 49. This understanding is also more compatible with John the Baptist's prediction of the Messiah baptizing rather than being baptized with fire. As a prerequisite for baptizing others with fire, the Messiah would need first to be baptized by fire himself (12.50), but this seems not to have been within John's line of vision. What John foretold was a baptism of fire that was 'expressive of the judgment that falls upon the wicked',[39] not a judgement that would fall upon the Messiah. Now 'Jesus desires the eschatological judgment that was promised by John' (3.9, 16-17).[40] The fire that Jesus has come to cast upon the earth, although related to the cross, is distinct from it. It is 'the eschatological conflagration'[41] that will befall the wicked. Nolland's succinct interpretation of vv. 49-53 is therefore apt: 'Jesus has been commissioned to cast the purging fire of the coming judgment upon the earth, but while he awaits God's timing for that, and as a prelude to it, he first anticipates his own baptism of disaster to come, and also the strife among people which he himself engenders, and indeed by which he is overwhelmed in the baptism he contemplates.'[42]

If the fire that Jesus has come to cast on the earth refers to the final judgement,

---

38 Morris, *Luke*, p. 219.
39 Marshall, *Luke*, p. 547.
40 Johnson, *Luke*, p. 207.
41 Hans Conzelmann, *The Theology of St Luke* (trans. G. Buswell; London: Faber and Faber, 1961), p. 109.
42 Nolland, *Luke*, p. 708.

then the relationship between Jesus' two sayings in vv. 49-50 is best explained as one of antithetical parallelism. These two exclamatory statements are to be contrasted rather than equated. Jesus agrees with John the Baptist that he has come to execute messianic judgement – to baptize with fire and to cast fire on the earth. But now Jesus adds a dimension that may never have occurred to John. Before he can baptize others with fire, he must first undergo a baptism of fire himself. Before he executes judgement, he must first experience judgement. This metaphorical understanding of baptism is unusual, but not unique. When James and John approached Jesus for special favours in his coming kingdom, Jesus asked them, 'Can you drink the cup I drink or be baptized with the baptism I am baptized with?' (Mk 10.38). The metaphor of the cup and the metaphor of baptism have the same meaning. Both symbolize judgement. Jesus is about to be inundated by the waters of divine judgement, an experience that will overwhelm him (cf. Isa. 21.4 LXX).[43] The imagery of floods representing persecution or judgement is common in the Old Testament (Pss. 18.4, 16; 42.7; 69.1-2; Isa. 8.7-8; 30.27-28; Jon. 2.3-6).[44] At the prospect of such a baptism Jesus is deeply distressed. The anguish that he experienced in Gethsemane in anticipation of drinking the cup in Matthew and Mark he now experiences in anticipation of the baptism he is to undergo. In both cases he is horrified at the prospect of divine judgement. Luke, however, differs from the other Synoptics in a significant way. Jesus' distress is introduced at a much earlier point in the narrative. He speaks of his distress in the present tense, a tense which in Greek implies continuity and progression. So what Jesus is describing is not a fleeting feeling but an overwhelming sense of distress which will accompany him until his baptism by fire is accomplished (cf. 18.31; 22.37).[45]

John the Baptist had prophesied that the Messiah would baptize with the Holy Spirit and with fire (3.16). Surprisingly, in Luke Jesus does neither, which is probably the reason for John's later consternation (7.18-20). Rather Jesus *is baptized* (passive voice) with the Spirit and fire. He is baptized with the Spirit at the Jordan and with fire at his crucifixion. These two baptisms provide the framework within which Jesus' ministry takes place in Luke's Gospel. Only when he has experienced this dual baptism is Jesus in a position to baptize others with the Spirit and with fire. But this has to wait until the book of Acts. In Luke the ministry of the Messiah is dominated by these two baptisms. His baptism with the Spirit results in exuberant joy (10.21). The prospect of his baptism by fire fills him with distress (12.50). It is a prelude to the Passion.

---

43 The verb *baptizō* is found four times in the LXX. Only in Isa. 21.4 is it used in a metaphorical sense, 'My heart wanders, and lawlessness *overwhelms* me.'

44 Thus Bock, *Luke*, p. 1194.

45 The verb that is used in the clause 'until it is completed' (NIV) or 'accomplished' (NASB) is *teleō*, the same verb that is later found on the lips of Jesus to refer to Old Testament prophecies that are to be *fulfilled* in his suffering and death (18.31; 22.37).

3.6 *Weeping (19.28-44)*

28 After Jesus had said this (i.e. the Parable of the Ten Pounds), he went on ahead, going up to Jerusalem.

29 As he approached Bethphage and Bethany at the hill called the Mount of Olives, he sent two of his disciples, saying to them,

30 'Go to the village ahead of you, and as you enter it, you will find a colt tied there, which no-one has ever ridden. Untie it and bring it here.

31 If anyone asks you, 'Why are you untying it?' tell him, 'The Lord needs it."

32 Those who were sent ahead went and found it just as he had told them.

33 As they were untying the colt, its owners asked them, 'Why are you untying the colt?'

34 They replied, 'The Lord needs it.'

35 They brought it to Jesus, threw their cloaks on the colt and put Jesus on it.

36 As he went along, people spread their cloaks on the road.

37 When he came near the place where the road goes down the Mount of Olives, the whole crowd of disciples began joyfully to praise God in loud voices for all the miracles they had seen:

38 'Blessed is the king who comes in the name of the Lord!' 'Peace in heaven and glory in the highest!'

39 Some of the Pharisees in the crowd said to Jesus, 'Teacher, rebuke your disciples!'

40 'I tell you,' he replied, 'if they keep quiet, the stones will cry out.'

41 As he approached Jerusalem and saw the city, *he wept over it*

42 and said, 'If you, even you, had only known on this day what would bring you peace – but now it is hidden from your eyes.

43 The days will come upon you when your enemies will build an embankment against you and encircle you and hem you in on every side.

44 They will dash you to the ground, you and the children within your walls. They will not leave one stone on another, because you did not recognize the time of God's coming to you.'

On two occasions in the Gospels Jesus weeps – at the tomb of Lazarus (Jn 11.35) and here on his approach to Jerusalem on Palm Sunday (Lk. 19.41). In each case the weeping occurs at a pivotal point in the development of the Gospel in which it is found. In Luke a significant juncture has been reached. The lengthy central section of the Gospel, the journey to Jerusalem (9.18–19.27) with its strong suffering motif, has drawn to a close.[46] The one who is being jubilantly hailed as the

---

46 Although there is widespread agreement as to where the journey section begins, its end cannot be determined with the same precision. Conzelmann, *Theology*, p. 60, sets the *terminus ad quem* of the journey at 19.27. Marshall, *Historian and Theologian*, pp. 150–51, sees the journey as filling the section 9.51–19.10. Jack D. Kingsbury, 'The Plot of Luke's Story of Jesus', *Interpretation* 48 (1994), p. 375, understands the dramatic power of Luke's narrative as being in large part due to the conflict around which the plot revolves, and hence detects a turning point at 19.47-48. Only when Jesus has entered Jerusalem and cleansed the temple do the

messianic king (19.38) finally has his destination in view – the royal city where suffering and death await him.[47]

From the English translation tradition it would appear that Jesus' weeping over Jerusalem is no different from his weeping at the tomb of Lazarus. In the Greek, however, a clear distinction is made as different verbs are used – *dakruō* in John and *klaiō* in Luke. In Jn 11.35 the well known words, 'Jesus wept', could more accurately be rendered 'Jesus burst into tears'[48] or 'broke out in tears'.[49] The main discernible difference between the two verbs lies in the 'emphasis upon the noise accompanying the weeping'[50] in the case of *klaiō*. Therefore *klaiō* refers to 'audible weeping' and 'any loud expression of pain or sorrow'.[51] It is a verb that is 'used of strong emotions'.[52] Warfield was therefore probably correct when he distinguished the two cases of Jesus weeping in the following way: 'The sight of Mary and her companions wailing at the tomb of Lazarus, agitated his soul and caused him tears (Jno. 11. 35); the stubborn unbelief of Jerusalem drew from him loud wailing (Lk. 19.41).'[53]

The fact that *klaiō* denotes emotion is uncontested. Although in some instances it expresses supreme joy (e.g. Gen. 29.11; 33.4; 42.24; 43.20; 46.29), it far more commonly designates sorrow and this is its consistent use in the New Testament. 'Sorrow may manifest itself in weeping or other outward demonstrations of grief, or remain concealed as inner anguish. In Gk. several verbs are used to express this range of emotions. *klaiō*, weep, cry out, expresses man's immediate and outward reaction to suffering.'[54]

When Jesus wept over Jerusalem (19.41), it would therefore seem to have been a loud demonstration of grief.[55] His weeping is all the more pronounced,

authorities look for an opportunity to destroy him. All are agreed, however, that the impending suffering of Christ is a strong motif in the journey section. Passages such as 9.51-53; 13.22, 31-35; 17.11 and 18.31-34 are clear pointers in this direction. Marshall, *Historian and Theologian*, p. 152, expresses a common view: 'Luke has used these markers to indicate that from the first prediction of the passion onwards (Luke 9:22) Jesus was conscious of the shadow of Jerusalem hanging over his ministry and had his ultimate destination in view . . . (Hence) what we find in the "journey" section is a heightened consciousness of suffering on the part of Jesus.'

47   This understanding of the destination has been carefully anticipated by the lengthy account of the journey from Galilee. As Conzelmann, *Theology*, p. 65, explains, 'The "journey" begins after the fact of suffering has been disclosed but not yet understood [i.e. by the disciples]. Now the place of the destination is fixed as the place of suffering required doctrinally . . . In other words, Jesus' awareness that he must suffer is expressed in terms of the journey.'

48   BDAG, p. 211.

49   EDNT 1, p. 274. So also A. T. Robertson, *A Grammar of the Greek New Testament in the Light of Historical Research* (London: Hodder and Stoughton, 1923), p. 834.

50   LN 1, p. 304.

51   G. Abbott-Smith, *A Manual Greek Lexicon of the New Testament* (Edinburgh: T & T Clark, 1937), p. 247.

52   EDNT 2, p. 293.

53   Warfield, *Person and Work of Christ*, p. 127.

54   NIDNTT 2, p. 416.

55   Norval Geldenhuys, *Commentary on the Gospel of Luke* (NICNT; Grand Rapids, MI:

not only because *klaiō* is used, but also because it stands in such stark contrast to the enthusiastic jubilation of the crowd (19.37) who recognized him as the messianic king of Old Testament promise (19.38 citing Ps. 118.26). So what was it that motivated Jesus' open expression of sorrow in the midst of the ecstatic joy of the chanting multitude?

Although the events of Palm Sunday are recorded in all four Gospels, Jesus' weeping is captured only by Luke's account. It is therefore likely that unique features of the Lukan narrative will provide the clue to Jesus' sorrow at this point. Large sections of Luke's travel narrative are unparallelled in the other Gospels. Also without parallel is Jesus' prophecy of the city's destruction, which accompanies his weeping (19.41-44).[56] The key to understanding the grief of Jesus in 19.41 should therefore probably be sought both within the travel narrative and in the pronouncement of doom spoken in the verses that follow.

The motif of messianic suffering has been a recurring refrain throughout the travel narrative (9.22, 23, 31, 44; 11.47-51; 12.50; 13.31-35; 14.27; 17.25; 18.31-33). The account of the journey proper opens on an ominous note, 'He resolutely set His face to go to Jerusalem' (9.51 NASB). As Howard Marshall observes, 'From the outset the goal of his journey is the passion and resurrection.'[57] This purpose is spelled out in the predictions that follow (13.33-35; 17.25; 18.31-33). Particularly significant for the present discussion is Jesus' prediction of suffering in 13.33-35: 'I must keep going today and tomorrow and the next day – for surely no prophet can die outside Jerusalem! O Jerusalem, Jerusalem, you who kill the prophets and stone those sent to you, how often I have longed to gather your children together, as a hen gathers her chicks under her wings, but you were not willing! Look, your house is left to you desolate. I tell you, you will not see me again until you say, "Blessed is he who comes in the name of the Lord."' This lament is absent from Mark, while in Matthew it occurs in a very different context – as the climactic statement concluding the seven woes against the scribes and Pharisees (Mt. 23.37-39). The fact that in Luke this lament over Jerusalem occurs 'as something of a midpoint in the journey'[58] from Galilee places the entire travel section in a particular light and also prepares the reader for Jesus' weeping when his destination is in view.[59] There is a painful paradox between the expectations of the crowd who hail Jesus as their triumphant king and his own predictions of his imminent suffering and death.

Nevertheless, it is not only the foreboding of his own death that gives rise

Eerdmans, 1951), p. 484, maintains that 'the word does not mean merely that tears forced themselves up and fell down His face. It suggests rather the heaving of the bosom, and the sob and cry of a soul in agony. We could have no stronger word than the word that is used here.'

56 See Kurt Aland (ed.), *Synopsis Quattuor Evangeliorum: Locis parallelis evangeliorum apocryphorum et patrum adhibiti* (Stuttgart: Deutsche Bibelgesellschaft, 3rd rev. edn, 1988), p. 236.

57 Marshall, *Historian and Theologian*, pp. 150–51.

58 Thus D. L. Tiede, *Prophecy and History in Luke-Acts* (Philadelphia: Fortress, 1980), p. 72.

59 The converse is also true. As Tiede, *Prophecy and History*, p. 73, explains, 'Luke 13:31-35 has been structured in close correlation to the third Gospel's account of Jesus' entry into Jerusalem where the suspense of this earlier pericope is largely resolved.'

to Jesus' tears. It is at least equally the coming fate of the city that lies before him. In a concise prophecy that anticipates the fuller Olivet discourse (21.5-36) he bewails the destruction of Jerusalem (19.42-44). Therefore it is both his own fate and that of the city that cause his sorrow. Moreover, the two are inextricably linked. His own rejection in Jerusalem will be the ultimate reason for the city's downfall (cf. 23.27-31). The messianic king has finally arrived in his royal city but, tragically, it did not recognize the time of its visitation (19.44). Hence Jesus' second, and now tearful, lament over the city. He weeps for two reasons that now have merged into one. As von der Osten-Sacken explains, 'The reason for the lament is his foreboding of rejection in the holy city. Then by way of explanation . . . Jesus brings together the destruction of the city and his own rejection.'[60]

In the Old Testament the greatest affinity to Jesus' weeping over Jerusalem is that of the prophets who are called upon to foretell calamities awaiting their own people.[61] Elisha weeps when he foresees the terror which Hazael will inflict on the sons of Israel (2 Kgs 8.11, 12). Isaiah weeps bitterly at the prospect of 'the destruction of the daughter of my people' (Isa. 22.4). Perhaps most telling is the weeping of Jeremiah. He exclaims that for the brokenness of his people he is broken (8.21) and wishes that he 'might weep day and night for the slain of the daughter of my people' (9.1). Again his eyes will weep bitterly 'because the flock of the Lord has been taken captive' (13.17; cf. 14.17).

This Old Testament background points to the conclusion that in Lk. 19.41 Jesus is portrayed as the sympathetic prophet weeping over the doom that will overtake his own people. Of the weeping prophets of the Old Testament Jeremiah is probably the most convincing antecedent to Jesus weeping over Jerusalem. On the basis of the prophetic evidence Nolland claims that Jesus' lamentation is especially reminiscent of that of Jeremiah and comments, 'The coming of the city into sight draws from Jesus, as a weeping Jeremiah, an announcement of its pending doom as a city that has failed to recognize in the ministry of Jesus the visitation of God.'[62]

This conclusion, that Jesus weeps as the sympathetic prophet at the doom of his people, is strengthened by a consideration of the language in which his

---

60 Peter von der Osten-Sacken, 'Jesu Weinen über sein Volk', in Ehrhard Blum et al. (eds), *Die hebräische Bibel* (Neukirchen-Vluyn: Neukirchener Verlag, 1990), p. 555 (author's translation).

61 In his chapter 'Weeping for Jerusalem', Tiede, *Prophecy and History*, pp. 79–86, regularly refers to Jesus as the 'prophet-king.' Nevertheless, in his opening paragraph on Lk. 19.41-44 he notes: 'It is finally the sympathy of the suffering prophet, of Deuteronomy's Moses, of Jeremiah, Isaiah, and Hosea, caught up in the rage, anguish, frustration, and sorrow of God for Israel that constitutes the pathos of this story' (p. 78). The closest affinity, however, is with Jeremiah. Citing L. Gaston, *No Stone on Another: Studies in the Significance of the Fall of Jerusalem in the Synoptic Gospels* (Leiden: Brill, 1970), pp. 359–60, Tiede further explains: 'That "the whole scene of Jesus weeping over Jerusalem could have come straight from the pages of Jeremiah" produces a striking effect, intensifying the rhetoric and pathos by reminiscence of a previous tragedy that is about to be repeated' (p. 82).

62 Nolland, *Luke*, p. 930.

prophecy is cast. Several of the key terms he uses occur only here in the New Testament, but are found in highly suggestive contexts in the LXX, namely *paremballō* ('set up'), *charax* ('barricade'), *perikukloō* ('encircle') in 19.43, and *edaphizō* ('raze to the ground') in 19.44. The language is clearly reminiscent of Old Testament passages where the destruction of Jerusalem is foretold, for example, Isa. 3.26; 29.3; Jer. 6.6; Ezek. 4.2. Hence, as Jesus predicts the destruction of Jerusalem that will occur in 70 AD, he is borrowing heavily from the prophetic descriptions of the original fall of Jerusalem in 586 BC. The earlier prophecies inform his, and he seems to be drawing particularly, though perhaps not exclusively, from the prophecies of Isaiah, Jeremiah and Ezekiel.[63] Like Isaiah and Jeremiah, he weeps at the prospect.

The link with Isaiah and Jeremiah is further strengthened by Luke's account of the cleansing of the temple which immediately follows (19.45, 46). Of all the Gospel accounts of this incident Luke's is by far the briefest. This makes Jesus' words of justification for his action stand in bold relief. He appeals to Scripture, quoting Isa. 56.7 ('My house shall be a house of prayer') and alluding to Jer. 7.11 ('a robbers' den'). By referring to Isaiah and Jeremiah he is making it clear that, albeit symbolically, Jerusalem's judgement has already begun. Jesus' situation, however, particularly parallels Jeremiah's. In Jesus' day the temple was being used for the same purpose as it was in the days of Jeremiah. By alluding to Jeremiah's famous temple sermon (Jer. 7.2-15) Jesus therefore exposes 'the people's foolish misconception that they can commit all manner of sin and then 'flee' to the Temple like a brigand to his cave'.[64] Not only does Jesus' denunciation draw upon Jeremiah's, even the leaders' desire to destroy Jesus (19.47) echoes Jeremiah's experience (Jer. 26.4-8).

The intensity of Jesus' weeping is further highlighted by the broken grammar that introduces his prophecy in 19.42. The opening sentence breaks off in mid course and therefore impressively reflects his emotional state.[65] A literal translation would read, 'If you had known on this day, even you, the things that make for peace . . .' This rough syntax is smoothed over in many English translations, for example, GNB, NEB, NIV, RSV. They bring out the highly emotive language either by the use of exclamation marks or powerful turns of phrase, but the English grammar remains intact.

Although the experts disagree as to the extent of the syntactical irregularity

63 Tiede, *Prophecy and History*, p. 82, detects another linguistic similarity, particularly with the prophecy of Jeremiah, in the concluding clause of Jesus' pronouncement (v. 44). In the LXX the conjunction *anth hōn* ('because', 'therefore') is used eight times in Jeremiah to speak of judgment 'in reference to the dire fate of the city, the temple and the exile from the land.' Although Tiede does not argue for a direct linguistic dependence on Jeremiah, he does suggest that this concluding statement of judgement 'is immersed in the precedent of such specific usage arising from interpretations of the first destruction of Jerusalem.'

64 Rikki E. Watts, *Isaiah's New Exodus and Mark*, Wissenschaftliche Untersuchungen zum Neuen Testament 2.88 (Tübingen: J. C. B. Mohr, 1997), p. 327.

65 Tiede, *Prophecy and History*, pp. 79, 86, twice refers to 'the fractured syntax of the passage' and notes that it 'compounds the effect of Jesus' weeping' (p. 79), but he does not develop the point further.

that marks Jesus' tearful statement in 19.42,[66] there can be little doubt about the strength of his emotion as he laments over Jerusalem and predicts the city's tragic downfall in 19.41-44. In his jeremiad over Jerusalem in these verses Jesus' weeping stands in stark contrast to the jubilation of the crowd (19.37). His weeping is best understood as an expression of emotion akin to that of Old Testament prophets – an outburst of sorrow and sympathy that seems to be strengthened by the disjoined syntax that marks the opening sentence of his prophecy (19.42a).

The sense of distress that Jesus would continue to experience until his baptism was completed (12.50) dogged his steps throughout the journey to Jerusalem. It will be relieved only at his death. As his destination comes into view this distress is compounded by his profound sympathy for the doomed city that lies before him. It is this powerful emotional combination of distress and sympathy that has him erupt into loud wailing. The prospect of his own fate and that of Jerusalem are intertwined and evoke in him a deep and disturbing sorrow. In the scheme of Luke and Acts, Jerusalem is the geographical centrepiece. The story moves towards it in Luke and away from it in Acts. Luke's narrative enters Jerusalem in ch. 19 and does not leave until Acts 8. It therefore occupies more than twelve chapters at the heart of his two-volume narrative. For Luke, Jerusalem is the city of destiny where the great events of salvation history take place. The crucifixion (Lk. 23), the resurrection (Lk. 24), the ascension (Acts 1), and Pentecost (Acts 2) all happen in or near Jerusalem. As the royal son of David, the King whose praises the whole crowd of disciples has been singing so loudly and joyfully (19.37-38), Jesus is about to enter his capital city.[67] But as he crosses the Mount of Olives range and catches his first glimpse of the city he breaks down and weeps. Before him lie both his destination and his destiny. Knowing more than his jubilant followers, he is overcome with grief. It may well be the last time Luke refers to an emotion of Jesus.

---

66   See the appendix at the end of this chapter.
67   Brent Kinman, 'Parousia, Jesus' 'A-Triumphal' Entry, and the Fate of Jerusalem (Luke 19:28-44)', *JBL* 118 (1999), pp. 284–89, strongly emphasizes the regal nature of Jesus' entry into Jerusalem. The kingship of Jesus is emphasized by his acceptance of the title 'son of David' (18.35-43), his identification with the man of noble birth in the immediately preceding parable (19.11-27), his commandeering of the animal he rides (19.28-35), the garments placed on the animal and thrown on the road (19.35-36), and of course most explicitly by his acclamation as 'king' (19.38). Given Jesus' royal status, Kinman concludes that 'in comparison to the lavish welcomes accorded to dignitaries in the Graeco-Roman world, Jerusalem's response to Jesus should be characterized as an appalling insult, which, in turn, explains his remarks about the coming destruction of the city' (p. 280). Particularly insulting, according to Kinman, was the absence of Jerusalem's social and religious elite (the chief priests, scribes and leaders of 19.47) from the welcoming crowd (pp. 292–93). While the regal nature of Jesus' entry cannot be denied, his loud wailing over the city (19.41) does not express the anger of an insulted dignitary but the sorrow and sympathy of a suffering sovereign and a lamenting prophet.

3.7 Anguish (22.39-46)

³⁹ Jesus went out as usual to the Mount of Olives, and his disciples followed him.

⁴⁰ On reaching the place, he said to them, 'Pray that you will not fall into temptation.'

⁴¹ He withdrew about a stone's throw beyond them, knelt down and prayed,

⁴² 'Father, if you are willing, take this cup from me; yet not my will, but yours be done.'

⁴³ An angel from heaven appeared to him and strengthened him.

⁴⁴ *And being in anguish*, he prayed more earnestly, and his sweat was like drops of blood falling to the ground.

⁴⁵ When he rose from prayer and went back to the disciples, he found them asleep, exhausted from sorrow.

⁴⁶ 'Why are you sleeping?' he asked them. 'Get up and pray so that you will not fall into temptation.'

In Matthew and Mark Jesus' emotions reach their peak of intensity in the Garden of Gethsemane. The same may also be the case with Luke, but only if vv. 43-44 are original. If these verses are a later scribal addition to Luke's text, then his version of Gethsemane lacks the anguish and the sweat like drops of blood, and becomes the most emotionally restrained account of Gethsemane that we possess. This would bring the scene in Gethsemane into line with Luke's crucifixion account which has no cry of dereliction and where Jesus' last words sound calm and confident, 'Father, into your hands I commit my spirit' (23.46). Can this same confident calm also be read back into Gethsemane or does Luke in fact describe an anguished Jesus whose agony and fervent prayer combine to produce sweat that 'was like drops of blood falling to the ground'?

A quick glance at a sampling of English translations soon reveals that we have a textual problem of major proportions on our hands. When it comes to vv. 43-44 our English Bibles can be divided into five categories: (1) those which include these verses in the main body of the text without comment (JB, KJV, Knox, LB, NKJV), (2) those which include these verses but with a footnote or marginal note to the effect that some early manuscripts do not have them (ESV, NASB, NEB, NIV, RV), (3) those which include vv. 43-44 but within square brackets (Holman, ML, NRSV, TEV), (4) the RSV which omits these verses from the main body of the text but includes them in a footnote, and (5) the paraphrase by J. B. Phillips which omits these verses completely.

These translations merely reflect the differences of opinion that exist within the world of New Testament scholarship. In the specialized and highly technical discipline of textual criticism the experts are still far from achieving a consensus.[68] The crux of the problem lies in the fact that some very ancient and

---

68 The omission of these verses is given an {A} rating (the highest of four) by the fourth revised edition of the United Bible Societies' Greek New Testament. This is a more negative assessment of their inclusion than that made by any previous edition. Metzger, *Textual Commentary*,

reliable manuscripts include these verses, while at the same time other equally ancient and reliable manuscripts omit them. This presents scholars with a genuine textual conundrum which continues to fuel debate. At this point in the debate and at our current level of knowledge it is probably safest to occupy the middle ground. This would mean affirming the historical reliability of the facts recorded in 22.43-44, but at the same time holding that these verses did not originally belong to Luke's Gospel.[69] So we need to take these verses seriously as providing a genuine insight into Jesus' suffering, but in isolation from the rest of Luke. For the purposes of our discussion they will therefore be taken as historically authentic, but also as a later scribal insertion into Luke's Gethsemane account.[70]

> p. 151, explains that the UBS Committee regarded this passage as a later addition to the text. Kurt Aland and Barbara Aland, *The Text of the New Testament: An Introduction to the Critical Editions and to the Theory and Practice of Modern Textual Criticism* (trans. E. F. Rhodes; Grand Rapids, MI: Eerdmans; 1987), p. 305, claim that 'these verses were not a part of the original text of the gospel of Luke', but that they are 'recognized as a very early tradition coming at least from the second century if not even earlier (attested by patristic quotations and allusions)'. According to Bart D. Ehrman and Mark A. Plunkett, 'The Angel and the Agony: The Textual Problem of Luke 22:43-44', *CBQ* 45 (1983), pp. 401–16, these verses are intrusions into the text. Not only do they disrupt a clear and concise chiasmus, but they also portray Jesus in a way that does not accord with the rest of Luke's Passion narrative. In a more recent article, 'Did Jesus Get Angry or Agonize? A Text Critic Pursues the Original Jesus Story,' *BibRev* 5 (2005), pp. 17-26, 49-50, Ehrman argues from the wider context of Luke's Passion account that these verses have no place there. 'Luke has gone to great lengths to counter the very view of Jesus that these verses embrace. Rather than entering his passion with fear and trembling, in anguish over his coming fate, the Jesus of Luke goes to his death calm and in control, confident of his Father's will until the very end' (p. 24). A strong case for rehabilitating these verses has been made by Raymond E. Brown, *Death of the Messiah: From Gethsemane to the Grave: A Commentary on the Passion Narratives in the Four Gospels* (2 vols; New York: Doubleday, 1994), vol. 1, pp. 179–190. Brown dismisses arguments based on chiasmus as exaggerated, and suggests that a copyist may have dropped the passage for fear that it 'might supply comfort to those who challenged the divinity of Jesus' (p. 184). Claire Clivaz, 'The Angel and the Sweat Like "Drops of Blood" (Lk 22:43-44): P[69] and *f*[13]', *HTR* 98 (2005), pp. 419–44, supports Brown by reappraising some of the manuscript evidence favouring the inclusion of these verses.

69   Metzger, *Textual Commentary*, p. 151, considers it likely that vv. 43-44 'were added from an early source, oral or written, of extra-canonical traditions concerning the life and passion of Jesus.'

70   Some manuscripts include these verses after Mt. 26.39. From this and other similar examples, J. M. Ross, 'Floating Words: Their Significance for Textual Criticism', *NTS* 38 (1992), pp. 154–55, concludes: 'If an additional sentence occurs at different places in different manuscripts, this is a sign not of inauthenticity but rather that the words, though absent from some manuscripts, were preserved in the belief that they were genuine, but there was uncertainty as to where they belonged.' T. van Lopik, 'Once Again: Floating Words, Their Significance for Textual Criticism', *NTS* 41 (1995), p. 287, disagrees with Ross, because 'in the Byzantine Church Luke 22.43-4 (usually with 45a) is read after Matt 26.39 in the lesson of Maundy Thursday.' Therefore 'the "omission" or "transposition" of Luke 22.43-4 (45a) in lectionaries is of no weight in the discussion about the Lukan authenticity of the passage'.

If these verses did not originally belong in Luke 22 but do describe Jesus in Gethsemane, it is probably best to compare them, at least initially, to the expressions of Jesus' emotions found in Matthew and Mark. Both of these Gospels observe that Jesus 'began to be sorrowful/deeply distressed and troubled' (Mt. 26.37/Mk 14.33). He also takes his inner circle of disciples into his confidence by admitting, 'My soul is overwhelmed with sorrow to the point of death' (Mt. 26.38; Mk 14.34). But what did Jesus' trouble, deep distress and overwhelming sorrow look like? How did these emotions come to outward expression? This is where Luke's floating verses make their contribution. Jesus was in agony and his sweat was like drops of blood falling to the ground. These words fill out the picture drawn by Matthew and Mark. They provide further insight into Jesus' titanic emotional and spiritual struggle in the Garden.

The order of these verses as they have been consistently transmitted in the textual tradition may at first seem puzzling. Jesus is first strengthened by an angel (v. 43) and is then described as 'being in anguish' and praying 'more earnestly' (v. 44). One might have expected these verses to be in reverse order. The traditional order, however, has its own spiritual logic. Jesus is given supernatural strength to continue in anguished, ardent prayer. This kind of angelic help is not without precedent. Daniel was strengthened by a heavenly messenger when he was in anguish because of a vision he had seen (Dan. 10.15-19). Likewise, the Servant of the Lord receives supernatural strength to accomplish the task appointed to him by God (Isa. 42.6).[71] Early in his own ministry Jesus had been attended by angels immediately following his temptation in the wilderness (Mt. 4.11; Mk 1.13). So this angelic assistance in Gethsemane is neither new nor unusual. What is unique is its effect. This is seen not only in Jesus' fervent prayer but also in the 'anguish' he experienced. This anguish is conveyed by the Greek noun *agōnia*, a word which admits of a rather specialized meaning.[72] Although etymologically related to our word 'agony', it occupies a somewhat different semantic field. In English 'agony' often means extreme pain, which is not quite the epicentre of the range of meanings associated with *agōnia* in New Testament times. By then it had come to 'designate the emotional tension, frequently connected with anxiety, experienced before a decisive conflict.'[73] Raymond Brown gives an imaginative illustration:

71 See William J. Larkin, 'The Old Testament Background of Luke XXII.43-44', *NTS* 25 (1979), pp. 252–53.

72 *Agōnia* is found only here in the New Testament, and three times in the LXX (2 Macc. 3.14, 16; 15.19). Of particular interest is the *agōnia* of the high priest Onias threatened by the prospect of the plundering of temple funds by Heliodorus, chargé d'affaires to King Seleucus of Syria. Like Jesus, Onias' anguish had visible physical manifestations: 'To see the appearance of the high priest was to be wounded at heart, for his face and the change in his color disclosed the *anguish* of his soul. For terror and bodily trembling had come over the man, which plainly showed to those who looked at him the pain lodged in his heart' (2 Macc. 3.16-17). The same sense of *distress* was felt throughout the whole city (2 Macc. 3.14). The one further occurrence of *agōnia* in the LXX refers to the *anxiety* of the inhabitants of Jerusalem over Nicanor's plan to attack Judas Maccabaeus and his men in the open country (2 Macc. 15.19).

73 *EDNT* 1, p. 27; cf. BDAG p. 17, 'apprehensiveness of mind, esp. when faced with impending

An athletic parallel offers an explanation for the profuse sweat that follows: The runner is tensed up to begin the trial, and sweat breaks out all over his body. In such an interpretation, the *peirasmos* or great trial, which Jesus now knowingly will enter, resembles an athletic contest. Gamba . . . compares the strengthening role of the angel to that of a trainer who readies the athlete; the prayer of Jesus is the last-minute preparation. Unlike the disciples who sleep, Jesus is now poised at the starting line.[74]

From the perspective of this analogy the order of these two verses makes good sense. Jesus is strengthened by the angel and as result not only prays more earnestly but is firm in his resolve to face the greatest contest of his life. Not without anguish and anxiety he steels himself for the mammoth struggle that lies ahead.

The athletic metaphor explains Jesus' sweat, but what about his blood? How are the sweat and the blood related? Commentators are generally quick to point out that 'his sweat was *like* drops of blood falling to the ground.' A simile is being employed. But if this is the case what is the point of the comparison? Was the sweat the colour of blood? Or is the stress on the falling rather than on the colour, so that the comparison is 'between profuse perspiration and copious drops of blood splashing to the ground'?[75] Or could it be argued that strictly speaking the comparison is not with blood but with drops of blood, and that therefore 'it could mean that the sweat became so profuse that it flowed to the ground as freely as if it were drops of blood'?[76] Or is all this simply a rhetorical expression like our 'tears of blood'?[77] Because these are 'floating' verses, they are bereft of context, and so the wider setting is of little help. A point that is often overlooked in determining the point of the comparison is the use of the term *hōsei*, which is employed here. This word does not have a one-to-one correspondence with the English preposition 'like'. It can also be translated by 'as', 'about' or 'approximately'. Sometimes it can be used to express identity, e.g. 'Make me *like* one of your hired men' (15.19). On other occasions it can be used for likeness that falls short of identity, for example, 'tongues *as* of fire' (Acts 2.3 NASB). As well as denoting comparison, *hōsei* can also denote approximation, for example, 'He withdrew *about* a stone's throw beyond them' (22.41).

While the precise level of comparison is difficult to determine, a convincing case can be made for a comparison approximating identity. The point has been argued strongly by Feuillet who appeals to the use of *hōsei* in Lk. 15.19 and Acts 2.3, and then adds: 'Moreover, it would be strange if the Evangelist simply intended to compare sweat with blood. Finally, it should be noted that in the Greek text (as in the Vulgate) the participial phrase "falling to the ground" refers not to the sweat but to the blood.'[78] There is therefore some merit to the view,

---

ills, *distress, anguish* (anxiety varying in degree of intensity).'

74 Brown, *Death of the Messiah* 1, p. 189.
75 Fitzmyer, *Luke*, p. 1444.
76 Brown, *Death of the Messiah* 1, p. 185.
77 Marshall, *Luke*, p. 832.
78 A. Feuillet, 'Le récit lucanien de l'agonie de Gethsémani (Lc XXII. 39-46)', *NTS* 22 (1976),

often repudiated by commentators, that the reference is to 'bloody sweat'. If this is so, the reference could be to the rare condition of hematidrosis, 'the actual mingling of blood and sweat as in cases of severe anguish, strain or sensitivity'.[79] This is different to the more common hyperhidrosis, which simply refers to sweating profusely due to extreme emotion or stress (such as a student may be under before an important exam).[80] Compared with hyperhidrosis, hematidrosis is an extremely rare condition, so much so that its occurrence has very often been seriously doubted. Until recently the evidence for this condition was largely anecdotal. In the words of Jane Manonukul and her colleagues,

> Hematidrosis, the excretion of bloody sweat, is such an extremely rare phenomenon that very few sporadic patients of this condition are reported in the medical literature. Many reports were before the twentieth century at a time when the present sophisticated laboratory procedures were unavailable. The authenticity of most of these reports remains in question and has been widely discussed in the past, yet without any conclusions being made.[81]

The authors' review of previous reports of hematidrosis yielded no satisfactory results. They found that its pathogenesis is unclear and that it was sometimes supposed to be mysterious in nature. Then they make a bold claim, 'It was our fortune to find this rare condition and to have the opportunity to explore this event . . . The psychogenic cause was found to occur in an acute emotional period, for example, *fear of death*, during stressful excitement or hypnosis.'[82] After a thorough investigation of the phenomena, complete with photographs and a detailed medical analysis, the researchers readily admit that this was after all only a single case. They therefore conclude that further investigation into this condition will be necessary. 'Finally', they write, 'although this condition is extremely rare, it is necessary to have another new eruptive case to conduct further studies. Immediate biopsy, right after bleeding, to determine the correct findings, is necessary and is recommended.'[83]

This recent research would seem to indicate that hematidrosis can no longer be relegated to the realm of hearsay and anecdotal evidence. At least this one case has been subjected to careful scientific investigation. One can only hope that

p. 403 (author's translation). Feuillet overstates his case, however, when on the basis of Lk. 12.49-50; 22.20 and Jn 19.34 he attaches redemptive significance to the blood of Gethsemane.

79 Kenneth Barker (ed.), *The NIV Study Bible* (Grand Rapids, MI: Zondervan, 1985), p. 1584.
80 Irwin M. Freedberg et al. (eds), *Fitzpatrick's Dermatology in General Medicine* (New York: Mc Graw-Hill, 6th edn, 2003), p. 703, under the heading of 'Emotional Sweating' discuss hyperhidrosis of the palms and soles as well as of the axillae (armpits). Such excessive sweating 'occurs during mental stress'.
81 Jane Manonukul et al. (eds), 'Hematidrosis: A Pathologic Process or Stigmata. A Case Report with Comprehensive Histopathologic and Immunoperoxidase Studies', *American Journal of Dermatopathology* 30 (2008), p. 135.
82 Manonukul, 'Hematidrosis', p. 136 (emphasis mine).
83 Manonukul, 'Hematidrosis', p. 139.

further medical research of this thorough and painstaking kind will take place in the future. Suffice it to say in the meantime that in Lk. 22.44 Jesus would seem to be experiencing hematidrosis rather than hyperhidrosis as is so commonly assumed. The extreme emotional stress that he experienced in Gethsemane and his physical reaction to it would seem to conform to the little that we know about the rare condition of hematidrosis.

If Lk. 22.43-44 is derived from a historically authentic tradition about Jesus, these verses provide a profound insight into the suffering he endured at Gethsemane. At that point, as perhaps at no other, 'he clothed himself with frail humanity'. Yet in spite of his weakness and vulnerability he was, paradoxically, at the same time supremely divine. His deep agony was not caused by some vague foreboding but by a precise foreknowledge of what lay ahead. Were it not for that divine foreknowledge, his suffering in the Garden would have lacked such painful intensity. Perhaps it would be no exaggeration to say that these 'floating words', with their emphasis on Jesus' anguish and agony, reveal the depths of Jesus' sufferings even more than the undisputed passages. In Gethsemane the terrors of the cross are seen more clearly than at Calvary.[84]

Conclusion

Luke may refer to only a handful of Jesus' emotions but they magnificently enhance the portrait of Jesus that he has set out to draw. Jesus is portrayed as the human son of Mary, the divine Son of the Most High and as the royal son of David. As a human, divine and royal personage he shows a most congenial sympathy for those he has come to save. He is surprised when a Gentile centurion is the first to recognize his authority for what it is. He shows divine compassion to a widow who has just lost her only son. He rejoices in the Spirit when he sees his mission being carried out and when he reflects on his intimacy with the Father. On a very human note he is distressed at the prospect of his death, and like a lamenting prophet of old he weeps as he enters his royal city knowing that he will die there and that the city is doomed. Yet at the same time his distress and even his weeping would be inexplicable apart from his precise knowledge of what awaited him. Jesus' emotions in Luke form a finely woven tapestry of his humanity, royalty and divinity.

If the reference to Jesus' agony did not originally belong to Luke's Gospel, it would be correct to say that Luke has given a very restrained Passion account. From this, however, it would be incorrect to conclude that he presents a very restrained Jesus. Luke has simply introduced the pathos at an earlier point in his Gospel. At the prospect of his baptism by fire Jesus is greatly distressed, and his first glimpse of Jerusalem produces a loud wailing. The weeping may be momentary, but his distress endures. It colours all that he does throughout the journey and in Jerusalem until the moment he dies.

84   Geldenhuys, *Luke*, p. 577.

The Broken Grammar of Luke 19.42a

The English translations that smooth over the grammar of this verse mask the trailing off of the conditional clause and the incompleteness of the sentence in the Greek. As a conditional sentence, v. 42a consists only of the protasis (the 'if' clause). Zerwick and Grosvenor call this construction 'an unfulfilled condition without apodosis' (the 'then' clause),[85] and give no hint of grammatical irregularity. Zerwick further explains that 'this is simply an "unreal" condition whose apodosis is suppressed (as in the regular English "if only . . .!")'.[86] This is the translation adopted by several English versions, for example, GNB, MLB, NEB, RSV. The question needs to be raised whether Zerwick and these translations are correct in their assumption that the syntax here is quite regular and unspectacular. Some other grammarians have detected an abruptness in Jesus' statement that calls for an explanation. In the protasis that stands in isolation they have recognized the figure of speech known as *aposiopesis*. Blass and Debrunner discuss the point, but somewhat curiously. They first claim that 'aposiopesis in the strict sense, i.e. a breaking-off of speech due to strong emotion or to modesty, is unknown in the NT',[87] but then proceed to give several examples – Lk. 19.42 among them! Robertson and Davis also cite this verse as an instance of aposiopesis, with the comment that 'the sudden breaking off is very effective'.[88] A fuller discussion of aposiopesis is found in Robertson's original *Grammar*. He first discusses this figure under the heading of elliptical conditions: 'An incomplete condition is really a species of ellipsis or aposiopesis and is common to all languages . . . There may be the absence of either protasis or apodosis'.[89] What distinguishes aposiopesis from ellipsis is the emotion involved. As he explains in a later discussion: '*Aposiopesis* stands to itself since it is a conscious suppression of part of a sentence under the influence of a strong emotion like anger, fear, pity . . . What differentiates [aposiopesis] from ellipses or abbreviations of other clauses . . . is the passion. One can almost see the gesture and the flash of the eye

---

85 Max Zerwick and Mary Grosvenor, *A Grammatical Analysis of the Greek New Testament* (Rome: Biblical Institute Press, rev. edn, 1981), pp. 260–61.

86 Zerwick, *Biblical Greek*, p. 138.

87 BDF, p. 255.

88 A. T. Robertson and W. Hersey Davis, *A Short Grammar of the Greek Testament* (Grand Rapids, MI: Baker, 10th edn, 1977), p. 399.

89 Robertson, *Grammar*, p. 1023.

in aposiopesis'.[90] In support of his argument Robertson is able to cite only a very modest number of unequivocal examples from the New Testament. Apart from Lk. 19.42 he mentions only Mk 11.32, Lk. 13.9, Jn 6.62 and Acts 23.9. Each example is found in direct speech. Only in Jn 6.62 do we have another undisputed example of aposiopesis on the lips of Jesus. The remaining three examples are all quotations from human speakers – whether real (Mk 11.32; Acts 23.9) or imagined (Lk. 13.9). Another biblical example that is worth mentioning is Exod. 32.32 where Moses pleads for the forgiveness of the people in highly emotive language: 'But now, if Thou wilt forgive their sin – and if not, please blot me out from the book which Thou hast written!' (NASB). Interestingly, the aposiopesis in this instance is found only in the Hebrew text. The LXX translators felt constrained to supply the apodosis after the first conditional clause by inserting the imperative *aphes* ('forgive'), thus removing the harshness of the construction. That Moses' speech here is emotionally charged is beyond question. In the original this is heightened by the use of aposiopesis.

---

90   Robertson, *Grammar*, p. 1203.

CHAPTER 4

The Loving Lord:
Jesus' Emotions in John's Gospel[1]

Of the sixty specific references to the emotions of Jesus in the Gospels, twenty-eight are found in John. More so than the other Gospels, John offers a close-up picture of Jesus' life and ministry. But although the Fourth Gospel refers to the emotions of Jesus more often than each of the others, the range of emotions it records is comparatively modest. The most frequent references are to Jesus' love (18x).[2] Three times it says that he is troubled, twice that he is deeply moved, and once that he rejoices and sheds tears. There are also two references to his joy and one to his zeal. This represents a total of only six different emotions.

The portrait of Jesus' emotions in the Gospel of John is both complementary to and markedly distinct from the Synoptic portraits of Jesus. Of the nine different Greek words John uses to describe Jesus' emotions, only the two verbs *agapaō* ('love') and *embrimaomai* ('sternly charge') are used of him in the Synoptics, and then only sporadically. The first of these verbs describes Jesus' affection for the rich man in Mk 10.21, while the second indicates his stern warnings to a cured leper (Mk 1.43) and to two men who have just been healed of blindness (Mt. 9.30). None of these incidents is found in John. It would therefore be safe to say that John's portrayal of Jesus' emotions is unique among the four Gospel accounts.

In the Synoptics, the references to the emotions of Jesus are distributed fairly evenly over the major divisions of each Gospel. The Galilee, Journey and Jerusalem sections all record his emotions. Moreover, the emotions are, with few exceptions, related to either the miracles or the Passion of Jesus. Can

---

1 For a more detailed discussion of this topic the reader is referred to my earlier work, *Jesus' Emotions in the Fourth Gospel – Human or Divine?* (London: T & T Clark, 2005), pp. 1–344.
2 These references are shared between the verbs *agapaō* (12x) and *phileō* (3x), and the noun *agapē* (3x).

similar patterns be detected in the Fourth Gospel? Or is John unique not only in the instances of emotions he has chosen to record but also in the ways they are distributed throughout his account? Do the emotions of Jesus in John tend to cluster around miracles and the Passion, or can other configurations be detected?

These questions can only be answered once the basic outline of the Fourth Gospel has been established. The simple tripartite geographical arrangement of the Synoptics does not apply to John. Other avenues will therefore need to be explored. While a number of convincing alternatives present themselves, the discerning of an unequivocal structure presents a challenge even to the most determined scholar. As D. A. Carson and Douglas Moo have suggested: 'One of the reasons that critics find so many mutually exclusive structures in John is that his repeated handling of only a few themes makes it possible to postulate all kinds of parallels and chiasms. Another is that various structures seem to serve as overlays to other structures.'[3] In spite of the inherent difficulties surrounding this question of structure, a sampling of scholarly discussion since the mid-twentieth century uncovers some illuminating trends in the literature.

Recent discussion of this issue can be taken back to the influential observations made by C. H. Dodd, who sees this Gospel as naturally dividing itself at the end of ch. 12.[4] The resulting two parts he refers to as 'The Book of Signs', which records seven of Jesus' miracles (chs 2–12), and 'The Book of the Passion,' which includes the Farewell, as well as Jesus' Passion and resurrection (chs 13–20). The former 'book' is preceded by a proem (ch. 1), and the latter is followed by a postscript (ch. 21).[5]

Raymond Brown detects essentially the same structure as Dodd, but with a significant modification – he renames the second major division 'The Book of Glory'.[6] The differences in nomenclature can easily be reconciled however, as in John 13–20 'the glorification of Jesus is virtually synonymous with his passion, resurrection and exaltation'.[7] These chapters can therefore appropriately be entitled 'The Book of Glory/Passion'.

Further modifications come with the imaginative outline offered by Richard Burridge. Burridge exploits the traditional association of John's Gospel with an eagle, a metaphor that can be traced back to patristic times. 'The Book of Signs' (1.19–10.42) and 'The Book of Glory' (13.1–20.31) form the two wings that are separated by a thin body, the 'Interlude' of chs 11 and 12. Extending the metaphor, Burridge proposes that the prologue (1.1-18) and the appendix (ch. 21)

---

3 D. A. Carson and Douglas J. Moo, *An Introduction to the New Testament* (Leicester: Apollos, 2005), p. 226.

4 C. H. Dodd, *The Interpretation of the Fourth Gospel* (Cambridge: Cambridge University Press, 1954), p. 289.

5 Dodd, *Fourth Gospel*, p. 290.

6 Raymond E. Brown, *The Gospel according to John* (2 vols; Garden City, NY: Doubleday, 1966-70), vol. 1, p. cxxxviii.

7 D. A. Carson, 'John and the Johannine Epistles', in D. A. Carson and H. G. M. Williamson, eds, *It is Written: Scripture Citing Scripture. Essays in Honour of Barnabas Lindars* (Cambridge: Cambridge University Press, 1988), pp. 248–49.

form extensions on the wingtips.[8] Particularly significant for our purposes is the insertion of an interlude between the two 'books' of the Fourth Gospel.

These examples of recent scholarship suggest that outlining this Gospel is no simple matter. There are, however, several lines of internal evidence that can be fruitfully explored so that the emotions of Jesus can be placed in a convincing context:

(a) As was noted by Dodd, there is a distinct shift in emphasis between chs 12 and 13. In 13.1 there is clearly a transition from Jesus' public to his private ministry. Moreover, 12.37-50 is cast as a summary of all that has gone before, first by way of editorial comments as to the effects of Jesus' ministry (vv. 37-43), and secondly by way of Jesus' final public appeal that captures the gist of his message (vv. 44-50).

(b) One of the distinguishing features of the Fourth Gospel is its emphasis on the feasts of Judaism. The most prominent of these is the Passover, which the Evangelist specifically names ten times. The Festival of Tabernacles is mentioned once, as is Dedication (Hanukkah). The Synoptics, on the other hand, only mention the Passover. This suggests that the feasts form a major theme for John.[9] He makes reference to six distinct feasts, and again a pattern can be detected: (i) the Passover during which Jesus cleansed the temple (2.12-25); (ii) 'a feast of the Jews' (5.1) during which Jesus healed the man at the pool of Bethesda (the precise identity of the feast being uncertain); (iii) a second Passover (6.4) that is described as being 'at hand' when Jesus fed the five thousand; (iv) the Feast of Tabernacles (7.2, 8, 10, 11, 14, 37) that would appear to be the setting for the events in ch. 7 (and possibly also for those in ch. 8); (v) the Feast of Dedication which supplies the context for Jesus' debate with the Jews in 10.22-39; and (vi) the final Passover (11.55, 56; 12.1, 12, 20; 13.1, 29; 18.39; 19.14) that is anticipated in chs 11 and 12, and is celebrated in chs 13–19.[10] It will be readily observed that the first five feasts belong to 'The Book of Signs' and the final Passover to 'The Book of Passion/Glory'. Under this arrangement, chs 11 and 12 form a period of transition.

---

8 Richard A. Burridge, *Four Gospels, One Jesus? A Symbolic Reading* (Grand Rapids, MI: Eerdmans, 1994), pp. 137–38.

9 N. T. Wright, *The New Testament and the People of God* (London: SPCK, 3rd impression, 1996), p. 412, explains the significance of these feasts for the Fourth Gospel: 'John . . . locates the ministry of Jesus in terms of Jewish sacred time, with each festival not only having a specific reference-point in past history but also giving a specific shape to the future expectation of the people. Jesus, it seems, is bringing Israel's history towards its intended goal.'

10 R. Alan Culpepper, *Anatomy of the Fourth Gospel: A Study in Literary Design* (Philadelphia: Fortress, 1983), p. 72, sees the Passovers as highly significant for an understanding of the flow of John's narrative: 'The three Passovers (2:14-3:21; 6:5-65; 13:1-19:42) provide annual intervals within which the rest of the narrative is structured.' The first year occupies only about 116 verses (3.22–6.2) and the second 295 verses (6.66–12.50). With the third Passover the narrative intensifies dramatically: 'John 12-20 covers a two-week period, and chapters 13–19 are devoted to the events of a single twenty-four hour period. The "speed" of the narrative reduces steadily, therefore, until it virtually grinds to a halt at the climactic day.'

(c) Jesus' 'hour' ('time' NIV) is referred to repeatedly in this Gospel. Again the occurrences follow a familiar pattern. On three occasions this hour is described as 'not yet come' (2.4; 7.30; 8.20), while on the remaining occasions it is said to have come (12.23, 27; 13.1; 17.1). Martin suggests that 'the hour' is a 'literary key to the Gospel' and a prism through which Jesus' life can be viewed.[11] His hour as 'not yet' is confined to the 'Book of Signs', while its arrival is heralded at the close of his public ministry in ch. 12. Jesus' hour therefore corresponds closely with the final Passover. It is his moment of glory, the time of his Passion. It is then that both he and the Father are supremely glorified (12.23, 27; 17.1). The repeated use of the word 'hour' gives the story a sense of dramatic suspense that is resolved only with the Passion. The approach and arrival of the 'hour' also correspond broadly to the division of the Gospel into two 'books'. Between these two however, it is appearing increasingly necessary to regard ch. 12 as a transition. This observation is further enhanced by the next line of evidence.

(d) The Old Testament quotations in John are less numerous than those in the Synoptics, but they perform a very distinct function and fall into a recognizable pattern: (i) the early quotations (1.23; 2.17; 6.31, 45; 10.34; 12.14, 15) are – with only one exception (1.23) – introduced by an 'it is written' formula; (ii) the later quotations (12.38-41; 13.18; 15.25; 19.24, 36, 37) are uniformly introduced by fulfilment formulae or are connected to such a formula.[12] The same pattern is reflected in the Old Testament allusions: (i) in 7.38, 42 'Scripture said . . .', (ii) in 17.12 and 19.28 the allusion is made 'so that the Scripture might be fulfilled . . .' The clustering is therefore almost absolute. Again, the transition between the two kinds of introductory formulae occurs in ch. 12. In vv. 14-15 it records an 'it is written' quotation and in vv. 38-40 a fulfilment quotation. In the earlier quotations the author is intent on establishing the identity of Jesus, while with the fulfilment quotations another purpose can be detected. As Carson explains: 'It appears as if the evangelist particularly wishes to stress the fulfilment of Scripture in connection with the passion of Jesus and the obduracy motif with which he links it . . . The fulfilment motif is more forcefully stressed the closer one gets to the rejection of Jesus culminating on the cross.'[13]

(e) The geographical structure of John's Gospel is more complex than that of the Synoptics. Instead of the relatively simple Galilee–Journey–Jerusalem

---

11 Ralph P. Martin, *New Testament Foundations: A Guide for Students* (2 vols; Grand Rapids, MI: Eerdmans, 1975–1978), vol. 1, p. 272.

12 John Carson, 'John and the Johannine Epistles', p. 248. Martin Hengel, 'Old Testament Quotations in the Fourth Gospel', *HBT* 12 (1990), p. 32, has also recognized this pattern: 'The *citation introductions* are themselves striking. John makes here a fundamental distinction between the formulas in the first part of the gospel, chapters 1-12, Jesus' public ministry in Israel, and the second part, after 12:38 with the farewell speeches and the Passion.'

13 Carson, 'John and the Johannine Epistles', p. 248.

structure, there are several Galilee–Jerusalem cycles. In the main body of the book the following pattern can be detected:

First Galilee/Jerusalem cycle (2.1–4.3)
Second Galilee/Jerusalem cycle (4.4–5.47)
Third Galilee/Jerusalem cycle (6.1–10.39)
Fourth and final journey to Jerusalem (10.40–20.31).[14]

The above observations make it increasingly clear that the Fourth Gospel cannot be easily divided between chs 12 and 13. While there is much evidence to support a distinction between 'The Book of Signs' and 'The Book of Glory/Passion', the dividing line between them has proved difficult to draw. Instead it would be helpful to regard ch. 12 as a transition between these two major divisions, particularly since the greatest and last of Jesus' seven signs (the raising of Lazarus) occurs in ch. 11. Under this arrangement the references to the emotions of Jesus fall out as follows:

Table 4.1 Jesus' Emotions within the Major Divisions of John's Gospel

Prologue and Introduction (Chapter 1)	
The Book of Signs	Zeal (2.17)
(Chapters 2–11)	Love (11.3, 5, 36)
	Rejoice (11.15)
	Deeply moved (11.33, 38)
	Troubled (11.33)
	Weeping (11.35)
Transition (Chapter 12)	Troubled (12.27)
The Book of Passion/Glory	Love – verb (13.1 [2x], 34; 14.21, 31; 15.9, 12)
(Chapters 13–20)	'The disciple whom Jesus loved'(13.23; 19.26; 20.2)
	Troubled (13.21)
	Love – noun (15.9, 10, 13)
	Joy (15.11; 17.13)
Epilogue (Chapter 21)	'The disciple whom Jesus loved' (21.7, 20)

From this table the clustering of Jesus' emotions in John becomes immediately apparent. Far from being evenly distributed, as was the case in the Synoptics, the references to the emotions are largely confined to two major events – the raising of Lazarus (ch. 11) and the Farewell Discourse (chs 13–17).[15] Apart from 2.17, 'The Book of Signs' associates the emotions of Jesus only with its final and

---

14 Cf. R. Alan Culpepper, 'The Plot of John's Story of Jesus', *Int* 49 (1995), p. 351.
15 Notable exceptions to this pattern are the references to 'the disciple whom Jesus loved' in 19.26; 20.2; 21.7, 20. Yet even this expression has its origin in the Farewell Discourse (13.23) and would seem to be used fairly stereotypically from that point on.

climactic sign. The only reference to an emotion in ch. 12 significantly relates Jesus' troubled soul to his 'hour' (v. 27). 'The Book of Passion/Glory' refers frequently to the emotions of Jesus but only in anticipation of the Passion rather than during the Passion itself. Like the Synoptics, therefore, the Fourth Gospel tends to link the emotions of Jesus with miracles and the Passion but it does so in its own unique way. Jesus' emotions are recorded only in connection with the climactic sign in 'The Book of Signs', while the Farewell Discourse indicates Jesus' emotions in anticipation of the Passion.

4.1 *John's Presentation of Jesus*

As was the case with the Synoptics, John's opening comments about Jesus set the stage for his ministry throughout the entire Gospel. In this case the significance of the introductory remarks about Jesus is beyond dispute. It is well recognized that John's prologue (1.1-18) is a microcosm of the Gospel as a whole.[16] This applies particularly to its presentation of Jesus.

¹ In the beginning was the Word, and the Word was with God, and the Word was God.

² He was with God in the beginning.

³ Through him all things were made; without him nothing was made that has been made.

⁴ In him was life, and that life was the light of men.

⁵ The light shines in the darkness, but the darkness has not understood it.

⁶ There came a man who was sent from God; his name was John.

⁷ He came as a witness to testify concerning that light, so that through him all men might believe.

⁸ He himself was not the light; he came only as a witness to the light.

⁹ The true light that gives light to every man was coming into the world.

¹⁰ He was in the world, and though the world was made through him, the world did not recognize him.

¹¹ He came to that which was his own, but his own did not receive him.

¹² Yet to all who received him, to those who believed in his name, he gave the right to become children of God –

¹³ children born not of natural descent, nor of human decision or a husband's will, but born of God.

¹⁴ The Word became flesh and made his dwelling among us. We have seen his glory, the glory of the One and Only, who came from the Father, full of grace and truth.

¹⁵ John testifies concerning him. He cries out, saying, 'This was he of whom

---

16 See Simon R. Valentine, 'The Johannine Prologue: A Microcosm of the Gospel', *EvQ* 68 (1996), pp. 291–304.

I said, "He who comes after me has surpassed me because he was before me."'

[16] From the fullness of his grace we have all received one blessing after another.

[17] For the law was given through Moses; grace and truth came through Jesus Christ.

[18] No-one has ever seen God, but God the One and Only, who is at the Father's side, has made him known.

In the prologue, the preliminary portrait of Jesus is sketched in a highly artful way. The prologue itself is a masterpiece in literary design. At the most basic level, vv. 1-2 form a neat *inclusio* with v. 18. Beyond this many have recognized the profound contrast between the Word being God (v. 1) and becoming flesh (v. 14). Various attempts have been made to capture these contrasts by way of chiastic structures.[17] Because of the prologue's tantalizingly poetic form it is possible to impose various a-b-c-c-b-a arrangements onto its overall structure. However, so many attempts have been made, and with such varying results, that they tend to cancel one another out and therefore cast serious doubt on the validity of the entire approach. It must be possible to find a better solution that does justice both to the prologue's artistic symmetry and to its profound Christology. A more comprehensive model than either the *inclusio* or the chiasmus is provided by the parabola.[18]

1. 'The Word' (v. 1)   'God the One and Only' (v. 18)

2. 'with God' (vv. 1-2)   'at the Father's side' (v. 18)

3. Creation – 'life and light' (vv. 3-5)   New Creation – 'grace and truth' (vv. 14-17)

4. The Testimony of John (vv. 6-8)   The Testimony of John (v. 15)

5. The Incarnation – 'light' (vv. 9-10)   The Incarnation – 'glory' (v. 14)

6. Human Response – negative (vv. 10-11)   Human Response – positive (vv. 12-13)

Figure 4.1 The Parabola of the Prologue

17   For example, Peder Borgen, 'Observations on the Targumic Character of the Prologue of John', *NTS* 16 (1970), pp. 288–95; R. Alan Culpepper, 'The Pivot of John's Prologue', *NTS* 27 (1980), pp. 1–31; Morna Hooker. 'John the Baptist and the Johannine Prologue', *NTS* 16 (1970), pp. 354–58.

18   For further discussion on this point see my article, 'John's Prologue: Beyond Some Impasses of Twentieth Century Scholarship', *WTJ* 63 (2002), pp. 15–44.

The parabola descends from eternity (vv. 1-2) down into human history and the incarnation and then ascends again into eternity (v. 18).[19] This great parabola is like the swoop of a mighty eagle, an image with which this Gospel has been associated since ancient times.[20] Unlike chiastic structures, the parabola allows for grand movement and broad conceptual parallels, without demanding those precise correspondences that can so easily smack of artificiality. This parabolic swoop illustrates the truth that Jesus is at such pains to emphasize later in the Gospel, that he is 'from above', 'from heaven', 'not of this world' and 'sent by the Father', and that he will return to the Father.

The flight of the Johannine eagle can therefore be charted from its cosmic origins 'with God' (vv. 1-2) to its heavenly destination 'at the Father's side' (v. 18). As the source of light and life it is involved in the creation of the universe (vv. 3-5). From there the flight descends into time in the testimony of John (vv. 6-8), reaches the earth by way of the incarnation (vv. 9-10) and arrives at its low point in human ignorance and rejection (vv. 10-11). The parabola begins its upward flight with the positive human response of acceptance and faith (vv. 12-13) and continues its ascent with another reference to the incarnation, but this time with a strong emphasis on glory (v. 14). The journey to ultimate glory continues again via John's testimony (v. 15) and now via the new creation that is qualified by grace and truth (vv. 14-17). Hence the prologue traces the eagle's majestic flight from eternity to eternity. Its course is broadly symmetrical in that its descent to earth is parallelled by its ascent back to heaven.

The artful simplicity of the parabola not only avoids the intricacies of more complex approaches, it removes the temptation of searching for the prologue's centre of gravity.[21] Under this arrangement no one element of the prologue carries more weight than any other. All contribute equally to the unity and symmetry of the whole. It would be an exegetical fallacy to assign a higher significance to any single aspect, as every concept introduced in the prologue will receive further elaboration in the narratives and discourses that follow. The parabola does, however, possess a balance that allows us to explore the message of the prologue in a coherent way and to discover parallels that have the potential of being mutually interpretive. The above diagram suggests six such parallels:

First, as the Word, Jesus is identified with God. On the basis of grammar alone v. 1 can be read as stating at the very least that the Word was divine. The further step of identifying the Word with God depends on contextual considerations. Evidence in this direction comes first from the expression 'God the One and Only', which translates the most probable of the variant readings in v. 18.

---

19   Cf. James T. Dennison, Jr., 'The Prologue of John's Gospel', *Kerux* 8 (1993), p. 3.

20   Burridge, *Four Gospels*, p. 26.

21   Cf. R. Alan Culpepper, 'The Pivot of John's Prologue', *NTS* 27 (1980), pp. 1–31. On the basis of the chiasm that he discovers in the prologue Culpepper argues that the chiastic structure pivots on v. 12b: 'and he gave them the authority to become the children of God.' From this he concludes that 'the Johannine community was identifying itself . . . as the heir to a role and standing which Israel had abdicated by her failure to receive the Son of God' (p. 31). To claim that this is the prologue's central thought is basing too much on the supposed chiasm that has been discovered.

Secondly, the identity of Jesus as God appears to be the presupposition of the Gospel as a whole. Barrett's comment on v. 1 has often been quoted in this connection: 'John intends that the whole of his gospel shall be read in the light of this verse. The deeds and words of Jesus are the deeds and words of God; if this be not true the book is blasphemous.'[22]

While Jesus can *be identified* as God, he is not to be *equated* with him. This becomes particularly clear from the phrases 'with God' (vv. 1, 2) and 'at the Father's side' (v. 18). Although these expressions indicate a relationship of the most intimate kind, they also underscore the distinction between the Word and God (vv. 1-2) or between Jesus Christ and the Father (vv. 17-18). This unique relationship supremely qualifies Jesus to reveal and explain God (v. 18b), which is arguably his chief function in John's narrative.

Jesus' divinity is further highlighted by his roles in creation (vv. 3-5) and in the new creation (vv. 14-17). The strong reminiscences of Genesis 1 in vv. 1-5 clearly align him with the Creator, particularly in his being portrayed as the source of life and light (vv. 4-5). Throughout the prologue the language further echoes the LXX of Genesis 1 so as to consistently place Jesus on the side of the Creator rather than of creation. In v. 14 this pattern alters markedly. Through his incarnation Jesus enters the creation and thereby transforms it with God's 'grace and truth' (vv. 14, 17). These attributes can be identified with Yahweh's covenant faithfulness and loving-kindness in the Old Testament. Hence the very qualities that characterized Yahweh under the old covenant are now being revealed through Jesus Christ.

A further aspect of Jesus' deity is conveyed through the witness of John the Baptist. The *subject* of his testimony is the light (vv. 6-8) which in the subsequent verses is clearly identified as Jesus, while its *content* is that Jesus, although coming after John, was in fact before him (v. 15). John therefore testifies to Jesus' pre-existence, which is precisely the doctrine that lies behind the opening paragraph (vv. 1-5) and is possibly picked up again in v. 18.

While we see that the prologue highlights Jesus' divinity – his identity as God, his intimacy with the Father, his roles in creation and the new creation, and his pre-existence – it is equally insistent in claiming his genuine humanity. Although his incarnation is obliquely mentioned in vv. 9-10, it is stated with force in v. 14. The choice of terminology is dramatic. The term 'flesh' is very descriptive and conveys the notion not only of humanity but also of mortality. This is probably the Gospel's first hint that Jesus must die. In the Bread of Life discourse Jesus repeatedly uses the word 'flesh' in this connection (6.51-56).

Finally, the human response to the 'Word become flesh' is both positive and negative. His own did not receive him (v. 11), while on the other hand there were those who both received and believed (v. 12). As the children of God, the latter group may be said to constitute the new covenant community (v. 12) and the beginning of the new creation (v. 13). Although he was shrouded in flesh they beheld the Word's glory (v. 14) and became the recipients of his grace and

---

22 C. K. Barrett. *The Gospel According to St John: An Introduction with Commentary and Notes on the Greek Text* (London: SPCK, 1955), p. 130.

truth (vv. 14, 16, 17). The distinction between these contrasting responses is seen consistently in the ensuing narrative. Many of the characters in the story saw in Jesus no more than 'flesh', while others recognized him as the divine Word or Logos, the covenant Lord.

These six points that grow out of the parabolic symmetry of the prologue lie on the surface of the text. A little probing into the Old Testament background to this passage reveals further symmetry at a deeper level. The first five verses, which introduce Jesus as the Word, are an exposition of Gen. 1.1-5. Jesus is immediately identified as the divine Word who spoke creation into being. The last five verses of the prologue (vv. 14-18), on the other hand, are loaded with Exodus imagery. The Word did not just become 'a man' or 'human' but 'flesh' – a strong term that brings out humanity's frailty, transience, vulnerability and mortality. Yet it is precisely in the flesh that the Word '*tabernacled* among us' (1.14 AV). John's choice of this unusual verb immediately evokes associations with the tabernacle of Exodus. Paradoxically, it is in the very frailty of human flesh that 'we have seen his glory' (1.14). Again images of the tabernacle come to mind. When this structure was completed at the end of Exodus, the account emphatically repeats the statement, 'and the glory of the Lord filled the tabernacle' (Exod. 40.34-35). The glory theme so prominent in Exodus becomes equally prominent in John. The glory of Yahweh, the Lord of the covenant, is now seen in Jesus Christ, the Word become flesh, who is full of grace and truth (1.14, 17; cf. Exod. 34.6).

If the prologue provides a lens through which the Gospel is to be read, then it also provides the reader with significant clues as to the identity of its main character. Jesus is to be understood as both divine and human, as Logos and flesh. One is not to be reduced to, or cancelled out by, the other. If this is how Jesus is understood in the prologue, is it also how his emotions are to be understood throughout the Gospel?

4.2 *Zeal (2.13-22)*

13 When it was almost time for the Jewish Passover, Jesus went up to Jerusalem.

14 In the temple courts he found men selling cattle, sheep and doves, and others sitting at tables exchanging money.

15 So he made a whip out of cords, and drove all from the temple area, both sheep and cattle; he scattered the coins of the money-changers and overturned their tables.

16 To those who sold doves he said, 'Get these out of here! How dare you turn my Father's house into a market!'

17 His disciples remembered that it is written: '*Zeal* for your house will consume me.'

18 Then the Jews demanded of him, 'What miraculous sign can you show us to prove your authority to do all this?'

¹⁹ Jesus answered them, 'Destroy this temple, and I will raise it again in three days.'

²⁰ The Jews replied, 'It has taken forty-six years to build this temple, and you are going to raise it in three days?'

²¹ But the temple he had spoken of was his body.

²² After he was raised from the dead, his disciples recalled what he had said. Then they believed the Scripture and the words that Jesus had spoken.

Following the prologue the remainder of ch. 1 is intent on establishing the messianic identity of Jesus Christ, the incarnate Word. This is done skillfully in a series of encounters between Jesus and his early followers. By the end of the chapter he has been given a number of messianic titles so that his credentials as the Messiah are left beyond doubt. John the Baptist testifies that Jesus is both the Lamb of God (1.29, 36) and the Son of God (1.34). Andrew calls him the Messiah (1.41), while Philip tells Nathanael, 'We have found the one Moses wrote about in the Law, and about whom the prophets also wrote – Jesus of Nazareth, the son of Joseph' (1.45). The most ringing affirmation comes with the confession of Nathanael, the 'true Israelite': 'Rabbi, you are the Son of God; you are the King of Israel' (1.49). But perhaps most revealing of all is Jesus' own declaration to his disciples in the closing verse: 'I tell you the truth, you shall see heaven open, and the angels of God ascending and descending on the Son of Man' (1.51).

Chapter 1 therefore ends on a high note. This is the first of the Gospel's twenty-five declarations on the lips of Jesus that open with the emphatic double *Amen*. This is also the first time Jesus refers to himself as 'the Son of Man', always a title of exaltation in John. The opening and closing expressions of this statement suggest that its content is important. The Son of Man is making a very significant declaration, the wording of which seems to be intentionally reminiscent of Jacob's dream at Bethel, 'in which he saw a stairway resting on the earth, with its top reaching to heaven, and *the angels of God were ascending and descending on it*' (Gen. 28.12, emphasis added). A superficial comparison of Jesus' allusion to its source would seem to suggest that the Son of Man be identified with Jacob's ladder and that Jesus is therefore identifying himself with the staircase to heaven. But this is not exactly correct. Strictly speaking, in Gen. 28.12 the angels ascend and descend *on* the ladder, while they ascend and descend *onto* the Son of Man in Jn 1.51.²³ Later in this Gospel Jesus insists that he is the way to the Father (14.6), but that is not his point here. In his allusion to Gen. 28.12 he is comparing himself not to Jacob's ladder but to Bethel, the place of Jacob's dream. Jacob specifically refers to Bethel – according to the etymology of its name – as 'the house of God' (Gen. 28.17), and that is also what he (re-)names the place (Gen. 28.19). In line with the prologue's declaration that he 'tabernacled among us' (1.14), Jesus is now subtly but unequivocally stating that as the Son of Man he is the house of God. In him God is dwelling with his people. This claim, so

---

23 This difference is seen most readily by comparing the LXX translation of Gen. 28.12 to the Greek of Jn 1.51. In both cases the preposition *epi* is used, but with the genitive in Genesis and with the accusative in John.

obliquely made in ch. 1, is stated with force in ch. 2. Between the two chapters a transition occurs. In ch. 1 the messiahship of Jesus is stated; in ch. 2 it is demonstrated. In the actions of ch. 2 the emphasis shifts from Jesus' messianic identity to his messianic authority.

Jesus' authority is initially demonstrated by his first miraculous sign, the changing of water into wine at the wedding reception in the Galilean village of Cana. Because of the huge quantity of quality wine that Jesus produced, this sign points primarily to the messianic age as an age of abundance (cf. 1.16; 6.13; 10.10; Gen. 49.11-12; Isa. 25.6; Jer. 31.12-14; Amos 9.13-14).[24] In the Christ, God is making abundant provision for his people. But a secondary purpose also seems to be at work. The water that Jesus used for his miracle filled 'six stone water jars, the kind used by the Jews for ceremonial washing' (2.6). So not only is Jesus changing water into wine, his miracle is also a sign that he is about to change the purification rites of Judaism. A major transformation is about to take place. The messianic age is dawning in spectacular fashion. The water of Judaism is becoming the wine of the age of salvation.

In the next episode Jesus raises the stakes considerably by setting his sights on a far bigger target than some relatively minor purification rites. His focus is now on the temple, the very heart of Jewish life, culture and religion. The occasion is the Passover, one of the pilgrim feasts for which Jewish males were expected to be in Jerusalem. But from ch. 1 we know that Jesus was no ordinary Jewish male. John the Baptist has already introduced him as the 'Lamb of God' (1.29, 36). It was dangerous for a lamb to be in Jerusalem at the Passover. For the attentive reader an element of narrative tension is introduced at this point. What will happen to this Lamb? Will he be slaughtered along with all the others? Yes, but not yet, for his hour has not yet come (2.4). First we are given a glimpse of the wrath of the Lamb.

What Jesus sees in the temple precincts at Passover is enough to make his blood boil. The temple area is hardly a serene place conducive to the reverent worship of God. The atmosphere is anything but worshipful. An environment that had been dedicated to the service of Yahweh had degenerated into a thriving place of business. Because of the large pilgrim crowds frequenting Jerusalem for the major Jewish feasts,[25] the temple had become a hub of economic activity. It was a thriving commercial centre, which may not have brought in the tourist dollar but it certainly brought in the pilgrim shekel. By the first century AD the temple had become the economic mainstay of Jerusalem.

---

24   As to the amount of wine that Jesus' miracle produced, estimates vary between 120 and 150 gallons or about 600 litres, the equivalent of roughly 800 standard-size bottles of wine. See Maximilan Zerwick and and Mary Grosvenor, *A Grammatical Analysis of the Greek New Testament* (Rome: Biblical Institute Press, rev. edn, 1981), p. 290.

25   Josephus, *Jewish War* 6, p. 425, gives some statistics for one of the Passovers celebrated during the reign of Nero (54–68): 'The count showed that there were 255,600 victims; the men, reckoning ten diners to each victim, totaled 2,700,000.' Although this is a generation after Jesus and granted that due allowances be made for exaggeration, it is reasonable to conclude that these feasts attracted huge numbers of pilgrims, which meant a financial boon for Jerusalem.

John gives his readers a brief glimpse of this brisk commercial activity (2.14-15). It is a very sober account of a situation where it is not difficult to imagine the lowing of cattle, the bleating of sheep, the fluttering of birds in cages, and men haggling over a fair rate of exchange. As the temple fees had to be paid in Tyrian coinage, many pilgrims would have needed to have their currency converted.[26] With the pilgrim throngs being what they were, the money changers must have been involved in lucrative business. But when Jesus sees what is happening, he is livid and cracks the whip over the entire enterprise.[27] It is not difficult to picture the chaos and commotion that results from his passionate reaction. Jesus sends the animals scurrying, no doubt with their owners chasing after them. He kicks over the tables of the money men with their neat piles of coins. But even stronger than his whip is the moral power of his words, 'Get these out of here! How dare you turn my Father's house into a market!' (2.16).

All this is most unusual for Jesus. We never see him getting so worked up again. But precisely what emotion is he expressing here? It is often said that Jesus was angry when he cleared the temple. But anger is too tame a word. The disciples were more accurate when they remembered a verse from the Old Testament, 'Zeal for your house will consume me' (2.17; cf. Ps. 69.9). Zeal is more than anger. It is the ardour of red-hot passion.[28] The quote is from a messianic Psalm. As a righteous sufferer, the Psalmist has a passion for the house of God – so much so that it is all-consuming.[29] It eats him up. Obviously the same is

---

26   Mary L. Coloe, 'Temple Imagery in John', *Int* 63 (2009), p. 372, explains the procedure: 'Since this tax could not be paid with Roman coins that offended Jewish law with the image of the emperor, the Roman money was exchanged with coins from Tyre that had no "graven image." Pilgrims, on entering the outer precincts of the temple could change their money, pay the temple tax, and buy an animal for sacrifice.'

27   The text is ambiguous as to how precisely Jesus used the whip. The word for 'all' (*pantas*) is a masculine accusative plural, which is in grammatical agreement with either 'the money-changers' (v. 14) or the 'cattle' (v. 15). After discussing the grammatical possibilities, Mark R. Bredin, 'John's Account of Jesus' Demonstration in the Temple: Violent or Nonviolent?" *BTB* 33 (2003), pp. 46–47, argues that if Jesus had used the whip on people he would most certainly have been in trouble. He concludes that 'John portrays Jesus using the whip on animals.' This may possibly have included the sheep as well.

28   The Greek word *zēlos* can denote either (a) 'intense positive interest in someth., zeal, ardor, marked by a sense of dedication', or (b) 'intense negative feelings over another's achievements or success, jealousy, envy' (BDAG, p. 427). John 2.17 is of course listed under (a), as is Heb. 10.27 which attracts the following comment: 'Of the fire of judgment which, with its blazing flames, appears like a living being intent on devouring God's adversaries' (BDAG, p. 427). *EDNT* 1, p. 100 states that, although the motivation can vary, *zēlos* designates 'a passionate commitment to a person or cause.' The papyrus evidence supports 'fervour' as the primary idea of the word (MM, p. 273).

29   Marvin E. Tate, *Psalms 51-100* (WBC 20; Dallas: Word, 1990), p. 192, discusses the difficulty of dating this Psalm and concludes that 'the determination of the exact context intended for the suppliant in the Psalm is very elusive'. This uncertainty makes it difficult to know whether 'your house' is to be understood as a reference to the temple or whether a metaphorical sense is intended.

true for Jesus when he uses the whip.[30] But an examination of the details reveals another level of meaning.

A careful comparison of the quote to its Old Testament source reveals a significant difference between the two. The Psalmist says, 'Zeal for your house *consumes* me' (present tense) or '*has consumed* me' (past tense). English translations render the Hebrew perfect tense by either the present or the past. John 2.17 takes neither of these options, but quotes the Psalm in the future tense, 'Zeal for your house *will consume* me.' Why, in quoting the Psalm, does John move from the present or the past to the future tense? The reason for the change lies in the nature of Jesus' zeal. In his case it is more than an all-consuming passion. Something is yet to happen. The Messiah must die. It is dangerous for the Lamb of God to be in Jerusalem for the Passover. Zeal for God's house will not just eat him up psychologically, as was the case with the Psalmist. Jesus has more than a passionate ardour for the house of God. He has a zeal that will consume him literally and totally. In this saying John sees a prediction of Jesus' death.[31]

The fulfilment of the prophecy that Jesus will be consumed (2.17) is fore-shadowed by his enigmatic response to the Jews' demand for a sign, 'Destroy this temple and I will raise it again in three days' (2.19). Jesus throws down the gauntlet by issuing a daring challenge. He is not only making a prediction but giving his questioners a command. He is telling them to 'destroy this temple'. The verb is an imperative. Taking his words at face value, the Jews don't have a clue as to what he is talking about. At that time the temple had been under

---

30   As Bredin, 'Jesus' Demonstration in the Temple', p. 47, argues: 'John emphasizes the passion of Jesus' act with the use of the whip and with remembrance of the Psalm. The whip reminds his readers of this quote . . . Jesus is ardent and utterly committed to put right that which offends him in the temple.'

31   Because the Psalms are Hebrew poetry their verb forms do not have a fixed tense. Whereas Hebrew prose usually provides clear indications of the time when an action takes place, poetry often gives no such clues. (See Alviero Niccacci, *The Syntax of the Verb in Classical Hebrew Prose* [JSOTSup 86; trans. W. G. E. Watson; Sheffield: Sheffield Academic Press, 1990], pp. 196–97.) This characteristic of Hebrew poetry may well go a long way towards explaining the differences in translation. In the case of Ps. 69.9 we have already seen that English translations fluctuate between the present and past tenses. Greek translations seem to have fluctuated too, but in a different way. The best textual evidence would suggest that the LXX translated the Hebrew perfect with an aorist (simple past) verb in Greek, i.e. 'consumed'. John 2.17, on the other hand, has the future tense, i.e. 'will consume.' But the apparent contradiction can be easily resolved. If in poetry there is nothing inherent in the form of the Hebrew verb to demand that it be translated by a certain tense in the receptor language, and if everything depends on exegetical and contextual factors, the differences between the LXX and John become understandable. The LXX translator apparently understood Ps. 69.9 as purely *descriptive* of the Psalmist's sufferings, in which case the simple past would be quite appropriate. The author of the Fourth Gospel, on the other hand, understood the same verse as also being *predictive* of Jesus' sufferings, in which case the future tense would be more appropriate. On the understanding that there is an underlying difference of exegesis behind the two renderings, each translation in its own way is legitimate and accurate. Together with other New Testament writers who make use of Psalm 69 (cf. Mt. 27.34, 48; Mk 15.23, 36; Lk. 23.36; Acts 1.20; Rom. 11.9-10; 15.3), John has detected its messianic typology and therefore accents its prophetic nature (see also 15.25; 19.29).

construction for forty-six years. Obviously his interlocutors had no intention of destroying their own temple. But Jesus was not talking about a temple constructed by architects and stonemasons. Being the wooden literalists that they were, his questioners did not have an inkling of Jesus' intended meaning. The Evangelist admits that even the disciples caught on only much later – 'after he was raised from the dead' (2.22). Were it not for the editorial comment, 'But the temple he had spoken of was his body' (2.21), most readers would be left completely in the dark as well. That the temple was Jesus' body makes the whole incident understandable. Ironically, it was *that* temple that the Jews would later seek to destroy and that Jesus would raise within the space of just three days. This would be the sign that he had the authority to clear the Jerusalem temple.[32] A little reflection soon shows that this sign would be an even greater feat than rebuilding Herod's temple in such a short period of time.

Only when Jesus had risen from the dead did all of this begin to make sense to the disciples. It was then that they recalled what he had said and that they believed the words that he had spoken (2. 22). This recollection would seem to apply to Jesus' challenge to the Jews (2.19). Only after the resurrection would his disciples understand what Jesus meant by destroying the temple and raising it in three days. It was also after the resurrection that 'they believed the Scripture' (2.22). The singular 'Scripture' should be seen as a reference to a specific passage, namely Ps. 69.9.[33] The disciples did not remember the Psalm immediately as Jesus was cleansing the temple. Only after he was raised did the whole incident come together in their minds. A similar comment is made about the events surrounding Palm Sunday, which is interpreted as a fulfilment of Zech. 9.9: 'At first the disciples did not understand all this. Only after Jesus was glorified did they realize these things had been written about him and that they had done these things to him' (12.16). Their later illumination seems to have been a result of their reception of the Holy Spirit (20.22; cf. 14.26). Only when they had received the Spirit did they have the hermeneutical insight to understand the true significance of the temple cleansing and the events that took place on Palm Sunday. By then the true temple had been destroyed and rebuilt in three days.

The temple theme that was introduced at an almost subliminal level in the opening chapter (1.14, 51) has become the main vehicle for predicting the Messiah's death and resurrection (2.19, 21). It is when the temple of his body is destroyed that zeal for God's house will have consumed him. Till that destruction occurs the Jerusalem temple remains 'my Father's house' (2.16). Because he is the Son of God (1.34, 49) the zeal that he shows for that house is therefore not

---

32 Cf. Gail R. O'Day, 'Piety without Pretense, Faith without Falsehood: The Lenten Journey According to John', *JP* 20 (1997), p. 11, 'The sign that Jesus gives as warrant for his actions in the temple, then, is his death and resurrection. Jesus has the authority to challenge the authority of the temple system because his life and death bear witness to the power and presence of God.'

33 Thus Richard B. Hays, 'Can the Gospels Teach Us How to Read the Old Testament?' *ProEccl* 11 (2002), p. 413, 'John is describing a retrospective act of memory and imagination after the resurrection: the disciples did not remember Psalm 69:9 at the time of the Temple protest action, but later, after he had been raised from the dead.'

only that of the righteous sufferer of Psalm 69 but also that of the divine Son who shares the holy zeal of God. So although the emphasis here is on the Christ's humanity, there are also overtones of deity that should not be missed. The distinctions are nuanced rather than absolute. Although the prediction of impending death would be inapplicable to God, the zeal that causes it is not exclusively human. The zeal of God could be conveyed through his representatives, such as Phinehas the priest (Num. 25.11; cf. 2 Macc. 2.54) and Paul the apostle (2 Cor. 11.2).[34] If their zeal could somehow be described as divine, it at least raises the possibility that – as *the* Representative of God – the Christ possesses such zeal in even greater measure. This perspective is further underscored by the fact that Yahweh's zeal/jealousy in the Old Testament comes to its most pointed and direct expression in contexts of worship. It is a divine emotion that is aroused particularly by Israel's idolatry (Exod. 20.5; 34.14; Num. 25.11; Deut. 4.23, 24; 6.14, 15; 29.20; 32.16, 21; Ps. 78.58).[35] The effect that Israel's idolatry had on Yahweh in the Old Testament, the Jerusalem temple now has on the Christ. The divine revulsion at idolatry is paralleled by Jesus' reaction to blighted worship.

Here again we see the paradox of Jesus' person. The zeal he expresses is that of God, but it is to result in his death. Moreover, he expresses zeal in his capacity as the divine Son. In this context it is precisely zeal for the Father's house (Jn 2.16) rather than simply the house of God (as in Psalm 69) that comes to such bold expression. Therefore we cannot place this emotion in a hermetically sealed compartment, whether human or divine. In that his zeal is intricately linked to his death, it accents Jesus' humanity; in that it reflects Yahweh's zeal against false worship, it expresses elements of the divine.

Jesus' zeal contains yet another paradox. The Old Testament quotation in which it is couched is the first to be introduced by an 'it is written' formula. Except for 1.23, this is how the quotations in the first half of the Fourth Gospel are introduced (6.31, 45; 10.34; 12.14-15). Fulfilment quotations which focus on the Messiah's sufferings commence only at 12.38. The paradox in the case of 2.17 lies in the fact that, although it is a prediction of the Messiah's death, the Old Testament quotation is introduced by 'it is written'. From this it could be argued that the pattern is broken before it is even begun. This would be an uncharitable judgement however, as the prediction of the Messiah's death by way of a Psalm citation links this first prediction with all the other Old Testament quotations that fulfil the same function (12.38-40; 13.18; 15.25; 19.24, 36-37). This lends an added dimension to the unity and symmetry of the Fourth Gospel. These connections forge further links to demonstrate that Jesus' all consuming zeal will ultimately devour him.

---

34 Cf. *TDNT* 2, p. 881, where Paul is not seen as the bearer of divine zeal per se, but where he describes his jealousy as 'God's jealousy in terms of the OT conception of God as One who with holy zeal seeks to keep His people from adultery with idols.'

35 See *TDNT* 2, p. 879: 'When the reference is to Yahweh, it is almost always a question of His relations to His people Israel. Yahweh's zeal is provoked when Israel worships idols and thus transgresses the commandment which has as its basis Ex. 20:5 . . .'

4.3 *Love and Joy over Lazarus (11.1-16)*

¹ Now a man named Lazarus was sick. He was from Bethany, the village of Mary and her sister Martha.

² This Mary, whose brother Lazarus now lay sick, was the same one who poured perfume on the Lord and wiped his feet with her hair.

³ So the sisters sent word to Jesus, 'Lord, *the one you love* is sick.'

⁴ When he heard this, Jesus said, 'This sickness will not end in death. No, it is for God's glory so that God's Son may be glorified through it.'

⁵ *Jesus loved Martha and her sister and Lazarus.*

⁶ Yet when he heard that Lazarus was sick, he stayed where he was two more days.

⁷ Then he said to his disciples, 'Let us go back to Judea.'

⁸ 'But Rabbi,' they said, 'a short while ago the Jews tried to stone you, and yet you are going back there?'

⁹ Jesus answered, 'Are there not twelve hours of daylight? A man who walks by day will not stumble, for he sees by this world's light.

¹⁰ It is when he walks by night that he stumbles, for he has no light.'

¹¹ After he had said this, he went on to tell them, 'Our friend Lazarus has fallen asleep; but I am going there to wake him up.'

¹² His disciples replied, 'Lord, if he sleeps, he will get better.'

¹³ Jesus had been speaking of his death, but his disciples thought he meant natural sleep.

¹⁴ So then he told them plainly, 'Lazarus is dead,

¹⁵ and for your sake *I am glad* I was not there, so that you may believe. But let us go to him.'

¹⁶ Then Thomas (called Didymus) said to the rest of the disciples, 'Let us also go, that we may die with him.'

When Jesus cleanses the temple in the Synoptics his opponents' reaction is extremely hostile. They are indignant (Mt. 21.15) and begin looking for ways to kill him (Mk 11.18; Lk. 19.47). In comparison, the Jews' demand for a sign in Jn 2.18 is a very mild reaction to what must have seemed a very provocative act on Jesus' part. Nevertheless, this is where Jesus' conflict with his opposition begins in John. It is centred in Jerusalem and it gains in intensity as the narrative unfolds. At first the conflict is merely verbal but it soon turns mortal (5.16-18). Jesus' conflict with his antagonists is one of the factors that drive his geographical movements in the Fourth Gospel. The other factor is the various religious feasts that Jesus attends in Jerusalem.

The city of Jerusalem therefore has a dual role in John. It is home to the various feasts that, as the Messiah, Jesus observes religiously, demonstrating that he in his own person is the fulfilment of their symbolism. For example, at the Feast of Tabernacles, with its water-pouring ceremony and the lighting of the candelabra, Jesus offers living water (7.38-39) and declares that he is the light of the world (8.12; 9.5). Yet it is precisely at times like this that Jerusalem takes on a second, more sinister role. Jesus' claims at these feasts arouse escalating opposition so that in John the city becomes the focal point of hostility against Jesus. From ch. 5 onwards this antagonism is deadly. His enemies want to kill him (5.18; 7.19, 20, 25; 8.37, 40; 11.53), preferably by stoning (8.59; 10.31; 11.8). Their opposition, however, is not fuelled by personal animosity. Nor do they oppose him mainly because they see him as a threat to the establishment. Their motives are religious. In their view he has broken the Law of Moses. He has desecrated the Sabbath and is guilty of blasphemy, and for that he deserves to be executed.

This dual role that Jerusalem plays in John creates a situation of narrative tension. For Jesus the city increasingly becomes the place both of fulfilment and of mortal danger. It is in Jerusalem that he makes messianic pronouncements (5.18; 7.17, 29; 8.55; 10.30, 38) that conform to what is claimed for him in the prologue (1.1-18). Yet these very pronouncements incite intense opposition. Jesus is therefore caught in a vortex from which he cannot escape. For safety's sake he leaves Jerusalem, but the feasts continually bring him back. Thus after Jesus' first recorded visit to Jerusalem for a Passover (2.13-3.21), he leaves Judea because he gets wind of the fact that the Pharisees had heard that he was making and baptizing more disciples than John (4.1). He therefore judiciously leaves for the relative safety of Samaria and Galilee (4.3-54). An unnamed Jewish feast has Jesus return to Jerusalem (5.1), but the healing of the cripple at the Pool of Bethesda on the Sabbath (5.1-15) inspires such hostility that Jesus retreats to the far shore of the Sea of Galilee (6.1). He remains in Galilee till the Feast of Tabernacles necessitates his presence in Jerusalem (7.10). This time he stays in Jerusalem, in spite of arrest attempts (7.30, 32, 44; 8.20) and death threats (7.25; 8.40, 59), apparently till the Feast of Dedication (10.22). If chs 7–10 are to be read as a continuous narrative in chronological order, this means that Jesus stayed in Jerusalem from October to December. At the Feast of Dedication, however, the situation becomes critical. While walking in Solomon's Colonnade in the temple Jesus is accosted by a group of Jews demanding to know whether he is the Christ. His unusually direct answer (10.25-30) ends on a provocative note, 'I and the Father are one' (10.30). For the Jews this is too much. They again attempt to stone him for blasphemy (10.31-33; cf. 8.59), but he eludes their grasp (10.39). This time he seeks refuge across the Jordan (10.40). The narrative has come full circle, as this was 'the place where John had been baptizing in the early days' (10.40; cf. 1.28). In spite of this connection, the precise location of 'Bethany on the other side of the Jordan' (1.28) is difficult to determine with any degree of certainty. But wherever it was, compared with the hostility in Jerusalem, it was a safe haven that provided some welcome relief. It was also a place of fruitful ministry (10.41-42).

It is in this setting of relative tranquility that Jesus receives an urgent message. Lazarus is sick. But that is not quite the way the sisters Mary and Martha word their message, 'Lord, *the one you love* is sick' (11.3). There is no specific mention of Jesus' love in Jn 1–10, but his love for Lazarus is emphasized repeatedly throughout ch. 11 (vv. 3, 5, 11, 36). Given the situation he is in, Jesus' love for his sick friend will be tested to the limit. Jesus can either stay in Bethany beyond the Jordan or return to Bethany near Jerusalem. The two sisters live three kilometres (just under two miles) from Jerusalem (11.18), too close for comfort to the epi-centre of deadly antagonism against Jesus. Will Jesus leave the relative safety of one Bethany for the mortal danger of the other? How strong is his love for his friend? Is Jesus' love great enough that he would be prepared to lay down his life for Lazarus (15.13)?

The love that Jesus has for Lazarus is shared by the sisters. Almost parenthet-ically the Evangelist notes that 'Jesus loved Martha and her sister and Lazarus' (11.5). The little trio at Bethany would seem to have had a special relationship with Jesus and were united to him, and presumably also to his disciples (11.11), in the bonds of a strong friendship (cf. Lk. 10.38-42). There could be more here, however, than meets the eye of the average reader of the English Bible. In 11.5 the Greek verb for 'love' is *agapaō*, while the love Jesus has for Lazarus individually is indicated by *phileō* (11.3, 36). Is this difference intentional? Commentators of an earlier generation certainly thought so. Thus B. F. Westcott understood Jesus' love for Lazarus as 'the natural affection of personal attachment,' whereas the use of *agapaō* in 11.5 'describes the Lord's affection for this family as that of moral choice.'[36] Benjamin Warfield is prepared to press these distinctions even further. For him *agapaō* is 'more elevated' and *phileō* 'more intimate'.[37] The latter is tactfully reserved for Jesus' affection for Lazarus so as to avoid the mis-conception that Jesus' love for Mary and Martha had anything of 'an amatory nature' about it.[38] More recent research has shown that such distinctions are quite artificial. Particularly in John, the verbs *agapaō* and *phileō* can be used synonymously and interchangeably, as for example to indicate Jesus' relationship to the Beloved Disciple (13.23; 19.26; 21.7, 20/20.2) and Peter's love for Jesus (21.15-16/21.15-17). There is therefore no fundamental difference between Jesus' love for Lazarus and that for his sisters. In Bethany beyond the Jordan the calibre of his love for all three is being severely tested.

At first Jesus' love for his friends seems to be put on hold: 'When he heard that Lazarus was sick, he stayed where he was two more days' (11.6). This is an odd response to an urgent request from close friends. One would have expected a true friend to suspend his plans immediately and rush to the aid of the one who is sick as quickly as possible.[39] But Jesus doesn't do this. Why? Is he taking his time to think through the issues and weigh up the pros and cons of the situation?

---

36   B. F. Westcott, *The Gospel According to St. John: The Authorized Version with Introduction and Notes* (Grand Rapids, MI: Eerdmans, 1954 [originally published in 1881]), p. 165.

37   Benjamin J. Warfield, *The Person and Work of Christ* (Philadelphia: Presbyterian & Reformed, 1950), p. 105.

38   Warfield, *Person and Work*, p. 106.

39   Francis J. Moloney, 'Can Everyone be Wrong? A Reading of John 11.1-12.8', *NTS* 49 (2003), p. 511: 'Judged by human standards, the juxtaposition of a description of Jesus' love for Lazarus and his sisters (v. 5) and his two-day delay when he hears of Lazarus' illness (v. 6) is extremely odd. This is not the way one behaves on receiving news of the fatal illness of a loved one. But on earlier occasions in the narrative Jesus' negative response to a request has led to unexpected consequences that transcend the intentions of the original request [2.1-11; 4.46-54; 7.2-14] . . . As in those earlier actions, Jesus' response cannot be measured by human standards.'

Does he need to reflect on the implications of what could easily be a very risky undertaking? What might be the repercussions not only for himself but also for the disciples, and perhaps even for the sisters who sent the message? While these questions may have crossed his mind during that two-day period, they hardly tell the whole story. As a matter of principle Jesus does not act on his own initiative, but always in concert with the Father's will (5.19, 30; 8.28; 12.49; 14.10), and this would seem to be the case in the present instance. However intense his affections and loyalty to his friends may be, his timing is always regulated by his Father's will. The timetable that Jesus is following is therefore not that of his friends, nor even his own, but his Father's.[40]

After the two-day delay Jesus has an announcement to make to his disciples: 'Let us go back to Judea' (11.7). Judging by their reaction it comes as quite a shock. 'But Rabbi', they protest, 'a short while ago the Jews tried to stone you, and you are going back there?' (11.8). The disciples still have vivid and bewildering memories of the attempted stoning not so long ago in Jerusalem (10.31-33). Under those circumstances no rabbi in his right mind would venture anywhere near Jerusalem. But Jesus has news for his disciples. Whether he acquired the information by natural or supernatural means the Gospel does not say, but during the two-day delay Lazarus' illness took a turn for the worse that resulted in his death. By using the metaphor of sleep, Jesus tries to break the news gently to his disciples, but they misunderstand (11.11-12). Wary of returning to Judea, they surmise that Lazarus has taken a turn for the better, thereby probably hoping that the hazardous journey could be avoided. So Jesus has to tell them quite bluntly that Lazarus has died (11.14), sweeping away any misunderstanding of Lazarus' condition as well as any false hopes of staying in the safety of Transjordanian Bethany. Jesus' love for his friends is such that it constrains him to return to Judean Bethany. Lazarus has died, but Jesus still needs to go. A sullen Thomas probably speaks for all the disciples, 'Let us also go, that we may die with him' (11.16). He seems to have little enthusiasm for the proposed journey, but is prepared to bow to the inevitable.[41]

Jesus does not share Thomas' sense of fatalism. In the same breath that he announces Lazarus' death (11.14), he provocatively declares that he is glad (11.15).[42] The juxtaposition is arresting to say the least. In the Greek it is even

---

40   Cf. Herman N. Ridderbos, *The Gospel According to John: A Theological Commentary* (trans. John Vriend; Grand Rapids, MI: Eerdmans, 1997), p. 388, 'The whole of vss. 5-7 shows how the human and the divine – his love for his own *and* his regard for the times appointed for him by the Father – are inseparably intertwined in Jesus' conduct and therefore in his glorification as the Son of God (vs. 4).'

41   Cf. Brendan Byrne, *Lazarus: A Contemporary Reading of John 11:1-46* (Homebush, NSW: St Paul Publications, 1991), p. 57: 'The deliberation ends with a resigned, pessimistic acceptance by Thomas of Jesus' proposal to go to Judea. That such a pessimistic appraisal of the likely future should come from Thomas is of a piece with what little emerges of his character in the rest of the gospel (cf. 14:5; 20:25). He is the realist who understands well enough that to follow Jesus means risking death. His statement underlines once again the fact that Jesus is putting his own life in mortal danger by going to Judea.'

42   The emotion is conveyed by the verb *chairō*. See 3.4 above. It means 'to be in a state of

more dramatic. A literal translation of the last words of v. 14 and the opening of v. 15 would read, 'Lazarus has died and I am glad for your sakes.' What gladdens Jesus is not the death of Lazarus, but the faith opportunity this presents to the disciples. Grammatically the whole sentence makes most sense if the words 'and I am glad for your sakes' are taken as a parenthesis. Jesus' entire statement would then read, 'Lazarus has died (and I am glad for your sakes) so that you may believe, because I was not there. But let us go to him.' If Jesus' gladness is parenthetical, 'Lazarus has died' becomes the main clause followed by two dependent clauses. These dependent clauses state both the purpose and the cause of Lazarus' death. To the question 'Why did Lazarus die?' Jesus' statement therefore gives two answers: (a) 'so that you may believe' and (b) 'because I was not there'. This also gives the reason for the parenthetical 'I am glad for your sakes.' Jesus is glad for the disciples because his absence from Bethany when Lazarus died would give him the opportunity to perform the greater miracle of a revivification[43] rather than a mere healing, and this in turn would lead to faith on their part.

The above explanation leaves one remaining problem. The purpose clause, 'so that you may believe', has long troubled commentators. Rudolf Bultmann claims that it is 'spoken as if 2:11 had not preceded it. There is no interest in the development of the disciples'.[44] Leon Morris disagrees, claiming that this clause cannot be understood as indicating the beginning of faith: 'The meaning will be that faith is progressive. There are new depths of faith to be plumbed, new heights of faith to be scaled. The raising of Lazarus will have a profound effect on them and give their faith a content that it did not have before.'[45] For Rudolf Schnackenburg, the purpose is that the disciples might 'receive a new and stronger stimulus for their faith': 'Strengthening the faith of the disciples is a constant concern of his, and all the more urgent as the passion approaches . . . The faith that Jesus wants to strengthen is not just faith in his power to cure diseases, or even to bring a dead man back to life, but faith in himself, the Messiah and Son of God.'[46]

The comments by Schnackenburg come closest to the heart of the issue, since 'so that you may believe' also occurs in 20.31. The purpose of Lazarus' death would then accord precisely with the purpose of the Gospel as a whole. The parallel between the two would seem to be more than incidental. Jesus is glad that the purpose of Lazarus' death (and his subsequent revivification) will be fulfilled in the faith of his disciples.[47] Likewise the purpose of the recording of the signs

---

happiness and well-being, *rejoice, be glad*' (BDAG, p. 1074).

43 In this context 'revivification' (restoration to life) seems preferable to both 'resurrection' (with its associations with the eternal resurrection body) and 'resuscitation' (which could have the connotation that Lazarus may not have been completely dead).

44 Rudolf Bultmann, *The Gospel of John: A Commentary* (ed. R. W. N. Hoare and J. K. Riches; trans. G. R. Beasley-Murray; Oxford: Blackwell, 1971), p. 400.

45 Leon Morris, *The Gospel According to John* (NICNT; Grand Rapids: Eerdmans, rev. edn, 1995), p. 583.

46 Rudolf Schnackenburg, *The Gospel According to St John* (ed. J. Massyngbaerde Ford, Kevin Smyth et al.; trans. Kevin Smyth et al. 3 vols; Tunbridge Wells, Kent: Burns & Oats, 1990-1993), vol. 2, p. 327.

47 Surprisingly, in the miracle's immediate aftermath nothing is said about the disciples' faith,

in the Fourth Gospel (which include the raising of Lazarus) is that the readers may believe 'that Jesus is the Christ, the Son of God' (20.31). A preliminary fulfilment of the Gospel's purpose is therefore the faith of the disciples that will ultimately result from Lazarus' death. The repetition of 'that you may believe' in 13.19; 14.29; 19.35 runs like a golden thread linking the purpose of Lazarus' death (11.15) to the purpose of the Gospel itself (20.31). Jesus' gladness at the prospect of the disciples believing because of Lazarus is therefore not eccentric, nor even difficult to comprehend, but is intimately connected to the Gospel's central theme.[48]

The journey between the two Bethanies is an unusual one in John. It is counter-intuitive. Rather than being repelled from Jerusalem because of its antagonism against him, Jesus is drawn to the city's environs because of his love for his friends and his gladness at the prospect of what it will mean for his disciples' faith. On this occasion Jesus' movements are not propelled by his messianic obligations, nor by antagonism against him, but by love and joy. Driven by these emotions, he is prepared to risk whatever dangers his journey to the vicinity of Jerusalem might entail. As it turns out, the disciples' protest (11.8) and Thomas' sense of resignation (11.16) are well grounded. In response to the news that Jesus has raised Lazarus the Sanhedrin meets for crisis talks (11.47), the upshot of which is that 'from that day on they plotted to take his life' (11.53). So Jesus is once again forced to seek asylum. This time he and his disciples head for the village of Ephraim (11.54). The old pattern has returned. It is a pattern that Jesus breaks only for the sake of his love for Mary, Martha and Lazarus and because of his joy over what this will mean for the faith of his disciples.

4.4 *Mixed Emotions at Lazarus' Tomb (11.32-44)*

32 When Mary reached the place where Jesus was and saw him, she fell at his feet and said, 'Lord, if you had been here, my brother would not have died.'

33 When Jesus saw her weeping, and the Jews who had come along with her also weeping, *he was deeply moved in spirit and troubled.*

34 'Where have you laid him?' he asked. 'Come and see, Lord,' they replied.

35 *Jesus wept.*

36 Then the Jews said, 'See how he loved him!'

37 But some of them said, 'Could not he who opened the eyes of the blind man have kept this man from dying?'

38 *Jesus, once more deeply moved*, came to the tomb. It was a cave with a stone laid across the entrance.

but Jesus does say that his prayer of thanksgiving to the Father at the tomb (11. 41-42) was for the benefit of the bystanders 'that they may believe that you sent me' (11.42).

48 Cf. Lk. 10.21 where Jesus' exultant joy comes to expression precisely as his mission is being fulfilled.

39 'Take away the stone,' he said. 'But, Lord,' said Martha, the sister of the dead man, 'by this time there is a bad odour, for he has been there four days.'

40 Then Jesus said, 'Did I not tell you that if you believed, you would see the glory of God?'

41 So they took away the stone. Then Jesus looked up and said, 'Father, I thank you that you have heard me.

42 I knew that you always hear me, but I said this for the benefit of the people standing here, that they may believe that you sent me.'

43 When he had said this, Jesus called in a loud voice, 'Lazarus, come out!'

44 The dead man came out, his hands and feet wrapped with strips of linen, and a cloth around his face. Jesus said to them, 'Take off the grave clothes and let him go.'

The geographical setting of the story has now moved to a location just outside the village of Judaean Bethany (11.30). It is there that Jesus meets first with Martha (11.20-27) and then with Mary (11.32-37). Ostensibly both sisters address Jesus in exactly the same way: 'Lord, if you had been here, my brother would not have died' (11.21, 32). However, there are significant differences between the two statements. In the Greek of Mary's statement, the possessive pronoun 'my' is placed in an emphatic position. This has the effect of making the entire sentence more emotional, as does the fact that when she speaks to Jesus she has fallen at his feet. Furthermore, Mary is weeping, and so are the Jews who have come with her (11.33). Jesus' encounter with Mary therefore takes place in an atmosphere that is highly charged with emotion. Where the meeting with Martha leads to a conversation, the meeting with Mary produces an outburst of emotion – not only from Mary, but from Jesus as well. Seldom are Jesus' reactions described in such intensely emotional terms.[49]

4.4.1 ANGRY (11.33, 38)

At the weeping of those around him Jesus 'was deeply moved in spirit and troubled' (11.33). This is followed by his own weeping (11.35). When Jesus comes to the tomb he is 'once more deeply moved' (11.38). As these references to Jesus' emotions begin and end with him being deeply moved, the overarching emotion would seem to be indicated by this verb. Thus at the purely visceral level Jesus' emotions are triggered by the sight of a weeping woman, a response for which the earlier narrative has duly prepared the reader (11.2, 5). Mary is no ordinary woman, but a close friend who has a deep devotion to Jesus. The complex cluster of Jesus' emotions depicted in 11.33-38 is very human in the sense that Jesus' feelings have been stirred by a grieving friend and her companions. But precisely how have Jesus' emotions been stirred? In what sense is he 'deeply

---

49 Only Matthew and Mark's accounts of Gethsemane could be said to equal the emotional intensity found here. See Mt. 26.37-38; Mk 14.33-34.

moved'? The Greek word behind this expression is *embrimaomai*, a verb we have already met on two previous occasions when Jesus sternly charged those he had just healed – a cleansed leper (Mk 1.43) and two men whose sight was restored (Mt. 9.30). On both occasions the underlying emotion was anger. Is that also the case here?

There is hardly a trace of this emotion in the more reputable English translations of Jn 11.33, 38. In these verses the verb is commonly rendered 'deeply moved' (ESV, NASB, NIV, RSV), 'groaned' (AV, RV), 'sighed heavily/deeply' (NEB), '(deeply) touched' (GNB), or 'greatly disturbed' (NRSV). Only the LB's paraphrase 'moved with indignation/deep anger' seems to convey the meaning suggested by the other occurrences. The English translation tradition is therefore almost unanimous in withholding anger from the complex equation of Jesus' emotions at this point.[50] This creates the overall impression that there is little more than an outpouring of human sympathy on Jesus' part. The sight of Mary and the other mourners causes him to be deeply moved and troubled within, and it brings tears to his eyes. Without the component of anger, Jesus' emotions would appear to be operating at this purely human level. If anger is present, it has the potential of introducing a different dimension.

As a matter of principle it is generally unwise to go against the trend of the English translation tradition, especially where that tradition is almost unanimous. On the other hand, it is also a matter of sound interpretation to translate a word as consistently as possible, particularly if that word occurs in Scripture only infrequently. In our earlier discussions of *embrimaomai* in Mt. 9.30 and Mk 1.43, the element of anger could not be avoided.[51] There was good reason for Jesus' anger in each case. On both occasions a comparison with Mk 14.5, the only New Testament occurrence of the verb without Jesus as its subject, proved to be instructive. In this instance the bystanders express their indignation by harshly rebuking the woman who anointed Jesus. In this case the emotion of anger lies on the surface of the text. Seeing that the other three occurrences of *embrimaomai* in the New Testament can be shown to have clear overtones of anger, the interpreter who wants to remove all traces of anger from Jesus' emotional reaction at the tomb of Lazarus must show cause.[52] Only if the context can be shown to eliminate anger should other possibilities be entertained. The problem with the current context is that motivations for Jesus' anger are not immediately obvious.

---

50 German translations in both the Luther and Zwingli traditions do not hesitate to render *embrimaomai* by the verb *ergrimmen* ('get angry, furious') in both verses. The Dutch authorized version ('Statenvertaling') has *bewogen* ('moved'), while the new translation of 1951 has *verbolgen* ('incensed', 'angry', 'wrathful'). The Vulgate uses *infremo* ('roar', 'rage') in v. 33, and *fremo* ('murmur', 'grumble', 'growl', 'rage') in v. 38.

51 See 1.3 and 2.2.1 above.

52 Barclay M. Newman and Eugene A. Nida, *A Translator's Handbook on the Gospel of John* (Stuttgart: United Bible Societies, 1980), p. 371, are insistent on this point: 'It is impossible to conclude that anything less than anger is meant here or in verse 38. The use of this verb and its cognates, both in the New Testament and elsewhere, clearly implies anger. Evidently the translations which attempt to remove the concept of anger from these verses do so on theological rather than linguistic or exegetical grounds.'

Before any such motivations are sought, it needs to be pointed out that Jesus' anger is internalized. He 'was deeply moved *in spirit*' (11.33) and at the tomb he was 'again being deeply moved *within*' (11.38 NASB). The inward nature of Jesus' anger is also suggested by the reaction of the Jews, 'See how he loved him' (11.36). This is a natural reaction to Jesus' weeping in the previous verse, but it would not have been an understandable response to an outward expression of anger. The onlookers can see only Jesus' tears, not the inner turmoil of his soul. But even if his anger is internalized, what causes this strong inner emotion? In the literature there are two main schools of thought.

It is often suggested that Jesus is angry at unbelief. Bultmann argues that the wailing of Mary and the Jews (11.33) provokes the height of agitation in Jesus.[53] Schnackenburg agrees and calls the lamenting Jews the 'representatives of unbelief'.[54] This explanation for Jesus' anger is not without force. It fits the wider context of the Gospel with its constant emphasis on the people's contrasting reactions of faith and unbelief. Nevertheless, this solution is not without its problems. Although there was to be unbelief in response to the raising of Lazarus (11.45-46), this is not what Jesus is responding to here. The verse in which the emotion first occurs (11.33) is unequivocal in declaring that Jesus' anger was triggered by the weeping of Mary and her companions, but it makes no mention of their lack of faith or the subsequent unbelief of some of the bystanders. In John's portrait of Jesus it would be quite out of character for him to be enraged at a weeping woman and her fellow mourners. Their wailing may have triggered his anger, but from this it does not follow that it was also the object of his anger. He may be angry *because of* their weeping, but this does not necessarily mean that he is angry *at* their weeping. The two are quite distinct. But if it is not unbelief that leads to Jesus' deeply emotional reaction, then the cause of his anger must be sought at a deeper level.

If Jesus is not angry at unbelief, the only other possibility allowed by the context is that he is enraged at death. Some of the more recent interpreters who hold this view have drawn their inspiration from Calvin. In his comments on 11.38 Calvin consciously distances himself from the explanation that Jesus' emotional reaction was 'because of that unbelief of which we have spoken'. The real reason for the stirrings within him lies elsewhere: 'Christ does not approach the sepulchre as an idle spectator, but as a champion who prepares for a contest . . . for the violent tyranny of death, which he had to conquer, is placed before his eyes.'[55]

In conscious dependence on Calvin, Warfield develops the point in greater detail:

It is death that is the object of his wrath, and behind death him who has the power of death, and whom he has come into the world to destroy. Tears of

---

53   Bultmann, *John*, p. 406.
54   Schnackenburg, *John*, 2, p. 336.
55   John Calvin, *Commentary on the Gospel According to John* (trans. William Pringle; 2 vols; Grand Rapids: Eerdmans, 1956), vol. 1, p. 442. Calvin does not shy away from attributing rage to Jesus and understands *embrimaomai* in this light.

sympathy may fill his eyes, but this is incidental. His soul is held by rage: and he advances to the tomb, in Calvin's words again, 'as a champion who prepares for conflict.' The raising of Lazarus thus becomes, not an isolated marvel, but – as indeed it is presented throughout the whole narrative (compare especially, verses 24-26) – a decisive instance and open symbol of Jesus' conquest of death and hell. What John does for us in this particular statement is to uncover to us the heart of Jesus, as he wins for us our salvation. Not in cold unconcern, but in flaming wrath against the foe, Jesus smites in our behalf.[56]

Jesus was indeed deeply moved. He was stirred to the very core of his being. 'He raged against death, that terrible enemy that had attacked this, and every, family.'[57] But as we gaze deeply into this text, and thus into the soul of Jesus as portrayed in this passage, there is more to be seen. In this episode with Lazarus Jesus foresees his own death. It is probably this that disturbs him most of all. At this point the combination of emotions becomes decidedly complex. As Jesus contemplates his own death, no single word can do justice to his emotional state. In considering this dimension we can no longer isolate Jesus' being deeply moved with anger from his being troubled. The pattern of these strong emotions, both in these verses and in the subsequent narrative (12.27; 13.21), suggests that it is Jesus' own death rather than merely death in general that moves him so deeply. In confronting Lazarus' death he must also confront his own. As R. Alan Culpepper explains, 'Jesus' emotion again in this instance is peculiar; it seems to arise from his foreknowledge of his own death.'[58]

4.4.2 TROUBLED (11.33)

A second strong emotion of Jesus in response to the weeping around him is conveyed by the word 'troubled.' It will be used again of Jesus in 12.27 and 13.21, and of the disciples in 14.1, 27. In each case it 'denotes a deep emotional disturbance'.[59] While the literal meaning of this verb (*tarassō*) is 'shake together' or 'stir up' (e.g. of water in Jn 5.7), its figurative meaning is far more prominent in the New Testament, and it is in this sense that it can refer to the emotions. In the active voice it means 'to cause inner turmoil', and can be translated *stir up, disturb, unsettle, throw into confusion.*[60]

Whether it is used literally or figuratively in John's Gospel, this verb almost invariably occurs in the passive voice. The only exception is the case under

---

56   Warfield, *Person and Work*, p. 117.
57   Walter G. Hansen, 'The Emotions of Jesus and Why We Need to Experience Them', *CT* 41/2 (3 February, 1997), p. 45.
58   Culpepper, *Anatomy*, p. 111.
59   Mark W. G. Stibbe, 'A Tomb with a View: John 11.1-44 in Narrative-Critical Perspective', *NTS* 40 (1994), p. 45.
60   BDAG, p. 990.

consideration. Here the verb is in the active voice and is used reflexively, that is, 'he troubled himself'. This raises the question whether the expression found here is equivalent to 'my heart is troubled' (12.27) and to 'Jesus was troubled in spirit' (13.21), the two other occasions when the verb *tarassō* is used to describe Jesus' emotional state. Are these three expressions synonymous or do they each carry their own nuances? More particularly, should the use of the reflexive construction in 11.33 be given its due weight (and therefore be translated quite literally as 'he troubled himself') or is it simply a stylistic variation of the more common passive usage (and therefore better translated as 'he was troubled')?

The English translation tradition has opted in favour of translating it as a passive rather than as a reflexive construction. The most common renderings are 'was troubled' (AV, NASB, NIV, RSV, RV) and 'was deeply moved' (GNB, NEB, NRSV). The paraphrases tend to give the verb even more emotional freight, for example, 'was deeply troubled' (LB) and 'was visibly distressed' (Phillips). However precisely the verb is translated, the passive voice prevails. In some translations a clear line can be drawn from 11.33 to 12.27 and 13.21 in that a conscious effort seems to have been made to render all the expressions as essentially equivalent in meaning (thus AV, NASB, NIV, RSV, RV). These translations completely assimilate the reflexive usage in 11.33 with the passives in 12.27 and 13.21.

The problem in equating the reflexive with a passive, and thereby not allowing it to have its full reflexive meaning, lies with the uniqueness of the construction as it stands. This is the only occurrence of the reflexive use among the seventeen occurrences of *tarassō* in the New Testament. Moreover, this verb is found $118x$ in the LXX, but is never used reflexively. Similarly in Josephus the passive is used $62x$, but never the reflexive. The expression in Jn 11.33 would therefore seem to stand alone in biblical and related Greek literature. Does this feature have any exegetical significance, and should its uniqueness therefore be reflected in translation? Although this question has been answered in the negative in the English translation tradition, other traditions appear to have been less hasty in drawing this conclusion. In some cases the Greek reflexive verb has been given its full weight in translation. Thus in German Luther translates 'betrübte sich selbst' ('distressed himself'), while the Zürich Bible has 'empörte sich' ('was enraged/furious'). The Dutch 'Statenvertaling' renders 'ontroerde Zichzelven' ('moved himself [emotionally]') and the Latin Vulgate 'turbavit seipsum' ('disturbed/agitated himself'). Taken together these versions represent a long and impressive history of translation from Jerome through the Reformation and beyond. They form a tradition that cannot be lightly dismissed, even though there is little evidence for it in English.

Among some English language commentators, however, the force of the reflexive verb has been staunchly defended. Thus B. F. Westcott states forthrightly: 'It cannot be supposed that the peculiar turn of phrase used here . . . is equivalent to *was troubled* . . . The force of it appears to be that the Lord took to himself freely those feelings to which others are subject; and this feeling of horror and indignation He manifested outwardly.'[61] Barrett is open to the possibility of taking the reflexive as it stands, but interprets it differently: 'If this is not a mere variation in the Johannine manner of similar expressions . . . it must be intended to underline the contention that Jesus was always master of himself and his circumstances.'[62] Morris observes that the expressions in 11.33; 12.27; 13.21 'form another example of John's habit of variation in repeated statements.' He nevertheless allows the reflexive its own sense: 'The expression is a way of showing that Jesus of His own free will entered fully into man's lot, identifying Himself with the griefs of his friends.'[63]

The difference between these two lines of interpretation is significant. If 'troubled' in 11.33 is read as passive, it gives the impression that Jesus is somehow overcome – if not overwhelmed – by emotion. The reflexive meaning, on the other hand, would indicate initiative on his part. He is exercising self-control and is master of the situation. This sense of initiative and self-mastery is the common denominator to the otherwise varied comments quoted in the last paragraph. Plausible though comments on both sides of the discussion may be, the uniqueness of the expression prevents commentators from giving firm exegetical anchorage to their views. Positions are stated, but seldom substantiated. In both directions there are significant gaps in the discussion at crucial points, the main problem being that the expression seems to be without precedent.

This is where the work by the German scholar Johannes Beutler has filled a void. He finds a precedent in the refrain in Pss. 41.6, 12; 42.5 (LXX):[64] 'Why are you deeply grieved, O my soul, and *why are you throwing me into confusion?*' (or more literally 'why are you troubling me?'). According to the LXX rendering, the Psalmist's soul troubles him. If 'my soul' stands for the self in this instance, there is a sense in which the Psalmist troubles himself. The Psalmist's experience therefore establishes a useful precedent for the present passage, a precedent which Jesus' words in Gethsemane, 'my soul is overwhelmed with sorrow', also evokes (Mt. 26.38; Mk 14.34). The choice of terminology to describe Jesus' emotion at this point is therefore not as unique and isolated as it first appeared. Via the Psalm reference, it has links with the synoptic Gethsemane tradition and is not to be severed from the later references to Jesus' being troubled in John's Gospel. Thus the expression of emotion in Jn 11.33 is indeed a foreboding of Jesus' death. As Beutler explains:

> From the perspective of the Fourth Evangelist not only the story of Jesus' anointing (12:1-8) and his violent emotion (12:27), but already his encounter with his dead friend, place Jesus' own suffering and death vividly before his eyes. Yet this suffering is not an experience that runs counter to the will of

61   B. F. Westcott, *The Gospel according to St. John: The Authorized Version with Introduction and Notes* (Grand Rapids, MI: Eerdmans, 1954), p. 171.
62   Barrett, *John*, p. 332.
63   Morris, *John*, p. 494.
64   Or Pss. 42.5, 11; 43.5 in English Bibles.

God. Rather it reveals Jesus as the righteous sufferer of which God himself had spoken in the Psalms.[65]

The unusual expression, 'he troubled himself', is therefore not necessarily intended to highlight Jesus' self-mastery, nor does it in any way diminish from his humanity, but – as so often is the case in this Gospel – he is identified as the righteous sufferer. Like the Psalmist, he was inwardly troubled. Unlike the Psalmist, he could foresee his own death. 'Jesus is troubled,' says Barrett, 'as in 12.27; 13.21, at the prospect of the *dénouement* of his ministry. In John *tarassō* always means such a fearful perturbation (cf. 14.1, 27).'[66]

Barrett's observation is pertinent and accurate as far as it goes. The figurative uses of *tarassō* in John do indeed consistently mean 'a fearful perturbation'. But does this meaning capture all the nuances of 'he troubled himself'? Is this not again a case of too readily assimilating this reflexive use with the later passives? Again a comparison with Psalms 41/42 (LXX) proves helpful. If the LXX translators sought to retain a sense of Hebrew parallelism, then 'deeply grieved' in the first half of the refrain provides a clue to the meaning of his soul troubling the Psalmist in the second half. Hence sorrow cannot be excluded from the complex of emotions affecting the Psalmist. This sorrow is not confined to the refrain, but permeates both Psalms. In both he asks: 'Why do I go *mourning* because of the oppression of the enemy?' (42.9; 43.2 NASB). He also laments the fact that his *tears* have been his food day and night (42.3 [41.4 LXX]). Similarly Jesus' sorrow comes to expression in his tears (11.35). As with the Psalmist, so with Jesus, sorrow forms a component of his trouble.

The Psalmist's soul troubles him because of conflicting emotions. On the one hand there is his present situation marked as it is by his mourning and tears, the outward expressions of his sorrow. On the other hand there are more positive emotions. They form a powerful contrast to his current sense of despair which is only intensified by being flanked on the one side by the memory of joyful and grateful worship in the house of God (42.4) and on the other by the hope that such joyful worship will be restored (43.4). The Psalmist is disturbed by the doleful reality of the present wedged between a joyous memory of the past and the hope that such joy will return in the future. He is thus torn between his trust in God and his despair over present circumstances. Small wonder that his soul troubles him.

Jesus also experiences this sense of being torn between conflicting emotions. In the account 'he troubled himself' stands between 'he was deeply moved (with anger)' (11.33) and 'Jesus wept' (11.35). Just as the Psalmist was caught between despair and hope, Jesus is caught between anger and sorrow. Although this is not an uncommon human predicament, it does have the effect of leaving him troubled.[67]

---

65   Johannes Beutler, 'Psalm 42/43 im Johannesevangelium', *NTS* 25 (1978), p. 44 (author's translation).
66   Barrett, *John*, p. 332.
67   Byrne, *Lazarus*, p. 73, has also recognized the fact that here Jesus is caught between

In the interpretation of 'he troubled himself,' it is therefore an oversimplification to understand the emotion of Jesus at this point as 'a fearful perturbation.' There are also overtones of sorrow and the sense of being torn between a strong inner sense of indignation and a grief that will openly express itself in the shedding of tears. Perhaps the sense of the words is best conveyed in the translation 'he was distressed' (Phillips). What is meant is a deeply internal emotion that is broad enough to encompass fear and sorrow, as well as the sense of being torn between anger and grief.

4.4.3 IN TEARS (11.35)

After the reply to Jesus' question as to the location of Lazarus' tomb (11.34), the account states tersely: 'Jesus wept' (11.35). Quite simply, he burst into tears. The weeping over Lazarus by Mary and the Jews is depicted by the verb *klaiō* (11.31, 33), while *dakruō* is used for the weeping of Jesus. It is possible that the careful choice of verbs is intended to contrast the quiet weeping of Jesus with the loud grief of Mary and the Jews. As Morris explains, 'The word used of them means a loud, demonstrative form of weeping, a wailing. That used here . . . signifies rather a quiet weeping. Jesus did not wail loudly, but he was deeply grieved.'[68] Yancey makes a further qualification: 'John does not say why Jesus wept. Since he had already revealed his plans to raise Lazarus from the dead, he surely did not feel the same grief as the devastated mourners.'[69]

Jesus' weeping in Jn 11.35 expresses a human emotion. This seems to be so even though (a) Jesus is about to perform a miracle that would appear to be intended as strong evidence of his divinity, and (b) some of the other emotions of Jesus in this context appear to spring from his foreknowledge of both the raising of Lazarus and his own impending death (11.15, 33, 38). Although the entire context is strongly permeated with the divine (both in terms of the foreknowledge that precedes Jesus' tears and the miracle that follows), this does not exclude the possibility that Jesus is expressing a purely human emotion here. According to Culpepper, 'Only his weeping in 11:35 and his gratitude to God in 11:41 are entirely normal human reactions.'[70] This point is developed further by Ridderbos:

> conflicting emotions, but he explains the dilemma (and the relationship between the relevant emotions) somewhat differently: 'Jesus, then, weeps at their grief, but their very grief intensifies the pressure upon him to restore Lazarus to them. At the same time as he feels this pressure he also knows that performing such a miracle will inevitably set in motion forces leading to death for himself. He is torn, then, between love for his friend and sympathy for the bereaved, on the one hand, and the shrinking from death that is part of human nature, on the other. His anger arises out of the impossible situation he is in and out of the conflict with the power of darkness now before him.' It is difficult to see how 'the impossible situation' could lead to anger at this point, since it was clearly foreseen by Jesus and had been the subject of conversation with his disciples (11. 8-16).

68 Morris, *John*, p. 495.
69 Yancey, *Jesus*, p. 177.
70 Culpepper, *Anatomy*, p. 111.

The Evangelist's portrayal of Jesus here is not of one who 'doth bestride the narrow world like a Colossus,' who, elevated far above and incapable of human suffering, does not tolerate tears in his presence. The Evangelist, precisely in the midst of his description of this incomprehensible and inconceivable miracle, includes his strongest expression of Jesus' existence as a human being. He does so to safeguard the sublimity of his message against all idealizing interpretations.[71]

The humanness of Jesus' response is also appreciated by Barrett who contributes the further insight that through his weeping Jesus took part in the lamentations of Mary and the Jews.[72] Jesus therefore fully enters into the sorrow of those around him. His rage at death (11.33) is now complemented by his sorrow at its devastating effects. 'Jesus' tears are an honest sharing in Mary's grief and perhaps in her anger at death, the enemy of all life,' writes Schneiders. 'Jesus, in his most fully human moment in the Fourth Gospel, legitimates human agony in the face of death, an agony he will feel for himself as he shrinks from the passion in chapter 12.'[73] Hence in the very chapter of John where we see Jesus' mightiest sign prior to his own resurrection, we also see his true humanity and identification. Although he knows he is about to reverse their sorrow, Jesus does not disregard the emotions of his friends. Rather he shares their sorrow. It is a poignant expression of his true humanity.

Thus, ch. 11 profoundly expresses both the humanity and divinity of Jesus' emotions. His love and his tears can be fully appreciated at the level of purely human considerations. On the other hand, his anger, gladness and distress cannot be adequately understood without attributing a degree of divine (or at least supernatural) foreknowledge to Jesus. If this factor is eliminated, his emotional reactions become difficult, if not impossible, to comprehend. Therefore, while Jesus' love and tears are quite normal human reactions and should be understood as such, the same cannot be said of his gladness, anger, and distress. These emotions are not normal, but stem from another agenda. They are driven by Jesus' foreknowledge. Jesus is glad because he knows that he will raise Lazarus and that the disciples will believe as a result. He is inwardly indignant and distressed because he foresees his own death and perceives the spiritual conflict involved. The Passion is looming, a prospect that arouses strong and unusual emotions in Jesus.

---

71 Ridderbos, *John*, p. 403. Among the 'idealizing interpretations' Ridderbos includes a docetic interpretation of Johannine Christology.
72 Barrett, *John* (1955), p. 334.
73 Sandra M. Schneiders, 'Death in the Community of Eternal Life: History, Theology, and Spirituality in John 11', *Int* 41 (1987), p. 54.

4.5 *A Troubled Soul (12.20-33)*

20 Now there were some Greeks among those who went up to worship at the Feast.
21 They came to Philip, who was from Bethsaida in Galilee, with a request. 'Sir,' they said, 'we would like to see Jesus.'
22 Philip went to tell Andrew; Andrew and Philip in turn told Jesus.
23 Jesus replied, 'The hour has come for the Son of Man to be glorified.
24 I tell you the truth, unless a grain of wheat falls to the ground and dies, it remains only a single seed. But if it dies, it produces many seeds.
25 The man who loves his life will lose it, while the man who hates his life in this world will keep it for eternal life.
26 Whoever serves me must follow me; and where I am, my servant also will be. My Father will honour the one who serves me.
27 '*Now my soul*[74] *is troubled*, and what shall I say? 'Father, save me from this hour'? No, it was for this very reason I came to this hour.
28 Father, glorify your name!' Then a voice came from heaven, 'I have glorified it, and will glorify it again.'
29 The crowd that was there and heard it said it had thundered; others said an angel had spoken to him.
30 Jesus said, 'This voice was for your benefit, not mine.
31 Now is the time for judgment on this world; now the prince of this world will be driven out.
32 But I, when I am lifted up from the earth, will draw all men to myself.'
33 He said this to show the kind of death he was going to die.

In ch. 12 the development of John's narrative reaches a major point of transition. With the climactic miracle of the raising of Lazarus, the Book of Signs has come to a dramatic close, but the Book of Passion/Glory is yet to open (13.1ff.). Jesus has entered Jerusalem for the last time (12.12-19) and his public ministry to Israel is about to conclude with a final appeal that encapsulates the essence of his message (12.44-50). Chronologically this chapter is set within the week prior to the last Passover (11.55; 12.1; 13.1), the feast that provides the larger context for the Book of Passion/Glory (13.1; 18.28, 39; 19.14). The transitional nature of John 12 comes to expression with particular clarity in the formulas that are used to introduce Old Testament quotations. In 12.14 the 'it is written' formula that had consistently introduced Old Testament quotations from 2.17 onwards is used for the last time. The Isaiah quotations in 12.38-40 are introduced by a fulfilment formula, thus setting the pattern that will be followed from this point on. In short, Jesus' Passion, by which he will be glorified at the Passover in Jerusalem, will be in direct fulfilment of the Old Testament.

In 12.20-36 it is made clear that this fulfilment will take place under the rubric of 'the hour'. On three occasions in the Book of Signs this hour is described as

---

74   Although the NIV reads 'heart', the more usual translation of *psychē* is 'soul.'

'not yet come' (2.4; 7.30; 8.20). When it finally strikes (12.23, 27), it is signalled in an unobtrusive and unlikely way. When Jesus is indirectly approached by some Greeks who were in Jerusalem for Passover, he announces: 'The hour has come for the Son of Man to be glorified' (12.23).[75] These Greeks, who seem to be requesting an interview with Jesus, disappear from the story almost as soon as they are introduced. Not only does their positive interest in Jesus stand in marked contrast to the plotting of the chief priests (12.10-11) and the envy of the Pharisees (12.19), their presence underscores the cosmic importance of what Jesus is about to undergo. In their observation that 'the whole world has gone after him' (12.19), the Pharisees had spoken more than they knew. The introduction of the Greeks in the very next verse highlights the irony of their remark. Presumably while the Greeks were still present, Jesus proclaimed the universal significance of his death (12.32): 'But I, when I am lifted up from the earth, will draw all men to myself.' The cosmic proportions of the events that will take place during Jesus' 'hour' are thus clearly stated in advance. The dual role of the Greeks in the narrative is to signal to Jesus that his moment has now arrived, and to indicate to the reader that it is to have universal implications.

The realization that his time has come overwhelms Jesus. In a rare instance of public self-disclosure of his inner feelings, he candidly declares: 'Now my soul is troubled' (12.27a). He seems to be overcome by emotion and does not hesitate to admit it. Before we examine the emotion itself, we will need to inquire as to its cause. Within this verse itself the emotion appears to be intricately related to 'this hour.' It puts him in two minds. On the one hand he would like God to rescue him from the hour. On the other hand he knows only too well why he has come to the hour. His ambivalence with respect to the hour lies at the root of his distress. In fact, the 'Now' during which Jesus' soul is troubled is synonymous with 'this hour.' But precisely why is the hour so troubling to Jesus? What features does it possess that it should disturb him so deeply? The defining hallmarks of the hour are indicated in 12.20-36, a passage that serves as an introduction to the Passion story, as Jesus openly states what his hour will mean for him.

The 'hour' is pre-eminently the time of Jesus' glorification (12.23). There is a sense in which Jesus had already been glorified through the signs he had performed (2.11; 11.4; cf. 17.4), but this element is secondary in comparison to the glory that will be his by virtue of the hour (17.1). The hour will indeed be his moment of glory. The way Jesus will attain this glory, however, is painfully paradoxical, as illustrated by the extended metaphor that follows. Only by falling to the ground and dying can a grain of wheat bear much fruit (12.24). This saying is deliberately ambiguous and is to be understood at two levels. At the most obvious level it refers to the one who hates his life in this world and serves Jesus, and this would appear to be the explanation provided by the context (12.25-26).

---

75   Francis J. Moloney, 'God so Loved the World: The Jesus of John's Gospel', *ACR* 75 (1998), p. 202, detects here some connections with events in the preceding chapter: 'The raising of Lazarus triggers the coming of the Greeks, the Jews' decision that he must die (11:49 50), and Jesus' proclamation that "the hour" has come for his glorification. The theme of the hour dominates his final days.'

At another level the grain of wheat is Jesus himself, the prototype of those who hate their lives in this world and keep them to eternal life (12.25). As the grain of wheat dies and bears fruit, so too will Jesus (12.24; cf. Isa. 53.10-12). In a veiled and figurative way Jesus is therefore indicating that he will be glorified supremely through his death (cf. 12.32-33).[76] Thus his death is the defining feature of 'the hour.'[77] For this reason his soul is troubled (12.27). As in the death of Lazarus he had foreseen his own death, and the prospect had filled him with distress; he now finds himself in a similar situation. With the arrival of the hour his death is imminent. Aware of his imminent death, his soul is troubled.

To restrict the reasons for Jesus' troubled state simply to his approaching death as such, however, is to do an injustice to the intensity of his emotions. It is not so much the fact of his death as the nature of his death that troubles him. The 'now' of 12.27 is repeated twice in 12.31: '*Now* is the time for judgment on this world; *now* the prince of this world will be driven out.' The hour involves more than the death of an individual man. His death also means that the world is judged, and its prince expelled. 'The hour' is the great showdown in a cosmic war, the decisive battle in the conflict between light and darkness (1.5). The expulsion of the cosmic ruler is indicated by the verb *ekballō*, the common word for the casting out of demons in the Synoptics. In a Gospel that records no exorcisms and that has no account of the temptation in the wilderness, this is a remarkable use of language. It is as though nothing is to detract from this great exorcism, that of Satan himself. This cosmic conflict in the death of Jesus is a dimension for which the reader has been steadily prepared (1.5, 10-12; 3.14-16, 19-21; 5.18; 7.1–10.39) and one which will be encountered time and again in the narrative that follows (13.2, 26-27; 14.30-31; 16.8-11). Jesus will tell his disciples that 'the prince of this world is coming' (14.30). Thus 'the world-ruler is presented as an active party in the conflict . . . he confronts Jesus by bringing about his crucifixion.'[78] But once again the account is laced with irony. The world ruler is exorcised (12.31) precisely when Jesus is lifted up from the earth, and it is then that he draws all to himself (12.31-32). The segment ends with Jesus' call to his audience to believe in the light and not walk in the darkness (12.35-36). The imagery of the cosmic battle underlies his appeal (cf. 1.5).

The reference to Jesus' troubled soul (12.27) is therefore flanked on either side by strong allusions to his death. In his death he is both glorified (12.23) and exalted (12.32). By it he bears much fruit (12.24) and draws all to himself (12.32). Such benefits are only possible, however, because his death at the same time entails Jesus' victory over the world and the devil. The cross is the locus of a cosmic battle in which Jesus, paradoxically, is triumphant through death. In

---

76 Moloney, 'God so Loved', p. 200, observes that the most crucial action of Jesus' life is his death: 'The Fourth Gospel is unique in the New Testament in presenting the death of Jesus as his most significant achievement, the moment when he brings to perfection the task given him by the Father, the one who sent him, glorifying God and achieving his own glory.'

77 So Barrett, *John*, p. 352: 'The hour is the hour of the death of Jesus.'

78 Judith L. Kovacs, '"Now Shall the Ruler of This World be Driven Out": Jesus' Death as Cosmic Battle in John 12:20-36', *JBL* 114 (1995), p. 230.

anticipation of such a conflict where he will be both the victim of death and the victor over his enemies, his soul is troubled.

When Jesus declares, 'Now my soul is troubled' (12.27), he is giving expression to a very human emotion. Behind this emotion, however, there is once again a supernatural knowledge of what lies ahead. Jesus is anticipating his death, but it will be no ordinary human death. Jesus is facing a superhuman feat, for the hour of his death is also the time of the world's judgement and the world-ruler's expulsion (12.31). Nevertheless, even as Jesus faces a titanic struggle with universal implications, we see in his reaction an indication of his true humanity. If anything, the paradox observed with the raising of Lazarus has now become even more intense. There Jesus displayed very human emotions in anticipation of a divine miracle heralding the new creation. Here the emotions are equally human, but now Jesus is facing events of which the death and raising of Lazarus was merely a foreshadowing. His fear and anxiety is real, and so is his assurance of victory.

4.6 *The Epitome of Love (13.1)*

> It was just before the Passover Feast. Jesus knew that the time had come for him to leave this world and go to the Father. *Having loved his own who were in the world, he now showed them the full extent of his love.*

In the Gospel's overall narrative, 13.1 plays a pivotal role. The chapters that follow stand under the rubric of both the Passover and the 'hour'. The timeframe is indicated by the opening sentence, 'It was just before the Passover Feast' (13.1), but precisely how long before the Passover is not specified. One may assume that events have now moved nearer the Passover than was the case in 11.55 and 12.1. With the strong anticipations of this feast throughout the preceding narrative (1.29, 36; 2.13-25; 6.1-15), the reader senses that the Gospel is beginning to reach a climax. The approach of the final Passover also corresponds to the arrival of Jesus' 'hour', and it is this connection that John wants his readers to make more than any chronological calculation. 'The hour', which in the previous chapter was introduced as 'the hour for the Son of Man to be glorified' (12.23), is now identified as the time for Jesus to 'depart out of this world to the Father'. The final Passover is therefore at the same time the hour of glorification and of departure. Paradoxically, this will also be the occasion of Jesus' ultimate expression of love for his own. Moreover, Jesus' love for his own, introduced in 13.1, is supremely demonstrated in the succeeding narrative. This supreme demonstration is clearly evident in the crucifixion, but it is not confined to that event. It also comes to expression in the acted parable of the foot-washing which, with its emphasis on cleansing (13.8-10), symbolically prefigures the significance of Jesus' death. Jesus' love for his own therefore comes to an immediate expression in the foot-washing, and to its ultimate expression in the crucifixion. Both take place within the 'hour'. Hence 13.1 introduces not only the remainder of the Gospel in general, but also the foot-washing episode in particular.

The great hour of love has struck. On this high note the Book of Passion/ Glory opens.

The main theme of ch. 13 can be honed to a fine point when its centre (13.19) is read in the light of its opening statement (13.1). It is precisely in his uncondi- tional love for those who do not love him in the same way (i.e. who betray and deny him), that Jesus shines forth as the *egō eimi* ('I am'), the true revelation of God. The chapter's overriding concern is not discipleship, but *the love of Jesus* that alone makes discipleship possible. In loving his own – specifically in washing the feet of Peter and in giving the morsel to Judas[79] – Jesus demonstrates that he is in fact the 'I am'. Already in the foot-washing episode Jesus begins to demonstrate that 'having loved his own who were in the world, he now showed them the full extent of his love' (or he 'loved them to the end' NASB). But how are these two expressions of love related? Is there any implied difference between 'having loved' (the past participle) and 'loved' (the simple past)? Is there a temporal distinction between the two or is it merely a matter of intensity?

If a temporal meaning is also admitted, this dual reference to Jesus' love can be related to the major periods of his ministry. The general meaning would then be that, although Jesus had certainly loved his own up to this point, he was about to demonstrate this love in a new and supreme way.[80] The time for its ultimate expression had now come. Because of the pivotal position of 13.1, it would per- haps not be going too far to say that the words 'having loved his own who were in the world' summarize Jesus' love for his own in the Book of Signs, while the principal clause, 'he now showed them the full extent of his love', summarizes that love in the Book of Passion/Glory. Both verbs refer to the love of Jesus for his own as a whole and in summary fashion. The temporal element, however,

---

79 The morsel (*psōmion*) which Jesus gave to Judas (13.26, 27, 30) is a term found only here in the New Testament. According to *EDNT* 3, pp. 503–504, dipping the morsel 'might refer to dipping of bitter herbs into fruit sauce, which was part of the Passover meal . . ., though it probably refers to dipping of a piece of bread into a common dish, a usual part of the Jewish meal.' Not all are agreed that this was an act of love on Jesus' part. Schnackenburg, *John 3*, p. 30, holds that 'this is a clear expression of Jesus' initiative, taken to remove the traitor.' In this action George R. Beasley-Murray, *John* (2nd edn; WBC 36; Waco: Word, 1999), p. 238, sees a sign of favour rather than of hostility toward Judas: 'He must make up his mind either to respond to Jesus' goodwill, and so repent of his plan to betray him, or spurn it and carry out his intentions.' D. A. Carson, *The Gospel According to John* (Leicester: Inter-Varsity Press, 1991), p. 474, takes matters further and calls Jesus' act 'a final gesture of supreme love (*cf.* v. 1).' Moloney, 'John 13:1-38', pp. 7–8, has gone so far as to argue for a eucharistic understanding of the morsel, but in a Gospel which has no account of the institution of the Eucharist such an interpretation, although it has a long tradition (Brown, *John 2*, p. 575), is unlikely. In a context where the love of Jesus for his disciples is so strongly emphasized (13.1, 23, 34), Jesus' offer of the morsel is best understood as his last, loving appeal to Judas to change his course. Whether this morsel consisted of bread, meat, or herbs is impossible to determine in our current state of knowledge, and is in any case immaterial to the present discussion.

80 Cf. Carson, *John*, p. 461: 'Jesus had loved his own all along; *he now showed them the full extent of his love*' [NIV translation in italics].

cannot be discounted. The participle looks back to the earlier narrative, while the main verb encapsulates the love that is yet to be shown.

In the Book of Signs explicit references to Jesus' love for his own were remarkably sporadic. Mary, Martha, and Lazarus were the only ones singled out as being the specific recipients of Jesus' love (11.3, 5, 36). In 13.1 the reader is reminded that Jesus' love was not the exclusive right of a privileged few, but was in fact for all who could be described as 'his own'. The choice of language is striking. Those whom Jesus loves are referred to as 'his own who were in the world', while in 1.11 it was precisely 'his own' who did not receive him. Clearly the two groups are not one and the same. Between the prologue and the introduction to the Book of Passion/Glory the terminology has been radically redefined. The key to this redefinition appears to lie in the expression 'his own sheep' (10.3). They are the sheep who hear Jesus' voice (10.3) and for whom he lays down his life (10.11). The reference in 13.1 is therefore to be understood in the light of the Good Shepherd discourse in ch. 10.[81] 'His own' are no longer those who rejected him, but those whom he loved 'to the end'.

The clause 'he loved' is modified by the phrase 'to the end' or 'to the uttermost' (NASB). In the Greek this adverbial phrase (*eis telos*) is ambiguous, as it can be understood in either a temporal or a qualitative sense. In other words, it could either indicate the extent or the intensity of Jesus' love. The qualitative meaning is probably dominant here, but particularly in view of 19.30 ('It is finished') the temporal meaning cannot be excluded.[82] 'Jesus loved up to the last moment of his life' and 'Jesus' love for his own was capable of any act of service or suffering.'[83] It is for this reason that the demonstration of Jesus' love refers both to the washing of the disciples' feet *and* to Jesus' death on the cross. It follows that 13.1 is an introduction not just to the Farewell Discourse (chs 14–17) but to the entire Book of Passion/Glory.[84] Jesus shows the full extent of his love not only through his death, but also in the events recorded in ch. 13.[85] His love for his own comes to particularly poignant expression when he washes the feet of Peter who will deny him and when he gives the morsel to Judas who will betray him. This is accentuated by the fact that he has a clear foreknowledge of both the betrayal (13.11) and the denials (13.38). In enduring that betrayal and those denials, Jesus becomes the quintessential righteous sufferer, revealing himself – again paradoxically – as the 'I am' (13.19).

---

81 Schnackenburg, *John* 3, pp. 15–16.
82 Thus Schnackenburg, *John*, 3, p. 16. There could be a play on words between *eis telos* ('to the end') in 13.1 and *tetelestai* ('it is finished') in 19.30, i.e. he loved them to the finish, to the very end of his life.
83 Barrett, *John*, p. 365.
84 Cf. Schnackenburg, *John*, 3, p. 16: 'This theologically very concentrated sentence . . . is therefore both the heading of the whole of the second main part of the gospel and the introduction to the washing of the feet.'
85 Beasley-Murray, *John*, p. 239, claims that the foot-washing 'is itself an act of love to the limit.' So also David Tripp, 'Meanings of the Foot-Washing: John 13 and Oxyrhynchus Papyrus 840', *ExpTim* 103 (1992), p. 237.

4.7 *A Broken Heart (13.18-21)*

¹² When he had finished washing their feet, he put on his clothes and returned to his place. 'Do you understand what I have done for you?' he asked them.

¹³ 'You call me "Teacher" and "Lord", and rightly so, for that is what I am.

¹⁴ Now that I, your Lord and Teacher, have washed your feet, you also should wash one another's feet.

¹⁵ I have set you an example that you should do as I have done for you.

¹⁶ I tell you the truth, no servant is greater than his master, nor is a messenger greater than the one who sent him.

¹⁷ Now that you know these things, you will be blessed if you do them.

¹⁸ 'I am not referring to all of you; I know those I have chosen. But this is to fulfil the scripture: "He who shares my bread has lifted up his heel against me."'

¹⁹ I am telling you now before it happens, so that when it does happen you will believe that I am He.

²⁰ I tell you the truth, whoever accepts anyone I send accepts me; and whoever accepts me accepts the one who sent me.'

²¹ After he had said this, *Jesus was troubled in spirit* and testified, 'I tell you the truth, one of you is going to betray me.'

The opening words of v. 21 – 'After he had said this' – refer to Jesus' direct speech that continued unbroken from 13.12b to 13.20. There are strains within this speech that would have troubled him deeply. He had said earlier that not all of his disciples were clean (13.10-11). This meant that not all of them would be blessed (13.17-18). He also indicated that one of the chosen would lift his heel against him (13.18). All ambiguity is removed in 13.21 where it is clear that Jesus is troubled in spirit because one of his disciples is about to betray him. He says so by way of solemn declaration in 13.21b. The solemnity of the prediction is highlighted by the double 'amen' with which it opens as well as by the two verbs of saying which introduce it, namely he 'testified and said' (NASB).[86] The announcement is therefore made with great emphasis. In the wider narrative Judas has already been designated as the traitor (6.71; 12.4). All that the disciples know, however, is that one of them is a devil (6.70) and that not all of them are clean (13.10). It is not Jesus' words to the disciples, but editorial comments for the benefit of the reader, that have disclosed Judas' true identity (6.71; 12.4; 13.2, 11). The narrative has therefore been carefully and gradually building up to this point. The account of the foot-washing has given strong indications to the reader as to what is to occur (13.2, 11) but the hints that Jesus has given the disciples (13.10, 18) are sufficiently vague that their full significance has passed them by. Particularly the significance of fulfilled Scripture (13.18) still escapes them.

The significance of this verse is likely to escape the reader as well. It comes

---

86 The verb 'testify' is usually associated with the witness of others *to* Jesus. Only rarely does it introduce statements *by* him (4.44; 7.7).

as the introduction to Jesus' announcement that one of his disciples will betray him (13.18-21). 'I am not referring to all of you,' he says, 'I know those I have chosen. But this is to fulfil the scripture: "He who shares my bread has lifted up his heel against me."' The NIV places a full-stop between 'I know those whom I have chosen' and 'But this is to fulfil the scripture.' This is a clever way of avoiding a knotty exegetical and theological problem.[87] But the reader will be asking how the two are related. How is Jesus' choice of his disciples related to the fulfilment of a scripture (Ps. 41.9) that predicts his betrayal? Does it mean that Jesus actually chose Judas so that Judas might betray him and thus fulfil the prophecy of the Psalmist? Although these questions are not answered by the immediate context, light is shed on them by the original introduction of Judas into the narrative of the Fourth Gospel. He is first mentioned in a context of mass defection by would-be disciples (6.60-71). Even before Judas is mentioned by name, an editorial comment reveals his role in the narrative, 'For Jesus had known from the beginning which of them did not believe and who would betray him' (6.64). Shortly afterwards the identity of the traitor is disclosed to the reader. In reply to Peter's confession that Jesus is 'the Holy One of God' (6.69), Jesus declares, 'Have I not chosen you, the Twelve? Yet one of you is a devil!' (6.70). The reader is then immediately informed that Jesus is referring to Judas who 'was later to betray him' (6.71). From the moment that Judas appears on the narrative scene of John's Gospel, the careful reader cannot avoid the uncomfortable conclusion that Jesus quite deliberately chose Judas, knowing that he was a devil who would betray him.

The strongly predestinarian character of ch. 6 pervades the present passage as well. The only logical way to relate 'I know those I have chosen' and 'this is to fulfil the scripture' is to understand the words 'I chose Judas' as filling the gap between the two statements.[88] Therefore Jesus is stating unequivocally that he chose Judas to be his traitor so that the prophecy of Ps. 41.9 might be fulfilled. This heavily predestinarian language would be quite out of place were it not for the fact that Jesus is about to refer to himself again as the divine 'I am' (13.19; cf. Exod. 3.14). Although most English translations supply a predicate (e.g. 'I am He'), there is no predicate in the Greek text. This is one of the few instances where *egō eimi* ('I am') is used absolutely (cf. 8.24, 28, 58). Jesus is therefore identifying himself with the great I AM who revealed himself to Moses at the burning bush (Exod. 3.1-22). Subtly but unmistakably he is identifying himself as the covenant Lord. As such he has the right to choose whom he wishes to carry out his sovereign will.

In the context of Jesus' predestination and foreknowledge, his disturbance of spirit becomes more difficult to account for. If the emotion is interpreted only within the setting of 13.21, the motivation behind it is readily understood. The

---

87 Literally the Greek reads, 'I know whom (plural) I have chosen, but . . . so that the Scripture may be fulfilled.' The major challenge facing the interpreter is how to fill in the ellipsis between the principal clause and the subordinate clause.

88 Thus M. J. J. Menken, 'The Translation of Psalm 41.10 in John 13:18', *JSNT* 49 (1990), p. 61.

reader's humanity can identify with being troubled in spirit by imminent betrayal. However, such comprehension seems to vanish in the light of the immediately preceding context. If Jesus chose Judas to be his betrayer so that Ps. 41.9 would be fulfilled, then his troubled spirit becomes all the more remarkable. Why should he be disturbed when all is going according to plan and the divine purpose is being fulfilled? Why be troubled if the train of events that he knowingly set in motion by choosing Judas (6.64, 70, 71) is now coming to pass?[89] These questions bring us to a profound mystery. The depth of the person of Jesus is beyond comprehension in John's presentation. In the present context, there are strong hints not only of supernatural foreknowledge but also of divine foreordination. Jesus knows whom he has chosen. Yet these overtones of divinity are not permitted to override his humanity. He is not surprised by what Judas is about to do, neither will the traitor thwart his plans, but he is still troubled – and deeply so.

Whenever the verb 'trouble' (*tarassō*) is used in this Gospel to denote an emotional reaction of Jesus, there seems to be a subtle and mysterious interplay between the divine and the human. He troubles himself outside the village of Bethany (11.33) even though he knows he will raise Lazarus from the dead, and it is for this very reason he made the journey back to Judea (11.8-16). His soul is troubled as his hour strikes (12.27), although he knows that the ruler of this world will now be cast out (12.31). He is troubled in spirit at the prospect of betrayal (13.21), in spite of the fact that he has chosen Judas so that the Scripture would be fulfilled (13.18). Judas was lost, but not unexpectedly or contrary to the divine purpose (17.12). Nevertheless, Jesus is troubled. Echoing Yahweh, he can say both 'I am' (13.19) and 'I have chosen' (13.18; cf. 6.70). At the same time his spirit can echo the Psalms of lament (13.21). Remarkably, John shows these apparently deep contradictions in Jesus' life rather than attempting to resolve them artificially.

The fact that the devil put it into the heart of Judas to betray Jesus (13.2), that Satan entered into him when he received the morsel (13.27), and that when Judas went out it was night (13.30), places the events of the upper room on a cosmic footing. This dimension enables us to trace the motivation for Jesus' emotion to

---

89   Cf. Menken, 'Translation', p. 72: 'John's view of Jesus [is] as one who "knows everything" (16.30; 21.17). Jesus sees through people (1.47-48; 2.24-25; 4:17-18; 5:6; 6.61), including Judas (6.64, 70-71); he knows what will happen to him in his passion (18.4; 19.28). This Johannine view of Jesus is very prominent in the context of 13.18.' Thus John is careful to quote Scripture in conformity with 'his ideas about Jesus' omniscience' (p. 73). Moreover, this omniscience is portrayed in John not as being merely superhuman insight or supernatural perception, but as a divine attribute. This characterization of Jesus is uniquely Johannine. As Culpepper, *Anatomy*, pp. 108–109, explains: 'He is omniscient, like the Father, and there is apparently nothing that the Father knows that Jesus does not know (in contrast to Mark 10:40; 13:32). Jesus knows who his betrayer is from the beginning (6:64) and speaks not only of his return to the Father but of his past in the history of Israel and his role on "the last day." He knows of his "hour" from the very beginning (2:4) and knows what is in the hearts of men (2:24; 1:47-48; 6:15). At times the evangelist takes extra pains to protect Jesus' omniscience, as in 6:6. Because he knows all things, Jesus never needs to ask for information and is never told anything he does not know.'

a deeper level. More is involved than the pain of betrayal by a close friend. Judas is not simply a traitor acting on his own accord, but has been duped by sinister forces to act on their behalf. His awareness of this factor also underlies Jesus' inner turmoil. As in 12.27, Jesus realizes that he must do battle with the ruler of this world. His overwhelming sense of foreboding that overtook Jesus on that occasion is now being experienced in a more intense way. The cosmic battle then anticipated in more general terms has now taken on a painfully personal dimension. The ruler of this world is about to win over a member of Jesus' intimate circle of friends. The enemy has struck at a point of vulnerability, a treasured relationship with a close associate (cf. Ps. 55.12-14). The cosmic battle is being brought home in a very direct way. Jesus is deeply wounded.

Throughout John 13 the strands of Jesus' love and knowledge are interwoven in intricate ways. Thus Jesus' love for Judas and his knowing selection of this disciple for betrayal are placed side by side. They stand together unharmonized and unreconciled. No attempt is made to explain the one in terms of the other. The author leaves the mystery unresolved and the antinomy unexplained. Jesus' supreme love for Judas (13.1) and his sovereign choice of Judas (13.18) reveal Jesus as the *egō eimi* (13.19). Jesus chose Judas even though he knew he was 'a devil' (6.64, 70, 71). Jesus loved Judas to the uttermost, washing his feet and giving him the morsel, even though he knew he would betray him. Although he is the sovereign Lord and the great I AM, it still breaks his heart.

4.8 *Love for the Disciples (13.31-38)*

31 When he [Judas] was gone, Jesus said, 'Now is the Son of Man glorified and God is glorified in him.

32 If God is glorified in him, God will glorify the Son in himself, and will glorify him at once.

33 'My children, I will be with you only a little longer. You will look for me, and just as I told the Jews, so I tell you now: Where I am going, you cannot come.

34 'A new command I give you: Love one another. *As I have loved you*, so you must love one another.

35 By this all men will know that you are my disciples, if you love one another.'

36 Simon Peter asked him, 'Lord, where are you going?' Jesus replied, 'Where I am going, you cannot follow now, but you will follow later.'

37 Peter asked, 'Lord, why can't I follow you now? I will lay down my life for you.'

38 Then Jesus answered, 'Will you really lay down your life for me? I tell you the truth, before the cock crows, you will disown me three times!'

At Judas' departure Jesus announces to the remaining disciples: 'Now is the Son of Man glorified' (13.31). The hour of Jesus' glorification, signaled by the coming of the Greeks (12.23) and culminating in his death (12.24), is now almost upon him: 'God . . . will glorify him at once' (13.32). The hour is about to strike with resounding finality, which means that Jesus will be with his disciples only a little longer (13.33). Prior to his departure he leaves them instructions as to how to live in his absence (13.34-35). He gives them 'a new commandment' – that of mutual love (13.34).

The age-old question regarding this commandment has to do with the precise nature of its newness. Although the 'new commandment' is mentioned again in 1 John 2.7, 8 and 2 John 5, the concept of newness is not well developed in the Fourth Gospel. Apart from Joseph's new tomb (19.41), the commandment stands alone in bearing this pristine quality. Moreover, the content of the command could hardly qualify as new in the light of the 'old commandment' to love one's neighbour as oneself (Lev. 19.18).

The commandment's newness can best be explained from within the text itself. At the heart of the command lies its rationale, 'as I have loved you'. Thus the newness of the command must be sought in the newness of its motive and scope.[90] A new standard has been set, the new quality of affection that believers are to have to one another on account of Christ's great love for them.[91] Their love for one another is to be a genuine reflection of his love for them.

But precisely how was that love demonstrated? For the disciples in the upper room the most obvious example of Jesus' love was still fresh in their minds. In the narrative time of the Gospel the foot-washing would have provided the readiest example of such love. Even so, the significance of Jesus washing Peter's feet and giving the morsel to Judas would not yet have penetrated their minds. The true depth of Jesus' love would become apparent only in his death, of which the foot-washing had been a symbolic anticipation. Thus the verb 'have loved' is not restricted to a single act, nor does it refer only to an event (or events) in the past. As in 13.1, it again depicts that love as a whole and in summary form. Thus the model for Christian love embraces both the foot-washing and the sacrificial death of Jesus, the first event prefiguring the second. The love of Jesus is epitomized in his death and this becomes the new standard of love (15.13; cf. 1 Jn 3.16).[92]

4.9 *Love for the Obedient Disciple (14.15-27)*

15 'If you love me, you will obey what I command.
16 And I will ask the Father, and he will give you another Counsellor to be with you for ever –
17 the Spirit of truth. The world cannot accept him, because it neither sees

---

90 Thus Westcott, *John*, p. 197.
91 Thus Morris, *John*, p. 633.
92 So Barrett, *John*, p. 377: 'The immediate reference is to the feet-washing (cf. vv. 14f.); but since this in its turn points to the death of Christ this last must be regarded as the ultimate standard of the love of Christians.'

him nor knows him. But you know him, for he lives with you and will be in you.

18 I will not leave you as orphans; I will come to you.

19 Before long, the world will not see me any more, but you will see me. Because I live, you also will live.

20 On that day you will realise that I am in my Father, and you are in me, and I am in you.

21 Whoever has my commands and obeys them, he is the one who loves me. He who loves me will be loved by my Father, and *I too will love him* and show myself to him.'

22 Then Judas (not Judas Iscariot) said, 'But, Lord, why do you intend to show yourself to us and not to the world?'

23 Jesus replied, 'If anyone loves me, he will obey my teaching. My Father will love him, and we will come to him and make our home with him.

24 He who does not love me will not obey my teaching. These words you hear are not my own; they belong to the Father who sent me.

25 'All this I have spoken while still with you.

26 But the Counsellor, the Holy Spirit, whom the Father will send in my name, will teach you all things and will remind you of everything I have said to you.

27 Peace I leave with you; my peace I give you. I do not give to you as the world gives. Do not let your hearts be troubled and do not be afraid.'

The opening statement of ch. 13.1 – 'now he showed them the full extent of his love' – not only explains what happened at the foot-washing and in the Passion but also undergirds Jesus' teaching in the Farewell Discourse (14.1–17.26). After Judas' departure the remaining disciples need to be reassured of Jesus' love. The reason for this is that their hearts are troubled (14.1, 27). The cause for their troubled hearts is obvious. In the foot-washing chapter Jesus had predicted both Judas' betrayal (13.18-30) and Peter's denials (13.38). But even more disturbing to the disciples is the prospect of Jesus' departure (13.33, 36). In the minds of the disciples his departure is somehow bound up with Judas' betrayal and Peter's denials. For those who have given up all to follow Jesus this is a deeply disturbing thought. No wonder their hearts are troubled.

The emotions the disciples are experiencing are ones Jesus himself undergoes. Not only does Jesus understand his disciples' emotions, he is experiencing them himself and for much the same reasons – his own impending death (11.33; 12.27) and the prospect of Judas' betrayal (13.21). With his own heart still pained at the thought of being betrayed, he tells his disciples, 'Do not let your hearts be troubled' (14.1). Later in the chapter he repeats exactly the same words (14.27). They form a tidy *inclusio* in the early part of the Farewell Discourse, and thus define the main body of what Jesus says between Judas' departure (13.30) and the exhortation to the remaining disciples to depart (14.31). This main body (14.1-27) is preceded by an introduction (13.31-38) and followed by a conclusion (14.28 31). Jesus' chief concern is to address the disciples' troubled hearts

(14.1, 27). It is in this context that Jesus vouches his love for the obedient disciple (14.21).

The main body of the discourse (14.1-27) can be divided into three major subsections. This division is based on the themes of departure and return, which are central to the discourse: (a) Jesus' departure and return (14.1-3), (b) Jesus' departure (14.4-14), and (c) Jesus' return (14.15-27).[93] This structure has important exegetical implications, not least of which is the fact that it places the references to the Holy Spirit (14.15-16, 26) within the theme of Jesus' return. The return in (a), however, is not synonymous with the return in (c). Jesus first refers to his ultimate, eschatological return, 'I will come back and take you to be with me that you also may be where I am' (14.3). The return in the latter half of the chapter, on the other hand, has to do with Jesus' immediate return in the coming of the Holy Spirit. The coming of the Spirit is therefore a way of describing the return of Jesus to the disciples. It is also in this setting that the love of Jesus and the Father (14.21, 23) is to be understood. The love of the Father and Jesus for the obedient disciple therefore comes to expression within the context of the promise of the Holy Spirit (14.15-27). Not only does the return of Jesus coincide with the coming of the Holy Spirit, but the Spirit's coming also constitutes the highest expression of the love that Jesus and the Father will extend to the obedient disciple. The love promised in 14.21 stands at the very heart of the passage that first introduces the Holy Spirit as the Paraclete ('Counsellor') into the Fourth Gospel (cf. 15.26; 16.7).[94]

Occupying such a central position within 14.15-27, v. 21 has direct connections with almost every other verse in the intricate web of thought that makes up this sub-unit. This is a clear instance where text and immediate context are mutually interpretive. To appreciate the role of 14.21 within this passage and its contribution to the overall meaning, we must consider each of its three constituent parts:

(a) *Whoever has my commands and obeys them, he is the one who loves me.*
    These words are the converse of 14.15, the opening verse of this section: 'If you love me, you will obey what I command.' The reciprocal relationship between the two sayings has been described by Westcott in his comments on 14.21, 'There active obedience is seen to be the consequence of love. Here active obedience is the sign of the presence of love.'[95] The two statements

---

93   This structure is developed in some detail by Fernando F. Segovia, 'The Structure, *Tendenz*, and *Sitz im Leben* of John 13:31-14:31', *JBL* 104 (1985), pp. 481–87.

94   The term 'Paraclete' is a transliteration of the untranslatable term *paraklētos*, which in the New Testament is confined to the Johannine literature. The Paraclete is with the disciples (14.16), instructs and reminds them (14.26), testifies about Jesus (15.26), and convicts the world of sin, righteousness and judgement (16.8-11). The term therefore has distinctly legal overtones, a note which is struck most strongly in 1 Jn 2.1 where Jesus Christ is described as 'an Advocate with the Father' (NASB). As the Paraclete, the Holy Spirit fulfils two major roles. In that he indwells and teaches the disciples he plays a comforting role in relation to the church. By testifying about Jesus he has a convicting role in the world.

95   Westcott, *John*, p. 207.

are two sides of the one coin. The condition of 14.15 is restated in slightly different terms in 14.23a: 'If anyone loves me, he will obey my teaching.' The negative corollary is stated in 14.24a: 'He who does not love me will not obey my teaching.' The correlation between love and obedience is therefore a strong theme in this passage and it is developed from various complementary perspectives. Within this development, 14.21a occupies a pivotal position. The unique contribution that it makes to this theme is that the one who loves Jesus not only 'keeps' his commandments/word(s) (in the sense of observing them in daily life), but he first 'has' them (in the sense of having 'grasped them with the mind'[96]).

(b) *He who loves me will be loved by my Father.* This promise is no less integrally related to the immediate context than is the first part of the verse. Just as 14.21a is related to 14.15, 14.21b is related to 14.16, namely the promise that the Father will give the disciples another Paraclete, the Spirit of truth (14.17). This promise is repeated in 14.26, where the Father will send the Paraclete in Jesus' name. The love of the Father for the obedient disciple is therefore epitomized in the giving and sending of the Spirit. This love is also shown in the accompanying promise that the Father and Jesus will come to the obedient disciple and make their home with such a person (14.23). This coming and abiding cannot be understood in isolation from the gift of the Spirit. In this way Jesus can promise his disciples that he will always be with them. Thus the 'little children' with whom he will be for only a little longer (13.33) will not be left as orphans (14.18). Their Father will always be with them. Through the coming of the Holy Spirit, the Father will in fact enter into a new relationship with the disciples. The promise of becoming God's children (1.12) is not yet a reality, but at this point is still an expectation to be realized in the future. Only the death of Jesus and the coming of the Spirit can actualize this promise.

(c) *And I too will love him and show myself to him.* Apart from the sudden change to the active voice, the love of Jesus is like that of the Father in every respect. If any distinction is intended by the change in voice, little if any attention is drawn to it. In 14.23 the Father's love is referred to in the active voice, as was the love of Jesus in 14.21. There seems to be no attempt to distinguish the nature of Jesus' love from that of the Father. In both cases the love is spoken of in the future tense and is directed to the obedient disciple, the one who loves Jesus. Furthermore, both the love of the Father and that of Jesus are experienced in terms of the presence of the Spirit within the community. Like the love of the Father, the future love of Jesus is also to be understood in the light of the coming of the Paraclete. Jesus' love is expressed in terms of his coming to the obedient disciple and making his home there (14.23). All these features combine to create the strong impression that the love of the Father and that of Jesus in this context are of the same character.

96   Thus Carson, *John*, p. 503.

The divine quality of Jesus' love is further demonstrated in the promise attendant upon this love, *and I will show myself to him*. Jesus' self-disclosure to the obedient disciple is an expression of love not attributed to the Father, but it is seen as no less divine. The verb used to designate this self-disclosure, *emphanizō*, is found only in these verses (14.21-22) in John, and never again in the New Testament in the same sense. Barrett has drawn attention to the fact that it is used of theophanies in both the LXX (Exod. 33.13, 18) and the Apocrypha (Wis. 1.2).[97] In a passage that places such a strong accent on divine love, the choice of this term seems therefore to be particularly appropriate. Although the future reference point for Jesus' self-disclosure is not explicitly stated in this verse, the context suggests the resurrection appearances (14.19) and Pentecost (14.16, 17, 26) as possibilities. In John's Gospel a choice between these two alternatives is not necessary, as the giving of the Spirit coincides with the first resurrection appearance to the disciples (20.22). Easter and Pentecost are collapsed into a single event – the self-disclosure of Jesus. It is a unique demonstration of Jesus' love for the obedient disciple, and yet in no way divorced from the love of the Father (14.23). When the Spirit is given, both the Father and the Son show their love to the obedient disciple by coming to him and making their home with him – but this will not occur until after Jesus' resurrection. It is then that they receive the Holy Spirit (20.22) and it is also then that Jesus keeps his promise that he will love them and show himself to them (14.21).

4.10 *Love for the Father (14.28-31)*

28 'You heard me say, "I am going away and I am coming back to you." If you loved me, you would be glad that I am going to the Father, for the Father is greater than I.

29 I have told you now before it happens, so that when it does happen you will believe.

30 I will not speak with you much longer, for the prince of this world is coming. He has no hold on me,

31 but the world must learn that *I love the Father* and that I do exactly what my Father has commanded me. "Come now; let us leave."'

The Gospel's sole reference to Jesus' love for the Father is found in the closing verse of the conclusion to the discourse of ch. 14. This concluding section (14.28-31) weaves together some of the major strands in the main body of the discourse (14.1-27) and at the same time anticipates the Passion of Jesus.[98] In performing this dual function, this conclusion contains three basic elements: '(1) an

---

97 Barrett, *John*, p. 388; cf. Brown, *John 2*, p. 647.

98 Thus Fernando F. Segovia, *Love Relationships in the Johannine Tradition: Agapē/Agapan in I John and the Fourth Gospel* (Society of Biblical Literature Dissertation Series 58; Chico, CA: Scholars Press, 1982), p. 159.

instruction concerning the proper attitude of the disciples with respect to Jesus' openly announced and impending glorification, vv. 28-29; (2) an explanation concerning the proper interpretation of that coming glorification as an encounter between Jesus and 'the ruler of the world,' vv. 30-31c; (3) a command to arise and depart, v. 31d.'[99] The reference to Jesus' love for the Father clearly falls within the second section. It forms an essential component in the interpretation of Jesus' glorification and as such anticipates the Passion. The love of Jesus in this instance therefore stands once again in the closest possible relationship with his imminent suffering and death (cf. 13.1).

Verse 30 opens with the strong suggestion that Jesus' departure and Passion are fast approaching: 'I will not speak with you much longer.' Little time is left, 'for the prince of the world is coming'. This is again a stark reminder that Jesus' Passion is to be viewed in terms of a cosmic conflict. In the ensuing narrative the only one who 'comes' is Judas (18.3), but the reader is already well aware that Judas has become the instrument of Satan (13.2, 27, 30). By his exit into the night he has joined the forces of darkness. Behind the dark deed of betrayal (18.5) stands the sinister figure of Satan, the ruler of this world, with whom Jesus must do battle. But the outcome has already been determined. The hour of Jesus' departure is also the hour when 'the prince of this world will be driven out' (12.31) and when he will be judged together with the world (12.31; 16.11).

Of this soon-to-be-expelled and judged ruler Jesus can confidently say, 'He has no hold on me.' Jesus is seeking to forestall any misunderstanding of his imminent death on the part of his disciples. In his Passion they are not to discern a Satanic victory. Contrary to appearances, this would be a profound misinterpretation. In the cosmic battle to be waged on the cross there will be no triumph for the ruler of this world. The negatives of 14.30 thus clear the way for the positive affirmation of 14.31. Jesus goes to his death out of love and obedience to the Father.

The nexus between love and obedience that has been emphasized repeatedly in the latter half of this chapter (14.15, 21, 23, 24, cf. 15.10) therefore finds its zenith in the obedience unto death that conclusively demonstrates Jesus' love for the Father. Just as the obedient disciple shows his love for Jesus by having and keeping his word(s)/commandments, so Jesus shows his love for the Father by doing just as the Father has commanded him. The specific commandments the Father gave Jesus in the Fourth Gospel had to do with what he was to speak regarding eternal life (12.49-50) and with laying down his life and taking it up again (10.17-18). Thus, Jesus' death was clearly implied in his obedience to what the Father had commanded him. Though his obedience was lofty, it does appear to be of the same order as the obedience expected of the disciples. Although more difficult to obey, the commands given him by the Father were not essentially different in character from the commands given to the disciples.

The nature of Jesus' love for the Father can thus only be understood in terms of the Father's love for him. The mutual love between the Father and the Son is the outworking of the relationship described in the prologue, where Jesus is

---

99   Segovia, 'Structure', pp. 487–88.

depicted as being 'in the bosom of the Father' (1.18 NASB). The image suggests a close and intimate relationship but, as the relationship unfolds on the pages of the Gospel, more is implied. Jesus' love for the Father is expressed in obedience, even to the point of willingly laying down his life (10.17, 18). Again, his death is not a victory for the prince of this world, but ultimately the most profound expression of Jesus' love for the Father.

4.11 *Love for His Friends (15.9-17)*

9 'As the Father has loved me, *so have I loved you*. Now remain in *my love*.
10 If you obey my commands, you will remain *in my love*, just as I have obeyed my Father's commands and remain in his love.
11 I have told you this so that my joy may be in you and that your joy may be complete.
12 My command is this: Love each other *as I have loved you*.
13 Greater *love* has no-one than this, that he lay down his life for his friends.
14 You are my friends if you do what I command.
15 I no longer call you servants, because a servant does not know his master's business. Instead, I have called you friends, for everything that I learned from my Father I have made known to you.
16 You did not choose me, but I chose you and appointed you to go and bear fruit – fruit that will last. Then the Father will give you whatever you ask in my name.
17 This is my command: Love each other.'

This paragraph is a unit that pivots on v. 12. 'My command is this: Love each other' anticipates v. 17, while 'as I have loved you', echoes v. 9. Love is therefore its unifying theme. According to Fernando Segovia, this central theme of love is developed as follows: '(1) the relationship of Jesus to the Father as constitutive for that of the disciples to Jesus, vv. 9-10; (2) an aside on the joy of the disciples, v. 11; (3) an exposition of the commandment of love, vv. 12-17.'[100]

Moreover, this paragraph is linked most intricately with the preceding one (15.1-8), which is an extended metaphor of the vine imagery introduced in v. 1. The elaborate connections between the two paragraphs can be seen most clearly in the four major parallels between them:[101]

(a) Each section is dominated by a single imperative: '*Remain* in me' (15.4) and '*remain* in my love' (15.9). These closely related commands represent a

---

100 Segovia, *Love Relationships*, p. 108. Following his arrangement, together with his claims that the references to joy in 15.11 are an aside, the exegesis of this verse will be omitted here, but will be undertaken in the next major section (4.12).
101 Bultmann, *John*, pp. 539–40.

parallel but also a development. The vine image can indicate dependence and intimacy, but not love. The disciples abide in Christ by abiding in his love.

(b) There is also a parallel between two similar statements: 'You are clean' (15.3) and 'You are my friends' (15.14). This is the indicative that is the basis for the imperative to 'remain'. The command is addressed to those who are clean (pruned) and therefore Jesus' friends (cf. 13.10).

(c) Both the pruned branch (15.2, 4, 8) and the friend of Jesus bear fruit (15.16).

(d) The highest point in the disciple's life is the assurance that the prayer will be heard (15.7, 16).

As well as beginning to unpack the metaphor of 15.1-8, v. 9 also introduces a hierarchy of love that will extend to the end of v. 17. The hierarchy is established by the opening word 'as'. A correspondence is drawn between the Father's love for Jesus and Jesus' love for the disciples. Verses 9-10 focus on the parallels between the love of the Father and the love of Jesus. The love of Jesus for the disciples is of the same order as the Father's love for Jesus. Both are indicated by 'love', the noun and the verb. Moreover, the disciples are to remain in Jesus' love in precisely the same way as he remains in the Father's love. Just as he has kept his Father's commands, so they are to keep his commands. Jesus' love is therefore the perfect paradigm for the disciples (15.12). His love for them is the model of their love for one another. Such love reaches its acme in the laying down of one's life (15.13). While 15.9-10 concentrates solely on the love of the Father and Jesus, in 15.12-17 the focus shifts to the mutual love between the disciples, which is to model itself on Jesus' love for them.

In this passage the hierarchy of love is therefore clearly spelled out:

(a) The Father's love for Jesus (15. 9-10);
(b) Jesus' love for the disciples (15. 9-10);
(c) The disciples' love for one another (15.12, 13, 17).

The Father shows his love to Jesus both by entrusting him with the task of revelation and by commanding him to lay down his life and take it up again (see above, 4.10). Hence Jesus remains in the Father's love by completing the task of revelation to the point of laying down his life and taking it up again. By way of anticipation Jesus can therefore claim, 'I have obeyed my Father's commands' (15.10). This is how he shows his love for the Father (14.31).

Just as the Father loved Jesus by assigning him his revelatory task, Jesus gives his disciples a similar assignment. This is a responsibility that Jesus is about to pass on to them because he loves them as his friends: 'I have called you friends, for everything that I learned from my Father I have made known to you' (15.15).[102] On this basis, and with the Paraclete's help, they will be called to the

---

102 The title *friends* is an appellation of rare distinction. The only other friends of Jesus specifically mentioned in this Gospel are Lazarus whom Jesus designates as 'our friend' (11.11), and John the Baptist who can refer to himself as the privileged 'friend of the bridegroom' (3.29). Outside the Fourth Gospel the designation is even more uncommon. Only in Lk. 12.4 does

revelatory task of bearing witness (15.26-27). So just as the Father loved Jesus by assigning him the task of Revealer (cf. 12.49, 50), so Jesus loved the disciples by making them his witnesses.

The parallel does not end, however, with the continuation of the revelatory task. Just as the Father commanded Jesus to lay down his life (10.17, 18; 14.31), so Jesus commands his disciples to love one another (15.12, 17), a mutual love which finds its highest expression in the laying down of one's life for the other (15.13). In displaying this quality of love as well as in fulfilling their assignment as witnesses, the disciples keep Jesus' commandments and thus abide in his love (15.10). The parallel between the Father's love for Jesus and Jesus' love for the disciples is therefore characterized by a precision that descends to the very details of the commands given and the obedience anticipated.

The commands of Jesus in 15.10 are reduced to the single command of mutual love in 15.12. After the parenthetical statement about joy in 15.11, Jesus returns to the hierarchy of love introduced in 15.9. The most important part of abiding in Jesus' love is the mutual love that the disciples are to display towards one another. The disciples can remain in the hierarchy of love only if they love one another. The Father loves Jesus. Jesus loves the disciples. The disciples must love one another. Only so will they abide in the vine. The paradigm for such love is the example of Jesus himself. The example alluded to in 15.12 ('as I have loved you') is the washing of feet, as it partly repeats the wording of the new commandment (13.34).

In the transition from 15.12 to 15.13 the standard for this mutual love is raised considerably. The high standard implied in the words 'as I have loved you' becomes immeasurably higher when compared to the pinnacle of such love in the next verse: 'Greater love has no one than this, that one lay down his life for his friends' (15.13).[103] No loftier love for a friend can be imagined than the sacrificial giving up of one's own life.[104] 'The giving of one's life for one's friends', writes George Beasley-Murray, 'is the greatest measure of altruistic human

---

Jesus again refer to his disciples as his friends. In Jas 2.23 the writer reminds his readers that Abraham 'was called the friend of God' (2 Chron. 20.7; Isa. 41.8). The only other Old Testament personage to be graced with such a title was Moses (Exod. 33.11). Significantly, both Abraham and Moses were key figures in the administration of the old covenant. There were also crucial points in salvation history when they 'knew what the master was doing' (e.g. Gen. 12.1-3; 18.16-33; Exod. 3.7-22; 33.7-11), a privilege that Jesus extends to the disciples in v. 15.

103 Stählin, *TDNT* 9, p. 153, cites several parallel sayings from classical antiquity: 'In many variations the supreme duty of a friend is to sacrifice himself for his friend even to the pt. of death. Thus Aristot. Eth. Nic., IX, 8, p. 1169a, 18-20 says: "To a noble man there applies the true saying that he does all things for the sake of his friends . . . and, if need be, he gives his life for them".'

104 Frances T. Gench, 'John 15:12-17', *Int* 58 (2004), p. 182, makes an astute observation on this emphasis in John: 'It is worth noting, in fact, that disciples are not asked to love one another as they love *themselves* (Mark 12:28-34; Matt 22:34-40; Luke 10:25-28), but as *Jesus* loved them. In this respect, John's love commandment, which points to the cross as the paradigm of love, is more radical than its synoptic analogues.'

love.'[105] The wording, however, suggests that more is in view than the epitome of altruism. The concept of sacrificially laying down one's life has its roots in the Good Shepherd imagery of John 10 (vv. 11, 15, 17, 18). Not only an altruistic, but also a sacrificial and vicarious death is in view. The laying down of the life is '*for* his friends'. (The Greek preposition *huper* with the genitive found here is used with an unequivocally substitutionary thrust in 10.11, 15; 11.50-52; cf. 1 Jn 3.16). Jesus personalizes the universal applicability of the saying in 15.13, when in the next verse he declares his table companions to be his friends. Little doubt is left that he will die on their behalf and that such love is now the new standard for their mutual love. Their love is to have its source in his redemptive love (cf. 1 Jn 4.19). In laying down his life for his friends he is also the Shepherd who lays down his life for his sheep. In this capacity he fulfils the roles of both the suffering Servant (Isa. 53) and the Lamb of God (1.29, 36).

Being prepared to lay down one's life for one's friends has already had an earlier application in that Lazarus was designated 'our friend' (11.11). By undertaking the hazardous journey into Judea Jesus was putting his own life in mortal danger. Clearly, the events that were set in train by the raising of Lazarus were to lead inexorably to Jesus' own death (11.45-53). As Brendan Byrne has pointed out: 'The Lazarus story, immediately preceding the Passion, powerfully enacts the truth that Jesus gives life at the cost of his own life.'[106] Therefore, although Jesus' love for Lazarus presents itself initially as warm, human affection for a friend, it also operates at a deeper level. He is one of those friends for whom Jesus lays down his life. Lazarus, by implication, becomes the recipient of redemptive love.

In the references to Jesus' love for his friends, 15.9-13 bring together some of the recurrent themes of the Fourth Gospel. In 15.9-10 Jesus is speaking the language of the covenant Lord. As Israel was to cleave to Yahweh by obeying his commands (Deut. 10.20; 11.22; 13.4; 30.20), so the disciples are to remain in Jesus' love by keeping his commandments. In 15.12-13 this covenant language is not abandoned. If anything, the emphasis on his commands now becomes even more pronounced (15.12, 14, 17). Yet, at the same time, the great paradox of the new covenant is introduced. The covenant Lord also becomes the covenant sacrifice (15.13; cf. 1.29, 36). As the supreme example of the one who lays down his life for his friends, Jesus fulfils the demands of the covenant in his own person. The great themes of Jesus as both covenant Lord and covenant sacrifice converge at this point. The axes along which the identity of Jesus is plotted in John's Gospel intersect in this passage. Seldom do the Gospel's central themes crystallize so succinctly. The covenant Lord who loves (15.9, 10, 12, 13; cf. Deut. 7.7-9) and elects his people (15.16, 19; cf. Deut. 7.6-7), and issues commandments that they are to keep (15.10, 12, 14, 17),[107] reveals his identity as

---

105   George R. Beasley-Murray, *John* (WBC 36; Waco: Word, 2nd edn, 1999), p. 274.
106   Brendan Byrne, *Lazarus: A Contemporary Reading of John 1:1-46* (Homebush, NSW: St Paul Publications, 1991), p. 105.
107   Not only God's electing love for Israel but also the giving and keeping of his commandments is a strong emphasis in Deuteronomy. In the LXX the verb 'command' occurs approximately 83*x* and the noun 'commandment' 44*x* in Deuteronomy, the combined total far outweighing

covenant Lord by laying down his life for them (15.13).[108] This is the highest manifestation of his love. Jesus' roles as covenant Lord and covenant sacrifice do not run parallel, nor do they merge only briefly. It is precisely when he offers himself as covenant sacrifice that he proves himself to be covenant Lord. It is in his flesh, his human mortality, that his disciples will behold his divine glory. The message of ch. 13 has now been transposed to a higher key. There the washing of feet demonstrated his identity as the divine 'I am.' Here his sacrificial death serves the same purpose. His death for his friends reveals a love that is sublime and divine. The love of the covenant Lord has come to its own.

4.12 *Joy Fulfilled (15.11; 17.13)*

Jesus says to the disciples:

> I have told you this so that *my joy* may be in you and that your joy may be complete (15.11).

Jesus prays to the Father:

> I am coming to you now, but I say these things while I am still in the world, so that they may have the full measure of *my joy* within them (17.13).

As indicated above, Jn 15.11 forms an aside within the hierarchy of love portrayed in 15.9-17. In spite of its parenthetical nature, however, it is most intricately linked to its context. First, it marks a transition between vv. 9-10 (with their exclusive focus on the love of the Father and Jesus) and vv. 12-17 (with the commandment of mutual love between the disciples as their *inclusio*). Secondly, the introductory words, 'I have told you this', are taken most naturally with the immediately preceding verses (15.9-10).[109] What Jesus says about the Father's love for him and his own love for the disciples, and about the appropriate response of obedience in each case, will therefore stand in the closest possible

---

that of any other Old Testament book.

108   Aelred Lacomara, 'Deuteronomy and the Farewell Discourse (Jn 13.31-16.33)', *CBQ* 36 (1974), pp. 65–84, shows a number of convincing parallels between Jesus and Moses and hence between the farewell speeches of each as recorded in Deuteronomy and in John 13–16. Although Lacomara is correct in detecting similarities between Moses and Jesus, the deeper continuity lies between Yahweh and Jesus. Like the covenant Lord in Deuteronomy, Jesus loves and chooses his disciples, gives them commands and makes promises that are conditional on their obedience. Although the word 'covenant' is never used, in the Farewell Discourse Jesus is entering into a covenant with his disciples as representatives of the new covenant people of God.

109   This expression occurs repeatedly throughout the Farewell Discourse (14.25; 15.11; 16.1, 4, 6, 25, 33), always with direct reference to what immediately precedes, although broader application to the discourse as a whole is at times not impossible.

relation to his own joy and that of the disciples in 15.11. To be specific, his keeping the Father's commands relates directly to his own joy, while the disciples' joy is dependent on their keeping his commands.

Within these three verses (15.9-11) there would also seem to be a strong correlation between love, obedience and joy. Love for the other is the motive for obedience. Obedience is the fitting response to the love of the other. Joy results from obedience. Hence obedience is the link between love and joy. Love is its source, and joy is its by-product. Here too Jesus serves as a paradigm for his disciples. Just as their love is to be modelled on his, so is their joy. He remained in the Father's love by keeping his commandments, pre-eminently the command to lay down his life. They likewise will remain in Jesus' love by keeping his commandments, especially the command to love one another. So just as Jesus' supreme joy lies in his relationship of obedience to the Father, the disciples' supreme joy lies in their relationship of obedience to Jesus.[110] That the disciples' mutual love should lead to joy is readily comprehensible. That Jesus' laying down his life should lead to joy is highly remarkable. Such joy is both inexplicable and unfathomable.

For both Jesus and the disciples, the joy in 15.11 can be defined as 'the sublime gladness of whole-hearted obedience'.[111] As Brown points out: 'Joy is presented as flowing from the obedience and love of which Jesus has spoken. Jesus' own joy springs from his union with the Father which finds expression in obedience and love (xiv 31).'[112] As the verse cited here contains an implicit reference to Jesus' death, one can only conclude that Jesus not only demonstrated his love to the Father by obeying the command to lay down his life, but also found joy in such obedience. Westcott refers to this as 'the joy of complete self-surrender in love to love.'[113] In absolute self-sacrifice Jesus finds the fullness of joy. Thus the joy of Jesus is sustained by love from two directions. By keeping the Father's commandments he both remains in the Father's love (15.10) and expresses his love to the Father (14.31). 'Such a relationship of love leads to joy to the uttermost,' says Beasley-Murray. 'Jesus experienced it, even when facing the dread hour of sacrifice.'[114] At this point John's Jesus forms a stark contrast to the agonizing figure in Gethsemane presented by Matthew and Mark.

However extraordinary Jesus' joy may appear in John, it is nevertheless a communicable quality. 'He revealed these things to his disciples that they might have the same joy in fullest measure.'[115] This becomes even more apparent in 17.13 where he no longer distinguishes his joy from theirs, but prays that 'they

110   In his love for Jesus the Father also assigned him the role of Revealer (12.49-50; cf. 3.35; 5.20). It can be assumed that Jesus took delight in fulfilling this obligation, just as the disciples would find joy in their calling to bear witness (15.26-27). In the immediate context, however, the most prominent command for Jesus to carry out is to lay down his life, while the disciples' primary obligation is mutual love.
111   D. A. Carson, *Jesus and His Friends: His Farewell Message and Prayer in John 14 to 17* (Grand Rapids: Baker, 1980), p. 99.
112   Brown, *John* 2, p. 681.
113   Westcott, *John*, p. 220.
114   Beasley-Murray, *John*, p. 274.
115   Beasley-Murray, *John*, p. 274.

may have the full measure of my joy within them.' A comparison between 15.11 and 17.13b indicates that the two statements are essentially parallel. Each consists of an introductory clause followed by a purpose clause:

Table 4.2 The Parallel Clauses in John 15.11 and 17.13b

Introductory Clause	*Purpose Clause*
I have told you this (15.11)	so that my joy may be in you and your joy may be complete. (15.11)
I say these things while I am still in the world (17.13b)	so that they may have the full measure of my joy within them. (17.13b)

As 'this' in 15.11 refers to the immediately preceding verses (15.9-10), so 'these things' of 17.13b may be taken to refer to the earlier part of the prayer (17.1-12).[116] As 15.9-10 speak of the obedience of Jesus and the disciples, the same subject may also be expected to surface in 17.1-12. Such is precisely the case. The obedience of Jesus to the commission entrusted to him by the Father is a strong motif in these verses. He had accomplished the work that the Father had given him to do (17.4). He manifested the Father's name to the disciples the Father had given him (17.6; cf. 17.26), and the words that the Father had given Jesus, he gave to them (17.8; cf. 17.14). Finally, he had kept them in the Father's name (17.12). According to the logic found in 15.9-11, the joy of Jesus in 17.13 springs from his obedience to the Father, in this case defined primarily in terms of his role as Revealer.

The disciples' obedience also features prominently in these verses, mainly in terms of their response to the revelation given. They kept the Father's word (17.6), they received the words that the Father gave Jesus, and they believed that the Father sent Jesus (17.8). Jesus prays that they may be one (17.11; cf. 17.21-23), presumably in the sense that they will carry out the command of mutual love (15.12-17). The disciples' joy will be a lasting characteristic if they remain faithful to the revelation received and maintain their unity by practising mutual love.

The similarity of wording between the two verses demands that the prayer of 17.13 be interpreted in the light of the saying in 15.11.[117] The two are clearly complementary and the context of 17.13 enlarges on the obedience that lay behind Jesus' joy and that is to be the key to the disciples' joy.[118] There is, however, a feature in 17.13 that is absent from 15.11, namely its opening clause, 'I am coming to you now'. This recalls another occasion when Jesus had announced that he would depart to the Father, a prospect that had not inspired the disciples with joy (14.28). This is a situation that Jesus had sought to correct in the intervening discourse (16.20-24). As his explanation of his departure appears to

---

116 Thus Brown, *John* 2, p. 761.
117 Thus Carson, *John*, p. 564; Morris, *John*, p. 729; Schnackenburg, *John* 3, p. 183.
118 Barrett, *John*, p. 425, makes the apt comment that the joy of both Jesus and the disciples in 17.13 springs 'from unsparing obedience to and unbroken communion with the Father'.

have reassured the disciples (16.29-30), he now prays that, even as he is about to depart, the disciples may experience the fullness of his joy. Inspired by obedience, their joy is strengthened by a greater understanding of the significance of his departure.

The reader cannot fail to be astonished by the few but powerful references to Jesus' joy in the Fourth Gospel. He rejoices in the face of Lazarus' death (11.15) and now again he expresses his joy as he anticipates his own death (15.11; 17.13). At the surface level the reason for his joy seems unusual, to say the least. Our investigation into Jesus' joy on the earlier occasion indicated that he did not rejoice in Lazarus' death as such. He was not glad that Lazarus had died. The death of his friend gave him no pleasure; quite the opposite (11.33-38). Rather, Jesus rejoices because the purpose of Lazarus' death (and his subsequent revivification) will be fulfilled in the faith of his disciples. Such faith will be a preliminary fulfillment of the purpose of the Gospel as a whole (20.30, 31). The same perspective applies here. Although Jesus experiences a remarkable fullness of joy in the face of his own death, this is not a macabre and masochistic delight in dying. The earlier references to his inner turmoil at the prospect of his own death (12.27; 13.21) should have pre-empted any such impression, for his horror at death is just as real here as in the Synoptics. His joy is not in his death as such, but in the *meaning* of his death. His death means that he has fully kept his Father's commands and that his mission as Revealer is complete. He will have loved his own to the end. What was anticipated by the death of Lazarus will finally be fulfilled. In short, as the Lord of the covenant, he finds joy in becoming the covenant sacrifice, in accordance with the will of the Father. In his death the new covenant will finally be ratified.

These references to Jesus' joy sit very comfortably with his repeated emphasis on love and peace in the Farewell Discourse. His love for the Father and the peace of the Holy Spirit provide the natural setting in which joy can flourish. Jesus' reflections on these truths not only reassure his disciples but bring comfort to his own soul as well. From being deeply troubled in both heart and spirit (12.27; 13.21), Jesus can move on to tell his disciples not to be troubled (14.1, 27) and then speak of his peace (14.27), love (14.21, 31; 15.9-13) and joy (15.11; 17.13). The tense atmosphere that pervaded the upper room during the foot-washing scene (13.2-30) is relieved by Judas' exit (13.30). Jesus is now among friends – troubled, fearful friends perhaps, one of whom will deny him, but friends nonetheless. As Jesus talks matters over with them, he reaches a level of acceptance of what lies ahead. So much is this the case that he can end his speech on a positively triumphant note: 'I have told you these things, so that in me you may have peace. In this world you will have trouble. But take heart, I have overcome the world' (16.33).

Yet this positive attitude on Jesus' part generates problems of its own. The last emotion that John attributes to Jesus before the Passion is joy. There is no account of Gethsemane in the Fourth Gospel. Yet the reader who is familiar with the Synoptics would be able to place Gethsemane quite confidently between Jn 18.1 (where Jesus and his disciples enter an olive grove across the Kidron Valley) and Jn 18.2-3 (where Judas enters the grove accompanied by soldiers and officials). Why John chose not to include any reference to Gethsemane is a matter of conjecture that cannot be resolved. It is wiser to simply note *that* John and the Synoptics vary at this point, rather than to speculate as to *why* they vary. Nevertheless, the contrasting and apparently conflicting pictures of Jesus that emerge from this comparison cannot be ignored. In John's account Jesus cuts a compelling, confident and triumphant figure who even at the point of his arrest twice declares himself to be the 'I am' (18.5-8) with dramatic consequences (18.6). On the other hand, the Synoptics – especially Matthew and Mark – portray Jesus struggling and anguished, a troubled soul overwhelmed with sorrow to the point of death (Mt. 26.37-38; Mk 14.33-34). Can these two images – the triumphant and the distressed – be reconciled?

The problem is actually more apparent than real. Those in the helping professions, such as pastors, doctors, counsellors and psychiatrists, will know only too well the emotional swings that can be experienced by those facing a crisis of life and death proportions. For example, a man has been diagnosed with a terminal illness and is preparing for his death. He has been able to work through the issue in conversation with family, friends and health care professionals. While still at home he has reached a point of quiet composure. Yet as soon as he arrives at the hospital for what he knows will be the last time, that composure quickly melts away. He goes through a brief but intense time of emotional turmoil before his composure returns. Acceptance comes at different levels. At home he accepted his impending death at an 'intellectual' level. In hospital he also has to accept it at an emotional level. The same pattern can be observed in patients awaiting surgery. A level of acceptance may be reached in anticipation of a potentially life-threatening operation, but often in the pre-operative situation there can be a brief but intense struggle. Again, acceptance comes at different levels and at different stages.

Jesus' experience is comparable to that of the man coming to terms with his impending death and of the patient facing major surgery. In the upper room, surrounded by his closest friends, he has reached a level of acceptance of what lies ahead. But then in the Garden he is faced by cold reality. Now there is nothing separating him from his arrest and he needs to accept his imminent suffering and death at a deeper level. Hence in Gethsemane he goes through a brief, intense period of struggle – perhaps for no more than one hour (Mk 14.37) – before his composure is regained. From a psychological point of view, therefore, there is no contradiction between John and the Synoptics. The emotional swings at a time of mortal crisis that the Gospels depict reflect perfectly normal human behaviour. The apparent discrepancies between the two traditions are not due to differing Christologies, the one with a greater emphasis on Jesus' humanity and the other on his divinity, but can be readily accounted for on purely psychological grounds. Both John and the Synoptics provide authentic accounts. They simply highlight different phases of Jesus coming to terms with the approaching crisis.

4.13 *The Beloved Disciple (13.23; 19.26; 20.2; 21.7, 20)*

On five occasions this Gospel refers to the Beloved Disciple as 'the disciple whom Jesus loved'. On four of those occasions this love is indicated by the verb *agapaō* (13.23; 19.26; 21.7, 20) and once by *phileō* (20.2) without any apparent distinction in meaning.[119] As these verbs are used with a high degree of synonymity in the Fourth Gospel, the feature to be observed in these occurrences is the consistent use of the imperfect tense in the Greek text.[120] In the LXX, the Apocrypha, Josephus, Philo, and the New Testament, neither verb is ever used in the imperfect with reference to God. Overwhelmingly, the imperfect of both verbs indicates human friendship and affection. In this Gospel another clear example of such usage depicts Jesus' love for Mary, Martha and Lazarus (11.5, 36). On the basis of this evidence it is reasonable to conclude that Jesus' love for the Beloved Disciple could be described in terms of human bonds of friendship and affection. Within his group of disciples there seems to have been one with whom he enjoyed a particularly warm and close relationship.

While the linguistic and grammatical evidence appears to point in this direction, this conclusion needs to remain tentative until the references to the Beloved Disciple have been examined in the light of their context. It appears significant that the Beloved Disciple is not introduced into the narrative until the opening chapter of the Book of Passion/Glory with its strong emphasis on the love of Jesus (13.1ff.). Moreover, he is mentioned only at crucial junctures within the narrative – the disclosure of Judas' betrayal (13.23), the crucifixion (19.26), the empty tomb (20.2), and during Jesus' final resurrection appearance (21.7, 20). Do these references cast him in the role of an especially loyal and privileged friend or could more be intended? Does his designation as 'the disciple whom Jesus loved' simply become a standard expression, or does its repetition serve to accentuate the depth of Jesus' affection for him? An overview of the five occurrences should at least begin to answer these questions.

A. AT THE SUPPER (13.23)

This is the first time that the Beloved Disciple is mentioned explicitly in the Gospel, although there could be a veiled reference to him as early as 1.35, where two disciples of John the Baptist hear Jesus introduced as the Lamb of God. Be that as it may, the Beloved Disciple is introduced as such directly after Jesus has predicted his betrayal. He therefore enters the narrative as Judas is about to exit (13.30). The Beloved Disciple would thus seem to be deliberately contrasted with Judas.[121] This feature is highlighted by the specific indication of the Beloved

---

119   The two verbs have been used interchangeably in the case of Lazarus (11.3, 5) and will be so used again in 21.15-17.
120   The Greek imperfect is roughly equivalent to the past continuous tense in English, e.g. 'he was loving'.
121   Thus Brown, *John* 2, p. 577: 'Perhaps the reason we have not heard of him [the Beloved

Disciple's position with respect to Jesus. At the supper he is described as leaning 'on Jesus' bosom' (13.23 AV). This expression may simply be intended to indicate the table arrangement at the supper, meaning that the Beloved Disciple was reclining to the right of Jesus during the meal.[122] One suspects, however, that more is being conveyed, especially in view of 1.18, where Jesus Christ is described as being 'in the bosom of the Father' (AV).

If the connection with 1.18 is intentional, then the relationship that Jesus has with the Father is paralleled by the relationship that the Beloved Disciple has with Jesus. However, the parallel may not be intended to be precise as different prepositions are used ('in' in 1.18 and 'on' in 13.23).[123] Although this could simply be a stylistic variation, it is likely that some distinction is intended. The parallel between the two sets of relationships therefore needs to be carefully qualified. Scholars have thus tended to make nuanced comments. Bartlett, for example, notes that the Beloved Disciple is '*almost* as close to the Son as the Son is to the Father'.[124] Carson is equally cautious: 'The verse before us may therefore suggest that the beloved disciple was in a relationship with Jesus *analogous* to the relationship Jesus enjoyed with his heavenly Father'.[125] What the similar expressions certainly have in common is the suggestion of a close family relationship.[126] In 1.18 it is the relationship between Father and Son; in 13.23, the nature of the family relationship is not spelled out. This is to be clarified with the next reference.

B. AT THE CROSS (19.26)

The precise family relationship between Jesus and the Beloved Disciple is disclosed here and in the next verse. Seeing his mother and the Beloved Disciple standing near the cross, Jesus says to his mother, 'Woman, behold, your son!' (19.26). Then he addresses the Beloved Disciple, 'Behold, your mother!' (19.27). The relationship of love between Jesus and the Beloved Disciple is thus defined as one between brothers. This relationship now transcends the level of human friendship that Jesus enjoyed with the family at Bethany. His love for the Beloved Disciple is to be understood at a deeper level than that of human friendship, even

---

Disciple] before . . . is that the evangelist wished to introduce him as an antithesis to Judas, showing the good and bad extremes in the spectrum of discipleship.'

122 Thus William Hendriksen, *New Testament Commentary: Exposition of the Gospel according to John* (2 vols; Grand Rapids, MI: Baker, 1953), vol. 2, p. 245; cf. Zerwick and Grosvenor, *Grammatical Analysis*, p. 329, who further explain that 'reclining on Jesus' right at table, the disciple could lean against him and speak wt [without] being overheard'.

123 The Greek has *eis* with the accusative in 1.18 and *en* with the dative in 13.23.

124 David L. Bartlett, 'Expository Articles: John 13:21-30', *Int* 43 (1989), p. 394 (italics mine).

125 Carson, *John*, p. 473 (italics mine). Less cautious is the comment by Brown, *John* 2, p. 577: 'The Disciple is as intimate with Jesus as Jesus is with the Father.'

126 Mary Coloe, 'Raising the Johannine Temple (John 19:19-37)', *ABR* 48 (2000), p. 54. Some of the family relationships indicated by these expressions in the LXX are between husband and wife (Gen. 16.5; Deut. 13.7; 28.56; 2 Sam. 12.8) and between mother and child (Num. 11.12; 1 Kgs 3.20; 17.19; Ruth 4.16; Isa. 49.22).

though such relationships have also been transposed to a higher key as Jesus lays down his life for his friends. At the cross a new relationship is established between the Beloved Disciple and the mother of Jesus, and hence also between the Beloved Disciple and Jesus. The family relationship hinted at in 13.23 now comes to concrete expression.

However, Jesus' brotherly love for the Beloved Disciple cannot be isolated from his Passion any more than can his friendship with Lazarus. While both these relationships display clear overtones of human affection, their essence is grounded in the death of Jesus. Jesus' love for each is the greatest love of all, in that they are friends for whom he lays down his life. This is the defining feature of his love.

C. AT THE EMPTY TOMB (20.2)

The implicit contrast that has emerged between the Beloved Disciple and Peter in chs 18–19 is further developed in the next reference to the Beloved Disciple. Running from the empty tomb to Peter and the Beloved Disciple, Mary Magdalene announces her discovery to the two disciples. What follows heightens the contrast between the two that has been latent since ch. 13, where Peter motions to the Beloved Disciple to ask Jesus who the betrayer is, but is then not privileged to know the answer to his question (13.24-30). Culpepper traces the contrast into the Passion narrative and beyond:

> Peter denies Jesus three times; the Beloved Disciple follows Jesus to the cross. The Beloved Disciple gets to the empty tomb first. Peter enters first, but only the Beloved Disciple perceives and believes. At the lake the Beloved Disciple is again the first to perceive who the stranger is. Peter will no longer boast that he loves Jesus more than the other disciples, among whom is the Beloved Disciple. When Peter begins to question the future role of the Beloved Disciple he is told that it is no concern of his. He is to follow Jesus just as the Beloved Disciple was already doing.[127]

The significant feature in this passage is the fact that the Beloved Disciple believed when he entered the empty tomb (20.8). By believing he also demonstrated that he was indeed a child of God (1.12). This is not yet said of Peter. The Beloved Disciple is therefore the first disciple of whom such a faith response is recorded, and in him the purpose of the Gospel (20.30-31) finds a preliminary fulfilment. This resurrection faith on the part of the Beloved Disciple is anticipated by Martha's confession that was also made in a resurrection context (11.27).

---

127 Culpepper, *Anatomy*, p. 122.

D. AT THE LAKE (21.7, 20)

In the Epilogue to the Gospel the contrast between the Beloved Disciple and Peter is drawn most sharply. He is the first to recognize Jesus on the shore of the lake and in the presence of Peter he proclaims, 'It is the Lord' (21.7). As the first to recognize Jesus and the first to have believed, the Beloved Disciple is qualified to bear witness (21.24). Although Peter would die a martyr's death, the Beloved Disciple would also fulfil Jesus' will. This is accomplished in the witness that he bears. In this, the Gospel's final reference to the Beloved Disciple, the account comes full circle. The parallel between the relationship of the Father to Jesus and that of Jesus to the Beloved Disciple manifests itself again at this point. As Jesus explained the Father (1.18), so the Beloved Disciple bears witness to Jesus (21.24; cf. 19.35), a task he shares with the other disciples in dependence upon the Paraclete (15.26, 27). Having been present at the supper, the cross, the empty tomb, and at the final appearance of the risen Jesus, the Beloved Disciple is above all the one qualified to bear true witness.

The Beloved Disciple is thus shown to be the ideal disciple, the one who understands who Jesus is, the one for all who follow to emulate. According to Collins, 'the Beloved is the epitome of discipleship; he is the disciple par excellence'.[128] He is a real historical person, but as such he has representative, paradigmatic and symbolic significance in John. With him there are no misunderstandings.[129]

E. EVALUATION

On the basis of Jesus' death not only the Beloved Disciple but all the disciples are called Jesus' brothers. They are specifically designated as such by the risen Jesus in his words to Mary Magdalene: 'Go instead to my brothers and tell them, "I am returning to my Father and your Father, to my God and your God"' (20.17). Although the disciples are now Jesus' brothers, his relationship to God and theirs are not identical. He is the Son of God (1.34 etc.), they are children of God (1.12). Nevertheless, in them the promise 'to become children of God' (1.12, 13) is fulfilled. God is their Father and they are Jesus' brothers.[130] By implication the love that Jesus has for the Beloved Disciple is now extended to them as well. They are now not only his friends (15.13-15), but also his brothers (20.17; 21.23). Both privileges were attained for them through Jesus' death.

This new relationship of Jesus to the disciples is, however, finely nuanced. They are his brothers (20.17), and are hence brothers to one another (21.23), but

---

128 Raymond F. Collins, 'From John to the Beloved Disciple: An Essay on Johannine Characters', *Int* 49 (1995), p. 367.

129 Thus Culpepper, *Anatomy*, p. 121; cf. Brown, *John* 2, p. 577: 'John does not present the Disciple as a pure symbol without historical reality.'

130 Since 'brothers' is used again in 21.23, its usage cannot be accidental. Discipleship in the Fourth Gospel is not gender-specific, nor confined to the Twelve, but includes all those regarded by Jesus as 'his own'. This clearly includes several of the women in John.

he is never called their brother, any more than he is called their friend in ch. 15. Likewise, in the Old Testament, Abraham and Moses are called friends of God, but he is never called their friend. Nowhere is the relationship a reciprocal relationship between equals.[131] Again a discreet distinction is maintained between Jesus as the Son of God and the disciples as children of God. Although they are now Jesus' brothers, the disciples still refer to him constantly as 'Lord' throughout chs 20 and 21. They are his brothers because of his death, yet as the risen one he remains their covenant Lord.

Conclusion

John's prologue introduces Jesus as the Word become flesh. Even a superficial reading of this opening passage suggests his dual identity as both human and divine. He is the divine Word who spoke creation into being. Through his incarnation Jesus assumes 'flesh', a powerfully descriptive term that definitively associates him with humanity in all its transience, vulnerability, frailty and mortality. The prologue therefore portrays Jesus as both perfectly human and completely divine. But this passage does more than provide a *locus classicus* for a high Christology. While it certainly performs this function, this does not exhaust its meaning. There is more to be mined from it. Comparisons with Genesis and Exodus allow the reader to explore the significance of Jesus at an even deeper level. The prologue lays the groundwork for the Fourth Gospel's presentation of Jesus as both the covenant Lord and the covenant sacrifice. As the divine Word of creation he is the covenant Lord, but his becoming 'flesh' sets the stage for his role as the covenant sacrifice. When Jesus becomes the covenant sacrifice, he most brilliantly displays the glory of the covenant Lord, the divine 'I am.' Therein lies the unique beauty of John's Gospel.

To understand the emotions of Jesus in the Fourth Gospel, it is not sufficient to place them in 'human' or 'divine' categories. Rather, as we have seen repeatedly, the emotions of Jesus often gain their significance as well as their poignancy in the interplay of Jesus' roles as the covenant Lord and the covenant sacrifice. Thus, in the very first emotion that is attributed to him, Jesus at the same time displays the all-consuming zeal of the righteous sufferer *and* the covenant Lord's holy zeal against false worship. Similarly, Jesus' love for the family at Bethany at first sight appears no more than an indication of close friendship, but as the story unfolds, this love gains in depth and intensity, and turns out to be redemptive in

---

131 Carson, *John*, p. 522, in his comments on 15.14-15 argues that when Jesus calls the disciples his friends, and when Abraham and Moses are called friends of God, 'mutual, reciprocal friendship of the modern variety is not in view'. Commenting on 15.16 Bultmann, *John*, p. 544, views the relationship somewhat differently: 'while the friendship between Jesus and his own is certainly reciprocal, there is no equality in it. If they are Jesus' friends, this is not because they had sought his friendship, nor does Jesus call himself their friend, but only them his friends.'

character. As in the Synoptics, other emotions that would appear human enough in themselves become virtually inexplicable apart from the divine foreknowledge that undergirds them. Thus Jesus' rejoicing at the news of Lazarus' death would be wholly inappropriate were it not for the fact that he could foresee what Lazarus' revivification would do for the disciples' faith. Likewise, his anger at Lazarus' tomb and his troubled state of mind at the prospect of his own death become comprehensible only from the perspective of foreknowledge. Only his tears of sympathy at the grief of Mary and her fellow-mourners could be regarded as expressing a human emotion pure and simple.

The use of *agapaō* in the Farewell Discourse, and with respect to the Beloved Disciple, is finely nuanced. In the imperfect (past continuous) tense, it is reserved for Jesus' love for the Beloved Disciple. The latter is portrayed as the ideal and representative disciple whom, because of his death, Jesus loves as a brother. In the aorist (simple past) tense, Jesus' love as covenant Lord is indicated – a sacrificial love by which he proves that he is the 'I am.' These variations in tense reflect functional differences. Jesus loves his disciples as his covenant people (aorist) and he loves the Beloved Disciple as his brother (imperfect). His love for the Beloved Disciple implies a family love possible only because of his death, after which it extends by implication to all the disciples. Henceforth he can refer to them all as brothers. The aorist and imperfect tenses of the verb *agapaō* thus signify two complementary roles exercised by Jesus, which are respectively the divine role of the covenant Lord and the human role of being brother to the Beloved Disciple (and thus to the other disciples, and ultimately to every believer).

So whether Jesus' love for his disciples is indicated by the aorist (simple past) or by the imperfect (past continuous) tense, the end-result is the same. Ultimately both loves are expressed supremely in his death. He died for his friends and thereby made them his brothers. The same relationship is thus viewed from two complementary perspectives. In the use of the aorist tense (13.1, 34; 15.9, 10, 12) he relates to them as the covenant Lord to his people. In the use of the imperfect tense he relates to the Beloved Disciple as his brother. The disciples also function in both roles. They are the new covenant people of God and also the children of God, and hence the brothers of Jesus. He therefore relates to them as both their covenant Lord and their brother. The expressions of his love in this Gospel are sufficiently finely tuned to reflect both realities. As such he functions in both a divine and a human role. He is both brother to the disciples and their covenant Lord.

The remaining tenses of *agapaō* once again cast Jesus in a divine role. The love that he will have (future tense) for the obedient disciple (14.21) is like that of the Father and coincides with the coming of the Paraclete (14.16, 17, 26). The love that he has (present tense) for the Father (14.31) comes to expression in his obedience even unto death, but at the same time flows from the mutual love between himself and the Father in whose bosom he resides (1.18).

While Jesus' love for the Father expresses itself in obedience, this obedience in turn results in joy (15.11; 17.13). This joy is an emotion shared with human characters in the Gospel, but because it springs from an obedience that entails the cross, it is a fullness of joy that is beyond comprehension. Jesus' joy is in the deepest sense paradoxical. As covenant Lord he rejoices at the prospect of becoming the covenant sacrifice.

Although John's presentation of Jesus' emotions is markedly different from that of the Synoptics, there is one feature that all four Gospels have in common. Their opening remarks about Jesus provide the matrix in which the emotions operate. In the case of the Fourth Gospel, the emotions of Jesus do little to prove how human he was. Rather, they highlight the complexity of his person as the Word become flesh. In taking time to reflect on what *motivates* Jesus' emotions, we see that they can only seldom be explained in purely human terms. As one who is aware of both his cosmic origins and divine destiny, Jesus experiences emotions that are extraordinary, paradoxical and at times also mysterious and incomprehensible. Often they lie beyond the realm of normal human experience.

Conclusion

The *Christianity Today* article which was used to introduce the present study closes with a conclusion that is as provocative as its opening paragraphs:

> I am spellbound by the intensity of Jesus' emotions: not a twinge of pity, but heartbroken compassion; not a passing irritation but terrifying anger; not a silent tear but groans of anguish; not a weak smile but ecstatic celebration. Jesus' emotions are like a mountain river, cascading with clear water. My emotions are more like a muddy foam or feeble trickle. Jesus invites us to come to him and drink. Whoever is thirsty and believes in him will have the river of his life flowing out from the innermost being (John 7:37-38). We are not merely to be spellbound by what we see in the emotional Jesus; we are to be unbound by his Spirit so that his life becomes our life, his emotions our emotions, to be 'transformed into his likeness with ever increasing glory.'[1]

Although the contrasts are overdone, to any thinking Christian these words constitute a considerable challenge. But the question needs to be asked whether Jesus' emotions should become our emotions. At the close of our investigation we are in a position to place this challenge under careful scrutiny. Does the *imitatio Christi* principle apply not only to ethics, life-style and personal relationships but also to the emotions that reflect the very core of our beings? Does spiritual transformation in the biblical sense mean increasingly a reproduction of the emotions of Jesus in the lives of his followers? These are penetrating questions that need to be answered at several levels.

The doctrine of Christ's incarnation needs to be appreciated for all its complexity and completeness. In Jn 1.14 this doctrine is radically expressed in the proposition that 'the Word became flesh'. As we have seen, this implies that, though divine, Jesus Christ fully embraced our humanity in all its frailty,

---

1 G. Walter Hansen, 'The Emotions of Jesus and Why We Need to Experience Them', *CT* 41, 2/2 (1997), p. 46.

transience, vulnerability and mortality. This means that his genuine humanity cannot be compromised. As a human being, Jesus therefore had a particular temperament. What that temperament was precisely, we do not have sufficient information to ascertain. But we can be sure that he had a particular temperament out of which he both acted and reacted. That temperament was as much a part of his humanity as his nationality, gender or physique. Because the Gospels do not provide the necessary information, no one can know whether or not they share Jesus' temperament. For the writers of the New Testament that is not the issue. Transformation into the likeness of Jesus is a transformation into his character, not into his temperament or personality.

A further perspective is gained from an appreciation of Jesus' messianic identity. He was confirmed as the Messiah at his baptism in the Jordan. Almost without exception his recorded emotions were expressed during a distinct period of his life, namely between his baptism and his death. Hence, it is precisely as he carries out his messianic ministry that Jesus is portrayed as expressing emotions. The emotions of Jesus are the emotions of the Messiah. As such they are found in two major contexts – in the performing of miracles and in anticipation of the Passion. At times they are driven by both concerns as, for example, prior to the raising of Lazarus. While John 11 is a window that gives a rare glimpse into his soul, it hardly provides a mandate for the way Christians are to feel at funerals. Those who mourn over the death of a dear friend may well be deeply moved and troubled as well as weep out of love and sympathy as Jesus did. But that is hardly the point of the passage where these emotions are recorded. These were the emotions of the Messiah. They were so intense partly because the terrors of the cross still lay before him. When Jesus stood at the tomb of Lazarus there had never yet been an Easter Sunday. The resurrection of Jesus was the greatest and most glorious event in all redemptive history. For believers in Christ it has given a new perspective on life, including the end of life.

Finally, although this emphasis is strongest in the Fourth Gospel, all four Gospels portray Jesus as divine. As God he can foresee the future. He knows in advance what is going to happen, and to an extent that drives his emotions. Again John 11 is a case in point. Early in the chapter he can genuinely be glad even though he bears the sad tidings that Lazarus has just died. At a purely human level this would be an unusual emotional reaction. But Jesus' divine foreknowledge casts this emotion in a completely different light. He knows that he will raise Lazarus from the grave and he can foresee what this will do for the disciples' faith. This is what motivates his gladness. On other occasions Jesus' knowledge of the future also provides the best interpretation of his emotions. His anger at a leper he has just cured and at two men whose sight he has restored would make no sense were it not for his divine foresight into the havoc these men would wreak on his ministry. The fact that he was deeply moved with indignation at Lazarus' tomb can be explained on similar grounds. Even his agony and mortal sorrow in Gethsemane can be attributed to his frighteningly accurate knowledge of what lay immediately before him. The intensity of Jesus' emotions that the *Christianity Today* article would have us emulate is often due to a detailed knowledge of the future that is seldom given to mere mortals.

Twenty-first-century Christians should therefore not be in too great a hurry to replicate the emotions of Jesus as precisely as possible. They may not share his human temperament and can definitely not lay claim to a messianic or divine identity. So does the experience of Jesus' emotions play any part in personal spiritual transformation? Should there be an expectation that any of the emotions of Jesus might be reproduced in the lives of Christians today? Is there not a place, for example, in Christian communities and local fellowships for an exuberant outpouring of love, compassion and joy?

These questions belong to the larger hermeneutical issue of Gospel genre. The Gospels, like the historical books of the Old Testament before them and the Acts of the Apostles after them, are primarily narrative, and it is not the nature of narrative to be normative. The stories of Scripture are generally descriptive rather than prescriptive. Therefore Bible readers are no more obliged to imitate the emotions of Jesus than they are the emotions of David, Peter or Paul.

However, this is not the whole story. Christians *are* to replicate the emotions of Jesus (and the emotions of David, Peter and Paul for that matter) when these emotions are enjoined in the more prescriptive passages of Scripture, such as in the Epistles and in the recorded teaching of Jesus. This is where G. Walter Hansen's article comes to its own. Christians are obliged to reproduce an emotion of Jesus when it is commanded in the normative portions of Scripture. They are therefore challenged to 'rejoice with those who rejoice' and to 'mourn with those who mourn' (Rom. 12.15), to 'love one another deeply from the heart' (1 Pet. 1.22), and to 'clothe themselves with compassion' (Col. 3.12). Above all, there is the first and greatest commandment to 'love the Lord your God with all your heart and with all your soul and with all your mind' (Mt. 22.37), and also the second that is like it, to 'love your neighbour as yourself' (Mt. 22.39). The New Testament is replete with emotional challenges without Christians trying to meticulously reproduce the emotions expressed by Jesus in the Gospels. Christians are not designed to be emotional clones of Jesus. Rather, it is through the transforming work of the Holy Spirit that believers are increasingly enabled to respond to situations in emotionally appropriate ways in conformity with their God-given temperament and personality.

If this is the case, we are left with one final question. Why did the Gospel writers take the trouble to portray the emotional life of Jesus with such richness and variety? Why is their picture of Jesus such a finely woven tapestry of feelings and emotions, if in this respect he is not intended to be a pattern and example? In their vivid portrayal of such scenes as Gethsemane and the raising of Lazarus they intend to highlight to the reader that the salvation of the people of God was won at great cost. Jesus went through deep emotional pain and spiritual trauma for the redemption of his people. This accounts for the basic emotional tenor of his life and ministry. 'Having loved his own who were in the world, he loved them to the end' (Jn 13.1 RSV).

Bibliography

Abbott-Smith, G., *A Manual Greek Lexicon of the New Testament* (Edinburgh: T&T Clark, 1937; repr. 1973).

Aharoni, Yohanan and Michael Avi-Yonah, *The Macmillan Bible Atlas* (New York: Macmillan, rev. edn, 1977).

Aland, Barbara, Kurt Aland, Johannes Karavidopoulos, Carlo M. Martini, Bruce M. Metzger, and Allen Wikgren (eds), *The Greek New Testament* (Stuttgart: Deutsche Bibelgesellschaft, 13th rev. edn, 1994).

Aland, Kurt (ed.), *Synopsis of the Four Gospels: Greek-English Edition of the Synopsis Quattuor Evangeliorum* (Stuttgart: German Bible Society, 7th edn, 1984).

—— *Synopsis Quattuor Evangeliorum: Locis parallelis evangeliorum apocryphorum et patrum adhibitis* (Stuttgart: Deutsche Bibelgesellschaft, 13th rev. edn, 1988).

——, and Barbara Aland, *The Text of the New Testament: An Introduction to the Critical Editions and to the Theory and Practice of Modern Textual Criticism* (trans. E. F. Rhodes; Grand Rapids, MI: Eerdmans, 1987).

Albright, W. F., and C. S. Mann, *Matthew*, AB 26 (New York: Doubleday, 1971).

Arndt, William F., and F. Wilbur Gingrich, *A Greek-English Lexicon of the New Testament and Other Early Christian Literature* (a translation and adaptation of the 4th rev. and augmented edition of Walter Bauer's *Griechisch-Deutsches Wörterbuch zu den Schriften des Neuen Testaments und der übrigen urchristlichen Literatur*; Chicago: The University of Chicago Press, 1957; 2nd edn rev. and augmented by F. Wilbur Gingrich and Frederick W. Danker from Walter Bauer's 5th edn; Chicago: The University of Chicago Press, 1979).

Atkinson, David, 'A Cry of Faith', *ExpTim* 96 (1985), pp. 146–47.

Atkinson, Rita L., Richard C. Atkinson, and Ernest R. Hilgard, *Introduction to Psychology* (San Diego, CA: Harcourt Brace Jovanovich, 1981).

Bailey, James L. 'Experiencing the Kingdom as a Little Child: A Rereading of Mark 10:13-16', *WW* 15 (1995), pp. 58–67.

—— 'Church as Embodiment of Jesus' Mission (Matthew 9:36-10:39)', *CurTM* 30 (2003), pp. 189–96.

Balz, Horst, and Gerhard Schneider (eds), *Exegetical Dictionary of the New Testament* (3 vols; Grand Rapids, MI: Eerdmans, 1990–1992). Translation of *Exegetisches Wörterbuch zum Neuen Testament* (Stuttgart: Kohlhammer, 1978–1980).

Barker, Kenneth (ed.), *The NIV Study Bible* (Grand Rapids, MI: Zondervan, 1985).

Barrett, C. K., *The Gospel According to St John: An Introduction with Commentary and Notes on the Greek Text* (London: SPCK, 1955).

Barnett, Paul, *The Servant King: Reading Mark Today* (Sydney: Anglican Information Office, 1991).

Bartlett, David L., 'Expository Articles: John 13:21-30', *Int* 43 (1989), pp. 393–97.

Bauer, David R., 'The Major Characters of Matthew's Story: Their Function and Significance', *Int* 46 (1992), pp. 356–67.

Beasley-Murray, George R., *John* (WBC 36; Waco: Word, 2nd edn, 1999).

Benner, David G. (ed.), *Baker Encyclopedia of Psychology* (Grand Rapids, MI: Baker, 1985).

Beutler, Johannes, 'Psalm 42/43 im Johannesevangelium', *NTS* 25 (1978), pp. 33–57.

Biblia Rabbinica: A Reprint of the 1525 Venice Edition Edited by Jacob Ben Hayim Ibn Adoniya (Jerusalem: Makor, 1972).

Blass, F., and A. Debrunner, *A Greek Grammar of the New Testament and Other Early Christian Literature* (trans. Robert W. Funk; Chicago: The University of Chicago Press, 1961).

Blomberg, Craig, *The Historical Reliability of the Gospels* (Downers Grove, IL: Inter-Varsity Press, 1987).

Bock, Darrell L., *Luke* (Baker Exegetical Commentary on the New Testament, vol. 3; Grand Rapids, MI: Baker, 1994–96).

Borgen, Peder, 'Observations on the Targumic Character of the Prologue of John', *NTS* 16 (1970), pp. 288–95.

Bredin, Mark R., 'John's Account of Jesus' Demonstration in the Temple: Violent or Nonviolent?' *BTB* 33 (2003), pp. 44–50.

Broadhead, Edwin K., 'Mark 1,44: The Witness of the Leper', *ZNW* 83 (1992), pp. 257–65.

Brodie, Thomas L., 'Towards Unravelling Luke's Use of the Old Testament: Luke 7.11-17 as an *Imitatio* of 1 Kings 17.17-24', *NTS* 32 (1986), pp. 247–67.

Brown, Colin (ed.), *The New International Dictionary of New Testament Theology* (3 vols; Exeter: Paternoster, 1975–1978). Translation, with additions and revisions, of *Theologisches Begriffslexicon zum Neuen Testament*, ed. Lothar Coenen, Erich Beyreuther, and Hans Bietenhard (Wuppertal: Rolf Brockhaus, 1971).

Brown, Raymond E., *The Death of the Messiah – From Gethsemane to the Grave: A Commentary on the Passion Narratives in the Four Gospels* (2 vols; New York: Doubleday, 1994).

Browne, S. G. 'Leprosy: The Christian Attitude', *ExpTim* 73 (1961–62), pp. 242–45.

Bultmann, Rudolf. *The Gospel of John: A Commentary* (ed. R. W. N. Hoare and J. K. Riches; trans. G. R. Beasley-Murray; Oxford: Blackwell, 1971). Translation of *Das Evangelium des Johannes* (Göttingen: Vandenhoeck & Ruprecht, 1964).

Burchard, Christoph, 'Miszellen: Zu Mattäus 8, 5-13', *ZNW* 84 (1993), pp. 278–88.

Burridge, Richard A., *Four Gospels, One Jesus? A Symbolic Reading* (Grand Rapids, MI: Eerdmans, 1994).

Byrne, Brendan, *Lazarus: A Contemporary Reading of John 1:1-46* (Homebush, NSW: St Paul Publications, 1991).

Calvin, John, *Commentary on the Gospel According to John* (2 vols; trans. William Pringle; Grand Rapids, MI: Eerdmans, 1956).

Carson, D. A., *Jesus and His Friends: His Farewell Message and Prayer in John 14–17* (Grand Rapids, MI: Baker, 1980).

—— 'Matthew', *The Expositor's Bible Commentary*, vol. 8 (Matthew, Mark, Luke) (Grand Rapids, MI: Zondervan, 1984).

—— 'John and the Johannine Epistles', in *It is Written: Scripture Citing Scripture: Essays in Honour of Barnabas Lindars, SSF* (ed. D. A. Carson and H. G. M. Williamson; Cambridge: Cambridge University Press, 1988), pp. 245–64.

—— *The Gospel According to John* (Leicester: Inter-Varsity Press, Leicester, 1991).

——, and Douglas J. Moo, *An Introduction to the New Testament* (Leicester: Apollos, 2nd edn, 2005).

Carter, Warren, 'Kernels and Narrative Blocks: The Structure of Matthew's Gospel', *CBQ* 54 (1992), pp. 462–81.

—— 'The Crowds in Matthew's Gospel', *CBQ* 55 (1993), pp. 54–67.

—— 'Matthew and the Gentiles: Individual Conversion and/or Systemic Transformation?', *JSNT* 26 (2004), pp. 259–82.

Cave, C. H., 'The Leper: Mark 1:40-45', *NTS* 25 (1979), pp. 245–50.

Clivaz, Claire, 'The Angel and the Sweat Like "Drops of Blood" (Lk 22:43-44): P[69] and *f*[13]', *HTR* 98 (2005), pp. 419–44.

Collins, Raymond F., 'From John to the Beloved Disciple: An Essay on Johannine Characters', *Int* 49 (1995), pp. 359–69.

Coloe, Mary, 'Raising the Johannine Temple (John 19.19-37)', *ABR* 48 (2000), pp. 47–58.

—— 'Temple Imagery in John', *Int* 63 (2009), pp. 368–81.

Conzelmann, Hans, *The Theology of St Luke* (trans. G. Buswell; London: Faber and Faber, 1961).

Cousland, J. R. C., 'The Feeding of the Four Thousand *Gentiles* in Matthew? Matthew 15:29-39 as a Test Case', *NovT* 41 (1999), pp. 1–23.

Cullmann, Oscar, *The Christology of the New Testament* (trans. S. C. Guthrie and C. A. M. Hall; Philadelphia: Westminster, rev. edn, 1963).

Culpepper, R. Alan, 'The Pivot of John's Prologue', *NTS* 27 (1980), pp. 1–31.

—— *Anatomy of the Fourth Gospel: A Study in Literary Design* (Philadelphia: Fortress, 1983).

—— 'The Plot of John's Story of Jesus', *Int* 49 (1995), pp. 347–58.

Daniel, F. Harry, 'Where is God? Matthew's Passion Narrative and the Triune God', *JP* 24 (2001), pp. 33–36.

Danker, Frederick William (ed.), *A Greek-English Lexicon of the New Testament and Other Early Christian Literature* (Chicago: The University of Chicago Press, 3rd edn, 2000). Based on Walter Bauer's *Griechisch-Deutsches Wörterbuch zu den Schriften des Neuen Testaments und der frühchristlichen Literatur*, ed. Kurt Aland and Barbara Aland, with Viktor Reichmann (6th edn) and on previous English editions by William F. Arndt, F. Wilbur Gingrich, and F. W. Danker.

Dennison, James T., Jr., 'The Prologue of John's Gospel', *Kerux* 8 (1993), pp. 3–9.

Derrett, Duncan M., 'Christ's Second Baptism (Lk 12:50; Mk 10:38-40)', *ExpTim* 100 (1989), pp. 294–95.

Dodd, C. H., *The Parables of the Kingdom* (London: James Nisbet, 1935).

Doty, Margie, '"Amazed" in Mark', *Notes on Translation* 4 (1990), pp. 49–58.

Edwards, James R., *The Pillar New Testament Commentary: The Gospel according to Mark* (Grand Rapids, MI: Eerdmans, 2002).

Ehrman, Bart D., 'Did Jesus Get Angry or Agonize? A Text Critic Pursues the Original Jesus Story', *BibRev* 5 (2005), pp. 17–26, 49–50.

——, and Mark A. Plunkett, 'The Angel and the Agony: The Textual Problem of Luke 22:43-44', *CBQ* 45 (1983), pp. 401–16.

Eichman, Phillip, 'The History, Biology & Medical Aspects of Leprosy', *The American Biology Teacher* 61 (1999), pp. 490–95.

Elliott, Bianca, *The Emotions of Jesus* (Martinsville, IN: Airleaf, 2006).

Elliott, Matthew, *Faithful Feelings: Emotion in the New Testament* (Leicester: Inter-Varsity Press, 2005).

Eubanks, Larry L., 'Mark 10:13-16', *Review and Expositor* 91 (1994), pp. 401–05.

Evans, Craig A., 'Luke's Use of the Elijah/Elisha Narratives and the Ethic of Election', *JBL* (1987), pp. 75–83.

—— *Mark 8:27-16:20* (WBC 34B; Nashville: Thomas Nelson, 2001).

——, and Stanley E. Porter, *Dictionary of New Testament Background* (Downers Grove, IL: Inter-Varsity Press, 2000).

Feuillet, A., 'Le récit lucanien de l'agonie de Gethsémani (Lc XXII. 39–46)', *NTS* 22 (1976), pp. 397–417.

Fitzmyer, Joseph A., *The Gospel According to Luke*, AB 28 (New York: Doubleday, 1981–85).

Forbes, Greg, 'Darkness over All the Land: Theological Imagery in the Crucifixion Scene', *RTR* 66 (2007), pp. 81–96.

France, Richard T., *The Gospel of Mark: A Commentary on the Greek Text* (Grand Rapids, MI: Eerdmans, 2002).

—— *The Gospel of Matthew* (Grand Rapids, MI: Eerdmans, 2007).

Freedberg, Irwin M., et al. (eds) *Fitzpatrick's Dermatology in General Medicine* (New York: McGraw-Hill, 6th edn, 2003).

Frijda, Nico H., 'The Psychologists' Point of View', in *Handbook of Emotions* ed. Michael Lewis, Jeannette M. Haviland-Jones, and Lisa Feldman-Barrett (London: The Guildford Press, 3rd edn, 2008), pp. 86–87.

Fryer, N. S. L., 'Matthew 14:14-21. The Feeding of the Five Thousand: A Grammatico-historical Exegesis', *IDS* 84 (1987), pp. 27–42.

Fuliga, Jose B., 'The Man Who Refused to be King', *AJT* 11 (1997), pp. 140–53.

Gagnon, Robert A. J., 'Luke's Motives for Redaction in the Account of the Double Delegation in Luke 7:1-10', *NovT* 36 (1994), pp. 122–45.

—— 'The Shape of Matthew's Q Text of the Centurion at Capernaum: Did It Mention Delegations?', *NTS* 40 (1994), pp. 133–42.

Garland, David E., *Mark: The NIV Application Commentary* (Grand Rapids, MI: Zondervan, 1996).

Geldenhuys, Norval, *Commentary on the Gospel of Luke: The English Text with Introduction, Exposition, and Notes* (Grand Rapids, MI: Eerdmans, 1951).

Gench, Frances T., 'John 15:12-17', *Int* 58 (2004), pp. 181–84.

Gibson, Jeffrey B., 'Mark 8:12a: 'Why Does Jesus "Sigh Deeply"?' *The Bible Translator* 38 (1987), pp. 122–25.

—— 'Jesus' Refusal to Produce a "Sign" (Mk 8:11-13)', *JSNT* 38 (1990), pp. 37–66.

—— 'Another Look at Why Jesus "Sighs Deeply" in Mark 8:12a', *JTS* 47 (1996), pp. 131–40.

Goleman, Daniel, *Emotional Intelligence: Why it Can Matter More Than IQ* (London: Bloomsbury, 1996).

The Gospel According to Thomas: Coptic Text Established and Translated (trans. A. Guillaumont et al.; San Francisco: Harper & Row, 1959).

Grässer, Erich, 'Jesus in Nazareth (Mark VI. 1-6a): Notes on the Redaction and Theology of St Mark', *NTS* 16 (1969), pp. 1–23.

Green, Joel B., *The Gospel of Luke* (NICNT; Grand Rapids, MI: Eerdmans, 1997).

Grosjean, François, *Life with Two Languages* (Cambridge, MA: Harvard University Press, 1982).

Guelich, Robert A., *Mark 1-8:26* (WBC 34A; Dallas: Word, 1989).

Gundry, Robert H., *Mark: A Commentary on His Apology for the Cross* (Grand Rapids, MI: Eerdmans, 1993).

Hagner, Donald A., *Matthew 1-13* (WBC 33A; Waco: Word, 1993).

—— *Matthew 14-28* (WBC 33B; Dallas: Word, 1995).

Hansen, G. Walter, 'The Emotions of Jesus and Why We Need to Experience Them', *CT* 41/2 (1997), pp. 43–46.

Harman, Allan M., 'Missions in the Thought of Jesus', *EvQ* 41 (1969), pp. 131–42.

Harrison, Everett F., *Introduction to the New Testament* (Grand Rapids, MI: Eerdmans, 1971).

Haslam, J. A. G., 'The Centurion at Capernaum: Luke 7:1-10', *ExpTim* 96 (1985), pp. 109–10.

Hays, Richard B., 'Can the Gospels Teach Us How to Read the Old Testament?' *ProEccl* 11 (2002), pp. 402–18.

Helm, Paul, 'B. B. Warfield on Divine Passion', *WTJ* 69 (2007), pp. 95–104.

Hendriksen, William, *New Testament Commentary: Exposition of the Gospel According to John* (2 vols; Grand Rapids, MI: Baker, 1953).

Hengel, Martin, 'The Old Testament in the Fourth Gospel', *HBT* 12 (1990), pp. 19–41.

Holmes, Michael W. (ed.), *The Apostolic Fathers: Greek Texts and English Translations of Their Writings* (trans. J. B. Lightfoot and J. R. Harmer; Grand Rapids, MI: Baker, 2nd edn, 1992).

Hooke, S. H., 'Jesus and the Centurion: Matthew viii. 5-10', *ExpTim* 69 (1957), pp. 79–80.

Hooker, Morna, 'John the Baptist and the Johannine Prologue', *NTS* 16 (1970), pp. 354–58.

Hunter, A. M., *According to John* (London: SCM, 1972).

Jennings, Theodore W., Jr., and Tat-Siong Benny Liew, 'Mistaken Identities but Model Faith: Rereading the Centurion, the Chap, and the Christ in Matthew 8:5-13', *JBL* 123 (2004), pp. 467–94.

Johnson, Luke T., *The Gospel of Luke* (Sacra Pagina Series, vol. 3; Collegevillle, MN: The Liturgical press, 1991).

Josephus, Flavius, *The Jewish War* (trans. G. A. Williamson; Harmondsworth, Middlesex, UK: Penguin, 1959), p. 221.

Kazmierski, Carl R., 'Evangelist and Leper: A Socio-Cultural Study of Mark 1.40-45', *NTS* 38 (1992), pp. 37–50.

Keener, Craig S., *Matthew* (Downers Grove: Inter-Varsity Press, 1997).

Kenneally, William J., '"Eli, Eli, Lamma Sabachthani?" (Mt. 27:46)', *CBQ* 8 (1946), pp. 124–34.

Kingsbury, Jack D., *Conflict in Mark: Jesus, Authorities, Disciples* (Minneapolis: Fortress, 1989).

—— 'The Plot of Matthew's Story', *Int* 46 (1992), pp. 347–56.

—— 'The Significance of the Cross within Mark's Story', *Intn* 47 (1993), pp. 370–79.

——'The Plot of Luke's Story of Jesus', *Int* 48 (1994), pp. 369–78.

Kinman, Brent, 'Parousia, Jesus' "A-Triumphal" Entry, and the Fate of Jerusalem (Luke 19:28-44)', *JBL* 118 (1999), pp. 279–94.

Kittel, Gerhard, and Gerhard Friedrich (eds), *Theological Dictionary of the New Testament* (trans. Geoffrey W. Bromiley, 9 vols; Grand Rapids, MI: Eerdmans, 1964–74).

—— *Theological Dictionary of the New Testament* (trans, and abridged in one vol. by Geoffery W. Bromiley; Grand Rapids, MI: Eerdmans, 1985).

Kovacs, Judith L., '"Now Shall the Ruler of This World be Driven Out": Jesus' Death as Cosmic Battle in John 12:20-36', *JBL* 114 (1995), pp. 227–47.

Kretch, David, Richard S. Crutchfield, and Norman Livson, *Elements of Psychology* (New York: Knopf, 2nd edn, 1969.

Lacomara, Aelred, 'Deuteronomy and the Farewell Discourse (Jn 13:31-16.33)', *CBQ* 36 (1974), pp. 65–84.

Lalleman, Pieter J., 'Healing by Mere Touch as a Christian Concept', *TynBul* 48 (1997), pp. 355–61.

Lane, William L., *Commentary on the Gospel of Mark* (NICNT; Grand Rapids, MI: Eerdmans, 1974).

Larkin, William J., 'The Old Testament Background of Luke XXII. 43–44', *NTS* 25 (1979): 250–54.

Law, Robert, *The Emotions of Jesus* (Edinburgh: T. & T. Clark, 1915).

Lewis, Charlton T., and Charles Short, *A Latin Dictionary* (Oxford: Clarendon, 1962).

Linnemann, Eta, *Is There a Synoptic Problem? Rethinking the Literary Dependence of the First Three Gospels* (trans. Robert W. Yarbrough; Grand Rapids, MI: Baker, 1992).

Little, William, H. W. Fowler, and J. Coulson, *The Shorter Oxford English Dictionary* (Oxford: Clarendon, 3rd edn, 1956).

Loader, William, 'Challenged at the Boundaries: A Conservative Jesus in Mark's Tradition', *JSNT* 63 (1996), pp. 45–61.

Louw, Johannes P., and Eugene A. Nida (eds), *Greek-English Lexicon of the New Testament Based on Semantic Domains* (2 vols, New York: United Bible Societies, 2nd edn, 1988–89).

McRay, John, *Archaeology and the New Testament* (Grand Rapids, MI: Baker, 1991).

Madigan, Kevin, 'Ancient and High-Medieval Interpretations of Jesus in Gethsemane: Some Reflections on Tradition and Continuity in Christian Thought', *HTR* 88 (1995), pp. 157–73.

Manonukul, Jane, et al. (eds), 'Hematidrosis: A Pathologic Process or Stigmata. A Case Report with Comprehensive Histopathologic and Immunoperoxidase Studies', *American Journal of Dermatopathology* 30 (2008), pp. 135–39.

Marshall, I. Howard, *The Gospel of Luke: A Commentary on the Greek Text* (The New International Greek Commentary; Exeter: Paternoster, 1978).

—— *Luke – Historian and Theologian* (Downers Grove, IL: Inter-Varsity Press, 3rd edn, 1988).

Martin, Ralph P., 'The Pericope of the Healing of the "Centurion's" Servant/Son (Matt 8:5-13 par. Luke 7:1-10): Some Exegetical Notes', in Robert A. Guelich (ed.), *Unity and Diversity in New Testament Theology: Essays in Honor of George E. Ladd* (Grand Rapids, MI: Eerdmans, 1978), pp. 14–22.

—— *New Testament Foundations: A Guide for Christian Students* (2 vols; Grand Rapids, MI: Eerdmans, 1975–1978).

Mays, James L., 'Prayer and Christology: Psalm 22 as Perspective on the Passion', *ThTo* 42 (1985), pp. 322–31.

—— '"Now I Know": An Exposition of Genesis 22:1-19 and Matthew 26:36-46', *ThTo* 58 (2002), pp. 519–25.

Meier, Paul D., Frank B. Minirth, Frank B. Wichern, and Donald E. Ratcliff, *Introduction to Psychology and Counselling: Christian Perspectives and Applications* (Grand Rapids, MI: Baker, 1991).

Metzger, Bruce M., *A Textual Commentary on the Greek New Testament* (Stuttgart: Deutsche Bibelgesellschaft, 2nd edn, 1994).

Moloney, Francis J., 'God so Loved the World: The Jesus of John's Gospel', *ACR* 75 (1998), pp. 195–205.

—— 'Can Everyone be Wrong? A Reading of John 11.1-12.8', *NTS* 49 (2003), pp. 505–27.

Morag, S., '*Ephphatha* (Mark VII: 34): Certainly Hebrew, Not Aramaic?' *JSS* 17 (1972), pp. 198–202.

Morrice, William G., *'Joy' in the New Testament* (Exeter: Paternoster, 1988).

Morris, Charles G., and Albert A. Maisto, *Understanding Psychology* (Upper Saddle River, NJ: Prentice Hall, 8th edn, 2008).

Morris, Leon, *The Gospel According to St. Luke: An Introduction and Commentary* (London: Inter-Varsity Press, 1974).

—— *The Gospel According to Matthew* (Grand Rapids, MI: Eerdmans, 1992).

—— *The Gospel According to John* (NICNT; Grand Rapids, MI: Eerdmans, rev. edn, 1995).

Moule, C. F. D., *An Idiom Book of New Testament Greek* (Cambridge: Cambridge University Press, 2nd edn, 1959).

Moulton, James H., and George Milligan, *The Vocabulary of the Greek Testament Illustrated from the Papyri and Other Non-Literary Sources* (London: Hodder and Stoughton, 1930; repr. 1972).

Neuner, Joseph, 'Immanuel, God with Us', *Vid* 62 (1998), pp. 562–66.

Newman, Barclay M., and Eugene A. Nida, *A Translator's Handbook on the Gospel of John* (Stuttgart: United Bible Societies, 1980).

Niccacci, Alviero, *The Syntax of the Verb in Classical Hebrew Prose* (Journal for the Study of the Old Testament Supplement Series 86; trans. W. G. E. Watson; Sheffield: Sheffield Academic Press, 1990).

Nolland, John, *Luke* (WBC, vol. 35; Dallas: Word, 1989–93).

Novakovic, Lidija, 'Jesus as the Davidic Messiah in Matthew', *HBT* 19 (1997), pp. 148–91.

O'Day, Gail R., 'Piety without Pretense, Faith without Falsehood: The Lenten Journey According to John', *JP* 20 (1997), pp. 10–13.

Osten-Sacken, Peter von der, 'Jesu Weinen über sein Volk: Predigt über Lukas 19,41-44', in *Die Hebräische Bibel und ihre zweifache Nachgeschichte: Festschrift für Rolf Rendtorff zum 65. Geburtstag*, ed. Erhard Blum, Christian Macholz, and Ekkehard W. Stegemann (Neukirchen-Vluyn: Neukirchener Verlag, 1990), pp. 555–59.

Paffenroth, Kim, 'Jesus as Anointed and Healing Son of David in the Gospel of Matthew', *Biblica* 80 (1999), pp. 547–54.

Pietersma, Albert, and Benjamin G. Wright (eds), *A New English Translation of the Septuagint and the Other Greek Translations Traditionally Included under That Title* (Oxford: Oxford University Press, 2007).

Powell, Mark A., 'The Plot and Subplots of Matthew's Gospel', *NTS* 38 (1992), pp. 187–204.

—— 'Toward a Narrative-Critical Understanding of Mark', *Int* 47 (1993), pp. 341–46.

Pryor, John W., *John: Evangelist of the Covenant People: The Narrative and Themes of the Fourth Gospel* (London: Darton, Longman & Todd, 1992).

Rhoads, David, 'Losing Life for Others in the Face of Death: Mark's Standards of Judgment', *Int* 47 (1993), pp. 358–69.

Richardson, Alan, 'The Feeding of the Five Thousand (Mark 6:34-44)', *Int* 9 (1955), pp. 144–49.

Ridderbos, Herman N., *The Bible Student's Commentary – Matthew* (trans. Ray Togtman; Grand Rapids, MI: Zondervan, 1987).

—— *The Gospel According to John: A Theological Commentary* (trans. John Vriend; Grand Rapids, MI: Eerdmans, 1997).

Roberts, Robert C., *Spiritual Emotions: A Psychology of Christian Virtues* (Grand Rapids, MI: Eerdmans, 2007).

Robertson, A. T., *A Grammar of the Greek New Testament in the Light of Historical Research* (London: Hodder and Stoughton, 1923).

——and W. Hersey Davis, *A New Short Grammar of the Greek Testament* (New York: Harper, 10th edn, 1933).

Ross, J. M., 'Floating Words: Their Significance for Textual Criticism', *NTS* 38 (1992), pp. 153–56.

Saddington, D. B., 'The Centurion in Matthew 8:5-13: Consideration of the Proposal of Theodore W. Jennings, Jr., and Tat-Siong Benny Liew', *JBL* 125 (2006), pp. 140–42.

Schilder, Klaas, *The Schilder Trilogy: Christ in His Suffering* (trans. Henry Zylstra; Grand Rapids, MI: Baker, 1979).

Schnackenburg, Rudolf, *The Gospel According to St John* (ed. J. Massyngbaerde Ford and Kevin Smyth et al.; trans. Kevin Smyth et al., 3 vols; 2nd and later impressions; Tunbridge Wells, Kent: Burns & Oats, 1990–1993).

—— *The Gospel of Matthew* (trans. Robert R. Barr; Grand Rapids, MI: Eerdmans, 2002).

Schneiders, Sandra M., 'Death in the Community of Eternal Life: History, Theology, and Spirituality in John 11', *Int* 41 (1987), pp. 44–56.

Segovia, Fernando F., *Love Relationships in the Johannine Tradition: Agapē/ Agapan in I John and the Fourth Gospel* (Society of Biblical Literature Dissertation Series 58; Chico, CA: Scholars Press, 1982).

—— 'The Structure, *Tendenz*, and *Sitz im Leben* of John 13:31-14:31', *JBL* 104 (1985), pp. 471–93.

Shaffer, Jack R., 'A Harmonization of Matt 8:5-13 and Luke 7:1-10', *MSJ* 17 (2006), pp. 35–50.

Smalley, Stephen S., *John: Evangelist and Interpreter* (Carlisle: Paternoster, 2nd edn, 1998.

Smith, Christopher R., 'Literary Evidences of a Fivefold Structure in the Gospel of Matthew', *NTS* 43 (1997), pp. 540–51.

Smith, Craig A., 'A Comparative Study of the Prayer of Gethsemane', *IBS* 22 (2000), pp. 98–122.

Smith, Karen E., 'Mark 14:32-42', *RevExp* 88 (1991), pp. 433–37.

Stein, Robert H., *The Synoptic Problem: An Introduction* (Grand Rapids, MI: Baker, 1987).

—— *Mark* (Baker Exegetical Commentary on the New Testament; Grand Rapids, MI: Baker, 2008).

Stevenson, J. (ed.), *A New Eusebius: Documents Illustrative of the History of the Church to A. D. 337* (London: SPCK, 1968).

Stibbe, Mark W. G., 'A Tomb with a View: John 11.1-44 in Narrative-Critical Perspective', *NTS* 40 (1994), pp. 38–54.

Stoldt, Hans-Herbert, *History and Criticism of the Marcan Hypothesis* (trans. and ed. Donald L. Niewyk; Macon, GA: Mercer University Press, 1980).

Streeter, Burnett H., *The Four Gospels: A Study of Origins* (London: Macmillan, 1956) (originally published in 1924).

Tate, Marvin E., *Psalms 51–100* (WBC 20; Dallas: Word, 1990).

Telford, George B., 'Mark 1:40-45', *Int* 36 (1982), pp. 54–58.

Thomas, Robert L. (ed.), *Three Views on the Origins of the Synoptic Gospels* (Grand Rapids, MI: Kregel, 2002).

Tiede, D. L., *Prophecy and History in Luke-Acts* (Philadelphia: Fortress, 1980).

Tolbert, Mary Ann, 'How the Gospel of Mark Builds Character', *Int* 47 (1993), pp. 347–57.

Tripp, David, 'Meanings of the Foot-Washing: John 13 and Oxyrhynchus Papyrus 840', *ExpTim* 103 (1992), pp. 237–39.

Trudinger, Paul, 'Did Schweitzer Get It Right? That "Cry of Dereliction" Revisited', *Faith and Freedom* 56 (2003), pp. 156–58.

Valentine, Simon R., 'The Johannine Prologue: A Microcosm of the Gospel', *EvQ* 68 (1996), pp. 291–304.

Van Lopik, T., 'Once Again: Floating Words, Their Significance for Textual Criticism', *NTS* 41 (1995), pp. 286–91.

Voorwinde, Stephen, 'John's Prologue: Beyond Some Impasses of Twentieth Century Scholarship', *WTJ* 63 (2002), pp. 15–44.

—— *Jesus' Emotions in the Fourth Gospel: Human or Divine?* (London: T & T Clark, 2005).

Wallace, Daniel B., *Greek Grammar beyond the Basics: An Exegetical Syntax of the New Testament* (Grand Rapids, MI: Zondervan, 1996).

Warfield, Benjamin B., 'On the Emotional Life of Our Lord', in Benjamin B. Warfield, *The Person and Work of Christ* (Philadelphia: Presbyterian & Reformed, 1950; article originally published by Charles Scribner's Sons, 1912), pp. 93–145.

—— *The Person and Work of Christ* (Philadelphia: Presbyterian & Reformed, 1950).

Watts, Rikki E., *Isaiah's New Exodus and Mark*, Wissenschaftliche Untersuchungen zum Neuen Testament 2.88 (Tübingen: J. C. B. Mohr, 1997).

Wefald, Eric K., 'The Separate Gentile Mission in Mark: A Narrative Explanation of Markan Geography, the Two Feeding Accounts and Exorcisms', *JSNT* 60 (1995), pp. 3–26.

Westcott, B. F., *The Gospel According to St. John: The Authorized Version with Introduction and Notes* (Grand Rapids, MI: Eerdmans, 1954; originally published 1881).

White, R. E. O., 'That "Cry of Dereliction" . . .?' *ExpTim* 113 (2002), pp. 188–89.

Whitters, Mark F., 'Why Did the Bystanders Think Jesus Called upon Elijah before He Died (Mark 15:34-36)? The Markan Position', *HTR* 95 (2002), pp. 119–24.

Wiarda, Timothy, 'Story-Sensitive Exegesis and Old Testament Allusions in Mark', *Journal of the Evangelical Theological Society* 49 (2006), pp. 489–504.

Wilkinson, John, 'The Seven Words from the Cross', *Scottish Journal of Theology* 17 (1964), pp. 69–82.

—— 'The Case of the Epileptic Boy', *ExpTim* 79 (1967), pp. 39–42.

—— *The Bible and Healing: A Medical and Theological Commentary* (Grand Rapids, MI: Eerdmans, 1998).

Williamson, Lamar, Jr., 'An Exposition of Mark 6:30-44', *Int* 30 (1976), pp. 169–73.

Wohlgemut, John R., 'Where Does God Dwell? A Commentary on John 2:13-22,' *Direction* 22 (1993), pp. 87–93.

Wojciechowski, Michal, 'The Touching of the Leper (Mark 1,40-45) as a Historical and Symbolic Act of Jesus', *BZ* 33 (1989), pp. 114–19.

Wright, N. T., *The New Testament and the People of God* (Christian Origins and the Question of God, vol. 1; London: SPCK, 1996).

Yancey, Philip, *The Jesus I Never Knew: Why No One Who Meets Him Ever Stays the Same* (London: Marshall Pickering, 1995).

Zerwick, Maximilian, *Biblical Greek Illustrated by Examples* (English edn, adapted from the 4th Latin edn by Joseph Smith S. J.; Rome: Biblical Institute Press, 1963).

—— and Mary Grosvenor, *A Grammatical Analysis of the Greek New Testament* (Rome: Biblical Institute Press, rev. edn, 1981).

Zias, Joseph, 'Lust and Leprosy: Confusion or Correlation?', *Bulletin of the American Schools of Oriental Research* 275 (1989), pp. 27–31.

Index of Scripture and Ancient Works

Subject Index

Index of Authors Cited